# Adoption Law

## A Practical Guide

Second Edition

# Adoption Law

## A Practical Guide

Second Edition

Nasreen Pearce

Wildy, Simmonds & Hill Publishing

ISBN: 9780854903085

British Library Cataloguing in Publication Data

A catalogue record for this book is available from the British Library



First edition 2020

This edition published in 2025 by

Wildy, Simmonds & Hill Publishing
Wildy & Sons Ltd
Lincoln's Inn Archway
Carey Street
London WC2A 2JD
www.wildy.com

Printed in Great Britain by CPI Group (UK) Ltd, Croydon CR0 4YY.

# Contents

# Table of Cases

*References are to page numbers*

# Table of Statutes

*References are to page numbers*

# Table of Statutory Instruments

*References are to page numbers*

# Table of European and International Material

*References are to page numbers*

# Table of Statutory Guidance, etc

*References are to page numbers*

# Table of Judicial Practice Directions and Guidance

*References are to page numbers*

# List of Abbreviations

| | |
|---|---|
| AAR 2005 | Adoption Agencies Regulations 2005 (SI 2005/389) |
| AAR 2013 | Adoption Agencies (Miscellaneous Amendments) Regulations 2013 (SI 2013/985) |
| ACA 2002 | Adoption and Children Act 2002 |
| ACACRR 2005 | Adopted Children and Adoption Contact Registers Regulations 2005 (SI 2005/924) |
| *Adoption Statutory Guidance 2013* | *Statutory Guidance on Adoption: For local authorities, voluntary adoption agencies and adoption support agencies* (Department for Education, July 2013); available at: www.gov.uk/government/publications/adoption-statutory-guidance-2013 |
| *Adoption Statutory Guidance 2014 (Draft)* | *Draft statutory guidance: For local authorities and voluntary adoption agencies* (Department for Education, July 2014); available at: https://assets.publishing.service.gov.uk/government/uploads/system/uploads/attachment_data/file/285718/Draft_adoption_statutory_guidance.pdf |
| AFER 2005 | Adoptions with a Foreign Element Regulations 2005 (SI 2005/392) |
| AIIS(PCA)R 2005 | Adoption Information and Intermediary Services (Pre-Commencement Adoptions) Regulations 2005 (SI 2005/890), as amended by SI 2014/2696 and SI 2015/1685 |
| ASAR 2005 | Adoption Support Agencies (England) and Adoption Agencies (Miscellaneous Amendments) Regulations 2005 (SI 2005/2720) |
| ASSR 2005 | Adoption Support Services Regulations 2005 (SI 2005/691), as amended by the Adoption Support Services (Amendment) Regulations 2014 (SI 2014/1563) |
| CA | Court of Appeal (in case citations)<br>Central Authority (in narrative text) |
| CAA 2006 | Children and Adoption Act 2006 |
| Cafcass | Children and Family Court Advisory and Support Service |
| ChA 1989 | Children Act 1989 |

| | |
|---|---|
| DAI(PCA)R 2005 | Disclosure of Adoption Information (Post-Commencement Adoptions) Regulations 2005 (SI 2005/888) |
| ECtHR | European Court of Human Rights |
| European Convention | European Convention for the Protection of Human Rights and Fundamental Freedoms 1950 |
| FC(CDB)Rules 2014 | Family Court (Composition and Distribution of Business) Rules 2014 (SI 2014/840) |
| FD | Family Division |
| FLRA 1969 | Family Law Reform Act 1969 |
| FPR 2010 | Family Procedure Rules 2010 (SI 2010/2955) |
| GDPR | General Data Protection Regulation |
| 1993 Hague Convention | 1993 Hague Convention on Protection of Children and Co-operation in Respect of Intercountry Adoption |
| 1996 Hague Convention | 1996 Hague Convention on Jurisdiction, Applicable Law, Recognition, Enforcement and Co-operation in Respect of Parental Responsibility and Measures for the Protection of Children |
| HFEA 2008 | Human Fertilisation and Embryology Act 2008 |
| IRD(AF)R 2009 | Independent Review of Determinations (Adoption and Fostering) Regulations 2009 (SI 2009/395) |
| MCA 2005 | Mental Capacity Act 2005 |
| NMS 2014 | *Adoption: national minimum standards* (Department for Education, July 2014); available at: www.gov.uk/government/publications/adoption-national-minimum-standards |
| SAR 2005 | Suitability of Adopters Regulations 2005 (SI 2005/1712) |
| SSWB(W)A 2014 | Social Services and Well-being (Wales) Act 2014 |
| UK CA | Central Authority in the United Kingdom |
| UNCRC | United Nations Convention on the Rights of the Child 1989 |

# Chapter 1

# Introduction

1.1 The law in relation to adoption of a child has developed over many years since the Poor Law Act 1899. However, although it was recognised then that there was a need to protect the adopted child and his carers and give them legal recognition, it was not until the Adoption and Children Act 1926 that adoption became part of English law and received some legal recognition. The Act provided for the transfer of the custody rights and duties of the birth parents to the adopters. It set out the conditions which had to be satisfied before an application for adoption could be considered. It confirmed that on the making of an adoption order the adopted child would be treated as if born to the adopters. It did not, however, confer any proprietary or inheritance rights on the adopted child.

1.2 Between 1958 and 1975 there was a series of statutory provisions dealing with situations that arose as a result of reform of the law relating to children. Following the publication of the Houghton Report in 1972, the law on adoption was further amended and consolidated in the Children Act 1975 and further consolidated in the Adoption Act 1976, which came into force on 1 January 1988. The 1976 Act provided the statutory framework of the law on adoptions subject to the several amendments until the Adoption and Children Act 2002 (ACA 2002), which came into force on 30 December 2005.

1.3 The ACA 2002 has been amended on a number of occasions to meet social changes, such as extending the categories of persons who may now apply to adopt a child; for example, permitting couples living in an enduring relationship or in a civil partnership pursuant to the Civil Partnership Act 2004 and married same sex couples when the Marriage (Same Sex Couples) Act 2013 came into force, to be eligible to adopt a child (Chapter 2). The Act as amended remains the main statutory instrument which sets out the law on adoptions in England and Wales. It is supplemented by regulations in relation to both domestic adoptions and adoptions with a foreign element. In respect of the latter, the principles which apply have been formulated by reference to international declarations and Conventions to which the United Kingdom is a party. These instruments provide the framework for the relevant domestic law as set out in the 1993 Hague Convention on Protection of Children and Co-operation in Respect of Intercountry Adoption (1993 Hague Convention) and the Adoptions with a Foreign Element Regulations 2005 (SI 2005/392) (AFER 2005), as amended (see Chapters 12–15).

1.4 Following in the footsteps of the Children Act 1989 (ChA 1989), the ACA 2002 makes the welfare principle the central focus of any decision-making in relation to the adoption of a child by a court or an adoption agency, for example when dispensing with parental consent, by providing that the paramount consideration must be the child's welfare throughout his life, and it sets out a list of factors that must be considered when determining the welfare of the child (ACA 2002, s 1(1)–(5)) (see Chapter 7). The ACA 2002 also requires the court and adoption agencies to consider a whole range of alternative options available under that Act and the ChA 1989, such as special guardianship orders. As the Supreme Court stressed in *Re B (A Child)* [2013] UKSC 33, adoption should be seen as 'a last resort', when all else fails.

1.5 The ACA 2002 also introduced a new process of placement for adoption orders, with a view to ensuring that all issues relating to the child's placement care and contact with birth parents and family are dealt with at an early stage. Hence, where a local authority intends to place a child in its care for adoption, it must either obtain the consent of the child's parents or apply to the court for a placement order. This enables the parents to challenge the care plan proposed by the local authority and allows the parents or other family members to put forward their proposals for contact as a better option to be determined by the court. The Court of Appeal in *Re R and C (Adoption or Fostering)* [2024] EWCA Civ 1302 confirmed that it is for the court – not the local authority or any other person – to determine, in proceedings for placement and adoption orders, whether there should be post-placement and post-adoption contact between siblings and between the child and his birth family; how the court should deal with the options put forward, and the procedure that should be followed by all professionals in dealing with the issue of contact. Consequently, the issue of ongoing contact will be given greater scrutiny in any care plan put forward and by the court. Additionally, the reference by the Court of Appeal to the President of the Family Division's two recent lectures, and in particular to his address to the Parents of Traumatised Adopted Teens Organisation (POTATO group) Conference on 17 May 2024, is likely to be given more weight notwithstanding the fact that the President stated that the address is 'neither a court judgment, Practice Direction nor other guidance from the President of the Family Division'. (See Chapters 4 and 8.)

1.6 The child's rights to his identity and family are specifically dealt with by ensuring that records are made and maintained of information relating to the child and his family, so that they are available should the adopted child wish to ascertain his background or make contact with his natural family. First and foremost, the ACA 2002 makes specific provisions in ss 26 and 46 for the court to provide for contact between the child and the natural parents following a placement and adoption order. However, the norm has been for post-adoption contact to be limited to letterbox contact and to be dictated by what is acceptable to prospective adopters, notwithstanding the statutory provisions. Access to the internet and social media has enabled adopted children to search out and make contact with their family, circumventing any order or regulations. Consequently, allowing prospective adopters and adopters autonomy in dictating whether and to what extent contact would be permissible post-adoption is no longer tenable. Additionally, considerable research confirms the benefit of post-adoption contact, and the President has in his recent lectures highlighted the need for adapting the approach to post-adoption contact. These issues and more are comprehensively covered in Chapter 8.

1.7 The Act as amended makes provisions for the Adopted Children Register and the Adoption Contact Register to be maintained in the General Register Office (see Chapter 19). The disclosure of information to the adopted person is sensitively dealt with, and provisions are made for the person to be provided with appropriate support services for those adopted pre- and post-30 December 2005 and for the birth families of such persons in relation to domestic adoptions, Convention adoptions and intercountry adoptions (see Chapters 17 and 18). A duty is placed on each local authority to maintain adoption support services to meet the needs of adopted children, their parents and guardians, and prospective adopters. These include providing financial support, where appropriate, and to ensure that all relevant information is available to the adopted person. Provision is also made in the ACA 2002 in ss 54, 56–65 and 79 for the nature of the information that the agencies are obliged to keep and the information that it must disclose to adopted adults and other relevant parties (see Chapters 16–18). Disclosure of information is a sensitive issue and therefore detailed provisions are made of what can be disclosed, to whom and how (see Chapter 20).

1.8 It can be seen from the brief outline above that the ACA 2002 sets out the statutory legal requirements which must be complied with in relation to all aspects of the adoption process. However, in all cases when dealing with the adoption of children and meeting those requirements, it is essential to ensure that the child's and his natural parents' basic human rights are not compromised, overlooked or denied. The United Nations Convention on the Rights of the Child 1989 (UNCRC) recognises the child's rights, as far as possible, to know and be cared for by his parents. European Convention for the Protection of Human Rights and Fundamental Freedoms 1950 (European Convention), Art 8 preserves the right of every person to respect for his private and family life and his home. It provides that there shall be no interference by a public authority with the exercise of the person's rights except in limited circumstances identified in Art 8(2). European Convention, Art 6 also requires that in the determination of his civil rights and obligation, everyone is entitled to a fair and impartial hearing, including the rights set out in Art 6. It is therefore essential, when advising a party in any proceedings in relation to the adoption of a child, to consider the issue of any infringements of these rights and how they may be avoided by adopting other available alternative options rather than making an adoption order. The issue of these rights now plays an important factor in all aspects of the adoption process. This ranges from interpretation of the ACA 2002 and all regulations, to determining whether, in the circumstances of the case, the statutory provisions are incompatible with Convention rights. If the court finds that the statutory provisions are incompatible with Convention rights, it will go on to determine whether the rights tip the balance in favour of those rights to justify the provisions being read down as is demonstrated in cases such as *Re H (Step-Parent: Adoption: Human Rights)* [2023] EWHC 3186 (Fam) (see Chapter 2); *Re X (Time-Barred Adoption)* [2024] EWHC 364 (Fam) (see Chapter 3); and *Re T (A Child: Refusal of Adoption Order)* [2020] EWCA Civ 797. The most recent examples are *Re A and B (Adoption: section 83 ACA 2002)* [2024] EWHC 2837 (Fam), *KA v FA and Others* [2024] EWHC 2855 (Fam) and *Re G (Recognition of Nigerian Adoption)* [2024] EWHC 2769 (Fam).

1.9 The chapters that follow set out an overview of the law and practice of each stage of placing a child for adoption and the adoption process, and the duties and responsibilities of the local authority and adoption agencies towards the child and all the relevant persons in the child's life, with the emphasis on the statutory principle that in coming to any decision relating to the adoption of a child, the paramount consideration is the child's welfare throughout his life.

# Chapter 2

# Who May Adopt?

## PEOPLE WHO MAY ADOPT

2.1 An application to adopt a child may be made by (a) a couple; or (b) one person, provided the required statutory conditions, set out in ACA 2002, s 49(2)–(3) and s 50 in relation to a couple and in s 51 in relation to adoption by a person, in each case are satisfied. These conditions relate to the age, domicile and residence of the applicants/applicant and the age of the child. These pre-requisite conditions are discussed below.

## ADOPTION BY A COUPLE

### Definition of 'a couple'

2.2 ACA 2002, s 144(4) defines 'a couple' to mean:

(a) a married couple – this includes single sex married couples; or
(b) two people who are civil partners of each other; or
(c) two people (whether of different sex or the same sex) living as partners in an enduring family relationship.

2.3 The reference to couple does not include two people one of whom is the other's parent, grandparent, sister, brother, aunt or uncle (ACA 2002, s 144(5)). These relationships may be of full or half-blood, or, in the case of an adopted person, such of those relationships as would exist but for the adoption, and include the relationship of a child with his adoptive or former adoptive parents, but do not include any other adoptive relationships (ACA 2002, s 144(6)).

## *Marriage or civil partnership*

2.4 The validity of the couple's marriage is a relevant factor when the court considers the application because Family Procedure Rules 2010 (SI 2010/2955) (FPR 2010) PD 14C, Section C, Part 1(e) requires the adoption agency to provide information on the prospective adopter's marital status or civil partnership status, and the date and place of the most recent marriage (if any) or civil partnership (if any). Part 1(h) of the PD also requires the adoption agency's report to provide information about the status of the couple's relationship and the assessment of the stability and permanence of the couple's relationship. The Adoption Application Form A58 requires documentary evidence of the applicant's/applicants' marriage or civil partnership to be filed with the application. The ACA 2002 is silent on whether a couple whose marriage is polygamous or potentially polygamous would qualify. Case law suggests that applicants whose marriage is polygamous or potentially polygamous are likely to be regarded as a 'married couple' (*Din (Imam) v National Assistance Board* [1967] 2 QB 213; *Alhaji Mohamed v Knott* [1969] 1 QB 1). The court is empowered to make a declaration concerning the validity of a marriage which was entered into under a law which permits polygamy (Matrimonial Causes Act 1973, s 47).

2.5 Where an adoption order is made in favour of a couple whose marriage is later found to be bigamous and therefore void, it does not nullify the adoption order. The court will not set it aside unless it is in the best interests and welfare of the adopted child/person (*Re F (Infants) (Adoption Order: Validity)* [1977] 2 All ER 777, CA).

2.6 The court may make an adoption order in favour of a married couple, notwithstanding the fact that the couple separated after the application was made, if the court finds that it is in the best interests of the child to do so (*Re CC (Adoption Application: Separated Applicants)* [2013] EWHC 4815 (Fam)). (See also *Re X (A Child: Foreign Surrogacy)* [2018] EWFC 15, a case for a parental order under ACA 2002, s 54(2)(a), but the same principle will be applied in adoption cases.)

## *Enduring family relationships*

2.7 The ACA 2002 does not define 'enduring family relationships'. Nor does it set a minimum period for which the relationship should have continued. Human Fertilisation and Embryology Act 2008 (HFEA 2008), s 54(2)(c) also requires partners to be in an 'enduring family relationship' with no statutory definition. Therefore, decisions made in applications for a parental order are, by analogy, relevant in applications for an adoption order when the issue relates to the nature and extent of the applicants' relationship. Since the objective of the legislation is the child's welfare throughout his life, it will be for the court to determine on the facts whether the applicants' relationship is sufficiently stable to provide for the child in the long term. In *Re T and M (Adoption)* [2010] EWHC 964 (Fam), Hedley J stated (at [16]) that:

> Clearly the crucial words are 'living as partners in an enduring family relationship.' These words are no doubt chosen so as not to require the residence of both in the same property. That is not surprising as historically many a parent has had to work abroad whilst the family remained at home without in any way imperilling an enduring family relationship. Nor is that unusual today with people having to move jobs often at short notice. What is required is: first an unambiguous intention to create and maintain family life, and secondly, a factual matrix consistent with that intention. That is clearly a question of fact and degree in each case.

2.8 The two women in the case were found to be living in a committed and exclusive relationship and shared the care of the child in question, and therefore were entitled to make a joint application for an adoption order (at [16]–[17]). In *P and B v Z* [2016] EWHC 1594 (Fam) (a case under HFEA 2008, s 54(2)), although the applicants had been in a relationship only for about two years, it was held that they were committed to each other and to the child. Similarly, in *Re Z (Parental Order: Child's Home)* [2021] EWHC 29 (Fam), a case under the Human Fertilisation and Embryology Act 2008, the court recognised the enduring relationship of a same sex couple and their commitment to the child and the child's welfare and granted a parental order although the child was living in foster care and not with them. In *Re Z (A Child) (Surrogate Father: Parental Order)* [2015] EWFC 73, approving the decision in *A and Another v P and Others* [2011] EWHC 1738 (Fam), it was held that where one of the applicants dies before the order is made, if, on the facts, family life is established, an adoption order may be made. The court will in such cases interpret the legislation in a way that is compliant with the European Convention. Similarly, where the couple separate after the adoption application is made but have agreed to and continue to co-parent the child and seek a joint adoption order, it is likely that an adoption order will be made, particularly if the evidence establishes that it is in the best interests and welfare of the child (*Re CC (Adoption Application: Separated Applicants)* [2013] EWHC 4815 (Fam)). See *DM and Another v SJ and Others (Surrogacy: Parental Order)* [2016] EWHC 270 (Fam), where despite the fact that the commissioning parents maintained separate households, the court ruled that the child had her home with them and that she did not have a home with anyone else. The court also went on to state that even if that conclusion was not correct, the European Convention applied, and the statute could be 'read down'. In *Re X (A Child – Foreign Surrogacy)* [2018] EWFC 15, the couple were married but in a platonic relationship, and they had separate homes, with the child spending time with each parent individually and both parents together. The court held that the child had a home with both of them. The issue of whether the parties are in an enduring relationship is fact-specific and much will depend on the strength of the evidence of the parties' relationship and ultimately on whether adoption is in the best interests and welfare of the child.

## AGE

2.9 ACA 2002, ss 50(1) and 51(1) require the applicant(s) to have attained the age of 21 years, but an adoption order may be made where one of the couple is a natural parent of the child and has attained the age of 18 years and the other has attained the age of 21 years. In all cases, age is attained at the commencement of the relevant anniversary of the person's date of birth (Family Law Reform Act 1969 (FLRA 1969), s 9(1)). There is no maximum age laid down in the Act. In the past, adoption agencies have imposed an upper age limit of 40 for a man, and 35 for a woman. The current thinking is that there should not be an age gap of more than 45 years, but these limits have not always been adhered to, particularly where the child in question has special needs (Jennifer Lord, *Adopting a child* (BAAF, 2016)). See, for example, *Re W (Adoption by Grandparents)* [1981] 2 FLR 161, where the grandparents were in their mid-60s when they applied to adopt their grandson who had lived with them since the age of seven; and *Re O (A Minor) (Adoption by Grandparents)* [1985] FLR 546, where the grandmother was 54 and the grandfather was 66 years of age and the child had lived with them since she was 10 months old. It should be noted, however, that in both the cases cited the adopters were grandparents of a child who had been in their sole care since childhood and there were exceptional circumstances. Additionally, the alternative of a special guardianship order was then not available.

2.10 Furthermore, although no upper age limit is imposed, it is of note that in the context of the interpretation of instruments concerning property, ACA 2002, s 69(5) provides that where it is necessary to determine, for the disposition of property effected by instrument, whether a woman can have a child, it must be presumed that once a woman has attained the age of 55 years, she will not adopt a person after execution of the instrument and if she does so, then (in spite of ACA 2002, s 67) that person is not to be treated as her child or (or if she does so as one of a couple) as the child of the other one of the couple for the purposes of the instrument.

## DOMICILE/HABITUAL RESIDENCE

2.11 At least one of the couple or the single applicant must be domiciled in a part of the British Islands. Alternatively, both of the couple or the single applicant must have been habitually resident in a part of the British Islands for a period of not less than one year ending with the date of the application (ACA 2002, s 49(2) and (3)).

2.12 The issue of domicile and habitual residence is a legal concept which is relevant in many legal situations which concern personal status and very much dependent on the circumstances of the case. No person can be without a domicile and a person cannot have more than one domicile at the same time. For the purposes of an adoption application, the domicile of a person is determined according to English law. Where a person's domicile or habitual residency is in issue, expert advice should be sought to ensure that the required condition is satisfied.

## Domicile of origin

2.13 A person acquires a domicile of origin at birth from his parents and it is capable of persisting during the lifetime of the person. The domicile of a legitimate child born during the lifetime of his father is that of the child's father. If the father dies before the birth of the child, the child acquires the domicile of his mother at birth and it will change if the parent(s) change their domicile, but the domicile acquired at birth will never be lost and is retained throughout a person's life.

## Domicile of choice

2.14 When a person attains the age of 16 years, he is free to acquire a domicile of choice by leaving the country of his domicile of origin and living in a country of his choice with the intention of making that country his permanent and settled home and living there indefinitely. The test is whether the person intended to make his home in the new country until the end of his days or until something happens to change his mind. If the person having acquired a domicile of choice then abandons that domicile and does not acquire another domicile of choice, he reverts to his domicile of origin until a new domicile of choice is established.

## Habitual residence

2.15 Habitual residence is not statutorily defined and is not a legal concept; it is purely a question of fact (*Re KL (A Child)* [2013] UKSC 75). Following the decision in *A v A (Children: Habitual Residence) (Reunite International Child Abduction Centre and Others Intervening)* [2013] UKSC 60, the European approach that habitual residence corresponds to the place that reflects some degree of integration of a person (in that case, a child) in a social and family environment has been adopted into UK domestic law. It will involve detailed consideration of the day-to-day life of the person, as referred to in *Re C and Another (Children) (International Centre for Family Law; Police and Practice Intervening)* [2018] UKSC 8, and the cases cited therein. Since then, there have been a number of cases in which the issue of what constitutes habitual residence has been considered. A useful summary of the issues raised and determined has been provided by MacDonald J in *J v E* [2024] EWHC 196 (Fam), [74]–[88].

### Losing and acquiring habitual residence

2.16 A distinction needs to be made between habitual residence and temporary presence. This distinction was highlighted by the Court of Justice of the European Union in Case C-497/1O PPU, *Mercredi v Chaffe*, ECLI:EU:C:2010:829 at para 51:

> Before habitual residence can be transferred to the host State, it is of paramount importance that the person concerned has it in mind to establish there the permanent or habitual centre of his interests with the intention that it should be of lasting character. Accordingly, the duration of the stay can serve only as an indicator in the assessment of permanence of the residence and that assessment must be carried out in the light of the circumstances of a fact specific to that case.

2.17 This approach has now been confirmed by the Supreme Court in *Re A (Children)* [2013] UKSC 60 and in a number of cases that have followed thereafter (see *Re KL (A Child)* [2013] UKSC 75; *AR v RN (Habitual Residence)* [2015] UKSC 35).

2.18 Although the above cases relate to child abduction, they are nevertheless significant in that they demonstrate the principle that applies and the factual enquiry that is necessary to establish the level of integration into the social environment of the new state needed to acquire habitual residence.

## ADOPTION BY A STEP-PARENT

2.19 A step-parent may make an application for an adoption order either as a single applicant on his/her own or as one of a married or unmarried couple or civil partner, as long as the applicant is able to satisfy the statutory requirements relating to age, domicile and residence as outlined at paras 2.9–2.17. This enables the partner of one of the child's birth parents to adopt that child without the biological parent having to adopt their own child. One of the major difficulties that adoption by a step-parent raises, however, is that the very concept of such an adoption does not sit comfortably with the child's right to know his own identity. This is because an adoption order has the effect of severing all ties between the child and one side of his family, thus depriving him of forming relationships with one of his birth parents and his/her extended family. In *Re J (Adoption Appeal)* [2018] EWFC 8, a step-parent adoption was set aside on the application of the natural father because the mother of the child and the applicant had misled the court and the local authority about their knowledge of the whereabouts of the child's father. In *Re H (Step-Parent: Adoption)* [2020] EWFC 86, the child was born in Thailand. The child's biological father was recorded on the child's birth certificate. However, he had disappeared few months after the child's birth and had not taken any part in the child's life. When the mother emigrated to the UK she left the child in Thailand with grandparents. In 2009 the mother married the stepfather in the UK, and in 2011 the child joined them. Thereafter, the child lived with the mother and stepfather. In 2019 the stepfather applied to adopt the child. Attempts were made to trace and identify the status of the child's biological father. Expert evidence in Thai law confirmed that the biological father would not be regarded as the child's father. The court held that it was proportionate and in the interests of the child's welfare and her rights under European Convention, Art 8 to make the order and to dispense with the father's consent (see *Soderback v Sweden)* [1999] 1 FLR 250). In *Re L (A Step-Parent Adoption)* [2021] EWCA Civ 801, an adoption order was made notwithstanding that the biological father had applied for and was granted contact with the child in 2013 but which he had not been exercising for several months. The stepfather had taken on the role of a father to the child and was described as having become the child's psychological parent. The father opposed the application. The judge concluded on the evidence that adoption was in the child's best interests. The father's appeal was dismissed, notwithstanding the fact that the issue of the father's contact was not considered by the court. King LJ distinguished the infringement of Art 8 rights of a child and his/her non-consenting biological parent and adoption by a step-parent, and between so-called stranger adoption, in that a stranger adoption is only justified when 'nothing else will do' whereas a step-parent adoption involves a lower degree of interference with those rights and may be more justified. Applying the decision in *Re P (Step-Parent Adoption)* [2014] EWCA Civ 1174, King LJ went on to add:

> It follows that the test in a step-parent adoption is lower. It is not an order of last resort and the 'nothing else will do' test found in *Re B (A Child)* [2013] UKSC 33, [2013] 2 FLR 1075, at [104], [130], [198], [215]. ('*Re B*') is not the correct test. The fact that the interference of a step-parent adoption is less extreme may render adoption proportionate in a case where the proposed adopter is a step-parent in circumstances where it may not be where the applicant is a stranger. ([49])

The Court of Appeal gave guidance (at [63]) that where there is a contact order in favour of the biological father the issue of contact should be dealt with as a specific issue, and that where a contact order is set aside this issue must be properly considered and specifically dealt with either in the judgment or in a recital to the order. It is clear that the court when determining an application by a step-parent will consider what is in the best interests of the child throughout their life and balance the family rights of the birth family and those of the child. In *Re H (Step-Parent Adoption: Human Rights)* [2023] EWHC 3186 (Fam), the child H's birth father was not married to H's mother and nor were they in a civil partnership. H's biological father was not registered on H's birth certificate, and he did not have parental rights. H had never had any contact with his birth father. The mother, who was an EU citizen, subsequently married a British citizen when H was two years old. When H was 13, his mother died. This consequently resulted in a situation where there was no one with parental responsibility for H. The stepfather applied to adopt H but the application ran into legal difficulties because, under ACA 2002, s 51(2), an adoption order may be made if the court is satisfied that the applicant is the partner of a parent of the child. In this case, since H's mother had died, when H's stepfather made the application, he was not a partner of H's mother due to her death. The court accepted that refusal of the stepfather's application to adopt H amounted to a breach of the Art 8 rights of both the stepfather and H. In considering the provisions of s 51(2) and to make it compatible with the Convention rights, the President stated that:

> the outcome that is sought by the applicant and by H is, to my eyes, entirely compatible with the preservation and enhancement of their respective rights under Art 8. Not only would an adoption order in favour of the applicant under section 51(2) bring him into the correct legal status with respect to H which mirrors their lived reality and indeed the reality that H has known since the age of 2 … but it will maintain the extant legal family life relationship that he had had with his mother and continues to have with his maternal family. [30]

The President concluded that the proposal put forward on behalf of the stepfather – that section 51(2) should be read down so that it ended with the words 'or was the partner until the time of the partner's death' – because to do so would be entirely compatible with the underlying policy of the Act. He therefore made the adoption order in favour of the applicant stepfather.

In *E v R and Others* [2023] EWFC 214, the child was born as a result of a surrogacy arrangement. The couple had been in a same sex relationship since 2000. They entered into a civil partnership in 2021. The child they wished to adopt had been born through a surrogacy arrangement and placed with the couple at birth. They applied for an adoption order rather than for a parental order. In determining the application, the court set out the advantages that an adoption would bring to the child as follows:

> 35. By making the step-parent adoption order it would have the effect of transforming the legal status of the child with the result that both E and L would be recognised as legal parents, both with parental responsibility with the added welfare benefit of recognising E's Italian heritage, her sense of identity and the family culture. The evidence demonstrates they are an international family; spending time in other countries and experiencing other cultures form a significant part of their shared identities. E and L identify H as being a child with Italian heritage, her name includes an Italian name and it is a heritage E

strongly identifies with. In the particular circumstances of this case the making of a step-parent adoption order is more likely to enable that heritage to be recognised in a tangible way for the benefit of H.

36. On the particular facts of this case the making of a step-parent adoption order will secure and safeguard, now and into the future, the established central relationship, legal and factual, between H and E and L and is the order that secures H's lifelong welfare needs, with identified welfare benefits. Any suggestion that a step-parent adoption order may not fully reflect H's background in the way a parental order would is met by the powerful evidence in this case. It demonstrates E and L are clear about the importance of H understanding from an early age her background and the circumstances of her conception. As a result of the secure ongoing meaningful relationships that exist between the relevant adults, in particular with R and the egg donor, their role in H's background will be an integral and lived part of H's life going forward. H's lifelong welfare and identity needs are best met by the court making a step-parent adoption order in favour of E.

## Factors to be taken into account

2.20 Consideration should also be given to the consequences if the marriage, relationship or partnership breaks down, and to the fact that an adoption order cannot be revoked. Security for both the carers of the child and the child is often referred to as the reason for making an adoption order. However, security depends upon the emotional attachment which a child develops with the adoptive parent, rather than on a legal document, and security can be provided from the wide range of alternatives now available which confer legal rights on the non-biological parent.

## Alternatives to adoption

2.21 The alternatives to an adoption order include entering into a 'parental responsibility agreement' with both the natural parents of the child; and the right to apply for parental responsibility for the child pursuant to the ChA 1989. The step-parent may also apply for a residence order, which will also confer parental responsibility for the child. The court may specifically direct that the order is to remain in force until the child reaches the age of 18 (ChA 1989, s 12(5)). These orders have the advantage that they may be varied or discharged if the circumstances change.

2.22 Additionally, it is now possible for a step-parent to acquire the right to apply for a special guardianship order under ChA 1989, ss 14A–14G if certain conditions are satisfied.

## Some important factors for consideration when opting for an adoption order

2.23 The approach taken by the ECtHR in *Soderback v Sweden* [2000] 29 EHHR 95, [1999] 1 FLR 250 gives some guidance on the factors which should, among others, be considered when determining step-parent adoption. The starting point is the fact that in breaking all ties with the parent with whom the child is not living, adoption amounts to an interference with respect to a parent's right to family life and leads to an irreversible change in the status of the child. The issue of evaluating proportionality will therefore be vital. Factors that will be essential to this evaluation process are:

(a) the duration of the relationship between the natural parent and the step-parent and how long the child has been living with them in an established family unit, and the emotional attachment of the child to the step-parent;
(b) the lack or absence of care given, and parental responsibility exercised by the other parent of the child;
(c) the infrequency or absence of contact between the child and the other parent;
(d) the best interests of the child;
(e) the wishes and feelings of the child, where the child is of sufficient age, maturity and understanding.

The case of *Re H (Step-Parent Adoption: Human Rights)* referred to at para 2.19 provides an ideal example where all these factors were considered by the court in granting the application.

2.24 In all cases the factors set out in the adoption welfare checklist under ACA 2002, s 1(4) (see Chapter 7) will also be relevant and will be balanced against all other relevant factors.

# SOLE APPLICANT

## Conditions that must be satisfied

2.25 A sole applicant may apply to adopt a child if the following conditions are satisfied:

(a) the applicant is domiciled in the British Islands or has been habitually resident in the British Islands for a period of not less than one year ending with the date of the application (ACA 2002, s 49(2) and (3));
(b) the applicant has attained the age of 21 years (ACA 2002, s 51(1));
(c) the applicant is not married or a civil partner, or if married or in a civil partnership, provided it can be established that:

- (i) the applicant's spouse/civil partner cannot be found; or
- (ii) the applicant has separated from their spouse/civil partner and they are living apart and the separation is likely to be permanent; or
- (iii) the applicant's spouse/civil partner is by reason of ill health, whether physical or mental, incapable of making an application for an adoption;

(d) the child has (unless the placement was by an adoption agency) had a home with the applicant for the relevant period within England and Wales; and

(e) the applicant has given notice to the appropriate local authority of their intention to apply for the adoption (ACA 2002, ss 42, 44 and 51(1)–(3A)).

## Parent as a sole applicant

2.26 An adoption order may only be made on the application of the mother or the father of the person to be adopted where the court is satisfied that:

(a) the natural parent is dead or cannot be found; or

(b) by virtue of Human Fertilisation and Embryology Act 1990, s 28 or ss 34–47 (disregarding HFEA 2008, ss 28(5A)–(5I) 39, 40 and 46), there is no other parent; or

(c) there is some other reason justifying the child's being adopted by the applicant alone (ACA 2002, s 51(4) and (5)).

2.27 Where in such cases the court makes an adoption order it must record that it is satisfied as to the facts mentioned under (a) and (b) (above). Where an order is made under (c) (above), the court must record the reasons for so doing. The reasons must be sufficient to outweigh the adverse consequences of an order which would result from the family ties being broken between the child and the other parent. Where 'the other reason' is relied on, the reason is likely to be exceptional for an order to be made. Before making the order, the court is required to consider the alternatives available under the ChA 1989 and confirm that the court considered the other alternative options available under that Act and found them not to be appropriate in the circumstances of the case (see para 2.19) (*Re B (Natural Parent)* [2001] UKHL 70).

# ADOPTION BY RELATIVES

2.28 Relatives of the child may adopt provided the requirements, relating to other applicants referred to at paras 2.9–2.17, are satisfied and the child has had his home with the applicant relative(s) for a period of not less than three years, whether continuous or not, during the five years ending with the date of the application unless the court has granted permission to make the application sooner (ACA 2002, s 42(5) and (6), and see further Chapter 3).

2.29 However, before embarking on an application for an adoption order the alternative options of a care arrangement order under ChA 1989, s 8 or a special guardianship order should first be considered. Of relevance will be the circumstances of the individual case and balancing the advantages and disadvantages of both of the alternative options against those of an adoption order. The case of *Re T (A Child: Refusal of Adoption Order)* [2020] EWCA Civ 797 is an example of the unusual facts and the factors that may be taken into account when the choice is between a special guardianship order and an adoption order. When allowing the appeal from a refusal to grant an adoption order to the maternal grandmother and step-grandfather, who were caring for the child under a guardianship order, the court took into account the following facts in deciding that an adoption order would be the preferable option:

> (i) it would reflect the reality of the child's life with his grandparents now and throughout the whole of his life;
> (ii) it would provide C and the grandparents with the security and reassurance that the C's future life was securely and permanently with them in fact and in law;
> (iii) it would sever the mother's legal relationship with C which is a Draconian step for any court to take, but it would remove the mother's ability to interfere in his life whether by making applications to the court and/or requiring and demanding information about the child's life;
> (iv) it would remove the obligation on the grandparents to seek the mother's consent to certain steps to be taken in C's life (e.g. remove him from the jurisdiction for a period in excess of three months);
> (v) it would enable the step-grandfather to be C's legal father as well as his social and psychological father in circumstances where the identity of C's biological father is unknown; and
> (vi) it would send the clear message to the wider world that C was lawfully the grandparent's child. ([58])
>
> 59. The Art 8 rights of the mother and C are engaged, but where there is tension between the rights of the child, on the one hand, and the rights of a parent on the other, the rights of the child prevail: *Yousef v The Netherlands* [2003]1 FLR 210.

The court concluded that in view of the unusual and grave circumstances of the case the child's welfare required him to be offered the greatest possible security in his placement with his grandparents. An adoption order would provide C with the degree of security he required in his welfare and best interests ([60]).

## RESTRICTIONS ON MAKING ADOPTION ORDER

2.30 The court may not hear an application for an adoption order in relation to a child where any application for an adoption order made in the British Isles or a

Scottish or Northern Irish adoption order or for an order for adoption made in the Isle of Man or any of the Channel Islands, in relation to the child by the same persons was refused by any court, unless it appears to the court that, because of the change of circumstances or for any other reason, it is proper to hear the application (ACA 2002, s 48). Where such an application is made the court must, as soon as practicable after the application is issued, consider whether it is proper to hear the application (FPR 2010), r 14.6(1)).

# Chapter 3

# The Child

## STATUTORY REQUIREMENTS

3.1 An application for an adoption order may only be made in respect of a child who: (a) is under the age of 18 years on the date of the application (ACA 2002, s 49(4)); (b) is not married or has not been married (ACA 2002, s 47(8)); (c) is not, or has not, been a civil partner (ACA 2002, s 47(8A)); (d) is in England and Wales when the application is made; (e) has had his home with one or both of the prospective adopter(s) during the relevant period (see paras 3.5–3.9) preceding the application; and where (f) sufficient opportunity to see the child with the applicant (or in the case of an application by a couple, both of them together) in the home environment has been given to the adoption agency or the local authority within whose area the home is situated (ACA 2002, s 42(7)). An adoption order may also be made even if the child to be adopted is already an adopted child (ACA 2002 s 46(5).

## AGE

3.2 The person to be adopted must be under the age of 18 years on the date of the application. An adoption order may therefore be made after the child's 18th birthday provided the proceedings were commenced before he attained that age. The case of *Mr and Mrs C v D and Others* [2023] EWFC 10 is an example where the application was made to adopt 10 days before the child's 18th birthday. She was 18½ at the date of the hearing of the application and when the order was made. In *Re X (Time Barred Adoption)* [2024] EWHC 364 (Fam) the application was made two days before the child's 18th birthday. However, an order may not be made if the child has attained the age of 19 years (ACA 2002, s 47(9)). This is significant in cases where, although the proceedings were commenced before the child's 18th birthday, exceptional circumstances have resulted in the final hearing for the adoption order not taking place before the child attains the age of 19 years. The age of 18 years is significant. ACA 2002, s 49(5) provides that references in the Act to a child, in connection with any proceedings (whether concluded or not) for adoption (such as a 'child to be adopted' or 'adopted child') include a person who has attained the age of 18 years before the proceedings are concluded. ACA 2002, s 144 defines 'a child' as a person who has not attained the age of 18 years. A similar definition is given in ChA 1989, s 105. The time at which a person attains a particular age expressed in years is the commencement of the relevant anniversary of the date of birth (Family Law Reform Act 1969 (FLRA 1969), s 9).

### Child is aged 18 or over at the final hearing

3.3 Where the child has attained the age of 18 years by the time the application for an adoption order is heard, the court's decision is, as in other cases, based on the application of the welfare principle; the particular circumstances of the case; the assessment of all the circumstances and the factors set out in ACA 2002, s 1(4) (see Chapter 7). The welfare of the child throughout his life is the paramount consideration (ACA 2002, s 1(2)). The court will also take into consideration the Art 8 rights of the child, to family life under the European Convention, as occurred in *Mr and Mrs C v D and Others* [2023] EWFC 10 (above). Other examples include *Re S and J (Adoption: Non-Patrials)* [2004] 2 FLR 111; *Re B (A Minor) Adoption Order: Nationality)* [1999] 2 AC 136; and *Re D (A Minor) (Adoption: Validity)* [1991] 2 FLR 66. Although these cases were determined under the Adoption Act 1976, they nevertheless illustrate the approach the court takes in relation to children over 18 years of age and echo the principles set out in the ACA 2002.

## PRESENCE IN ENGLAND AND WALES

3.4 For the English court to have jurisdiction, the child must either be habitually resident and present in England or Wales or be physically present in England and Wales when the application is made (*Re M (Care Orders: Jurisdiction)* [1997] 1 FLR 456; see also the ChA 1989). Where the child is habitually resident outside England and Wales, the requirements of AFER 2005, Pt 2 will need to be satisfied before the child can be brought into the United Kingdom (see Chapters 12–15).

## HOME WITH THE PROSPECTIVE ADOPTER(S)

### Time limits

3.5 ACA 2002, s 42 prescribes time limits for which the child must have had his home with the applicants, or one of them, before an application to adopt may be made. The period depends on how the child came to be placed with them.

3.6 If the child was placed with the applicant(s) by an adoption agency, or in pursuance of an order of the High Court (for example, in wardship proceedings), or the applicant is a parent of the child, the child must have had his home with the applicant or in the case of a couple with one or both of them at all times during a period of 10 weeks before the proceedings are commenced (ACA 2002, s 42(2)).

3.7 Where the applicant or one of them is the partner of a parent of the child, the child must have had his home with the applicant(s) at all times during the period of six months before proceedings are commenced (ACA 2002, s 42(3)).

3.8 Where the applicant(s) are local authority foster parents, the period is one year preceding the application (ACA 2002, s 42(4)).

3.9 In all other cases, for example where the applicant(s) are relatives of the child, the condition is that the child must have had his home with the applicant, or in the case of an application by a couple, with one or both of them, for not less than three years preceding the application (whether continuous or not) during the five years preceding the application (ACA 2002, s 42(5)). This longer period may be to stress the inappropriateness of relatives applying for adoption save in exceptional circumstances and for them to consider other options such as a care arrangement (residence) order under ChA 1989, s 8 or a special guardianship order under ACA 2002, s 115.

## Permission for the application to be made after a shorter period

3.10 In the case of an application made by a local authority foster parent or a person other than a partner of a parent, the court may grant permission to make the application before the relevant statutory period (ACA 2002, s 42(6)).

3.11 The Act does not set out the criteria which the court should apply, but clearly the principles relevant to the exercise of the court's discretion whether to grant permission are identical to those that apply under ACA 2002, s 24(2) for permission to apply for a revocation of a placement order and identified in *M v Warwickshire County Council* [2007] EWCA Civ 1084. Hence, the welfare of the child is relevant, but not a paramount consideration; the prospect of success is also relevant, and the court is also likely to consider the motives and reasons for making the application. In the case of an older child, the views and wishes of the child, the guardian's analysis and the child's rights under Art 8 of the European Convention too, will be relevant: *Mr and Mrs C v D and Others* [2023] EWFC 10. This test applies to all categories of applicants. See *Coventry City Council v CC and A* [2007] EWCA Civ 1383; *Re MW (Leave to Apply for Adoption)* [2014] EWHC 385 (Fam), where the applicant applied to adopt her 17-year-old cousin from Pakistan who had lived with her for only 16 months. On the facts, the court considered that the application was made in good faith and for good and appropriate reasons, and had not been contrived to gain immigration status in the United Kingdom. Contrast with *Re IH (A Child) (Permission to Apply for Adoption)* [2013] EWHC 1235 (Fam), where the mother had entered the United Kingdom with the child on the pretext of seeing her sick grandmother and left the child with his uncle and aunt. The application made after the child's visa had expired was refused because the court found there had not been any estrangement between the child and his birth family, and the applicants had no true desire or other reasons to adopt a child. They had five children of their own. Their motive was to give the child a better life in the United Kingdom.

## Had his home with the applicant

3.12 The home does not have to be maintained in the same location throughout the relevant period. Whether or not a child had his home with the applicant will depend on the circumstances (*ECC v M and Others* [2008] EWHC 332 (Fam)). When a child is temporarily absent, for example, at a boarding school, the question whether the child has his home with the applicant(s) is determined by reference to whether the applicant(s) continue to exercise parental control over him and some significant time is spent with the applicant at home with them. See *Re X (Adoption Application: Gateway Requirements)* [2013] EWHC 689 (Fam), where the application by the mother's partner to adopt the mother's daughter failed because the mother's partner had spent very little physical time with the daughter. It was held that the focus of the issue should not be on the relationship between the applicant and the child. If relationship considerations were relevant for computing the time limits, the statutory provision would have expressly made reference to this. Therefore, although on the facts there were powerful welfare considerations for allowing the application, these, the court held, could not overrule the statutory gateway requirements. Contrast with the case of *Re X (A Child: Foreign Surrogacy)* [2018] EWFC 15, where it was held that the child had his home with a married couple who had never lived together. The court took the view that it was not for the court to question the couple's sexual relationship during the marriage.

3.13 The case of *Re TY (Preliminaries to Inter-country Adoption)* [2019] EWHC 2979 (Fam) illustrates how the court deals with the circumstances of the individual case and makes its decision on the basis of the welfare of the child and the protection of the applicant's and the child's rights under European Convention, Art 8. The case concerned a child (T) adopted in Jamaica in 2014 by his aunt who lived in England. Due to delays in the entry visa being granted, T did not make his home with her until 2018. When she applied to adopt him in England, one of the issues raised was whether T had 'his home' with the applicant for the relevant period preceding the application. The court held that T had had his home with the applicant notwithstanding that he had not physically lived with the applicant for the whole of that period because the applicant and T had a parent/child relationship while he remained in Jamaica, and the applicant had arranged his daily routine and provided for him. Other relevant factors which the court took into account were their mother/son relationship; the fact that the applicant and T had been in daily contact when not together; they had lived together for 22 of the 26 weeks required; the applicant's younger son had visited T in Jamaica and they had spent time together as a family; the separation between the applicant and T was not by choice but due to the delay in the Home Office issuing a visa (see [33]–[36] of the judgment).

## OPPORTUNITIES TO SEE THE CHILD AND THE PROSPECTIVE ADOPTER(S) AT HOME

3.14 An adoption order may not be made unless the court is satisfied that sufficient opportunities to see the child with the applicant, or in the case of a couple, both of them together, in the home environment have been given to the adoption agency which placed the child with the applicant(s); or in any other case, to the local authority within whose area the applicant's/applicants' home is (ACA 2002, s 42(7)). The relevant authority means any unitary authority or any county council. The applicant(s) must thus have a home within England and Wales (ACA 2002, s 144(1)).

3.15 Therefore, where a child is placed for adoption by an adoption agency the home environment may be outside England and Wales. Under ACA 2002, s 42(7)(a) the home environment may be outside England and Wales because in this instance the phrase 'home environment' could have been but has not been geographically defined by the Act (*Re A (A Child)* [2009] EWCA Civ 41).

3.16 Where the child has not been placed for adoption with the applicant(s) by an adoption agency, the home must be within a local authority in England and Wales (ACA 2002, s 42(7)(b); *Re SL (Adoption: Home in Jurisdiction)* [2004] EWHC 1283 (Fam)). Additionally, the applicant(s) are required to give notice to the appropriate local authority of their intention to adopt no more than two years nor less than three months before the date on which the application to adopt is made: ACA 2002, s 44(2), (3). Thus, at least three months' notice is required. The appropriate local authority is the local authority for the area in which at the time of giving the notice of intention to adopt, the applicant(s) have their home. If the applicant(s) are seeking permission to apply before the statutory time limit set out in ACA 2002, s 42(5) (see paras 3.9–3.11) has been met, the notice of intention to adopt may not be given until the application is finally determined by the court and permission is granted to the applicant(s) to apply for an adoption order.

3.17 In *Re A (A Child: Adoption Time Limits s 44(3))* [2020] EWHC 3296 (Fam), the notice to the local authority had been given more than two years before the adoption application was made. Keehan J referred to a number of cases where, despite the failure to meet strict compliance with procedural time limits, the courts had considered the purpose of the legislation ([24]–[30]), and held that a purposive approach should be applied to the provisions of ACA 2002, s 44(3), and if he was wrong on this, he was satisfied that pursuant to the Human Rights Act 1998, s 3, the Art 8 rights of the child required him to read down the provisions of s 44(3) of the Act to make it compatible with the European Convention right to family life. Keehan J concluded that 'to do otherwise would be to deny A [the child] the transformative benefits of an adoption order such an outcome would be nonsensical and an affront to public policy' ([50]).

3.18 In *Andrew v Beatrice and Others* [2023] EWFC 114, the court gave permission for the application to proceed notwithstanding that notice to the local authority was given at the time the application was made, instead of the required minimum of three months prior to the application being made. The court, applying Keehan J's purposive approach, held that the notice requirements in s 44(2) and (3) were directory rather than imperative. Account was also taken of the fact that the failure to comply with the notice requirements had not prejudiced any party or the court; the local authority had not been impeded in the preparation of its reports; the non-compliance was accidental. The court therefore exercised its discretion and allowed the adoption application to proceed to a final hearing.

3.19 Similarly, in *Re X (Time Barred Adoption)* [2024] EWHC 364 (Fam), the notice given was less than three months before the date of the adoption application. This was an application by a step-parent Mr X who had adopted the child in Ukraine in 2015. The court, in exercising its discretion in permitting the application to be made, applied the purposive approach taken in previous cases and took into consideration the fact that the child had lived with his mother and Mr X for 16 years since he was two years old. The local authority was supportive of the application, and it was clear that adoption was in the best interests and welfare of the child.

# Chapter 4

# Placement for Adoption and Placement Orders

## INTRODUCTION

4.1 ACA 2002, ss 18–41 set out the provisions which apply to the placement of a child for adoption by an adoption agency. The objective is to ensure that issues leading up to an adoption order are dealt with at an early stage, providing greater certainty, a smoother route to placement with the prospective adopter(s) and a non-adversarial adoption hearing. (See, for example, the observations of Peter Jackson LJ in *Re W (A Child Leave to Oppose Adoption)* [2020] EWCA Civ 16 at [40].) The parent(s) must be involved before it is decided to place the child for adoption by either giving their consent or being given the opportunity of challenging the proposals during the court process for the application for a placement order, i.e. an order made by a court authorising a local authority to place a child for adoption with any prospective adopter(s) chosen by the authority (ACA 2002, s 21(1)). If the parent consents to the child being placed for adoption or the court, on the application of the local authority, makes a placement order in consequence of which the child is placed with prospective adopter(s), the child's parent(s) have limited opportunity to apply for revocation or variation of the placement order or to oppose any application for an adoption order.

4.2 The statutory provisions are supplemented by those set out in the AAR 2005 and the Care Planning Placement and Case Review (England) Regulations 2010 (SI 2010/959) or, in relation to Wales, the Care Planning Placement and Case Review (Wales) Regulations 2015 (SI 2015/1818) (W 261). The regulations set out the procedures that must be followed by the local authority or other adoption agency when deciding whether a child should be placed for adoption and in relation to a child who is in the care of, and accommodated by, the local authority.

## BY WHOM AND WHEN MAY A CHILD BE PLACED FOR ADOPTION?

4.3 ACA 2002, s 18(1) provides that an adoption agency (see below) may place a child for adoption with prospective adopter(s), or where it has placed a child with any person (whether under the ACA 2002 or not), leave the child with them as prospective adopter(s), except where the child is less than six weeks old (ACA 2002, s 18(1); see below). It may, however, only do so provided it is satisfied that the child ought to be placed for adoption (ACA 2002, s 18(2)). Additionally, AAR 2005, reg 33 requires the adoption agency to take into account any recommendation made by the adoption panel when it decides to place the child with any prospective adopters. Any reference to placing a child for adoption by an agency and to a child who is placed for adoption by an agency is to be interpreted accordingly (ACA 2002, s 18(5)). An adoption agency is defined in the Act as a local authority or registered adoption society (ACA 2002, s 1(2)).

4.4 A child who is placed or authorised to be placed for adoption by a local authority is a 'looked after' child (ACA 2002, s 18(3)), and therefore the local authority will be responsible for the child as required under the ChA 1989 until an adoption order is made.

4.5 An adoption agency may place the child for adoption with prospective adopter(s), either with the consent of each parent or guardian of the child or, in the case of a local authority, if that local authority has obtained a placement order. The local authority, however, is not prevented from placing a child with foster carer(s) who are also registered as local authority foster carer(s) and prospective adopter(s). Furthermore, pursuant to the amendments made to the ChA 1989 by the Children and Families Act 2014, where a local authority is considering adoption but has not yet obtained a placement order, it is now required to consider placing the child with local authority foster carer(s) who are also prospective adopter(s) (ChA 1989, s 22C). Since July 2014 the local authority is also permitted to place the child with approved adopter(s) who are not yet approved as local authority foster carer(s) on the basis that the person(s) is approved as a temporary foster carer (see Care Planning, Placement and Case Review (England) Regulations 2010 (SI 2010/959), reg 25A, and Care Planning, Placement and Case Review (Wales) Regulations 2015 (SI 2015/1818) (W 261), reg 28).

4.6 In such cases the local authority is authorised to grant temporary approval only if it is satisfied that the placement is the most appropriate placement for, and it is in the best interests of, the child to be placed with that person(s) but provided that it has:

(a) assessed the suitability of that person to care for the child as a foster carer; and
(b) considered that, in all the circumstances and taking into account the services to be provided by the local authority, the proposed arrangements will safeguard and promote the child's welfare and meet the child's needs as set out in the care plan (Care Planning, Placement and Case Review (England) Regulations 2010 (SI 2010/959), reg 25). See also the statutory guidance on *Early Permanence Placements and Approval of Prospective Adopters as Foster Carers*, available at https://dera.ioe.ac.uk/id/eprint/20575/.

4.7 The temporary approval will come to an end:

(a) on termination of the placement by the local authority;
(b) on the prospective adopter(s)' approval being terminated;
(c) on the approved prospective adopter(s) being approved as foster carer(s);
(d) if the approved prospective adopter(s) give 28 days' written notice to the local authority that they no longer wish to be temporarily approved as foster carers, where the 28-day period will start from the date when the local authority receives the notice; or
(e) on the child being placed for adoption with the approved prospective adopter(s) pursuant to the ACA 2002.

4.8 Where a child is placed on a temporary basis with prospective adopter(s) as foster carer(s), the local authority must inform the birth parents, including a father without parental responsibility, of the placement and the legal implications of the placement (AAR 2005, reg 14). AAR 2005, reg 14(3) provides that where the local authority is aware of the identity of a father without parental responsibility and it considers that it is appropriate to do so, it should contact the father and take steps to explain the legal process for placement and adoption of the child and its legal implications to him. The adoption agency is also required to ascertain his wishes and feelings about the child being placed for adoption and being adopted and his future contact with the child. It should also inform him of his right to apply for parental responsibility and for a care arrangement order under the ChA 1989. If the adoption agency has any doubts about the appropriateness of contacting the father without parental responsibility, an application should be made to the court for directions (see FPR 2010, Pt 14). This usually occurs in cases where the child is relinquished at birth by the birth mother who, for a number of reasons, may wish to conceal the birth from the father and family members. The issue of notification to the father of the child with or without parental responsibility and members of the family is discussed in detail in paras 16.29–16.39. The procedure for applying to the court for directions on the issue of whether the father of the child or family members should be notified of the placement of the child for adoption and the court's approach to such an application are dealt with in Chapter 16.

## Placing children with parental consent

4.9 An adoption agency is authorised to place a child for adoption where each parent or guardian who has parental responsibility for the child has consented to the child being placed for adoption with the prospective adopter(s) identified in the consent, or with any prospective adopter(s) who may be chosen by the agency and has not withdrawn the consent (ACA 2002, s 19(1)). The child will continue to be so placed notwithstanding that the parent's/parents' consent is subsequently withdrawn (ACA 2002, ss 19(4) and 52(5)). Where it is not clear whether parental consent to the placement has been given, the local authority may apply to the court for clarification (*A Local Authority v GC* [2008] EWHC 2555 (Fam), [2009] 1 FLR 299).

4.10 However, an adoption agency may not place a child for adoption unless it is satisfied that adoption is in the best interests of the child and account has been taken of any recommendation made by the adoption panel, as required by AAR 2005, reg 33. Additionally, once the decision is taken to place the child for adoption, the adoption agency must notify the decision, in writing, to each of the following persons:

(a) the parent(s) or guardian of the child;
(b) the father of the child (where this is appropriate) where AAR 2005, reg 14(3) applies (see para 4.8).

4.11 Where the child is of sufficient age and understanding, consideration must also be given to explain the decision to the child.

4.12 It should be noted, however, that the consensual route to placement does not apply where care proceedings are pending or where a care order has been made but the appropriate local authority has not been authorised to place the child for adoption. In such cases the appropriate local authority must apply for a placement order if it is satisfied that the child ought to be placed for adoption (ACA 2002, s 19(3)).

# CHILD UNDER SIX WEEKS OLD

4.13 An adoption agency may place a child who is less than six weeks old for adoption with the voluntary agreement of the parent(s) given in writing (AAR 2005, reg 35(4)). Such a placement, however, is not an authorised placement within the provisions of the ACA 2002. It follows that the parents continue to have parental responsibility for the child.

4.14 Before placement of such a child, however, the process set out under AAR 2005, Pt 5 must be complied with (see Chapter 16). Once the child reaches the age of six weeks, the adoption agency must either obtain the formal consent of the parent(s) to continue the placement or the local authority must apply for a placement order (*A Local Authority v GC* [2008] EWHC 2555 (Fam)). Although a child under six weeks old may be placed for adoption, consent to the making of an adoption order, given by the mother, is ineffective if given less than six weeks after the child's birth (ACA 2002, s 52(3)).

## CONSENT

### Meaning of consent

4.15 'Consent' means 'consent given unconditionally and with full understanding of what is involved, but a person may consent to adoption without knowing the identity of the person in whose favour the order will be made' (ACA 2002, s 52(5)). As set out in ACA 2002, s 19(2), consent may be:

(a) specific to identified adopters or to the adoption agency in Form A101; or
(b) general, i.e. to adoption by any prospective adopter(s) who may be chosen by the adoption agency in Form A100; or
(c) combined, i.e. consent to placement with specified prospective adopter(s), or with any other prospective adopter(s) who may be chosen by the adoption agency if the child is removed from, or returned by, the identified prospective adopter(s) in Form A102.

### Advance consent for the child to be adopted

4.16 ACA 2002, s 20 provides that a parent or guardian who consents to the child being placed for adoption may give advance consent to a child being adopted in the future:

(a) at the same time as consent for placement for adoption;
(b) at any subsequent time;

in relation to:

- (i) prospective adopter(s) who are identified;
- (ii) adoption by any prospective adopter(s) who may be chosen by the adoption agency or the local authority (ACA 2002, s 20(2)).

4.17 Advance consent to adoption should be given using Form A103. Where one parent has given consent for placement for adoption and at a later date the other parent acquires parental responsibility, the other parent is treated as having given consent at the same time as that given by the first parent (ACA 2002, s 52(9) and (10)). Advance consent may be withdrawn provided it is withdrawn before an application for an adoption order has been made (ACA 2002, s 20(4); and see para 4.22). A parent who gives advance consent to the making of an adoption order may, at the same time or at any subsequent time, give notice to the adoption agency stating that he does not want to be informed of any application for an adoption order. The notice will have effect from the time it is received by the adoption agency. However, such a notice if given may be withdrawn (ACA 2002, s 20(4) and (5)).

## Consent in relation to a child less than six weeks old

4.18 See paras 4.13–4.14.

## Counselling

4.19 The adoption agency is required to provide a counselling service for the parent(s) or guardian of the child, and to explain the procedure for placement and the legal implications of giving consent and 'advance consent', and of the placement and adoption orders. In addition, the parent(s) or guardian must be provided with written information. The agency also has a duty to ascertain the parent's/parents' or guardian's wishes and feelings about the child and in relation to contact, and their religious and cultural views (AAR 2005, reg 14). (See further in Chapter 16.)

## Obtaining consent

4.20 The agreement of the parent(s) or guardian to placement of the child for adoption must be:

(a) given on the appropriate statutory form, i.e.: (i) Form A100 for placement with any prospective adopter(s); (ii) Form A101 for adoption with identified adopter(s); (iii) Form A102 for adoption with identified adopter(s); and, if the placement fails, with any prospective adopter(s); (iv) Form A103 for advance consent;
(b) witnessed by the appropriate officer: in England and Wales, it must be witnessed by a Children and Family Court Advisory and Support Service (Cafcass) officer; if the child is ordinarily resident in Wales, by a Welsh family proceedings officer; in Scotland by a Justice of the Peace or Sheriff; and in Northern Ireland by a Justice of the Peace (AAR 2005, reg 20). It is

the responsibility of the adoption agency to contact the appropriate Cafcass office and inform them of the need for a Cafcass officer to witness the consent. In all other cases the form should be witnessed by a British Consul, a notary or a person who is authorised by the law of the country where the document is signed to administer an oath;

(c) valid: for the consent given to be valid the person authorised as above to witness the consent given will need to be satisfied that the parent(s) or guardian fully understand the consequences of giving the consent and that it is unconditionally given. If the person is not so satisfied or has doubts about the competence or capacity of the parent(s) to give valid consent, they should inform the agency of this fact;

(d) current: where an application for a care order has been made, any consent previously given is ineffective while proceedings under ChA 1989, s 31 are pending or where a care order has been made after the consent was given (ACA 2002, s 19(3)). If the care plan is for the child to be placed for adoption and the child is made the subject of a care order, the local authority should apply for a placement order and, if that application is granted, it is that placement order which will provide authorisation to the local authority to place the child for adoption and not the previous consents, if any, given by the parent(s) (ACA 2002, ss 19 and 22(3)).

## Consequences of consent to placement for adoption

4.21 Where parental consent is given to place the child for adoption, a number of consequences arise, some of which are irrecoverable. These include:

(a) when an adoption agency is authorised to place a child for adoption, parental responsibility is given to the agency (ACA 2002, s 25(2));

(b) while a child is placed with prospective adopter(s), they will acquire parental responsibility while the child remains with them (ACA 2002, s 25(3));

(c) a child arrangement order providing for contact under ChA 1989, s 8 or for contact under ChA 1989, s 34 will come to an end, resulting in any contact between the child and his parent(s) being determined by the adoption agency (ACA 2002, s 26). However, the court may make an order under ACA 2002, s 26 requiring the person with whom the child lives or is to live to allow the child to have contact with the person named in the order (ACA 2002, s 26(2)(b));

(d) a parent or guardian may not apply for a care arrangement order under the ChA 1989 or an order for contact under s 34 of that Act;

(e) no person may cause the child to be known by a new surname without the court's permission (ACA 2002, s 28(2) and (3)(a));

(f) no person may remove the child from the UK without the court's permission (ACA 2002, s 28(2) and (3)(b));

(g) a parent or guardian may not oppose an application for an adoption order without the court's permission (ACA 2002, s 47). The court may only grant permission if there has been a change of circumstances since consent to the placement of the child was given;
(h) the parent's ability to require return/removal of the child is restricted (see below).

## Withdrawal of consent

4.22 Consent, including advance consent, given by a parent(s) or guardian for their child to be placed for adoption may be withdrawn at any time until an application is made for an adoption order. For such withdrawal to be valid and effective it must be made:

(a) on the statutory Form 106 or by written notice given to the adoption agency (ACA 2002, s 52(8) and s 144(1)); and
(b) before an application for an adoption order is made (ACA 2002, s 52(4)).

## Consequence of withdrawal of consent – return of the child

4.23 Where a child has not been placed for adoption and is being accommodated by an adoption agency and the parent or guardian withdraws consent and informs the agency that he wishes the child to be returned, the agency must return the child to the parent(s) or guardian within seven days 'beginning with the request' (see below), unless an application is or has been made for a placement order and the application has not been disposed of (ACA 2002, s 31(2)). The local authority must nevertheless review the situation and, where necessary, apply for a placement order (AAR 2005, reg 38; and see also paras 4.30–4.31).

4.24 Where the child is placed for adoption by an adoption agency when consent is withdrawn, and the parent(s) or guardian inform the agency that they wish the child to be returned, the child must be returned to the agency by the prospective adopter(s) unless an application is or has been made for a placement order and that application is pending (ACA 2002, s 32). Where the agency is a registered adoption society it is obliged to consider whether it is appropriate to notify the local authority in whose area the child is living (AAR 2005, reg 38) (see also paras 4.30–4.31).

4.25 The agency must notify the prospective adopter(s) of the withdrawal of consent and request the return of the child. The prospective adopter(s) must return the child to the agency within 14 days beginning with the day on which notice is given (ACA 2002, s 32(1) and (2)) unless an application is or has been made for a placement order. A prospective adopter who fails to return the child is guilty of an offence and liable on summary conviction to imprisonment for a period not exceeding three months or a fine under level 5 on the standard scale or both (ACA 2002, s 32(3)). As soon as the child is returned to the adoption agency by the prospective adopter(s), the agency must return the child to the parent or guardian (ACA 2002, s 32(4)). If, however, before the notice is given, an application for an adoption order, special guardianship order or residence order, or for permission to apply for a special guardianship order or residence order, was made in respect of the child and the application is still pending, the prospective adopter(s) are not required to return the child to the agency unless the court so orders (ACA 2002, s 32(5)).

4.26 The term 'beginning with the request', read literally, means from the date of the request. If the request is sent by second-class post, the local authority will barely have time to make an application for a placement order or prepare the child for removal. It could be argued that the provision is not one which sufficiently takes into account the welfare of the child. Where the child has been placed, the obligation on the adoption agency is to return the child to the parent as soon as the child is returned by the prospective adopter(s) to the adoption agency. The prospective adopter(s) are obliged to return the child 'within 14 days beginning with the day on which notice is given'. Again, the issue could arise whether time begins to run from the date the notice is sent, or the date the notice is received. ACA 2002, s 32(2) imposes a duty on the adoption agency to give notice of the withdrawal to the prospective adopter(s), but it does not specify the form of such notice or the period within which it must be given. It follows that the return of the child within 14 days of the withdrawal of consent by the parent may prove difficult unless notice is given by email or special delivery service and followed by notice served by post. However, applying the decision of the court in *Prospective Adopters v Sheffield City Council* [2000] EWCA Civ 1591 (referred to in para 4.39), it is suggested that it is preferable to give written notice.

4.27 Where a child placed for adoption is less than six weeks old or the agency has at no time been authorised to place the child for adoption, and the parent informs the agency that he wishes the child to be returned to him, the agency must give notice of the parent's wish to the prospective adopter(s) and they must return the child to the agency within a period of seven days beginning with the day on which notice is given, unless an application is or has been made for a placement order and the application is pending (ACA 2002, s 31(3) and (4)). Immediately on the child being returned to the agency, it must return the child to the parent(s) or guardian of the child (ACA 2002, s 31(6)). A prospective adopter who fails to return the child commits an offence liable on summary conviction to imprisonment for a term not exceeding three months or a fine under level 5 of the standard scale or both (ACA 2002, s 31(5)).

4.28 The meaning of 'seven days beginning with the day on which notice is given' may need to be determined. Presumably, the notice referred to is the notice given by the local authority to the prospective adopter(s), but it is not clear whether the period of seven days runs from the date inserted in the notice sent, or the date when the notice is received. ACA 2002, s 110 provides that any notice or information may be sent by post. If time begins to run from the date the notice is sent, and the notice is sent by second-class post, it may be two or three days before it is received. In many cases this will not give sufficient time to prepare the child for the move and could be both emotionally and psychologically damaging. It would be advisable to ensure that the notice is sent by special delivery or delivered personally. In view of the fact that non-compliance with these provisions is made a criminal offence, any issues arising under the provisions will have to be considered with sensitivity, applying the welfare principle and the overriding objective.

### Dispensing with consent

4.29 For grounds, see Chapter 6, and for how to request for consent to be dispensed with, see paras 4.88–4.89.

## PROHIBITION ON REMOVAL FROM PLACEMENT

### Removal by an adoption agency

4.30 Where the child is placed for adoption by an adoption agency and the agency is of the opinion that the child should not remain with the prospective adopter(s) and gives them notice of their opinion, the prospective adopter(s) must return the child to the agency not later than the end of seven days beginning with the giving of notice. A prospective adopter who fails to return the child is guilty of an offence punishable on summary conviction of imprisonment for a term not exceeding three months or a fine within level 5 of the standard scale or both (ACA 2002, s 35(4)).

4.31 However, if, before the notice was given an application was made for an adoption order, including a Scottish or Northern Irish adoption order, or a special guardianship order, care arrangement order or permission to apply for such an order, the prospective adopter(s) are not required to return the child unless the court so orders (ACA 2002, s 35(5)).

### Return/removal of a child in an emergency

4.32 Where the local authority seeks the return/removal of a child as a matter of urgency without giving the required notice or at short notice, an application should be made for an emergency protection order or an interim order to the Family Court (*DL and ML v Newham Borough Council and Secretary of State for Education* [2011] EWHC 1127 (Admin)).

## Removal from consensual placement under ACA 2002, s 19

4.33 No person, including the parents of the child, may remove from the prospective adopter(s) a child who has been placed for adoption by an adoption agency under ACA 2002, s 19 (consensual placement), or a child so placed who is either less than six weeks old or whom the agency has not been authorised to place for adoption (ACA 2002, s 30(1)). Only the adoption agency may remove the child. The parent or guardian must inform the agency if he wishes the child returned.

4.34 Where a child has not yet been placed for adoption but is being accommodated by a local authority and the local authority has applied for a placement order which is pending, only the local authority may remove the child from his accommodation. Any other person will need to apply to the court for permission to do so and can remove the child only if the court grants permission to do so (ACA 2002, s 30(2)).

4.35 Where a child is not for the time being placed for adoption but is accommodated by an adoption agency and that agency is authorised to place the child for adoption with the parent's/parents' consent or would be so authorised if any consent to placement had not been withdrawn, no person other than the agency may remove the child from the accommodation (ACA 2002, s 30(3)); only the agency is permitted to do so. If the parent or guardian of the child wants the child returned, he must request the return of the child (see para 4.22).

4.36 Where the child is placed for adoption by an adoption agency and either the child is less than six weeks old or the agency has at no time been authorised to place the child for adoption, and a parent or guardian of the child informs the agency that he wishes the child returned to him, the agency is under a duty, unless an application is or has been made for a placement order which is pending, on receipt of such a notice, to notify the prospective adopter(s) of the request. They, in turn, have a duty to return the child to the agency within seven days of the day on which the notice is given. On the child's return to the agency, the agency must return the child to the parent as soon thereafter as possible (ACA 2002, s 31(3)–(6)) (see further paras 4.23–4.28).

## Removal after placement order

4.37 Where a placement order: (a) is in force; or (b) has been revoked, but the child has not been returned by the prospective adopter(s), or remains in any accommodation provided by the local authority, only the local authority may remove the child from the prospective adopter(s) or from the accommodation provided by the local authority (ACA 2002, s 34(1)). A person who removes a child in contravention of this provision is guilty of an offence (ACA 2002, s 34(2)).

4.38 If a placement order is revoked, and the court determines that the child should not remain with the prospective adopter(s) with whom the child is placed, the prospective adopter(s) must return the child to the local authority within such period as determined by the court (ACA 2002, s 31(3)). The court may determine that the child be returned to his parent or guardian, in which case the local authority is required do so as soon as the child is returned to the local authority or within such period as directed by the court. If the child is accommodated by the local authority, it must return the child immediately (ACA 2002, s 34(4)).

4.39 Where a child is placed for adoption and the prospective adopter(s) give notice to the agency of their wish to return the child, the agency must receive the child within seven days of the notice being given, and the agency must notify the parent or guardian of the child of the prospective adopter's/adopters' decision to return the child (ACA 2002, s 35(1)). The prospective adopter's/adopters' notice to the agency of their wish to return the child permanently must be clear and unequivocal that the prospective adopter(s) no longer wish to be considered as prospective adopter(s) for the children and wish the agency to remove the child from their care, and must show that the prospective adopter(s) understand that they are withdrawing from the plan. Notice given by email is insufficient to amount to notice within the meaning of ACA 2002, s 35(1). Where it is evident that there may be a crisis in the placement, the local authority should take steps to investigate and identify the problem and offer support before permanently removing the child from the placement. Furthermore, where following the request to remove the child, the local authority removes the child and comes to the conclusion that the child should not be returned/remain with the prospective adopters, it must give notice to the prospective adopters of its opinion. It is insufficient to refuse to return the child on the basis that the request by the prospective adopters for the temporary removal was sufficient indication that the placement had come to an end. The notice from the local authority required under ACA 2002, s 35(2) must be in writing and the birth parents must be notified of the situation so that they can exercise their right to apply to revoke the placement order. Notice cannot be inferred from the local authority's conduct. (See *Prospective Adopters v Sheffield City Council* [2000] EWCA Civ 1591.)

4.40 Similarly, where the adoption agency takes the decision that the child should not remain with the prospective adopter(s) and gives notice to them of its decision, the child must be returned by the prospective adopter(s) to the agency within seven days of notice being given to them (ACA 2002, s 35(2)). The agency must also give notice to any parent or guardian of the child of the obligation to return the child to the agency (ACA 2002, s 35(3)). If, however, before such notice is given to the prospective adopter(s), an application for an adoption order, special guardianship order or residence order, or for permission to apply for a special guardianship order or residence order, was made in respect of the child and the application has not been disposed of, the prospective adopter(s) are not required to return the child to the agency unless the court so orders (ACA 2002, s 35(5)) (see also the case of *Prospective Adopters v Sheffield City Council* [2000] EWCA Civ 1591 on what constitutes notice; *R v Devon County Council ex parte O (Adoption)* [1997] 2 FLR 388; and *RCW v A Local Authority* [2013] 2 FLR 95). In those circumstances the local authority's remedy is to make an application for an emergency protection order, and application for the removal of the child or reconsideration of the decision to remove (ChA 1989, s 43). The local authority is required to give reasons for the removal/refusal to return the child to the prospective adopters (see *DL and ML v Newham London Borough Council* [2011] EWHC 1127 (Admin).

4.41 Non-compliance by the prospective adopter(s) or the local authority, or removal by any person of a child from its placement without the authority of the court, is an offence. On summary conviction an offender is liable to imprisonment for a term not exceeding three months or a fine, or both (ACA 2002, s 34(5)).

## RESTRICTIONS ON REMOVAL IN PENDING PROCEEDINGS

### From foster parents

4.42 Where a child has been in the care of foster parents and has had his home at all times with them for the preceding five years, and the foster carers have given notice of intention to adopt or have applied for permission to apply for an adoption order and the application has not been disposed of, the child may only be removed by a person who has permission from the court to do so or by a local authority or other person in the exercise of a power conferred by any enactment other than ChA 1989, s 20(8) or Social Services and Well-being (Wales) Act 2014 (SSWB(W)A 2014), s 76(5) (ACA 2002, s 38(1)–(3)).

4.43 If the child has not had his home with the foster parents for the preceding five years, but has had his home with them at all times during the preceding one year and the foster parents have given notice of intention to adopt, the only persons who may remove the child are:

(a) a person with parental responsibility for the child who is exercising the power under ChA 1989, s 20(8) or SSWB(W)A 2014, s 76(5); or
(b) a person who has the court's permission; or
(c) a local authority or other person in the exercise of a power conferred by any enactment other than the ChA 1989 or SSWB(W)A 2014, s 76(5) (ACA 2002, s 38(4)–(5)).

4.44 If the foster carer has given notice of intention to adopt a child in their care, they may, to prevent removal of the child from their care, apply to the court for an injunction prohibiting removal (see *Re B (Children) (Adoption)* [2012] 3 WLR 208, CA).

## From partners of parents

4.45 Where a child has his home with a partner of a parent and the partner has given notice of intention to adopt, then if the child's home has been with the partner for not less than three years (whether continuous or not) during the preceding five years, only a person who has the court's permission or a local authority or other person in the exercise of a power conferred by any enactment other than ChA 1989, s 20(8) or SSWB(W)A 2014, s 76(5) may remove the child from the partner's home (ACA 2002, s 39(1) and (2)). In all other cases a parent or guardian of the child or a person who has the court's permission or a local authority or other authorised person in the exercise of a power conferred by any enactment other than ChA 1989, s 20(8) or SSWB(W)A 2014, s 76(5) may remove the child (ACA 2002, s 39(3)).

## From non-agency placement

4.46 At any time when a child's home is with any persons ('the people concerned') with whom the child is not placed by an adoption agency, but the people concerned:

(a) have applied for an adoption order with respect to the child and the application has not been disposed of;
(b) have given notice of intention to adopt;
(c) have applied for permission to apply for an adoption order under ACA 2002, s 42(6) (see paras 3.10–3.11) and that application has not been disposed of,

no person may remove the child other than in accordance with the scheme set out at para 4.48 in relation to other applicants. However, a notice of intention to adopt will be disregarded if more than four months have elapsed since the notice was given without the people concerned applying for an adoption order, or if the notice is a second or subsequent notice of intention to adopt and was given during the period of five months beginning with the giving of the preceding notice (ACA 2002, s 36(1) and (2)).

4.47 Where the people concerned have been given permission to apply for an adoption order, the placement will remain protected for three days thereafter to enable them to make the application to adopt (ACA 2002, s 36(3)).

### In any other non-agency case

4.48 In any other case which does not fall under any of the above provisions, provided the people concerned have given notice of intention to adopt or have applied for permission to make the application to adopt, a child may only be removed by a person with the court's permission or a local authority or other person in exercise of a power conferred by any enactment other than ChA 1989, s 20(8) or SSWB(W)A 2014, s 76(5) (ACA 2002, s 40).

## BREACH OF RESTRICTIONS ON REMOVAL – RECOVERY ORDERS

### When and by whom can a breach be enforced?

4.49 Where a child has been removed:

(a) in contravention of the provisions set out above or there are reasonable grounds for believing that a person intends to remove a child in contravention of those provisions; or
(b) there is a failure to comply with the statutory requirements under ACA 2002, s 31(4), s 32(2), s 33(2), s 34(3) or s 35(2) to return the child,

any person may apply to the court for a recovery order.

### Orders the court is empowered to make

4.50 Where it appears to the court that a child has been removed as set out at para 4.49, it may:

(a) direct any person who is in a position to do so, to produce the child on request to any person mentioned in the order or a constable or a person authorised by the adoption agency;
(b) authorise the removal of the child by any of the persons named in the order or a constable or a person authorised by the adoption agency;

(c) require any person who has information about the child's whereabouts to disclose the information to a constable or officer of the court;
(d) authorise a constable to enter any premises specified in the order and search for the child, using reasonable force if necessary (ACA 2002, s 41(1), (2) and (4)).

4.51 Where a court requires a person to disclose information, that person must comply with the request even if the information sought might constitute evidence that he had committed an offence (ACA 2002, s 41(6)), but except in relation to a charge of perjury, that person is protected from evidence relating to the information being adduced in the proceedings and from being questioned in relation to the information, by or on behalf of the prosecution (ACA 2002, s 41(7)–(8)).

4.52 Any person who intentionally obstructs any person in the exercise of a recovery order is guilty of an offence liable on summary conviction to a fine not exceeding level 3 on the standard scale (ACA 2002, s 41(5)).

### Review of child's case

4.53 Where an adoption agency is authorised to place a child for adoption either by consent of the parents or by a placement order, until the child is placed for adoption, the agency must carry out a review of the child's case as required by the Care Planning, Placement and Case Review Regulations 2010 and AAR 2005, reg 36.

## PROCEDURE FOR APPLICATION FOR A RECOVERY ORDER

4.54 The procedure is governed by FPR 2010, rr 14.1–14.17.

### Form of application

4.55 An application for a recovery order must be made on Form A57, which is available at:

www.justice.gov.uk/courts/procedure-rules/family/formspage

4.56 The application may be made without notice. If the application is made as a matter of urgency outside normal court hours and by telephone, the application should be filed on the next business day thereafter (FPR 2010, r 14.20(1) and (2)).

## Who should be made respondents?

4.57 The respondents to the application are:

- all the parties to pending placement or adoption proceedings or proceedings under ACA 2002, s 84;
- any adoption agency authorised to place the child for adoption or which has placed the child for adoption;
- any local authority to whom notice under ACA 2002, s 44 (notice of intention to adopt or apply for a s 84 order) has been given;
- any person having parental responsibility for the child;
- any person in whose favour there is provision for contact;
- any person who was caring for the child immediately prior to the making of the application; and
- any person whom the applicant alleges to have effected, or to have been or to be responsible for, the taking or keeping of the child (FPR 2010, r 14.20(3)).

## Procedure following issue of proceedings

4.58 The application will proceed under FPR 2010, rr 14.1–14.17 (see para 4.73).

# PLACEMENT UNDER A PLACEMENT ORDER

4.59 A placement order is an order made by the court authorising the local authority to place a child for adoption with prospective adopter(s) chosen by the local authority (ACA 2002, s 21(1)). Parental responsibility for the child will pass to the local authority and when the child is placed with the prospective adopter(s) and so long as the child remains in the placement, also to them (ACA 2002, s 25). The local authority may, however, determine that the parental responsibility of any parent or guardian or of the prospective adopter(s) is to be restricted to the extent specified in the determination (ACA 2002, s 25). On the making of the placement order the court does not have any powers to impose conditions upon the placement for an adoption order (*Re A (Placement Order: Imposition of Conditions on Adoption)* [2013] EWCA Civ 1611).

## Grounds for applying for a placement order

4.60 A placement order cannot be made unless:

(a) the child is the subject of a care order; or
(b) the court is satisfied that the threshold criteria in ChA 1989, s 31(2) are met; or
(c) the child has no parent or guardian; or

(d) each parent or guardian of the child has consented to the child being placed for adoption with any prospective adopter(s), or with those chosen by the local authority and has not withdrawn consent; or
(e) the parent's/parents' or guardian's consent should be dispensed with under ACA 2002, s 52 (ACA 2002, s 21(2) and (3)).

4.61 However, the court will only make a placement order if it considers that the paramountcy consideration set out in ACA 2002, s 1 is met and that options other than adoption have been explored (see *Re H (Care and Adoption Assessment of Wider Family)* [2019] EWFC 10 and the cases cited in the judgment; see further para 4.69 and Chapter 7).

4.62 A child who is 'looked after' but not subject to a care order will come within these provisions, where the threshold criteria in ChA 1989, s 31(2) referred to under (b) (above) are met (*LB v London Borough of Merton and CB* [2013] EWCA Civ 476).

## Requirement for local authority to apply for a placement order

4.63 In addition, the local authority must apply for a placement order where a child is placed for adoption by the authority or being provided with accommodation and:

(a) no adoption agency is authorised to place the child for adoption; and
(b) the child has no parent or guardian, or the authority considers that the threshold criteria under ACA 2002, s 31(2) are met; and
(c) the authority is satisfied that the child ought to be placed for adoption (ACA 2002, s 22(1); see also *London Borough of Merton v CB* [2013] EWCA Civ 476; *Surrey County Council v S* [2014] EWCA Civ 601).

4.64 The local authority must also apply for a placement order where proceedings for a care or supervision order are pending in which a care order might be made in respect of a child; or the child is a subject of a care order but the appropriate local authority is not authorised to place the child for adoption, provided it is satisfied that the child should be so placed, after having made the decision to that effect under AAR 2005, reg 19 and considered the child's permanence report and medical reports on the child and the parents (ACA 2002, s 22(2) and AAR 2005, reg 19).

4.65 The local authority has a discretion to apply for a placement order where a child is the subject of a care order and it is the appropriate local authority authorised to place the child for adoption by reason of parental consent pursuant to ACA 2002, s 19 (ACA 2002, s 22(3)). The above provisions do not apply where any person has given notice of intention to adopt the child unless more than four months have elapsed since the notice and an application to adopt has not been made.

## MATERIAL THAT MUST BE CONSIDERED BY AGENCY DECISION MAKER

4.66 The Court of Appeal has given the following guidance in *Re B (Placement Order)* [2008] EWCA Civ 835, [81]–[82]:

> ***Guidance***
> … First and foremost, of course, the provisions of the 2002 Act and the Regulations must be followed, and not by-passed. More specifically, the guardian suggested the following [must be provided to the adoption panel]:
>
> (1) expert reports which have been filed and served in care proceedings and which address the present and future needs of the subject child (including, but not exclusively, dealing with placement issues) should be provided to members of an adoption panel in advance of the relevant meeting and to decision makers for pre-reading;
> (2) where such reports are voluminous, as a minimum those sections of the reports setting out the experts' opinion, conclusions and/or recommendations should be provided in advance to the members of the panel and to the decision maker;
> (3) a summary of the expert(s)' opinions should only be provided to the panel members and the decision maker in substitution for the reports if:
>
> (a) the summary is in writing;
> (b) all parties to the care proceedings agree in writing that the summary is fair and accurate and should be provided to the panel and the decision maker in substitution for the reports; and
> (c) copies of the reports are available at the meeting for the members of the panel and the decision maker to consult if desired;
>
> (4) a clear, full and accurate minute of the panel meeting should be made during the meeting with particular attention given to:
>
> (a) recording the documentation considered by the members of the panel; and
> (b) the questions asked by members of the panel and the answers given by the social worker(s) present; and
>
> (5) the social workers who attend the panel meeting to present the child's case should be invited to approve the record of the note of the questions asked of and answers given by them during the meeting.
>
> It is imperative that the decision to ratify the AAP's [Agency Adoption Panel's] decision and to begin the process of applying for a placement order must never be a simple rubber stamp. The circumstances in which the decision is taken should be

> transparent, and ... Whilst it may well be that in practice the decision to take proceedings for a placement order will be made by an individual rather than a group, the source and substance of the information given to the decision maker must be clear, and both the decision itself and the reasons for it minuted.

4.67 Where a court has made a placement or adoption order in ignorance of the fact that the local authority had failed to adhere to the provisions of AAR 2005 when deciding to apply for a placement order, the order will stand. The court is only bound to declare that an existing order is void if the error made by a local authority relates to the court's jurisdiction to make the order. None of the statutory criteria for jurisdiction to make a placement order and adoption order turns on the local authority's adherence to the requirements of AAR 2005. In such circumstances, at its highest, the order would be voidable and subject to challenge by way of an appeal on the facts of any specific case. If necessary, an application for permission to appeal out of time should be made. Alternatively, an application for leave to apply for revocation of the order pursuant to ACA 2002, s 24 may be made. However, in both alternatives the court is required to consider the prospects of success of any appeal or application when determining whether to grant permission (*Somerset County Council v NHS Somerset Clinical Commissioning Group and Others* [2022] EWFC 31).

4.68 The adoption agency is required to notify the child's family of the plan to place the child for adoption, and the intention (if this be the case) of contacting the father of the child who is unaware of the birth of the child and the plan to place the child for adoption, see paras 16.29–16.39.

## CRITERIA THAT MUST BE APPLIED

4.69 Whenever the court or the adoption agency is considering a decision relating to the adoption of a child, the paramount consideration must be given to the child's welfare throughout his life but at all times bearing in mind, in general, that any delay in coming to the decision is likely to prejudice the child's welfare. In coming to its decision, the court or the adoption agency must have regard to the following matters (among others) set out in ACA 2002, s 1(4):

- (a) the child's ascertainable wishes and feelings regarding the decision (considered in the light of the child's age and understanding);
- (b) the child's particular needs;
- (c) the likely effect on the child (throughout his life) of having ceased to be a member of the original family and become an adopted person;
- (d) the child's age, sex, background and any of the child's characteristics which the court or agency considers relevant;
- (e) any harm (within the meaning of the Children Act 1989) which the child has suffered or is at risk of suffering;

(f) the relationship which the child has with relatives and with any other person in relation to whom the court or agency considers the relationship to be relevant, including—

(i) the likelihood of any such relationship continuing and the value to the child of its doing so;
(ii) the ability and willingness of any of the child's relatives, or of any such person, to provide the child with a secure environment in which the child can develop, and otherwise to meet the child's needs;
(iii) the wishes and feelings of any of the child's relatives, or of any such person regarding the child.

4.70 ACA, s 1(4)(f) makes the issue of contact post-placement or post-adoption an important factor to be taken into account when determining whether adoption would be in the best interests of the child concerned. Furthermore, s 27(4) requires that:

> Before making a placement order, the court must:
>
> (a) consider the arrangements which the adoption agency has made, or proposes to make, for allowing any person contact with the child, and
> (b) invite the parties to the proceedings to comment on those arrangements.

4.71 In the case of *Re R and C (Adoption or Fostering)* [2024] EWCA Civ 1302, the Court of Appeal made it clear that it is for the court – not a local authority or any other person – to determine whether contact between the child and their siblings and birth family should take place. It is, therefore, not the absolute decision of prospective adopters or the local authority or adoption agencies to dictate what, if any, contact should be permitted between the child and any member or members of their family. Recent developments in adoption policy and the increased public discussions on adoption law generally, but in particular relating to open adoption, emphasise the issue of ongoing contact to be a specific need of the child which should be given as much importance as, for instance, a physical or health need of the child. Attention is also drawn to the comprehensive discussion of these developments by the President in his two recent lectures and, in particular, 'Adapting Adoption to the Modern World', given on 17 May 2024 at the 2024 POTATO Group Conference (see further Chapter 8). Due consideration must also be given to the child's religious persuasion, racial origin(s) and cultural and linguistic background. The order should be made only after giving due consideration to the whole range of options available, and only if the court or adoption agency considers that making the order would be better for the child than not doing so (ACA 2002, s 1(5) and (6)).

4.72 These criteria apply to: (a) any decision; (b) application for a placement and adoption order; or (c) the revocation of such an order, or contact or revocation of contact; granting permission in respect of any action which may be taken by the adoption agency or individual under the Act. For relevance of rights under European Convention, Art 8, see *D McG v Neath Port Talbot County Borough Council* [2010] EWCA Civ 821, [2010] 2 FLR 1827; *Re H (Step Parent: Adoption Human Rights)* [2023] EWHC 3186 (Fam); *Re A Child (Adoption Time Limits)* [2020] EWFC 3296 (Fam); and *Re X (Time Barred Adoption)* [2024] EWHC 364 (Fam).

## PLACEMENT ORDER APPLICATION PROCEDURE

4.73 FPR 2010, Pt 14 and PDs 14A–14E outline the procedure for an application for a placement order and an adoption order (including contact orders under the ACA 2002). These provisions are subject to the overriding objective, in FPR 2010, Pt 1, the General Case Management Powers set out in Pt 4 and the rules relating to forms and other procedural requirements set out in Pt 5.

### Overriding objective

4.74 The overriding objective which is set out in FPR 2010, r 1.1(1) requires that the court must deal with cases 'justly, having regard to any welfare issues involved', which includes, so far as is practicable:

(a) ensuring that it is dealt with expeditiously and fairly;
(b) dealing with the case in ways which are proportionate to the nature, importance and complexity of the issues;
(c) ensuring that the parties are on an equal footing;
(d) saving expenses; and
(e) allotting to it an appropriate share of the court's resources while taking into account the need to allot resources to other cases.

4.75 The parties are also required to help the court to further the overriding objective (FPR 2010, r 1.3).

### Case management duties and powers

4.76 FPR 2010, r 1.4(1) requires the court to further the overriding objective by actively managing cases, including:

(a) setting timetables or otherwise controlling the process of the court;
(b) identifying at an early state the issues and who should be a party to the proceedings;
(c) deciding promptly which issues need full investigation and hearing and which do not and the procedure to be followed in the case;

(d) deciding the order in which issues are to be resolved;
(e) controlling the use of expert evidence;
(f) encouraging the parties to use a non-court resolution procedure if the court considers that appropriate, and facilitating the use of such procedure;
(g) helping the parties to settle the whole or part of the case;
(h) encouraging the parties to co-operate with each other in the conduct of proceedings;
(i) considering whether the likely benefits of taking a particular step justify the cost of taking it;
(j) dealing with as many aspects of the case as it can on the same occasion;
(k) dealing with the case without the parties needing to attend at court;
(l) making use of technology; and
(m) giving directions to ensure that the case proceeds quickly and efficiently.

4.77 These provisions must be read alongside the court's general case management powers set out in FPR 2010, rr 4.1–4.8 and any other powers given to the court by any other rule. This inevitably will require consideration to be given to what, if any, steps should be taken to ensure that appropriate measure are put in place, if necessary, for the effective participation of vulnerable witnesses as set out in FPR 2010, Pt 3A. FPR 2010, r 4.1 provides the Family Court with wide-ranging and flexible powers of case management, including the power 'to take any other step or make any other order for the purpose of managing the case and furthering the overriding objective'. Early identification and notification of vulnerability is essential when a witness or party is identified as being vulnerable such that their ability to effectively participate in the hearing is compromised. The Court of Appeal in *Re N (A Child)* [2019] EWCA Civ 1997 has emphasised that there is a duty under FPR 2010, PD 3AA for legal representatives actively to consider whether their client might be a vulnerable witness. The court should be notified as soon as possible so that it can consider what, if any, adjustments need to be made to ensure that hearings are fair. See *Re TG (Care Proceedings: Case Management: Expert Evidence)* [2013] EWCA Civ 5 for a reminder that the overriding objective of the FPR must be complied with (see also *Re H-L (Expert Evidence: Test for Permission)* [2013] EWCA Civ 655, [2013] 2 FLR 1434; *Re S-W (Children)* [2015] EWCA Civ 27, [2015] 2 FLR 136).

## Venue gatekeeping and allocation

4.78 Applications for placement and adoption orders are issued in the Family Court and are then allocated to either lay justices or the level of judiciary as regulated by the Family Court (Composition and Distribution of Business) Rules 2014 (SI 2014/840) (FC(CDB)Rules 2014); President's Guidance on Continuity and Deployment (Private Law) and (Public Law), 22 April 2014, which is available at:

www.judiciary.uk/wp-content/uploads/2013/02/private-law-continuity-and-deployment-guidance.pdf

and the Guidance on Allocation and Gatekeeping under ChA 1989, Pt II.

4.79 An application for a placement order will usually be made during the course of proceedings for a care order under the ChA 1989 and therefore will be made in existing proceedings. Hence the application will be allocated to the level of judge (lay justices) dealing with the existing proceedings, provided that that level of judge has authority to grant the order (see FC(CDB)Rules 2014, Sch 2). Where the original proceedings have concluded, the application for a placement order or an adoption order should be made to the level of judge who last dealt with the proceedings to which the current application relates, unless excluded under FC(CDB)Rules 2014, Sch 2.

4.80 Where there are no proceedings pending or concluded relating to the child who is the subject of the current proceedings, then FC(CDB)Rules 2014, Sch 1, para 5 provides for the following applications to be allocated to lay justices:

(a) placement order (ACA 2002, s 21);
(b) order varying a placement order (ACA 2002, s 23);
(c) order revoking a placement order (ACA 2002, s 24);
(d) contact order (ACA 2002, s 26);
(e) variation or revocation of contact order (ACA 2002, s 27);
(f) order permitting the child's name to be changed or the removal of the child from the United Kingdom (ACA 2002, s 28(2) and (3));
(g) adoption order, except where:

    (i) a local authority is a party;
    (ii) where the application is for an overseas adoption under ACA 2002, s 87; or
    (iii) for a Convention adoption within the meaning of ACA 2002, s 66(1)(c) (see Chapter 13);

(h) post-adoption contact (ACA 2002, s 51A(2)(a) or (b)); ACA 2002, s 55(e)); or
(j) an application seeking an amendment of an order under ACA 2002, Sch 1, para 4.

4.81 Where care proceedings have been concluded, applications for an adoption order under ACA 2002, s 46 where a local authority is a party to the application, or the application relates to an overseas adoption under ACA 2002, s 87 or a Convention order under ACA 2002, s 66(1)(c), the application will be allocated to the level of judge who is dealing with or dealt with the proceedings relating to the same child, or if there are or were no such proceedings, to a district judge (FC(CDB)R 2014, Sch 1, para 6).

4.82 These provisions should be read alongside the President's Guidance on Continuity and Deployment (Private Law) and (Public Law), 22 April 2014, which is available at:

> www.judiciary.uk/wp-content/uploads/2013/02/private-law-continuity-and-deployment-guidance.pdf

and the Guidance on Allocation and Gatekeeping under ChA 1989, Pt II.

4.83 Applications under ACA 2002, s 60(3) for an order to disclose or to prevent disclosure of information to an adopted person and under ACA 2002, s 79(4) for an order for the Registrar General to give information will be allocated to a judge of High Court Judge level subject to the President's Guidance on the Allocation of Work to Section 9 Judges (December 2016).

## Transfer of proceedings to another court

4.84 A court may transfer a case to another court either on its own initiative or on the application of one of the parties if:

(a) the parties consent to the transfer;
(b) the court has determined at a hearing that a transfer should be ordered; or
(c) the circumstances set out under para 4.81 (above) apply (FPR 2010, r 29.17(1)).

4.85 The court may also transfer a case without a hearing if the court has notified in writing that it intends to order a transfer and no party has, within 14 days of the notification being sent, requested a hearing to determine whether the transfer should be ordered (FPR 2010, r 29.17(2)).

4.86 Where a decision is taken that a case or any part of it should be heard by a High Court Judge, the order for transfer should be to a High Court Judge sitting in the Family Court and not a transfer to the Family Division of the High Court. A case may only be transferred from the Family Court to the High Court if the transfer is directed by: (a) the President of the Family Division; or (b) an ordinary judge of the Court of Appeal or a puisne judge of the High Court (FPR 2010, r 29.19(3) and (4), and see the President's Guidance, Jurisdiction of the Family Court: Allocation of Cases Within the Family Court to High Court Judge Level and Transfer of Cases From the Family Court to the High Court, 24 May 2021, which is available at:

> www.judiciary.uk/wp-content/uploads/2022/07/PFD-Guidance-Jurisdiction-of-the-Family-Court-May-2021.pdf

## STARTING PROCEEDINGS – PLACEMENT ORDER

### The application

4.87 The application for a placement order is in Form A50. If the child's address is not to be disclosed, the address should be omitted from the Form A50 and given instead on Form A65 (Confidential Information) (FPR 2010, PD 5A Forms), which should then be filed. The applicant will be the relevant local authority.

### Request for dispensing with consent

4.88 Where the applicant wants to ask the court to dispense with consent of any parent or guardian of a child to the child being placed for adoption, the applicant must give notice of the request in the application form or at a later stage by filing a written request setting out the reasons for the request and file a statement of facts setting out a summary of the history of the case and any other facts to satisfy the court of the grounds relied on, i.e. that the parent or guardian cannot be found or is incapable of giving consent or that the welfare of the child requires the consent to be dispensed with (FPR 2010, r 14.9) (see further Chapter 6). The statement of facts must be framed so that it does not disclose the identity of the prospective adopter(s), if known.

4.89 On receipt of the notice, the court officer will inform the parent(s) or guardian of the child of the request and send a copy of the statement of facts relied on to them and to any children's guardian, reporting officer or children and family reporter (FPR 2010, r 14.9(4)). If the applicant considers that the parent or guardian is incapable of giving consent, the court must consider whether to appoint a litigation friend for the parent or guardian under FPR 2010, r 15.5(1) or give directions for an application to be made under FPR 2010, r 15.6(3), unless a litigation friend has already been appointed for that parent or guardian (FPR 2010, r 14.9(4)(b)).

### Who should be made respondents?

4.90 The respondents to the application will be:

(a) each parent who has parental responsibility for the child or any guardian of the child;
(b) any person in whose favour an order under the ChA 1989 is in force in relation to the child;
(c) any adoption agency or voluntary organisation which has parental responsibility for, is looking after, or is caring for, the child;

(d) the child; and
(e) the parties or any persons who are or have been parties to proceedings for a care order in respect of the child where those proceedings have led to the application for the placement order (FPR 2010, r 14.3).

4.91 The court may at any time direct that a child who is not already a respondent to proceedings be made a respondent to the proceedings where the child wishes to make an application; or has evidence to give to the court or a legal submission to make which has not been given or made by any other party; or where there are other special circumstances (FPR 2010, r 14.3(2)). Where the biological parent does not have parental responsibility for the child, there is a presumption that he should be joined unless there is a good reason for refusing his application. However, if the parent has delayed in making the application to be joined, the court will consider the principle that delay is prejudicial to the child and the fundamental rights under European Convention, Arts 6 and 8 of all the parties and balance these against the rights of the child and the child's needs for a conclusion of the proceedings and certainty in his life (*Re P (Care Proceedings: Father's Application to be joined as a Party)* [2001] 1 FLR 781).

4.92 The court may also at any time direct that any other person or body be made (or removed as) a respondent (FPR 2010, r 14.3(3)).

4.93 FPR 2010, PD 14A, para 1 also requires that any appointed children's guardian, children and family reporter and reporting officer should receive a copy of the application form.

## Documents that must be filed with Form A50

4.94 The application form must be accompanied by three copies of the application form and the court fee. In addition, the form requires the following further documents referred to in Form A50 to be submitted:

- a certified copy of the full entry in the Register of Live Births that relates to the child or, where the child has been adopted, a certified copy of the entry in the Adopted Children Register;
- any written consent of the parent or guardian to the child being placed for adoption, and any notice of withdrawal of such consent;
- if the applicant is asking the court to dispense with the consent of any parent or guardian to the child being placed for adoption, a brief statement of the facts relied on in support of the request, and two copies of the statement;
- a copy of any final care order relating to the child;

- if available, a copy of any parental responsibility order or parental responsibility agreement relating to the child;
- if the authority was a party to the proceedings, a copy of any other final order relating to the child that has effect and, if available, a copy of any maintenance agreement or maintenance award relating to the child;
- if the authority was a party to the proceedings, a copy of any final order relating to a full, half- or step-brother or step-sister of the child that has effect.

The applicant local authority (if directed to do so) must file a report on the child and birth family containing the matters set out in PD14C Annex B.

## Steps the court will take

4.95 As soon as practicable after the application for a placement order has been filed the court must set a date for the first directions hearing, which must be within four weeks of the date when the application was filed unless the court considers it appropriate to give the directions required by FPR 2010, r 14.8 (see also paras 4.91–4.92) without a hearing (FPR 2010, rr 14.10 and 14.6(4)). The court will:

- appoint a guardian or a reporting officer, as the case may be, in accordance with FPR 2010, r 16.3(1) or r 16.30. If a parent has consented to or is willing to consent to placement for adoption, a reporting officer will be appointed. Proceedings for a placement order are 'specified proceedings' under ChA 1989, s 41; the child is therefore a party to the proceedings and a guardian will be appointed unless it is not necessary to safeguard the interests of the child (FPR 2010, r 16.3). Where an appointment is made, the person in the first instance should be the guardian who is acting in any pending proceedings or has acted in previous proceedings relating to the child;
- consider whether a report relating to the welfare of the child is required and, if so, request a report in accordance with FPR 2010, r 16.33;
- consider whether a report giving the local authority's reason for placing the child for adoption is required and, if so, direct the local authority to prepare such a report (FPR 2010, r 14.6(3);
- set a date for the hearing of the application;
- ask Cafcass (or the National Assembly for Wales) to file any form of consent to the child being placed for adoption;
- if the applicant is asking for the consent of the parent or guardian to be dispensed with, the court officer will send a copy of the statement of facts filed as set out at para 4.89.

## Service

4.96 The court will:

- serve a copy of the application form but not the documents filed with it, to each parent who has parental responsibility for the child or guardian of the child and any other person directed by the court to receive a copy;
- send a copy of the birth certificate or entry in the Adopted Children Register, any health reports attached to the application form to any guardian, reporting officer or children and family reporter;
- if a request has been made to dispense with consent of the parent(s) or guardian of the child, inform the parent(s) or guardian of the request and send a copy of the statement of facts to them and to the children's guardian, reporting officer or children and family reporter and any adoption agency which has placed the child for adoption (FPR 2010, r 14.6).

## First directions hearing

4.97 The first directions hearing must, unless the court otherwise directs, take place within four weeks of the application. The parties and their legal representatives must attend this hearing unless the court otherwise directs (FPR 2010, r 14.8(4)). The court will consider giving directions on the following matters at the first directions hearing:

(a) fix a timetable for the filing of:

  (i) any report relating to the suitability of the applicants to adopt a child;
  (ii) any report from the local authority;
  (iii) any report from a children's guardian, reporting officer or children and family reporter;
  (iv) if a statement of facts has been filed, any amended statement of facts;
  (v) any other evidence; and
  (vi) give directions relating to the reports and other evidence;

(b) consider whether the child or any other person should be a party to the proceedings and, if so, give directions in accordance with FPR 2010, r 14.3(2) or (3) joining that child or person as a party;
(c) give directions relating to the appointment of a litigation friend for any protected party or child who is a party to, but not the subject of, proceedings unless a litigation friend has already been appointed;

(d) consider whether the case needs to be transferred to another court and, if so, give directions for the transfer of the proceedings to another court;
(e) give directions about:

  (i) tracing parents or any other person the court considers to be relevant to the proceedings;
  (ii) service of documents;
  (iii) subject to paragraph (2), disclosure as soon as possible of information and evidence to the parties;
  (iv) participation of any vulnerable party and any special measures required; and
  (v) the final hearing.

4.98 Directions may also be given at any stage of the proceedings of the court's own initiative or on the application of a party or the children's guardian or reporting officer. In such an event a further directions hearing will be listed and notice of this will be given to all the relevant parties and the guardian, reporting officer or the children and family reporter (FPR 2010, rr 14.5 and 14.6).

## Disclosure of confidential reports

4.99 Reports prepared by the adoption agency or local authority children's guardian or reporting officer or a children and family reporter in relation to the proceedings and provided to the court are considered confidential. The court may, however, give directions for any reports filed to be disclosed to the parties to the proceedings. In determining whether directions for disclosure should be given, the court will consider whether any information contained in the report should be deleted, including information which discloses or is likely to identify the person with whom the child is placed and who has been assigned a serial number under FPR 2010, r 14.2(2), and personal details of any person who has given notice to the court that they do not wish their details to be disclosed (FPR 2010, r 19.1(2)). FPR 2010, r 14.3 also empowers the court to direct that a confidential report should not be disclosed to a party to the proceedings. In addition, in *Re D (Minors) (Adoption Reports: Confidentiality)* [1995] 2 FLR 687, HL, the House of Lords (now the Supreme Court) set out the principles in relation to disclosure of confidential reports in adoption proceedings as follows:

> 42. It is a fundamental principle of fairness that a party is entitled to the disclosure of all materials which may be taken into account by the court when reaching a decision adverse to that party. This principle applies with particular force to proceedings designed to lead to an order for adoption, since the consequences of such an order are so lasting and far-reaching.
>
> 43. When deciding whether to direct that notwithstanding rule 53(2) of the Adoption Rules 1984 a party referred to in a confidential report supplied by an

adoption agency, a local authority, a reporting officer or a guardian ad litem shall not be entitled to inspect the part of the report which refers to him or her, the court should first consider whether disclosure of the material would involve a real possibility of significant harm to the child.

44. If it would, the court should next consider whether the overall interests of the child would benefit from non-disclosure, weighing on the one hand the interest of the child in having the material properly tested, and on the other both the magnitude of the risk that harm will occur and the gravity of the harm if it does occur.
45. If the court is satisfied that the interests of the child point towards non-disclosure, the next and final step is for the court to weigh that consideration, and its strength in the circumstances of the case, against the interest of the parent or other party in having an opportunity to see and respond to the material. In the latter regard the court should take into account the importance of the material to the issues in the case.
46. Non-disclosure should be the exception and not the rule. The court should be rigorous in its examination of the risk and gravity of the feared harm to the child, and should order non-disclosure only when the case for doing so is compelling.

4.100 Hence when disclosure is sought steps should be taken as soon as practicable to bring this to the attention of the court and where appropriate to apply to the court to consider the issue and give directions. Where withholding disclosure of information relating to an adult is desired, an application should be made relying on any infringement of Convention rights, for example Art 8 rights (see *Re B (Disclosure to Other Parties)* [2001] 2 FLR 1017 and *Re X (Adoption: Confidential Procedure)* [2002] EWCA Civ 828, [2002] 2 FLR 476).

## Proof of the child's identity

4.101 The inclusion of the child's birth/adoption birth certificate is deemed to be sufficient evidence of the child's identity and that any parental/guardian consent set out in any form of consent relates to the child who is the subject of the proceedings. Similarly, where the child's place of birth cannot be proved to the satisfaction of the court, the child may be treated as having been born in the registration district and sub-district of the court where it is probable the child may have been born within the United Kingdom or the Channel Islands or the Isle of Man. In all other cases the particulars of the country of birth may be omitted.

## Reports by adoption agency or local authority

4.102 A local authority that is directed to prepare a report on the placement of the child for adoption must file the report covering the matters set out in FPR 2010, PD 14C, Annex B, which include information in relation to the child and the birth family, relationships, contact, matters relating to the child's and the family's wishes and feelings; and a summary of the actions taken by the adoption agency in relation to, for instance, consent (see Chapter 6), within the timetable directed by the court (FPR 2010, r 14.11).

### Final hearing

4.103 Any person who is a party to the proceedings and the children's guardian, reporting officer or children and family reporter will be notified of the date and place where the application will be heard and of the fact that unless the person wishes or the court requires, the person need not attend the hearing but the legal representative of the applicant to an application for a placement order must attend (FPR 2010, r 14.16(9)). However, any person who has been given notice of the hearing may attend the final hearing and be heard on the question of whether a placement order should be made (FPR 2010, r 14.16). The children's guardian should consider the child's permanence report filed with the court before the final hearing. The AAR 2005 provide that the permanence report should contain an analysis of the options available for the future care of the child, i.e. the documentation that records in original form the pros and cons of each of the realistic care options and the social work reasoning behind the local authority's decision to apply for a placement order (*Re M (A Child: Leave to Oppose Adoption)* [2023] EWCA Civ 404).

### Placement order – form of order

4.104 A standard form for a placement order is not set out in FPR 2010, PD 5A, Table 1.

## DURATION

4.105 A placement order continues in force until:

(a) it is revoked by a court order under ACA 2002, s 24; or
(b) an adoption order is made in respect of the child; or
(c) the child marries or forms a civil partnership; or
(d) the child attains the age of 18 (ACA 2002, s 21(4)).

## CONSEQUENCES OF A PLACEMENT ORDER

4.106 The consequences of a placement order are as follows:

- Parental responsibility is shared between the parents with parental responsibility and the local authority. When the child is placed with the prospective adopter(s), parental responsibility is also given to them and shared with the parents and the local authority. However, the agency may make a determination to restrict the parental responsibility of the parent(s) but in so doing they must exercise their discretion judiciously and take into account the welfare factors set out in ACA 2002, s 1(4) (see ACA 2002, s 25). The grant of parental responsibility to a prospective adopter is a factor when determining whether or not the European Convention, Art 8 right to family life is established between them and the child (*DL and ML v Newham London Borough and Secretary of State for Education* [2011] EWHC 1127 (Admin)).
- Any existing orders for contact under ChA 1989, s 8 or s 34 will cease to have effect (ACA 2002, s 29(2)) and an application under ChA 1989 cannot be made while the adoption agency remains authorised to place the child for adoption or where the child is placed for adoption, but see AAR 2005, reg 26 which places a duty on the agency to consider contact arrangements. The agency is also obliged to review contact arrangements in the light of the views of the prospective adopter(s) and any advice given by the adoption panel but the views of all the persons affected by any decision taken must also be taken into account. However, an application may be made under ACA 2002, s 26 for a contact to be considered by the court. Additionally, the court may, on making a placement order, on its own initiative make an order for contact (see further Chapter 8).
- Where a child is placed with the consent of the parent(s), or the agency is authorised to place a child for adoption, or a placement order remains in force, no person may change the child's surname or remove the child from the United Kingdom (save for a period of less than a month by a person who provides the child with a home), unless the court has given permission to do so (ACA 2002, s 28(2)(4)).
- A prohibited steps, residence or specific issue order; supervision or child assessment order may not be made (ACA 2002, s 29(3)).
- Any existing care order in respect of the child will cease to have effect while the placement order remains in force. The care order does not cease, it is merely suspended. On the revocation of the placement order the care order revives without any further order of the court (ACA 2002, s 29(1)).
- No special guardianship order may be made in respect of the child until an application for an adoption order is made. At that stage the guardian of the child may apply for a special guardianship order with permission of the court (ACA 2002, s 47(5)) and any other person who is entitled to apply for such an order may do so but only with the court's permission (ACA 2002, s 29(5)).

# REVOCATION OF A PLACEMENT ORDER

## Who may apply for revocation of a placement order?

4.107 The child or the local authority may apply for revocation of the order as of right. All other persons, including the child's parent(s) or guardian, may only do so if:

(a) the court gives permission, which will not be granted unless the court is satisfied that there has been a sufficient change of circumstances since the placement order was made; and
(b) the child has not been placed for adoption by the authority (ACA 2002, s 24(2) and (3)).

If the court is satisfied that there has been a change of circumstances, the court will then go on to consider whether or not to exercise its discretion to grant.

## What constitutes a change of circumstances?

4.108 The Court of Appeal in *Re P (Adoption: Leave Provisions)* [2007] EWCA Civ 616 ruled that the change could embrace a wide range of different factual situations and need not relate to the circumstances of the parent(s). The test must not be set too high as parents should not be discouraged from improving their situation or from seeking to prevent the adoption of their child by imposing too high a bar that was unachievable. The change of circumstances is a matter of fact to be decided by the good sense and sound judgment of the court hearing the application (at [30]–[32]). See also *Re LG (Adoption: Leave to Oppose)* [2015] EWFC 52. Belatedly obtained fresh evidence which relates to the findings of the original proceedings will not suffice to found an application for permission in the absence of a decision on appeal (*Re M (Adoption: Leave to Oppose)* [2009] EWHC 3643 (Fam)). In *The Prospective Adopters v IA and London Borough of Croydon* [2014] EWHC 331 (Fam), the father's application for permission to oppose the adoption application was allowed on the basis that it was unclear whether the first instance court had applied the test in *Re B (A Child) (Care Proceedings: Threshold Criteria)* [2013] UKSC 33 and *Re B-S (Children) (Adoption Order: Leave to Oppose)* [2013] EWCA Civ 1146. In *Re B-S* the Court of Appeal applied the test set out by Wall LJ in *Re P* (above), where he stated (at [26]) that ACA 2002, s 47(5) involves a two-stage process:

> First of all, the court has to be satisfied, on the facts of the case, that there has been a change in circumstances within section 47(7). If there has been no change in circumstances, that is the end of the matter, and the application fails. If, however, there has been a change in circumstances within section 47(7) then the door to the

exercise of a judicial discretion to permit the parents to defend the adoption proceedings is opened, and the decision whether or not to grant leave is governed by section 1 of the 2002 Act. In other words, 'the paramount consideration of the court must be the child's welfare throughout his life'.

4.109 The Court of Appeal in *Re B-S* then went on to give the following guidance on how an application under ACA 2002, s 47(5) should be approached:

> 74. In relation to the second question – If there has been a change in circumstances, should leave to oppose be given? – the court will, of course, need to consider all the circumstances. The court will in particular have to consider two inter-related questions: one, the parent's ultimate prospect of success if given leave to oppose; the other, the impact on the child if the parent is, or is not, given leave to oppose, always remembering, of course, that at this stage the child's welfare is paramount. In relation to the evaluation, the weighing and balancing, of these factors we make the following points:
>
> i) Prospect of success here relates to the prospect of resisting the making of an adoption order, *not*, we emphasise, the prospect of ultimately having the child restored to the parent's care.
>
> ii) For purposes of exposition and analysis we treat as two separate issues the questions of whether there has been a change in circumstances and whether the parent has solid grounds for seeking leave. Almost invariably, however, they will be intertwined; in many cases the one may very well follow from the other.
>
> iii) Once he or she has got to the point of concluding that there has been a change of circumstances and that the parent has solid grounds for seeking leave, the judge must consider very carefully indeed whether the child's welfare really does necessitate the refusal of leave. The judge must keep at the forefront of his mind the teaching of *Re B*, in particular that adoption is the 'last resort' and only permissible if 'nothing else will do' and that, as Lord Neuberger emphasised, the child's interests include being brought up by the parents or wider family unless the overriding requirements of the child's welfare make that not possible. That said, the child's welfare is paramount.
>
> iv) At this, as at all other stages in the adoption process, the judicial evaluation of the child's welfare must take into account *all* the negatives and the positives, *all* the pros and cons, of *each* of the two options, that is, either giving or refusing the parent leave to oppose. Here again, as elsewhere, the use of Thorpe LJ's 'balance sheet' is to be encouraged.
>
> v) This close focus on the circumstances requires that the court has proper evidence. But this does not mean that judges will always need to hear oral evidence and cross-examination before coming to a conclusion. Sometimes, though we suspect not very often, the judge will be assisted by oral evidence. Typically, however, an application for leave under section 47(5) can fairly and should appropriately be dealt with on the basis of written evidence and submissions: see *Re P*, paras 53–54.

vi) As a general proposition, the greater the change in circumstances (assuming, of course, that the change is positive) and the more solid the parent's grounds for seeking leave to oppose, the more cogent and compelling the arguments based on the child's welfare must be if leave to oppose is to be refused.

vii) The mere fact that the child has been placed with prospective adopters cannot be determinative, nor can the mere passage of time. On the other hand, the older the child and the longer the child has been placed the greater the adverse impacts of disturbing the arrangements are likely to be.

viii) The judge must always bear in mind that what is paramount in every adoption case is the welfare of the child 'throughout his life'. Given modern expectation of life, this means that, with a young child, one is looking far ahead into a very distant future – upwards of eighty or even ninety years. Against this perspective, judges must be careful not to attach undue weight to the short term consequences for the child if leave to oppose is given. In this as in other contexts, judges should be guided by what Sir Thomas Bingham MR said in *Re O (Contact: Imposition of Conditions)* [1995] 2 FLR 124, 129, that 'the court should take a medium-term and long-term view of the child's development and not accord excessive weight to what appear likely to be short-term or transient problems.' That was said in the context of contact but it has a much wider resonance: *Re G (Education: Religious Upbringing)* [2012] EWCA Civ 1233, [2013] 1 FLR 677, para 26.

ix) Almost invariably the judge will be pressed with the argument that leave to oppose should be refused, amongst other reasons, because of the adverse impact on the prospective adopters, and thus on the child, of their having to pursue a contested adoption application. We do not seek to trivialise an argument which may in some cases have considerable force, particularly perhaps in a case where the child is old enough to have some awareness of what is going on. But judges must be careful not to attach undue weight to the argument. After all, what from the perspective of the proposed adopters was the smoothness of the process which they no doubt anticipated when issuing their application with the assurance of a placement order, will already have been disturbed by the unwelcome making of the application for leave to oppose. And the disruptive effects of an order giving a parent leave to oppose can be minimised by firm judicial case management *before* the hearing of the application for leave. If appropriate directions are given, in particular in relation to the expert and other evidence to be adduced on behalf of the parent, *as soon as* the application for leave is issued and *before* the question of leave has been determined, it ought to be possible to direct either that the application for leave is to be listed with the substantive adoption application to follow immediately, whether or not leave is given, or, if that is not feasible, to direct that the substantive application is to be listed, whether or not leave has been given, very shortly after the leave hearing.

x) We urge judges always to bear in mind the wise and humane words of Wall LJ in *Re P*, para 32. We have already quoted them but they bear repetition: 'the test should not be set too high, because ... parents ... should not be discouraged either from bettering themselves or from seeking to prevent the adoption of their child by the imposition of a test which is unachievable'.

4.110 In *Re M (A Child: Leave to Oppose Adoption)* [2023] EWCA Civ 404, the Court of Appeal approved the above guidance given in *Re B-S (Children) Adoption Order: Leave to Oppose)* and added that:

(a) 'the prospect of success in opposing an adoption if leave is granted is an important element to which the court must have regard but it is not a test in itself, still less an exclusive one' (at [21]); and
(b) 'the essential question for the court at the second stage is this: Taking account of all the circumstances and giving paramount consideration to this child's lifelong welfare, should the court revisit the plan for adoption that it approved when making the placement order? By asking this question, the court ensures that it focuses firmly on the individual child's welfare in the short, medium and long term with reference to every relevant factor, including the nature and degree of the change that it has found, the parent's prospects of success, and the impact on the child of contested proceedings.' (at [23]).

The court disapproved the suggestion advanced in *Prospective Adopters v SA* [2015] EWHC 327 (Fam) at [16]–[19] and in *Prospective Adopters v London Borough of Tower Hamlets* [2020] EWFC 26 at [5] that the change must be unexpected or unforeseen.

4.111 The approach set out in *Re W (A Child) (Adoption Order: Leave to Oppose)* [2010] EWCA Civ 1535; *Re H (Children) (Adoption Order: Leave to Oppose)* [2013] EWCA Civ 1177 has also been disapproved. However, this does not mean that the child will be returned to the parent's care (*Re M (Adoption: Leave to Oppose)* [2009] EWHC 3643 (Fam); *S-H v Kingston Upon Hull City Council* [2008] EWCA Civ 493). The case of *Re JL (Leave to Apply to Revoke Placement Order* [2020] EWCA Civ 1253 is an example where the Court of Appeal held that a grandmother's move to a significantly larger and better accommodation and her ability to offer J a home was a clear change in her circumstances and for the child to be brought up in a close relationship with his siblings and with his grandmother, mother and other family members. The Court also held that the potential advantage of securing J's placement with his family immediately and the fact that the law requires, where possible, for children to be brought up by their natural families outweighs the disadvantage of the delay which would occur in finding a placement for J. The placement with the grandmother was therefore in the circumstances in J's interests. The court therefore granted the grandmother leave to apply to revoke the placement order and to apply for a special guardianship order. See also *Re G and H (Leave to Revoke Placement Order)* [2023] EWCA Civ 768.

4.112 In *Re C (Revocation of Placement Orders)* [2020] EWCA Civ 1598, on the substantive application to revoke a placement order, the Court of Appeal endorsed (at [23]) the following principles applied by the first instance judge from the extensive case law which has developed, and in particular from the Supreme Court's decision in *Re B (A Child)* [2013] UKSC 33 as providing a clear and comprehensive summary of the approach:

(a) the paramount consideration for a court when considering an outcome for a child is that child's welfare;
(b) it is a principle of the law that the welfare of a child is best met by maintaining the connection with birth parents to as full an extent as possible;
(c) that principle is underpinned by application of the least interventionist principle enshrined in s.1(6);
(d) adherence to those principles reflects and respects both the importance of the right to family life set out in Article 8(1) of ECHR and the limited scope for interference with that right as set out in the exceptions in Article 8(2);
(e) interference in the right to family life, which is the right both of the parent and of the child, is parametered by necessity, proportionality and legality.
(f) As a consequence, the permanent severing of ties between a child and her birth parents is an outcome only to be ordered in exceptional circumstances and where motivated by overriding requirements pertaining to the child's welfare.
(g) To arrive at that conclusion the possibility of parental care or, in the alternative, care by members of the wider birth family must be shown to be options which are not realistic either by reason of unavailability (i.e. they do not exist) or because such care cannot meet the welfare needs of the child. [In *Re N (Children: Revocation of Placement Orders)* [2023] EWCA Civ 1352, the Court of Appeal revised this to read that the family's case must not only be realistic but that revocation must be in the child's interests.]
(h) That option of parental or family care should not be rejected if identified deficits could be remedied through appropriate and proportionate support provided by the Local Authority, even if such support would be necessary for an extended period of time.
(i) In order to arrive at a valid conclusion that a child's welfare requires their permanent removal from parental/family care it is necessary to consider individually all of the competing options for care, to assess their respective strengths and weaknesses and then to look at those options against each other to ensure that every option is fully considered against every other option.
(j) Having done so and identified the outcome most able to meet the welfare needs of the child it is necessary to consider whether that outcome is itself a proportionate interference in the rights of the child.

In *Re H (Children: Placement Orders)* [2023] EWCA Civ 1245, the Court of Appeal has expanded on the above by ruling that where a child has said his final goodbyes to his birth family and has been prepared for adoption, rehabilitation with his family should only be considered if there is convincing evidence of the success of the move.

## When is a child said to be placed for adoption?

4.113 Before a child can be said to be placed for adoption with prospective adopter(s): (a) the adoption panel must have recommended the child suitable for adoption; (b) a placement order must have been obtained; and (c) the adoption panel must have recommended that the child may be adopted by identified and approved prospective adopter(s) (*Re S (Placement Order: Revocation)* [2008] EWCA Civ 1333). A child is not said to be placed until he has begun to live with the prospective adopter(s). Where the child has been living with foster carer(s) who wish to adopt him, he is regarded as being placed only when the agency changes the foster carer's/carers' status to that of a prospective adopter (*Coventry City Council v O (Adoption)* [2011] EWCA Civ 729).

## How does the court exercise its discretion whether or not to grant permission?

4.114 A two-stage test (see para 4.103) is applied by the court when determining whether or not to grant permission. The first relates to determining whether there has been a change in circumstances. Once the court is satisfied on this issue it will go on to consider whether or not the application has a real prospect of success. This will necessarily involve consideration of the child's welfare and best interests, but welfare is not the paramount consideration as it is when the application is for permission under ACA 2002, s 47 to oppose an adoption application (see *Re JL (Leave to Apply to Revoke Placement Order* [2020] EWCA Civ 1253; *Re G (Adoption: Leave to Oppose)* [2014] EWCA Civ 432).

4.115 The court may also revoke the placement order if at the final hearing of the application of an adoption order it determines not to make the adoption order (ACA 2002, s 24(4)).

4.116 Where an application for a revocation of a placement order is pending and the child is not placed for adoption, the child may not be placed for adoption unless the court grants permission to do so (ACA 2002, s 24(5)). If the child has not yet been placed when the application for permission to apply for the revocation of a placement order is at an advanced stage, the local authority should not deliberately, and in order to frustrate the parent's application, place the child with prospective adopter(s). If it does it can be challenged by way of judicial review (*Re F (Placement Order)* [2008] EWCA Civ 439). Where a parent's intention to challenge a placement order is known to the local authority, it must inform the parent of its decision to place the child and the parent's right to apply for permission to challenge the placement order under ACA 2002, s 24 (*R (EL) v Essex County Council* [2017] EWHC 1041 (Admin)).

## REVOCATION OF PLACEMENT ORDER PROCEDURE

### Form of application

4.117 An application for the revocation of a placement order should be made on Form A52, which is available at:

> www.justice.gov.uk/courts/procedure-rules/family/formspage

4.118 The application for permission should be made on Form FP2 and the procedure set out in FPR 2010, Pt 18 should be followed. The application for permission should set out in detail the change of circumstances relied on and the reasons for making the application and why it is considered that it would be in the best interests of the child for the placement order to be revoked. On the application being issued the court will fix a hearing date for the first direction hearing and set a timetable for the application to be heard.

### Who should be made a respondent?

4.119 FPR 2010, r 14.3 sets out the persons who should be made respondents to the application for a revocation of a placement order under ACA 2002, s 24 as follows:

- the parties to the proceedings leading to the placement order which it is sought to have revoked; and
- any person in whose favour there is provision for contact.

### Venue

4.120 The application should be made to the court which made the placement order. The procedure set out in FPR 2010, Pt 18 will apply to the proceedings. The court may deal with the application without a hearing if the court does not consider a hearing to be necessary.

## VARIATION OF A PLACEMENT ORDER

4.121 The court may vary a placement order so as to substitute another local authority for the local authority in whose favour the placement order was made. The application for variation must be made jointly by both local authorities (ACA 2002, s 23).

### Form of application

4.122 The application is made on Form A51, which is available at:

> www.justice.gov.uk/courts/procedure-rules/family/formspage

4.123 The application must be made jointly by both authorities. The procedure set out in FPR 2010, Pt 18 should be followed. A draft of the order sought should be attached to the application form.

### Who should be made a respondent?

4.124 The respondent to the application will be:

- the parties to the proceedings leading to the placement order which it is sought to vary, except the child who was the subject of the proceedings;
- any person in whose favour there is provision for contact (FPR 2010, r 14.3).

### Who should be served?

4.125 Persons who are entitled to receive a copy of the application form include each parent with parental responsibility for the child or the guardian of the child; any appointed children's guardian, reporting officer and children and family reporter; and any other person directed by the court.

### Venue

4.126 The application should be made to the court which made the placement order. The FPR 2010, Pt 18 procedure applies. The case will be allocated to the judge who made the placement order, if available. The court may decide to deal with the application without a hearing if it considers that a hearing is not necessary.

## POWER TO GRANT INJUNCTION

4.127 The Family Court has jurisdiction to grant an injunction in prospective or pending proceedings pursuant to Senior Courts Act 1981, s 37, the County Courts Act 1984, or under Human Rights Act 1998, s 8(1)). The power to grant this relief is also available under FPR 2010, r 20.2(1)(a).

## APPLICATION FOR A CHILD'S NAME TO BE CHANGED

### How to make the application

4.128 Application for a child's surname to be changed is governed by the provision set out in ACA 2002, s 28 and the procedure in FPR 2010, Pt 14. The application should be made on Form A55, which is available at:

> www.justice.gov.uk/courts/procedure-rules/family/formspage

### Who may apply?

4.129 The application may be made by any person, including the adoption agency or the local authority authorised to place the child, or which has placed the child for adoption.

### Who should be the respondents?

4.130 The respondents to the application for a change of name are:

- the parties to the proceedings leading to any placement order;
- the adoption agency authorised to place the child for adoption, or which placed the child for adoption;
- any prospective adopter(s) with whom the child is living;
- each parent with parental responsibility or guardian of the child (FPR 2010, r 14.3);
- the child who is not a party to the proceedings may also be made a party on the direction of the court where the child expresses a wish to make an application or has evidence to put before the court, or to make submissions which have not been given by any other party, or where there are exceptional circumstances ((FPR 2010, r 14.3(3));
- any other person or body may be made a party to the proceedings or be removed as a respondent if the court so directs.

## Service

4.131 On the application being filed the court is required to serve a copy of the application form, but not the supporting documents, to all the parties, any appointed guardian for the child, reporting officer or a children and family reporter and any other person directed by the court (FPR 2010, r 14.6(1)(b)(ii) and PD 14A).

# REMOVAL OF A CHILD FROM THE UNITED KINGDOM

4.132 Where a child is placed for adoption with parental consent under ACA 2002, s 19, or an adoption agency is authorised to place the child for adoption, or a placement order is in force, the child may not be removed from the United Kingdom without the permission of the court or without the written consent of each parent or guardian of the child. The only exception to this rule is that a person who provides a home for the child may remove the child in his/her care for a period of less than a month (ACA 2002, s 28(2)–(4)).

4.133 The application for permission to remove the child from the United Kingdom should be made in Form A56. The applicants and respondents to the application are the same as for an application to change a child's name (see paras 4.129–4.130).

# Chapter 5

# Conditions for Making an Adoption Order

## INTRODUCTION

5.1 The conditions that must be met before an adoption order may be made are set out in ACA 2002, s 47. This provides that an adoption order may not be made if the child has a parent or guardian unless one of the following three conditions is met, namely:

(1)

- (a) The parent or guardian of the child consents to the making of the adoption order;
- (b) the parent or guardian has consented under s 20, and has not withdrawn the consent, and does not oppose the making of the adoption order; or
- (c) the parent's or guardian's consent should be dispensed with.

(2)

- (a) The child has been placed for adoption by an adoption agency with the prospective adopter(s) in whose favour the order is proposed to be made; and
- (b) either:
    - (i) the child was placed for adoption with the consent of each parent or guardian, and the mother's consent was given when the child was at least six weeks old, or
    - (ii) the child was placed for adoption under a placement order, and
- (c) no parent or guardian opposed the making of the adoption order.

(3) The child is free for adoption by virtue of a Scottish permanence order (as defined under ACA 2002, s 47(10)) which includes authority for the child to be adopted, or is free for adoption by an order made under art 17(1) or art 18(1) of the Adoption (Northern Ireland) Order 1987 (SI 1987/2203) (NI 22).

5.2 In agency cases, the issue of consent arises at the time when the decision is taken to place the child for adoption. In non-agency cases, such as adoption by a step-parent, a partner or spouse of a parent of the child, or a relative, it does not arise until the adoption stage. Where consent is not forthcoming it can be dispensed with provided that one or both situations set out in ACA 2002, s 52(1)(a) is/are met and the welfare of the child requires consent to be dispensed with (ACA 2002, s 52(1)(b)). The issue of dispensation of consent is dealt with in Chapter 6.

## THE FIRST CONDITION – PARENTAL CONSENT

5.3 In relation to the requirement of parental consents referred to in para 5.1 (1)(a) and (b) (above), see further paras 4.5–4.22. Consent given by the mother if given less than six weeks after the birth of her child is ineffective (ACA 2002, s 52(3)). Consent should be given unconditionally and with full understanding of what is involved (ACA 2002, s 52(5). Although there is no specific requirement that consent should be given freely, consent obtained under pressure or by reason of undue pressure will not constitute valid consent, but consent given reluctantly (as is often the case when a parent does not wish to give up his child but recognises that adoption is in the best interests of the child) will nevertheless be effective consent. In adoption proceedings, consent of the parent or guardian must be to the particular adoption order which the court is being asked to make, even if (as is often the case) the identity of the adopters is not known to the parent (ACA 2002, s 52(5)).

5.4 A parent who has given advance consent pursuant to ACA 2002 s 20 and has not withdrawn the consent before the application for adoption is made may not oppose the making of an adoption order unless the court gives permission to do so (ACA 2002, s 47(3)). Permission may be granted by the court only if it is satisfied there has been a change of circumstances since the consent was given (ACA 2002, s 47(3) and (7)).

### Who is a parent?

5.5 'Parent' means a parent who has parental responsibility for the child under the CA 1989 (ACA 2002, s 52(6)). This will include the birth mother and the natural father if:

(a) the natural father is married to or in a civil partnership with the mother at the date of the child's birth; or
(b) the natural father and the mother have subsequently married or entered into a civil partnership (Legitimacy Act 1976, s 2; FLRA 1987); or

(c) in the case of birth after 1 December 2003, the natural father is registered as the child's father on the birth certificate (ChA 1989, s 4); or
(d) the natural father has entered into a parental responsibility agreement with the mother (ChA 1989, s 4); or
(e) the natural father has obtained an order granting him parental responsibility (ChA 1989, s 4(1));
(f) it may also include the child's adoptive parent(s) where the adoption has broken down and the adopted child is the subject of a subsequent adoption application.

It is therefore clear that a father with parental responsibility has a right to be notified of an application for adoption of his child.

5.6 Where an order is made in a foreign country depriving the natural parents of their parental authority it will be for the courts in England and Wales to determine the validity of that order and to determine whether the family law concepts correspond to those in England and Wales. Expert evidence on the law in the foreign country may be required to establish the extent and effect of any such order. The court will also be mindful of judicial comity when determining the issue of recognition of such an order: *Re AMR (Adoption Procedure)* [1999] 2 FLR 807.

## Father without parental responsibility

5.7 The consent of a father who does not have parental responsibility is not required under the ACA 2002. However, pursuant to AAR 2005, reg 14. which applies not only to parents and guardians of the child but to 'others' as well, if the identity and whereabouts of a father without responsibility are known to the agency and it is considered appropriate in the circumstances of the case to do so, the adoption agency is required to: (a) provide counselling services to him; (b) explain the procedure in relation to the placement for adoption and adoption; (c) explain the legal implications of adoption; (d) ascertain his wishes and feelings regarding the child's placement for adoption and the child's adoption; (e) ascertain any wishes and feelings about the child's religious and cultural upbringing and contact. These requirements do not apply if the agency is satisfied that they have been undertaken by another agency.

5.8 The agency must also ascertain whether the father wishes to acquire parental responsibility, or intends to apply for a child arrangement order under ChA 1989, s 8 (he does not require permission to make the application: ChA 1989, s 10(4)); or, if the child is the subject of a care order, to apply for contact with the child under ChA 1989, s 34.

5.9 Where adoption proceedings have commenced, the adoption agency or the local authority (as the case may be) may apply to the court for direction that the father be made a respondent to the proceedings under FPR 2010, r 14.4(3)(a). However, his exclusion and that of extended family members from the adoption process, or being notified of the adoption proceedings, will very much depend on the facts of the case. Where the mother wishes to conceal the birth of her child from the father or extended family, the reasons for so doing should be fully investigated and balanced against what is in the best interests and welfare of the child (but not the paramount consideration); and the various interests involved. The following guidance given in *Re A, B and C (Adoption: Notification of Fathers and Relatives)* [2020] EWCA Civ 41 at [89], whilst not obligatory, may be useful:

> The principles governing decisions (by local authorities as adoption agencies or by the court) as to whether a putative father or a relative should be informed of the existence of a child who might be adopted can be summarised in this way.
>
> 1. The law allows for 'fast-track' adoption with the consent of all those with parental responsibility, so in some cases the mother alone. Where she opposes notification being given to the child's father or relatives her right to respect for her private life is engaged and can only be infringed where it is necessary to do so to protect the interests of others.
> 2. The profound importance of the adoption decision for the child and potentially for other family members is clearly capable of supplying a justification for overriding the mother's request. Whether it does so will depend upon the individual circumstances of the case.
> 3. The decision should be prioritised and the process characterised by urgency and thoroughness.
> 4. The decision-maker's first task is to establish the facts as clearly as possible, mindful of the often limited and one-sided nature of the information available. The confidential relinquishment of a child for adoption is an unusual event and the reasons for it must be respectfully scrutinised so that the interests of others are protected. In fairness to those other individuals, the account that is given by the person seeking confidentiality cannot be taken at face value. All information that can be discovered without compromising confidentiality should therefore be gathered and a first-hand account from the person seeking confidentiality will normally be sought. The investigation should enable broad conclusions to be drawn about the relative weight to be given to the factors that must inform the decision.
> 5. Once the facts have been investigated the task is to strike a fair balance between the various interests involved. The welfare of the child is an important factor but it is not the paramount consideration.
> 6. There is no single test for distinguishing between cases in which notification should and should not be given but the case law shows that these factors will be relevant when reaching a decision:

(1) *Parental responsibility.* The fact that a father has parental responsibility by marriage or otherwise entitles him to give or withhold consent to adoption and gives him automatic party status in any proceedings that might lead to adoption. Compelling reasons are therefore required before the withholding of notification can be justified.

(2) *Article 8 rights.* Whether the father, married or unmarried, or the relative have an established or potential family life with the mother or the child, the right to a fair hearing is engaged and strong reasons are required before the withholding of notification can be justified.

(3) *The substance of the relationships.* Aside from the presence or absence of parental responsibility and of family life rights, an assessment must be made of the substance of the relationship between the parents, the circumstances of the conception, and the significance of relatives. The purpose is to ensure that those who are necessarily silent are given a notional voice so as to identify the possible strengths and weaknesses of any argument that they might make. Put another way, with what degree of objective justification might such a person complain if they later discovered they had been excluded from the decision? The answer will differ as between a father with whom the mother has had a fleeting encounter and one with whom she has had a substantial relationship, and as between members of the extended family who are close to the parents and those who are more distant.

(4) *The likelihood of a family placement being a realistic alternative to adoption.* This is of particular importance to the child's lifelong welfare as it may determine whether or not adoption is necessary. An objective view, going beyond the say-so of the person seeking confidentiality, should be taken about whether a family member may or may not be a potential carer. Where a family placement is unlikely to be worth investigating or where notification may cause significant harm to those notified, this factor will speak in favour of maintaining confidentiality; anything less than that and it will point the other way.

(5) *The physical, psychological or social impact on the mother or on others of notification being given.* Where this would be severe, for example because of fear arising from rape or violence, or because of possible consequences such as ostracism or family breakdown, or because of significant mental health vulnerability, these must weigh heavily in the balancing exercise. On the other hand, excessive weight should not be given to short term difficulties and to less serious situations involving embarrassment or social unpleasantness, otherwise the mother's wish would always prevail at the expense of other interests.

(6) *Cultural and religious factors.* The conception and concealed pregnancy may give rise to particular difficulties in some cultural and religious contexts. These may enhance the risks of notification, but they may also mean that the possibility of maintaining the birth tie through a family placement is of particular importance for the child.

(7) *The availability and durability of the confidential information.* Notification can only take place if there is someone to notify. In cases where a mother declines to identify a father she may face persuasion, if that is thought appropriate, but she cannot be coerced. In some cases the available information may mean that the father is identifiable, and maternal relatives may also be identifiable. The extent to which identifying information is pursued is a matter of judgement. Conversely, there will be cases where it is necessary to consider whether any confidentiality is likely to endure. In the modern world secrets are increasingly difficult to keep and the consequences, particularly for the child and any prospective adopters, of the child's existence being concealed but becoming known to family members later on, sometimes as a result of disclosure by the person seeking confidentiality, should be borne in mind.

(8) *The impact of delay.* A decision to apply to court and thereafter any decision to notify will inevitably postpone to some extent the time when the child's permanent placement can be confirmed. In most cases, the importance of the issues means that the delay cannot be a predominant factor. There may however be circumstances where delay would have particularly damaging consequences for the mother or for the child; for example, it would undoubtedly need to be taken into account if it would lead to the withdrawal of the child's established carers or to the loss of an especially suitable adoptive placement.

(9) *Any other relevant matters.* The list of relevant factors is not closed. Mothers may have many reasons for wishing to maintain confidentiality and there may be a wide range of implications for the child, the father and for other relatives. All relevant matters must be considered.

7. It has rightly been said that the maintenance of confidentiality is exceptional, and highly exceptional where a father has parental responsibility or where there is family life under Article 8. However exceptionality is not in itself a test or a short cut; rather it is a reflection of the fact that the profound significance of adoption for the child and considerations of fairness to others means that the balance will often fall in favour of notification. But the decision on whether confidentiality should be maintained can only be made by striking a fair balance between the factors that are present in the individual case.

See further also under Chapter 4.

## Guardian of the child

5.10 'Guardian' has the same meaning as in the ChA 1989 and includes a special guardian (ACA 2002, s 144). Under ChA 1989, s 105, a guardian of a child means a guardian (other than a guardian of the estate of a child) appointed in accordance with the provisions of ChA 1989, s 5. The court may, by order, appoint a guardian for a child on the application of any person, or of its own motion in family proceedings if:

(a) the child has no parent with parental responsibility for him;
(b) a care arrangement order (residence order) has been made with respect to the child in favour of a parent, guardian or special guardian of his who has died while the order was in force; or
(c) point (b) (above) does not apply and the child's only or last surviving special guardian dies (ChA 1989, s 5(1) and (2)).

5.11 A parent with parental responsibility may appoint a person to be the child's guardian in the event of the parent's death, and in turn the guardian may appoint another person to take his place in the event of his death (ChA 1989, s 5(3) and (4)). The appointment of the guardian by the parent must be in writing, dated and signed; or, if the appointment is made by a will, the will must be attested in accordance with the requirement of the Wills Act 1837.

5.12 A person appointed as a child's guardian under ChA 1989, s 5 has parental responsibility for the child. A special guardian also has parental responsibility for the child and is included within the meaning of a guardian.

5.13 There may be situations where the application of the above conditions involves a foreign child or a foreign adoption order. In such cases it is for the court in England and Wales to determine whether the guardian appointed by the foreign court falls within the meaning of the ChA 1989. Expert evidence may be relied on to determine the issue. The decisions in the following cases under the Adoption Act 1976 may provide some guidance: *Re AMR (Adoption: Procedure)* [1999] 2 FLR 807; *Re D (Adoption: Foreign Guardianship)* [1999] 2 FLR 865; *Re AGN (Adoption: Foreign Adoption)* [2000] 2 FLR 431. These decisions were referred to in *Re J (Adoption: Consent of Foreign Public Authority)* [2002] EWHC 766 (Fam) in which Charles J held (at [30)] that when considering whether a person in another jurisdiction is, or is to be treated as, a guardian under the adoption legislation and therefore a person whose consent to an adoption order has to be given or dispensed with the court should consider:

> (i) the extent to which that person's duties, rights and responsibilities equate to those of a person (a) who has parental responsibility in English law, and (b) whose consent to an adoption has to be given or dispensed with before the order can be made;
> (ii) whether in all the circumstances that person's consent to an adoption order should be given or dispensed with, before such an order is made.

5.14 Where difficult issues arise in relation to foreign orders and jurisdiction, a transfer of the proceedings to a High Court Judge sitting in the Family Court should be considered. On issuing the application it should be referred to the Designated Family Judge (DFJ) for consultation with the Family Division Liaison Judge on whether the application should be referred to a High Court Judge or a Deputy High Court Judge. (For the procedure for making an application, see Chapter 9.)

## THE SECOND CONDITION – PLACEMENTS AND PLACEMENT ORDERS

5.15 The second condition, which may be considered when determining whether the court has jurisdiction to make an adoption order as an alternative to consent, is that:

- the child has been placed for adoption by an adoption agency with the prospective adopter(s) in whose favour the order is proposed to be made and either:
  - the child was placed for adoption with the consent of each parent or guardian and the consent of the mother was given when the child was at least six weeks old; or
  - the child was placed for adoption under a placement order, and
- no parent or guardian opposes the making of the adoption order (ACA 2002, s 47(4)).

### Permission to oppose an adoption order

5.16 Where the parent or guardian has given advance consent for the child to be placed for adoption under ACA 2002, s 20, and consent has not been withdrawn, the parent may not oppose the application for an adoption order unless the court grants permission to do so. Permission will not be granted unless the court is satisfied that there has been a change of circumstances since the consent was given or the placement order was made (ACA 2002, s 47(7)) (*A Local Authority v GC and Others* [2008] EWHC 2555 (Fam)). Where permission to oppose is given, the court may still dispense with consent on the ground that the child's welfare so requires (ACA 2002, ss 47(2) and 52(1)(b)) (see further Chapter 6).

### Dispensing with consent

5.17 If consent remains an issue, or permission is given to oppose the application, it is open to the applicants to seek an order that consent be dispensed with (see Chapter 6). The child's welfare is the principal ground for dispensing with parental consent. Where there is a conflict between the child's welfare, and therefore the child's rights, and the parent's rights, the court will carry out a balancing exercise between the competing rights of the child and those of the parents under the European Convention.

## THE THIRD CONDITION – SCOTTISH AND NORTHERN IRISH PERMANENCE/FREEING ORDER

5.18 It is clear from ACA 2002, s 47(6) that a Scottish permanence order which includes authority for the child to be adopted and a freeing order made by a court in Northern Ireland will be recognised in adoption proceedings, and therefore an adoption order may be made without determining the issue of consent (see ACA 2002, ss 105 and 106). See *Re A and O (Children) (Adoption)* [2017] EWHC 35 (Fam), where the court was concerned with a number of cases in which applicants living in England were seeking from the (English) Family Court an adoption order pursuant to the ACA 2002 in relation to a Scottish child who had been placed with them by a Scottish local authority following the making by a (Scottish) Sheriff Court of a permanence order with authority to adopt under Adoption and Children (Scotland) Act 2007, ss 80 and 83. In each case, the application was being made in accordance with ACA 2002, s 47(6)(a). The court held that it had jurisdiction based on the domicile/habitual residence of the prospective adoptive parents, and that the Scottish local authority had acted as an adoption agency, and therefore the case fell within ACA 2002, s 42(2)(a).

5.19 In *Re A and O (Children: Scotland)* [2017] EWHC 1293 (Fam), the Scottish adoption and permanence panel recommended that the children be adopted. Following an application for a permanence order, the children were matched with the applicants who lived in England and the children placed with them. Applications were made in England for an adoption order in accordance with ACA 2002, s 47(2). One of the issues before the court was whether the children had been lawfully placed in England and whether the proceedings should have been commenced in Scotland. The court held that the English court had jurisdiction to hear the application irrespective of where the children were habitually resident and to dispense with the consent of the parents notwithstanding the fact that the parents were not habitually resident in England. However, since the parents were in Scotland, the court held that:

> the imperative demands of justice and fairness, and the equally pressing demands of humanity and common decency, require that the State, which at the behest of one State agent [the local authority] and through the actions of another – the Family Court – is being invited to dispense with the parents' consent … must, if these proceedings are to remain in the Family Court, meet the parents' costs, not merely of travel to and from the court for the final hearing but also of their overnight accommodation near the court starting on the night before the final hearing commences and thereafter for the duration of the hearing. If and to the extent that these … wholly necessary, costs will not be met by the Legal Aid Agency … then they must be met by [the local authority].' (at [65])

The court also suggested that where an adoption application is made to an English court relying on a Scottish order, whether a compulsory supervision order or a permanence order with authority to adopt, the papers should be referred to the designated family judge at the outset with a view to making an order joining the Scottish local authority before the first directions hearing ([68]).

## OTHER REQUIREMENTS

5.20 Reference should be made to Chapters 2 and 3, which set out the statutory requirements in relation to who may be adopted and those who wish to adopt, where the child is placed by an adoption agency, for the child to live with the adoptive parents for a trial period and for the adoption agency to be given sufficient opportunity to see the child with the applicants before an application for an adoption order is made.

5.21 In the case of a non-agency placement, the statutory requirements for giving notice of intention to adopt, must be given to the appropriate local authority before the date on which the application for an adoption order is made.

# Chapter 6

# Dispensing with Parental Consent

## GROUNDS FOR DISPENSING WITH CONSENT

6.1 ACA 2002, s 52 provides for only two grounds for dispensing with parental consent to a child being placed for adoption or to the making of an adoption order. These are that:

(a) the parent or guardian cannot be found or lacks capacity (within the meaning of the Mental Capacity Act 2005 (MCA 2005)) to give consent; or
(b) the welfare of the child requires the consent to be dispensed with.

### When will it be necessary to apply for dispensation of parental consent?

6.2 The circumstances when there will be a need to consider making an application for dispensing with parental consent may arise at various stages in the adoption process:

(a) initially, when parental consent has been given but consent is subsequently withdrawn, and it is considered necessary to apply for a placement order;
(b) where the local authority's care plan for the child to be adopted is opposed and an application is made for a placement order;
(c) where consent having been given or a placement order made, the parent applies for and is granted permission to oppose the making of the order;
(d) in non-agency cases (i.e. by relatives) where the application is opposed.

### How is the application for dispensation made?

6.3 The application for dispensing with parental consent must be made by the applicant within the application form if it is known that the application for a placement order or for an adoption order is opposed. If consent having been given it is later withdrawn after the proceedings are issued, the application should be made by filing a written request. In both instances, the request must set out the reasons for the request and a written statement of facts must be filed setting out a summary of the history of the case and any other facts to satisfy the court of the grounds for dispensation (FPR 2010, r 14.9(2)).

### What criteria will the court apply in determining dispensing with consent?

6.4 Although the ACA 2002 in s 1 makes it clear that whenever a court makes a decision relating to the adoption of a child, the child's welfare is the paramount consideration and hence there is a single consideration, the decision relating to dispensation of consent involves a two-stage process. The court will consider whether adoption is in the best interests of the child, and if so, whether a ground for dispensing with consent has been made out (see para 6.1). In determining the welfare issue the court is required to take into account the factors set out in ACA 2002, s 1(3) and (4) (see Chapter 7). The protection of rights under the European Convention and balancing the respective rights of the parents and the child and determining whether any infringement of those rights is proportionate to safeguard the child's interests will also be relevant, but it is the child's welfare that will trump the exercise. Dispensation of consent per se is not incompatible with Convention rights (*Re CB (A Child) (No 2) (Adoption Proceedings: Vienna Convention)* [2015] EWCA Civ 888).

## PARENT OR GUARDIAN CANNOT BE FOUND

6.5 Much of the case law under the Adoption Act 1976 provides guidance on how this can be established. In *Re F (R) (An Infant)* [1969] 3 WLR 853, the Court of Appeal stated that the words 'cannot be found' mean 'cannot be found by taking all reasonable steps' to try to contact the parent. Hence every effort should be made to locate the parent by all means available, including through relatives of the missing parent. In *Re S (Adoption)* [1999] 2 FLR 374, applying the test in *Re F (R)*, the court held that the proper approach to construing the words 'cannot be found' is 'all reasonable steps must be taken, and even if only one reasonable step is omitted, one cannot say that the person cannot be found'. However, in *Re R (Adoption)* [1967] 1 WLR 34, the court held that if there are no 'practical means' of communicating with the parent, the person cannot be found. The difference in these two interpretations was reconciled by Charles J in *Re A (Adoption of a Russian Child)* [2000] 1 FLR 539, who stated that what is 'reasonable' and what is practical will often overlay, and the question the court should ask is whether there are any reasonable steps that can now be taken to inform the mother of the proposed adoption and to seek her properly informed views. In asking that question, the court should consider whether any proposed or possible step is practical and if it would not be then it would not be a reasonable step. These days, where social media plays such a significant part in many people's lives, attempts should be made through this means to locate a missing parent. The cases of *Re A* and *Re R* can also be distinguished from *Re F (R)* and *Re S* on the facts. *Re A* and *Re R* both involved the adoption of a foreign child, and in both there was evidence of risk: in *Re R* the risk was of endangering life or causing embarrassment; in *Re A* the risk was to the applicants and third parties. In *Re A* the mother had given up her child for adoption, had consented to the adoption and had taken no part in the Russian proceedings, whereas in *Re F (R)* and *Re S* the mother had not given up her child for adoption and had had no inkling that the child might be adopted, nor was there any evidence of any risk to the applicants or the natural parent in making inquiries. In *B (An Infant)* [1958] 1 QB 12, where the applicants had failed to serve the mother with notice of the proceedings notwithstanding the fact that they were aware of her address, the adoption order was set aside.

6.6 It is thus essential to take all practical and reasonable steps to locate the person whose consent is required. It is the duty of legal advisers to ensure that the applicants are made aware of the serious consequences which may follow, should the parent later appear and seek to have the order set aside. The usual avenues of inquiry are to contact members of the person's extended family and friends, and to consult the Electoral Register, the Council Tax Register and relevant government or local government departments, for example the Department of Work and Pensions. Where the inquiry relates to a person who is resident in England, an application may be made to the court for an order addressed to HM Revenue & Customs, directing the disclosure of the person's whereabouts and last known address to the court. Communication can then be made with the person through the court. In the digital world it will be advisable to seek the court's permission to use social media such as Facebook, Instagram, WhatsApp, etc. to locate the parent. See, for example, *West Sussex County Council v Jade Alma* [2016] EWHC 2009 (Fam), where a public campaign was launched, and the national press and television channels were used to reach the parents.

## LACKS CAPACITY TO GIVE CONSENT WITHIN THE MEANING OF THE MCA 2005

### Incapacity within the meaning of the MCA 2005

6.7 MCA 2005, s 2(1) provides that:

> a person lacks capacity in relation to a matter if at the material time he is unable to make a decision for himself in relation to the matter because of impairment of, or a disturbance in the functioning of, the mind or brain.

6.8 It does not matter whether the impairment or disturbance is permanent or temporary (MCA 2005, s 2(2)). MCA 2005, s 2(3) provides that a lack of capacity cannot be established merely by reference to:

> (a) a person's age or appearance; or
> (b) a condition of his, or an aspect of his behaviour, which might lead others to make unjustified assumptions about his capacity.

## When is a person unable to make a decision?

6.9 Determining whether the person is unable to make a decision involves eliciting information from him and then assessing his ability to retain information and to weigh up the information given to him. MCA 2005, s 3 sets out what constitutes inability to make decisions. It provides that a person is unable to make a decision for himself if he is unable:

(a) to understand the information relevant to his decision. This includes information about the reasonably foreseeable consequences of:

    (i) deciding one way or another; or
    (ii) failing to make the decision (MCA 2005, s 3(4)).

    However, a person is not to be regarded as unable to understand the information relevant to a decision if he is able to understand an explanation of it given to him in a way that is appropriate to his circumstances using simple language, visual aids or any other means (MCA 2005, s 3(2));
(b) to retain the information. The fact that a person is able to retain information relevant to a decision for a short period does not prevent him from being regarded as able to make the decision (MCA 2005, s 3(3));
(c) to use or weigh that information as part of the process of making the decision; or
(d) to communicate his decision (whether by talking, sign language or any other means).

In relation to an underage mother, it is appropriate to apply the *Gillick* competency test to determine the competence of the young person. In order to maintain consistency of approach it is now accepted that the key provisions of the MCA 2005 are relevant to assessing *Gillick* competence of both adults and children, but the threshold under the MCA 2005 should not be set artificially high. With regard to a child parent, they should be able to have sufficient understanding of the 'salient' facts around adoption, and the nature and quality of the transaction and should not need to be concerned with the peripheral: *Re A (Child as Parent: Adoption Consent)* [2017] EWHC 2729 (Fam), [60]–[61] and *A and Another v B and Another* [2022] EWHC 2962 (Fam). See further paras 6.13–6.17.

6.10 Incapacity, therefore, is not limited to mental illness in the traditionally accepted way. It is a broader concept based on impairment of the thought process. Thus, people with learning difficulties may come within this broad definition. It will be essential, at a very early stage in the proceedings, for the parent whose consent it is sought to dispense with to be assessed by a qualified psychiatrist or psychologist, or both, with experience and expertise in dealing not only with persons with mental illness, but also with persons with learning difficulties. The purpose would be to ascertain the extent of the disability and whether, having regard to the provisions of the section, there are any practical steps that can be taken to assist the person's understanding, particularly, as suggested in the section, by visual aids or other means.

## How should inability to make decisions be assessed?

6.11 The assessment should deal with the extent of the ability of the person to retain relevant information and to make an informed decision. It is the duty of the adoption agency, as far as is reasonably practicable, to ascertain the wishes and feeling of the parent of the child and:

(a) to provide counselling services for the parent;
(b) to explain to the parent the procedure in relation to placement for adoption and adoption, including the legal implications of giving consent and of the adoption order, and to provide written information about these matters.

6.12 The assessment should deal with whether the ability to retain information, even briefly, leads in the particular case to an affirmative conclusion about the person's understanding of the relevance of the information; the importance and effect of the consequences, both to the person and in relation to the welfare of the child; and the person's ability to make an informed decision on the whole process of adoption. In some cases, it may be necessary to show that all attempts have been made to relay the information by assisted means.

## What are the principles that apply when considering whether a person lacks capacity?

6.13 The incapacity must be referable to an impairment of, or a disturbance in, the functioning of the mind or brain. It is therefore doubtful whether cases such as *Re R (Adoption)* (above), and *Re A (Adoption of a Russian Child)* (above) would fall within the new provisions. MCA 2005, s 1 requires that, in arriving at any decision, certain principles should be applied when considering whether a person lacks capacity. These are:

(a) a person must be assumed to have capacity unless it is established that he lacks capacity;
(b) a person is not to be treated as unable to make a decision unless all practicable steps to help him to do so have been taken without success;
(c) a person is not to be treated as unable to make a decision merely because he makes an unwise decision;
(d) an act done, or decision made, under the Act, on behalf of a person who lacks capacity must be done or made in his interests; and
(e) before the act is done, or decision is made, regard must be had to whether the purpose for which it is needed can be as effectively achieved in a way that is less restrictive of the person's rights and freedom of action.

6.14 The question of capacity is therefore issue-specific and subject-specific, particularly in relation to understanding the legal process and the legal proceedings. It is also important to consider whether, in the light of the expert evidence, the person in question has the personal autonomy to make a decision without being influenced by any third party.

## How can an incapacitous person be assisted?

6.15 MCA 2005, s 16 specifically deals with the power of the court to appoint a deputy to make decisions on behalf of a person who is found to lack capacity in relation to matters concerning his personal welfare and personal property and affairs. 'Personal welfare' includes decisions relating to contact with others (MCA 2005, s 17(1)(b)); and 'property and affairs' includes the conduct of legal proceedings in the person's name or on his behalf (MCA 2005, s 18(1)(k)). It will thus be necessary for the court to consider inviting the Official Solicitor to act on behalf of a parent who lacks capacity.

6.16 In addition, consideration should be given for arrangements to be made for the person to have an independent mental capacity advocate, even where the Official Solicitor has agreed to act and the person has legal representation, in order to offer support to the person throughout the proceedings. Some local authorities provide this service. MCA 2005, s 35 introduces provision for the appointment of 'independent mental capacity advocates'. It imposes on the Secretary of State and the National Assembly for Wales a duty to make such arrangements as they consider reasonable, to enable independent mental capacity advocates to be available to represent and support persons in acts or decisions relating to medical treatment and the provision of accommodation. The ambit of this section does not extend to adoption proceedings, but MCA 2005, s 41 authorises the Secretary of State to expand the role of the independent mental capacity advocate and to adjust the obligation imposed by MCA 2005, s 35. There is therefore scope for extension of this service. Additionally, it should be recognised that persons with learning disabilities are vulnerable persons and should be provided, where appropriate, with support and assistance throughout the whole legal process. Consideration should be given to providing a vulnerable person with the assistance and support of an intermediary or lay advocate.

6.17 *Re S (Parent as Child: Adoption; Consent)* [2017] EWHC 2729 (Fam) is an example of a case where the court was troubled with a child mother's competence to consent to the adoption of her three-month-old child, although she had clearly expressed the wish for the child to be adopted as soon as possible. The issue that faced the court was how it should assess the competence of the mother as decision maker; what the test was for establishing competence of the child parent to consent to placement/adoption; whether steps should be taken to help the parent to reach a decision; in what circumstances the threshold was likely to be met in relation to a relinquished baby, and where a placement order had been refused and there was no valid consent. Even in relation to whether the mother was *Gillick* competent, the court had to be satisfied that she was able to understand the nature and implications of the decision and the process of implementing that decision; to understand the implications of not pursuing the decision; to retain the information long enough for the decision-making process to take place; to weigh up the information, arrive at a decision and communicate that decision; and the fact that even if she was regarded as competent to agree to the child being accommodated, it did not mean that she was competent to consent to adoption as the evaluation of competence was decision-specific. The observations made by Cobb J in his judgment when arriving at his decision are set out below as a guide for future reference:

> 57. While this assessment is helpful in providing general background about S's functioning, and while Professor Beail has additionally furnished some useful advice about how to convey information to, and discuss issues with, S, the report is of minimal assistance in relation to the *specific* issue with which the court is now concerned. A specific assessment is therefore required, and reasonably urgently, on her capacity to consent to adoption. As a prelude to that assessment, S should receive some 'age-appropriate information about adoption in an age-appropriate way in order to enhance her decision-making potential' ...
>
> ...
>
> 62. By way of summary and conclusion, I distil the following principles from my analysis above:
>
> i) The test of competence for decision-making of a young person is that set out in the House of Lords decision of *Gillick v West Norfolk and Wisbech Area Health Authority* [1985] 3 WLR 830, [1986] 1 AC 112 ('*Gillick*') ('a sufficient understanding and intelligence to enable him or her to understand fully what is proposed'); in this regard, the child should be able to:

a) Understand the nature and implications of the decision and the process of implementing that decision;
b) Understand the implications of not pursuing the decision;
c) Retain the information long enough for the decision-making process to take place;
d) Be of sufficient intelligence and maturity to weigh up the information and arrive at a decision;
e) Be able to communicate that decision.

ii) The determination of a child's competence must be decision-specific and child-specific; it is necessary to consider the specific factual context when evaluating competence;
iii) Just because a child lacks litigation competence in (for example) care or placement order proceedings does not mean that she lacks subject matter competence in relation to consent to section 20 CA 1989 accommodation of her baby, or indeed to the adoption of the baby;
iv) The assessment of competence must be made on the evidence available;
v) When considering the issue of *Gillick* competence of a child parent, an important distinction must be drawn between the determination of competence to make the decision, and the exercise by that young person of their competent decision making;
vi) The relevant information that a child under 16 would need to be able to understand, retain and weigh up in order to have competency to consent to the section 20 accommodation of a child would be:

a) That the child will be staying with someone chosen by the local authority, probably a foster carer;
b) That the parent can change her mind about the arrangements, and request the child back from accommodation at any time;
c) That the parent will be able to see the child.

vii) The salient or 'sufficient' information which is required to be understood by the child parent regarding extra-familial adoption is limited to the fundamental legal consequences of the same; this would be:

a) Your child will have new legal parents, and will no longer be your son or daughter in law;
b) Adoption is final, and non-reversible;
c) During the process, other people (including social workers from the adoption agency) will be making decisions for the child, including who can see the child, and with whom the child will live;
d) You may obtain legal advice if you wish before taking the decision;
e) The child will live with a different family forever; you will (probably) not be able to choose the adopters;
f) You will have no right to see your child or have contact with your child; it is highly likely that direct contact with your child will cease, and any indirect contact will be limited;

g) The child may later trace you, but contact will only be re-established if the child wants this;

h) There are generally two stages to adoption; the child being placed with another family for adoption, and being formally adopted;

i) For a limited period of time you may change your mind; once placed for adoption, your right to change your mind is limited, and is lost when an adoption order is made.

viii) When determining the competence of a child parent in these circumstances, 'all practicable steps to help' her, as the decision-maker, to make the decision, must have been taken; a young person under the age of 16 will be treated as understanding the information relevant to a decision if she is able to understand an explanation of it given to her in a way which is appropriate to her circumstances (using simple language, visual aids or any other means);

ix) The decision to consent to adoption is significant and life-changing; there is a greater onus on ensuring that at the decision-making stage the child understands and is able to weigh the information;

x) Before exercising her decision-making, the child parent should freely and fully understand the information set out on the consent forms (which information is drawn from the ACA 2002 and from the Regulations); the information should be conveyed and explained to the young person in an age-appropriate way; there is no expectation that the young person would be able to understand the precise language of the consent forms;

xi) The question whether the threshold criteria is established in a relinquished baby case (section 21(2) ACA 2002) is one of fact;

xii) If there is any doubt about the competence of a child parent to give consent to adoption or placement for adoption, the issue should be referred to a court.

# THE CHILD'S WELFARE

## Paramount consideration

6.18 The court cannot dispense with the consent of any parent or guardian when deciding the making of a placement order or an adoption order unless it is satisfied that the welfare of the child *requires* the consent to be dispensed with (ACA 2002, s 52(1)(b)). This makes the welfare test the dominant test, and read together with the provision of ACA 2002, s 1(1) and (2), it is evident that in deciding whether to dispense with parental consent the paramount consideration must be the welfare of the child throughout his life. In deciding the issue, therefore, the court must take into account the factors set out in ACA 2002, s 1(4) and (5) (see Chapter 7). Additionally, in all applications the court has a duty also to consider the implications of the rights protected by the European Convention. Case law since the ACA 2002 came into force provides guidance on the approach to be adopted in dispensation cases.

## Child's welfare requires consent to be dispensed with

6.19 The interpretation and significance of 'requires' in ACA 2002, s 52(1)(b) was considered in *Re P (Placement Orders: Parental Consent)* [2008] EWCA Civ 535. Wall LJ reviewed the statutory provisions of ACA 2002, ss 1 and 52 and the implications of European Convention, Art 8 and related case law, and concluded that the word 'requires' has the 'connotation of the imperative, what is demanded rather than what is merely optional or reasonable or desirable' (at [125]); what has to be shown is that the child's welfare (at [126]):

> 'requires' *adoption* as opposed to something short of adoption. A child's circumstances may 'require' statutory intervention, perhaps may even 'require' the indefinite or long-term removal of the child from the family and his or her placement with strangers, but that is not to say that the same circumstances will necessarily 'require' that the child be adopted. They may or they may not. The question, at the end of the day, is whether what is 'required' is adoption. (original emphasis)

6.20 But 'this does not mean that there is some enhanced welfare test to be applied in cases of adoption ... The [vital] difference ... is ... between section 1 of the 1989 Act and section 1 of the 2002 Act' (at [127]). ACA 2002, s 1(2) requires a judge to focus on the child's welfare 'throughout his life'. This emphasises that adoption, unlike other forms of order made under the ChA 1989, is something with lifelong implications. The judge has to be satisfied that the child's welfare, now, throughout the rest of his childhood, into adulthood and indeed throughout his life, requires that he be adopted. Furthermore, the welfare checklist in ACA 2002, s 1 feeds into the ultimate question under ACA 2002, s 52(1)(b): Does the child's welfare throughout his life require adoption as opposed to something short of adoption (at [127]–[128])? See *Re T (A Child: Refusal of Adoption Order)* [2020] EWCA Civ 197, where the Court of Appeal ruled that the child's welfare required him to be afforded with the security in his placement with the adopters who were his grandparents, and that in the circumstances of the case only an adoption order would provide the degree of security his welfare interests required. Contrast with *Re E (A Child) (Care and Placement Orders)* [2024] EWFC 170(B) where the court decided to make a care order and dispensed with parental consent on the grounds of the child's best interests and concerns over the paternal grandmother's ability to care for the child. See also *ANS v ML (Scotland)* [2012] UKSC 30, which considered the equivalent legislation in Scotland and ruled that 'required' meant that it is 'necessary' and that there is an overriding need for adoption.

## Guidance on the approach to be adopted

6.21 The two leading cases which offer guidance and are often relied on are *Re B (Care Proceedings: Appeal)* [2013] UKSC 33 and *Re B-S (Adoption: Application of s 47(5))* [2013] EWCA Civ 1146. The guidance has been further explained and clarified by the Court of Appeal in a number of subsequent cases. A brief outline of the principles which have emerged from these decisions is set out below.

6.22 In *Re B*, the Supreme Court pointed out the need for proportionality when determining whether or not to place a child for adoption. It stated that adoption should be approved as an option of 'last resort' – when all else fails and where the child's welfare dictates that 'nothing else will do'.

6.23 In *Re B-S*, having reviewed the statutory provisions, European Convention, Art 8 implications and relevant case law, the Court of Appeal gave the following guidance on the approach to be adopted:

(1) there must be proper evidence from both the local authority and the guardian which addresses all the options which are realistically possible and which must contain an analysis of the arguments for and against each of the options (at [34]);
(2) it is essential that there is an adequate and reasoned judgment which gives proper focused attention to the specifics and a global holistic evaluation taking into account the positives and negatives (at [41]). In this respect, Munby P drew attention (at [43]) to what was stated in *Re G (A Child)* [2013] EWCA Civ 965 by McFarlane LJ:

> In most child care cases a choice will fall to be made between two or more options. The judicial exercise should not be a linear process whereby each option, other than the most draconian, is looked at in isolation and then rejected because of internal deficits that may be identified, with the result that, at the end of the line, the only option left standing is the most draconian and that is therefore chosen without any particular consideration of whether there are internal deficits within that option.
> The linear approach … is not apt where the judicial task is to undertake a global, holistic evaluation of each of the options available for the child's future upbringing before deciding which of those options best meets the duty to afford paramount consideration to the child's welfare.

6.24 And Munby P went on to add:

> 44. We emphasise the words 'global, holistic evaluation'. This point is crucial. The judicial task is to evaluate *all* the options, undertaking a global, holistic and

(see *Re G*, para 51) multi-faceted evaluation of the child's welfare which takes into account *all* the negatives and the positives, *all* the pros and cons, of each option. To quote McFarlane LJ again (para 54):

> 'What is required is a balancing exercise in which each option is evaluated to the degree of detail necessary to analyse and weigh its own internal positives and negatives and each option is then compared, side by side, against the competing option or options.'

45. McFarlane LJ added this important observation (para 53) which we respectfully endorse:

> 'a process which acknowledges that long-term public care, and in particular adoption contrary to the will of a parent, is "the most draconian option", yet does not engage with the very detail of that option which renders it "draconian" cannot be a full or effective process of evaluation. Since the phrase was first coined some years ago, judges now routinely make reference to the "draconian" nature of permanent separation of parent and child and they frequently do so in the context of reference to "proportionality". Such descriptions are, of course, appropriate and correct, but there is a danger that these phrases may inadvertently become little more than formulaic judicial window-dressing if they are not backed up with a substantive consideration of what lies behind them and the impact of that on the individual child's welfare in the particular case before the court. If there was any doubt about the importance of avoiding that danger, such doubt has been firmly swept away by the very clear emphasis in *Re B* on the duty of the court actively to evaluate proportionality in every case.'

6.25 In *Re W (Care Proceedings: Functions of Court and Local Authority)* [2013] EWCA Civ 1227, the Court of Appeal re-emphasised the need for a welfare evaluation and the need to address the question of what, if any, orders engage European Convention, Art 8 rights and the evaluation of the proportionality test that has to be undertaken and articulated. In *Re M (A Child: Long-term Foster Care)* [2014] EWCA Civ 1406, the court observed that the Supreme Court's decision in *Re B* (see above) required an evaluation of all the circumstances and the realities in the child's life assessed alongside the checklist set out in ACA 2002, s 1. On this point, in *CM v Blackburn with Darwen Borough Council* [2014] EWCA Civ 1479, the Court of Appeal rejected any suggestion that the 'nothing else will do test' in *Re B* and *Re B-S* had re-drawn the statutory landscape, but stated that what it did was to explain the existing law and require a process of deductive reasoning applying the welfare test alongside the relevant parts of ACA 2002, ss 21 and 52. This judgment goes on to highlight recent cases in which the proportionality evaluation had been misconstrued by practitioners.

6.26 In *Re M-H (A Child) (Placement Order: Correct Test to Dispense with Consent)* [2014] EWCA Civ 1396, the mother wanted the child placed in foster care so that she could continue to have contact with her six-year-old child. The Court of Appeal confirmed the test set out in *Re B*, but explained that: (a) *Re B* must be read as stated, that the orders are to be made 'only in exceptional circumstances and where motivated by the overriding requirements pertaining to the child's best interests' (at [8]); (b) that in any contested application there will always be another option, with some being finely balanced and calling for critical and often anxious scrutiny, but 'the fact that there is another credible option worthy of examination will not mean that the test of "nothing else will do" automatically bites' (at [9]); (c) that (at [11]):

> [t]he 'holistic' balancing exercise of the available options that must be deployed in applications concerning adoption is not so as to undertake a direct comparison of what probably would be best but in order to ascertain whether or not the particular child's welfare demands adoption. In doing so it may well be that some features of one or other option taken in isolation would produce a better outcome in one particular area for the child throughout minority and beyond. It would be intellectually dishonest not to acknowledge the benefits. But this is not to say that finding one or more benefits trumps all and means that it cannot be said that 'nothing else will do'. All will depend upon the judge's assessment of the whole picture determined by the particular characteristics and needs of the child in question no doubt often informed by the harm which s/he has suffered or been exposed to.

6.27 Options which are unrealistic should be discarded at an early stage. The test set out in *Re B* does not mean that every 'stone needs to be uncovered'. There needs to be something more than just a hope that 'something will turn up'. Placement orders are made more often in anticipation of finding adoptive parents than with ones in mind. Plans go awry. Some adoption plans are over ambitious. Inevitably, there will be contingency plans, often for long-term fostering. It will still remain for the court to consider the paramountcy of the welfare of the child (*Re R (A Child)* [2014] EWCA Civ 1625). See also *Re J (A Child)* [2015] EWCA Civ 222, in which the Court of Appeal once again set out a reminder to advocates and courts of the principles to be applied in adoption cases. Where the court does not have the evidence of the kind referred to in *Re B-S*, the case should be adjourned even if this results in delay. Where on the analysis of the evidence the court concludes that adoption can be only said to benefit the child if further requirements are satisfied, it is unlikely that the court in those circumstances can hold that the welfare of the child requires that consent should be dispensed with (*Re A (Placement Order: Imposition of Conditions)* [2013] EWCA Civ 1611).

6.28 In *Re N (Refusal of Placement Order)* [2023] EWCA Civ 364, the Court of Appeal drew attention to the distinction between the welfare paramountcy provision in the ACA 2002 and CA 1989 and the factor in ACA 2002, s 1(4)(f) which emphasises the child's existing relationships, which were an important component of any analysis of the child's welfare 'throughout life' and that 'a sibling relationship is a paradigm example because unlike nearly every other relationship, it is likely to be lifelong (at [29]).

The ECtHR has also held that, when assessing the child's welfare and best interests, considerations must be borne in mind of the child's relationships with family and for these to be maintained except where the family have proved to be unfit, and of the need to ensure the child's development in a safe and secure environment: *YC v United Kingdom (Application No 4547/10)* (2012) 55 EHRR 33, [2012] 2 FLR 332, ECtHR. See also *Ibrahim v Norway (Application No 15379/16)* [2022] ECtHR (Grand Chamber), where the court held that in depriving the mother of parental responsibility in respect of her child and authorising adoption by the child's foster carers, the domestic authorities had failed to attach sufficient weight to the mother's and the child's Art 8 rights of family ties and the possibility for them to maintain contact.

## PROCEDURE FOR DISPENSING WITH CONSENT

6.29 See paras 4.87–4.88, and see paras 4.89–4.103 for the procedural steps to the final hearing.

Chapter 7

# Criteria to Be Applied – Welfare Must Be the Paramount Consideration

## INTRODUCTION

7.1 The ACA 2002 makes the welfare of the child the central principle to be applied whenever a court or adoption agency makes any decision concerning the adoption of a child. ACA 2002, s 1(1) and (2) provides that whenever a court or an adoption agency is coming to a decision relating to the adoption of a child, the paramount consideration of the court or the adoption agency *must* be the child's welfare throughout his life. This is wider than the paramountcy test in ChA 1989, s 1(1), which requires the paramountcy test to be considered with respect to the child's upbringing. Similarly, when considering whether to dispense with parental consent, the court cannot do so unless the welfare of the child 'requires' the consent to be dispensed with (s 52(1)(b)). It is thus clear that both provisions are mandatory 'rather than merely optional or reasonable or desirable' (*Re P (Placement Orders: Parental Consent)* [2008] EWCA Civ 535. This paramountcy principle is given a wide interpretation and includes all matters (such as acquisition of British citizenship) that may affect the child not only during his childhood, but also into adulthood and beyond (*FAS v Secretary of State for the Home Department and Another* [2015] EWCA Civ 951; *Re P (Placement Orders: Parental Consent)* [2008] EWCA Civ 535). In determining where the child's interests lie, the court will need to consider the child's family ties and to ensure the child's development in a safe and secure environment (*YC v United Kingdom (Application No 4547/10)* (2012) 55 EHRR 33, [2012] 2 FLR 332, ECtHR). This includes decisions not only on an adoption order, but also on a placement order (or revocation of an adoption or placement order), dispensing with consent, contact, and decisions about granting permission in respect of any other action (ACA 2002, s 1(7)). See also *D McG v Neath Port Talbot County Borough Council* [2010] EWCA Civ 821, [2010] 2 FLR 1827, where it was held that all options towards rehabilitation should be explored before a placement order is sought, and the guidance given in *Re H (Care and Adoption Assessment of Wider Family)* [2019] EWFC 10 at [49]–[56]. See also *Re B (A Child)* [2013] UKSC 33, where Baroness Hale stated (at [34]) that the 'test for severing the relationship between parent and child is very strict; only in exceptional circumstances and where motivated by overriding requirements pertaining to the child's welfare. In short, where nothing else will do' (see the guidance set out at para 4.66).

## CRITERIA TO BE APPLIED TO WELFARE CONSIDERATION

7.2 When considering the welfare of the child, the court or adoption agency must have regard to the following factors set out in ACA 2002, s 1(4) (among others):

(a) the child's ascertainable wishes and feelings regarding the decision (considered in the light of the child's age and understanding);
(b) the child's particular needs;
(c) the likely effect on the child (throughout his life) of having ceased to be a member of the original family and become an adopted child;
(d) the child's age, sex, background, and any of the child's characteristics which the court or agency considers relevant;
(e) any harm (within the meaning of the ChA 1989) which the child has suffered or is at risk of suffering;
(f) the relationship which the child has with relatives, and with any other person in relation to whom the court or agency considers the relationship to be relevant, including:
    (i) the likelihood of any such relationship continuing and the value to the child of its doing so;
    (ii) the ability and willingness of any of the child's relatives, or of any such person, to provide the child with a secure environment in which the child can develop, and otherwise to meet the child's needs;
    (iii) the wishes and feelings of any of the child's relatives, or of any such person, regarding the child (ACA 2002, s 1(4)).

7.3 Since 25 July 2014, in placing a child for adoption, an adoption agency in Wales is required to give due consideration to the child's religious persuasion, racial origin and cultural and linguistic background (ACA 2002, s 1(5)).

7.4 In addition, decision makers must at all times: (a) bear in mind that, in general, delay in coming to a decision is likely to prejudice the child's welfare; and (b) consider the whole range of options available to them in the child's case, whether under the ACA 2002 or the ChA 1989, and the court must not make any order in relation to the child unless it considers that making the order would be better for the child than not doing so (ACA 2002, s 1(6)). The cases of *Re T (A Child: Refusal of Adoption Order)* [2020] EWCA Civ797 and *Torbay v M and*

*Others (A Child: Refusal of Adoption Order)* [2023] EWFC 126 provide examples of the various factors which are taken into account from the perspective of the child's welfare, the child's best interests, security and reassurance throughout the child's life in determining the benefits of adoption as opposed to a special guardianship order/foster care placement, or in some exceptional surrogacy cases a parental order (*E v R and Others* [2023] EWFC 214), and both a parental and an adoption order (*FG and Another v IJ and Others* [2024] EWHC 586 (Fam) for the child concerned given the circumstances of the case.

## THE CHILD'S WISHES AND FEELINGS

7.5 The reference to the child's ascertainable wishes and feelings considered in the light of his age and understanding is in terms similar to those in ChA 1989, s 1(3)(a). In addition, under ChA 1989, s 25(5)(a), a local authority is obliged, before making any decision with respect to a child whom it is looking after, or proposing to look after, to give due consideration 'having regard to his age and understanding, to such wishes and feelings of the child as they have been able to ascertain'. While there is no requirement to comply with the child's wishes and feelings, these are nevertheless matters which the local authority is specifically required to consider from the moment the child comes into its care. The ACA 2002, while not giving this factor greater weight than any of the others referred to, nevertheless reinforces the importance of giving it proper consideration. It is one among many other elements which must be considered, and usually has greater importance the older the child. Much depends on the circumstances of the case, and on the age, maturity and intellectual understanding of the child. Also relevant may be whether the child's views have been influenced by any other person, and if so, by whom.

7.6 The child's wishes and feelings must be 'considered in the light of the child's age and understanding'. How then is this to be assessed? In most cases, assessments are carried out during care proceedings and/or proceedings for a placement order, so there will have been opportunities to ascertain the child's wishes and feelings, not least through the child's guardian within those proceedings. In *Re S (Independent Representation)* [1993] Fam 263, on the issue of 'understanding', Sir Thomas Bingham MR (at page 276B–C; see also pages 279H–280E) stated that:

> in the ordinary way it is no doubt true (at least of children) that understanding increases with the passage of time. But the rule eschews any arbitrary line of demarcation based on age, and wisely so. Different children have differing levels of understanding at the same age. And understanding is not an absolute. It has to be assessed relatively to the issues in the proceedings. Where any sound judgment on these issues calls for insight and imagination which only maturity and experience can bring, both the court and the solicitor will be slow to conclude that the child's understanding is sufficient ...

> The 1989 Act enables and requires a judicious balance to be struck between two considerations. First is the principle, to be honoured and respected, that children are human beings in their own right with individual minds and wills, views and emotions, which should command serious attention. A child's wishes are not to be discounted or dismissed simply because he is a child. He should be free to express them and decision-makers should listen. Second is the fact that a child is, after all, a child. The reason why the law is particularly solicitous in protecting the interests of children is because they are liable to be vulnerable and impressionable, lacking maturity to weigh the longer term against the shorter, lacking the insight to know how they will react and the imagination to know how others will react in certain situations, lacking the experience to measure the probable against the possible. Everything of course depends on the individual child in his actual situation. For the purposes of the Act, a babe in arms and a sturdy teenager on the verge of adulthood are both children, but their positions are quite different; for one the consideration will be dominant, for the other the first principle will come into its own. The process of growing up is, as Lord Scarman pointed out in *Gillick* [1986] AC 112 at p 186B, [1986] 1 FLR 224 at p 250H a continuous one. The judge has to do his best, on the evidence before him, to assess the understanding of the individual child in the context of the proceedings in which he seeks to participate.

7.7 In addition, UNCRC, Art 12(1) requires states to assure to the child who is capable of forming his own views the right to express those views freely in all matters affecting him, the views of the child being given due weight in accordance with his age and maturity. UNCRC, Art 12(2) provides that 'the child shall in particular be provided with the opportunity to be heard in any judicial and administrative proceedings affecting the child, either directly, or through a representative or an appropriate body, in a manner consistent with the procedural rules of national law'.

7.8 See also the European Convention on the Exercise of Children's Rights, 25 January 1996 (not ratified by the United Kingdom), Arts 3–6, 9 and 14. A case such as *Re H (Step Parent: Adoption: Human Rights)* [2023] EWHC 3186 (Fam)) is an example of where the wishes and feelings of H, the subject of the application, that he supported the application by the applicants to adopt him were respected. Additionally, he was given the opportunity to attend all the hearings and be separately represented. H was also permitted to express his views (in favour of adoption) by writing to the judge. (See further under paras 2.19 and 2.33.)

## THE CHILD'S PARTICULAR NEEDS

7.9 Unlike the ChA 1989, the ACA 2002 does not specify the particular needs of a child which must be taken into account. The ChA 1989, in s 1(3)(b), specifically refers to physical, emotional and educational needs. These must be as relevant in adoption proceedings as they are in other proceedings relating to a child and therefore the needs referred to in the ACA 2002 must encompass these three aspects. Of particular relevance will be any needs relating to the child's health, whether physical or mental, and any learning or intellectual difficulties which the child may have. In a case where the child has complex needs, it is essential that those making the decision undertake an analysis of the welfare principles and highlight the facts that tip the balance in favour of adoption rather than any other option, so that the parents can understand the reasons for the decision that is taken.

## THE LIKELY EFFECT ON THE CHILD THROUGHOUT HIS LIFE

7.10 The likely effect on a child of the fact that on adoption the natural parents' parental responsibility is extinguished and all family ties with the birth family come to an end, so that the child ceases to be a member of the birth family and becomes an adopted person, is more relevant in relation to older children, who are likely to have memories of their family and friends and therefore to be emotionally sensitive. In this respect the child's rights under European Convention, Art 8 and UNCRC, Arts 8 and 9 will be relevant. The loss of family ties will need to be balanced against the need to ensure the child's safety and security which he will enjoy in the adoptive home, and the commitment to him that the adoptive parents will provide which his birth family cannot (*Re M (Adoption or Residence Order)* [1998] 1 FLR 570, page 589; and *Re H (Step Parent: Adoption: Human Rights)* [2023] EWHC 3186 and *Re T (A Child: Refusal of Adoption Order)* [2020] EWCA Civ797 are recent examples) (see also para 7.1).

## AGE, SEX, BACKGROUND AND ANY RELEVANT CHARACTERISTICS

7.11 The requirement in ACA 2002, s 1(4)(d) to consider the child's age, sex, background and any characteristics which are considered relevant mirrors the provision of ChA 1989, s 1(3)(d). These matters become particularly important when dealing with children who have strong family and cultural links. The word 'characteristic' is wide enough to include racial issues (see *Re M (Section 94 Appeals)* [1995] 1 FLR 546).

## HARM THE CHILD HAS SUFFERED OR IS AT RISK OF SUFFERING

7.12 The requirement to take into account any harm the child has suffered or is at risk of suffering is to be assessed on the same basis as under ChA 1989, s 1(3)(e). In ChA 1989, s 31(9), 'harm' is defined as 'ill-treatment or the impairment of health or development including, for example, impairment suffered from seeing or hearing the ill-treatment of another'; 'development' means physical, intellectual, emotional, social or behavioural development; 'health' means physical or mental health; and 'ill-treatment' includes sexual abuse and forms of ill-treatment which are not physical. Where the question of whether harm suffered by a child is significant turns on the child's health or development, his health or development is to be compared with that which could reasonably be expected of a similar child (ChA 1989, s 31(10)).

7.13 'Harm' also includes exposure to domestic violence, and violence and ill-treatment generally (*Re L; Re V; Re M and Re H (Children) (Contact: Domestic Violence)* [2000] EWCA Civ 194). On this issue, see also the provisions of FPR 2010, PD 12J and, in particular, paras 3–4, 'Children as victims of domestic abuse'. The criteria under ChA 1989, s 31(2) must be satisfied at the date when proceedings are commenced, or if the child has been accommodated and the arrangements have remained in place continuously, the date on which those arrangements were first made (*Re M (A Minor) (Care Order: Threshold Criteria)* [1994] 2 FLR 577, HL), but relevant information obtained subsequently can be taken into account where the information is indicative of risk of harm that was not exposed earlier and establishes risk of significant harm (*Re G (Care Proceedings: Threshold Condition)* [2001] EWCA Civ 968). As regards risk of future harm to the child, the evidence must establish a real risk that cannot be ignored having regard to its gravity in the circumstances of the case and the reasons why it is suggested that the child is at risk of suffering harm (*Re B (Care Proceedings: Appeal)* [2013] UKSC 33). In the majority of cases, the placement of a child for adoption is likely to occur after care proceedings are concluded, and where the child is made the subject of a care order. In this case, the requirement under ChA 1989, s 31(2) that the child concerned is 'suffering, or likely to suffer, significant harm and that the harm, or likelihood of harm is attributable to the care given to the child or likely to be given to given to him if the order were not made' will have been adjudicated upon. However, it is when the parents subsequently wish to challenge the decision to place the child for adoption, on the basis of change of circumstances, that it will be important to reassess the risk.

## THE CHILD'S RELATIONSHIP WITH RELATIVES AND OTHERS

7.14 ACA 2002, s 1(4)(f) requires the courts and adoption agencies to have regard to the child's relationships with relatives and others in a very wide context. Unlike the provisions in the ChA 1989, it requires the decision maker to consider the child's relationship with the relative or other person who is a prospective adopter and any other person in relation to whom it is considered the question to be relevant. This includes consideration of the likelihood of any such relationship continuing and the value to the child of it doing so, the ability and willingness of that person(s) to provide a secure environment for the child in which the child can develop, and otherwise to meet the child's needs and to consider the wishes and feelings of such relative or other person: s 1(4)(f). The term 'relative' is defined to include the child's mother and father, grandparents, brother, sister, uncle or aunt, whether of full blood or half-blood or by marriage or civil partnership. The reference to 'any other person' clearly indicates that the child's relationship with any person which is important to the child, such as with grandparents or a foster carer (see *Re T (A Child: Refusal of Adoption Order)* [2020] EWCA Civ 797; *Re M'P-P (Children) Adoption Proceedings: Value to be Placed on Status Quo)* [2015] EWCA Civ 584), or a prospective adopter with whom the child has been placed, will be a relevant factor. In *Re W (Adoption: Approach to Long Term Welfare)* [2016 EWCA Civ 793, the court observed (at [40]) that 'it should be evident that a prospective adopter with whom a child has been placed under a placement for adoption order will automatically be 'any other person' within the context of s 1(4)(f) of ACA 2002'. The strength and value of the relationship which the child has with a relative, for example a sibling, or any other person, and its continuation, along with the wishes and feelings of the child and those with whom he has a relationship, will be relevant in the analysis of the child's welfare and best interests, and in the context of future contact or where considering alternatives to adoption. See, for example, *Re N (Refusal of Placement Order)* [2023] EWCA Civ 364; *Re T and R (Refusal of Placement Order)* [2021] EWCA Civ 71; *Re S (Adoption Order or Special Guardianship Order)* [2007] EWCA Civ 54.

7.15 The strength and value of the child's relationship with their parents and other family member(s) will also be relevant in determining post-placement and post-adoption contact between the child and birth family members (see further Chapter 8).

### The child's relationship with others

7.16 The ACA 2002 defines 'relationships' to extend beyond legal relationships, and pursuant to the Children and Social Work Act 2017, as from 31 October 2017, they include prospective adopter(s) (see *Re W (Adoption: Approach to Long-Term Welfare)* [2016] EWCA Civ 793). It may include the child's relationship with foster carer(s) (*Re M'P-P (Adoption Proceedings: Value to be Placed on Status Quo)* [2015] EWCA Civ 584).

## RELIGIOUS, RACIAL, CULTURAL AND LINGUISTIC ISSUES

7.17 Children and Families Act 2014, s 3 repealed this requirement in England with effect from 13 May 2014, but it remains a requirement in relation to Wales.

However, notwithstanding the repeal, welfare issues may still require this element to be considered in applying the welfare paramountcy principle, especially when dealing with a child of mixed race heritage where issues relating to the child's status in the child's or his parent's country of origin may not be recognised or may result in the child facing difficulties in future. See, for example, *Re T and R (Refusal of Placement Order)* [2021] EWCA Civ 71; *Re LC (A Child) (Placement Order)* [2020] EWCA Civ 787, in which cultural identity was a factor taken into account and *Re N (Children: Welfare Decision)* [2016] EWFC 44; *Re Z (A Child) (English Adoption: Egyptian Orphanage)* [2016] EWHC 2963 (Fam). In *Re N (Adoption: Jurisdiction)* [2015] EWCA Civ 1112, Munby P stated:

> 105. It cannot be emphasised too much that the court in such a case must give the most careful consideration, as must the children's guardian and all the other professional witnesses, in particular to those parts of the checklist which focus attention, explicitly or implicitly, on the child's national, cultural, linguistic, ethnic and religious background. Moreover, it must always be remembered that, in the context of such factors, the checklist demands consideration of the likely effect on the child *throughout her life* of having ceased to be a member of her original family. Mere lip service to such matters is not enough. The approach, both of the witnesses and of the judge, must be rigorous, analytical and properly reasoned, never forgetting that adoption is permissible only as a 'last resort' and only if a comprehensive analysis of the child's circumstances in every aspect – including the child's national, cultural, linguistic, ethnic and religious background – leads the court to the conclusion that the overriding requirements of the child's welfare justify adoption. (original emphasis)

7.18 This requirement still remains in relation to Wales and therefore earlier decisions where the issue was given consideration may still be relevant. In *Re E* [1964] 1 WLR 51, the child's mother was Roman Catholic but the child was placed with a Jewish couple who wished to adopt him. The mother objected as she wanted the child to be brought up in her faith. The prospective adopters were willing to undertake to bring the child up as a Catholic. In wardship proceedings, Wilberforce J said (at page 57):

> These authorities establish the basis on which I deal with this case, namely that in wardship proceedings the paramount consideration is the welfare of the child. Welfare is not limited to material welfare. The religious upbringing is an element of great importance. An illegitimate child's mother's wishes are of great significance and must not merely not be disregarded; they must be very seriously regarded by the court. The court will certainly not substitute its views for hers, but they must be considered with all other matters bearing on the welfare of the child (both long term and immediate). The court is not bound to give effect to them when satisfied that the child's welfare requires otherwise, and in giving effect to them the court has power to do so in such a manner as it may consider to be best in the child's interest.

7.19 In *Re J (A Minor) (Adoption Application)* [1987] 1 FLR 455, a child of mixed race was placed with white foster parents who were Jehovah's Witnesses. The mother objected to the adoption. Her objections were upheld on the basis that the child had West Indian characteristics and that this would lead to the child's drifting from the adoptive parents and seeking out his own ethnic origins. It would therefore not be in the child's best interests to lose his links with his mother. In *Re N (Minor) (Adoption)* [1990] 1 FLR 58, the fact that the concept of adoption is not recognised in the parent's home country, and the distress and shame which adoption would bring to the paternal family and the consequences for the child were weighed against the security of an adoption order to the foster carer. Applying the welfare test, it was held that adoption was not in the best interests of the child. The adopters' ability to understand the child's family background and willingness to accommodate this in the child's upbringing too will be relevant (*Re C (Adoption: Religious Observance)* [2002] 1 FLR 1119). However, the ultimate test that the welfare of the child is the paramount consideration will dictate the result, and religious beliefs or cultural heritage issues can never tip the balance when considering the welfare of the child. Rights under the European Convention and the UNCRC too will be a relevant consideration (*Re A (Children) (Placement Orders: Cultural Heritage)* [2015] EWCA Civ 1254; *Haringey London Borough Council v CE and Another* [2006] EWHC 1620 (Fam); *Re S; Newcastle City Council v Z* [2005] EWHC 1490 (Fam)).

## DELAY

7.20 ACA 2002, in s 1(3), provides that the court or adoption agency must at all times bear in mind that, in general, any delay in coming to a decision is likely to prejudice the child's welfare. This provision is not dissimilar to that set out in ChA 1989, s 1(2), which provides that 'in proceedings in which any question with respect to the upbringing of a child arises, the court shall have regard to the general principle that any delay in determining the question is likely to prejudice the welfare of the child'. Taken together, the provisions emphasise the need to avoid delay. A number of steps have been taken to ensure that the care and adoption processes are considered together and not in isolation. Thus, the avoidance of delay applies not only within the adoption proceedings, but also across all aspects of any decision relating to a child. The welfare of the child now being paramount in both care proceedings and applications for placement orders and adoption orders, the court should be able to deal with applications for a care and placement order at the same time, or within a relatively short period after a care order has been made where the care plan is for adoption. However, while adoption agencies and the courts are required to have regard to delay, they are not obliged to do so at the expense of the child's welfare. In appropriate cases, delay, if it is necessary, proportionate and fair, and planned and purposeful – for example, with a view to rehabilitation with the birth family, or to provide the court with detailed information on which an informed and considered decision can be made – may be justified (see *Re T (A Child)* [2016] EWCA Civ 1210), and (although they are decisions in ChA 1989 proceedings) *Re W (Welfare Reports)* [1995] 2 FLR 142; *Hounslow London Borough Council v A* [1993] 1 WLR 291).

## THE NO ORDER PRINCIPLE

7.21 ACA 2002, s 1(6) provides that the court must not make any order under the Act unless it considers that making the order would be better for the child than not making it. This is akin to the fundamental principle which is applied in all applications under the ChA 1989, and set out in ACA 2002, s 1(5), namely, that where a court is considering whether or not to make one or more orders under the Act with respect to a child, it shall not make the order or any of the orders unless it considers that doing so would be better for the child than making no order at all. The effect of the provisions is to encourage those who make decisions about children to consider the least interventionist approach in preference to a draconian measure. To this extent it is in line with the decisions of the European Court of Human Rights (see, for example, *Johansen v Norway* [1997] 23 EHRR 33, page 108). It is also in line with the principle of proportionality embedded in the European Convention and Art 8 – the right to family life. This principle complements the requirement that the court and the adoption agency should consider the wide range of options available as an alternative to adoption (see paras 8.34–8.42.)).

## RANGE OF POWERS

7.22 ACA 2002, s 1(6) requires the court and the adoption agency to consider the whole range of powers available in the child's case, whether under the ACA 2002 or the ChA 1989. The powers or orders which the court should consider on an application for an adoption order, starting from the least interventionist, include:

(a) applying the 'no order principle' and making no order;
(b) in an application for adoption by a step-parent, granting parental responsibility;
(c) granting a residence order;
(d) granting a residence order with a contact or specific issue order, such as a change of name;

(e) granting a residence order with a restriction under ChA 1989, s 91(14) to prevent repeated applications;
(f) granting a special guardianship order, with or without contact;
(g) placing a child with long-term foster parents;
(h) offering additional support to the birth family with a view to rehabilitation;
(i) granting an adoption order.

7.23 Going through each of these options, the court and the adoption agency must weigh up and balance all the factors, and the effect of the available options, their advantages and disadvantages and arrive at a decision which is in the interests of the child (*Re M (Adoption or Residence Order)* [1998] 1 FLR 570). In *T and R (Refusal of Placement Order)* [2021] EWCA Civ 71, when dismissing the application for a placement order, the first instance judge invited the local authority to reconsider its care plan so as to enable the children to remain in long-term foster care. The local authority's appeal against that decision was dismissed on the ground that the judge was entitled to conclude that the case was not one where adoption was the only option that would meet the children's needs.

Chapter 8

# Post-placement and Post-adoption Contact

## INTRODUCTION

8.1 Before a placement or adoption order is made, contact between the child and his parents or extended family is governed by the provisions in the ChA 1989 either under s 8 in a child arrangement order or under s 34 where the child is the subject of a care order. Once a placement order is made, any contact provisions in a child arrangement order under ChA 1989, s 8 will cease to have effect. Similarly, an order under s 34 providing for parental contact when a care order is made will also come to an end (ACA 2002, s 26(1)). No application may be made for a child arrangement order under s 8 or an order for contact under s 34. However, this does not mean that contact between the child and his parents also comes to an end. Post-placement, or on the making of an adoption order or post-adoption of the child, any issue relating to parental contact is governed by the provisions set out in ACA 2002, ss 26 and 27 when an adoption agency is authorised to place for adoption or a child is placed for adoption, and under ss 46(6), 51A and 51B where an adoption agency has placed or is authorised to place a child for adoption and the court is making or has made an adoption order in respect of the child.

## CONTACT POST-PLACEMENT ORDER

8.2 ACA 2002, s 27(4) imposes a mandatory duty on the court before making a placement order to consider the arrangements which the adoption agency has made or proposes to make for allowing any person contact with the child and to invite the parties to commence proceedings to comment on those arrangements. The adoption agency is therefore under a duty before applying for a placement order to deal with the issue of contact. Its decision must be taken applying the welfare checklist set out in ACA 2002, s 1. The agency must also have regard to the wishes and feelings of the parent, and if appropriate, a father without parental responsibility and the advice of the adoption panel (AAR 2005, reg 46).

8.3 Any person involved in the care of the child or having an interest in maintaining contact with the child when dealing with an application for a placement order should consider carefully the proposals for contact put forward by the adoption agency. If those proposals are not acceptable, the person should raise or challenge these proposals by making an application under ACA 2002, s 26 within the placement proceedings for the court to make a contact order requiring the person with whom the child lives, or is to live, to allow the child to visit or stay with the person named in the order, or for the person named in the order and the child otherwise to have contact with each other. ACA 2002, s 26(3) provides for such an application to be made:

(a) by the child or the agency;
(b) by any parent, guardian or relative;
(c) by any person in whose favour there was provision for contact under ChA 1989, s 8 or s 34 but which will cease when a placement order is made;
(d) if a child arrangement order was in force immediately before the adoption agency was authorised to place the child for adoption or (as the case may be) placed the child for adoption at a time when the child was less than six weeks old, by any person named in the order as a person with whom the child was to live;
(e) if a person had care of the child immediately before that time by virtue of an order made in the exercise of the High Court's inherent jurisdiction with respect to children, by that person; and
(f) by any other person who has obtained permission from the court to make the application.

8.4 The court hearing the placement application is also empowered, notwithstanding that an application under ACA 2002, s 26 has not been made by any person, on its own initiative to make an order for contact (ACA 2002, s 26(4)).

8.5 When considering whether to make an order for contact pursuant to ACA 2002, s 26, the court must apply the paramountcy test, i.e. the paramount consideration must be the welfare of the child and in so doing apply the welfare checklist set out in ACA 2002, s 1. The need for care, sensitivity and intellectual rigour on the part of judges hearing applications for placement orders is reinforced by the fact that applications for placement orders will, regularly, be heard and will be determined immediately after the court has made a care order in relation to the same child. Equally, where an application for a placement order is sought against the background of a care order with the care plan for adoption and the application is heard by a judge who has not made the previous care order, the judge considering the application for a placement order will in particular need to consider with care the way in which the judge who approved that care plan expressed himself in relation to the issue of adoption, the extent to which that judge addressed himself in terms not merely to ChA 1989, s 1, but also to ACA 2002, s 1, and the extent to which, since the care plan was approved, there has been any change in the circumstances or in the assumptions which underlay the care plan and, in particular, which underlay the plan for adoption. Because of the fundamental importance of preserving the children's relationship with each other, when there are other siblings, and with the birth parents, the question of contact is a matter for the court and not for the local authority or for the authority in agreement with the prospective adopter(s). The existence of placement orders should not be an inhibition on the ability of a parent to apply to the court to determine the questions of contact and, in particular, between siblings. In *Re P (Placement Orders: Parental Consent)* [2008] EWCA Civ 535 at [132]–[133] and [147]–[150], the Court of Appeal, in relation to the circumstances in the case, also went on to state that 'the placement of the children with adopters or foster carers, who are unwilling, in particular, to facilitate contact between D and S (the siblings) would provide a basis for leave to be granted' to revoke the placement order. The court ruled (at [147]) that:

> In our judgment, the judge in the instant case was plainly right to make a contact order under section 26 of the 2002 Act, and in our judgment the question of contact between [the children], and between the children and their parents, should henceforth be a matter for the court, not for the local authority, or the local authority in agreement with prospective adopters.

The court went on to add that, having regard to the facts of the case, it was accepted that the relationship between the siblings needed to be preserved and while the local authority was seeking the placement order with the children being separated, the question of contact 'between the two children is not a matter for agreement between the local authority/adoption agency and the adopters: it is a matter which, ultimately is for the court. It is the court which will have to make adoption orders or orders revoking the placement orders'. It is the court which has the responsibility to make contact orders under s 26 of the ACA 2002 if contact is required in the interests of the children. The court went on to add (at [152]):

> In our judgment, the making of placement orders in the instant case requires additional safeguards for the two children over and above the fact that the court has made contact orders under section 26 of the 2002 Act. We accordingly direct that all further applications in the case, including any application for either child to be adopted, should be listed before the same judge, and that all further applications in the case be reserved to him. Whilst we cannot, of course, fetter the future exercise of his discretion, which he must exercise as he thinks fit on the facts of the case, we are satisfied that he must retain control of the case, and that no final step should be taken in relation to either child without his imprimatur'.

The court went on to emphasise that the relationship between the two children was of fundamental importance and must be maintained even if the children were placed in separate adoptive placements or if one was adopted and the other fostered. It is not:

> a proper exercise of judicial powers given to the court under the 2002 Act to leave contact between the children and their natural parents to the discretion of the local authority and /or the prospective carers (of the children) be they adoptive parents or foster carers. It is the court which must make the necessary decisions if the contact between the siblings is in dispute, or if it is argued that it should cease for any reason. (at [153])

At [154] the court went on to rule that where the stakes are sufficiently high the court should retain control over the question of contact and make orders for contact post-adoption in accordance with s 26 of the ACA 2002 and ChA 1989:

> This is what Parliament has enacted. In section 46(6) of the 2002 Act Parliament has specifically directed the court to consider post adoption contact, and in section 26(5) Parliament has specifically envisaged an application for contact being heard at the same time as an adoption order is applied for. All this leads us to the view that the 2002 Act envisages the court exercising its powers to make contact orders post adoption, where such orders are in the interests of the child concerned.

8.6 This approach was adopted in *Re R and C (Adoption or Fostering)* [2024] EWCA Civ 1302. The case was a local authority's appeal from the refusal of the first instance judge to make placement orders in relation to two children on the basis that adoption was inconsistent with the children's need for continuing contact with members of the birth family and in particular with their two older siblings who were to be placed in foster care. In allowing the appeal the Court of Appeal concluded that the judge had failed to provide a sufficient, robust and rigorous analysis of the advantages and disadvantages of the available options for the children, as set out in *Re G* [2013] EWCA Civ 965, and that when determining an application for a placement order the court needs to undertake a balancing exercise in which each option is evaluated to the degree of detail necessary to analyse and weigh its own positives and negatives. This requires the local authority and the children's guardian and the court to carry out a robust and rigorous analysis of the advantages and disadvantages of realistic options for the child and for the court to provide an analysis in a reasoned judgment. In determining the appeal, the court reviewed case law on this issue and referred to the developments in adoption policy and in particular to the President's two recent lectures (see paras 8.43–8.44). For recent developments on adoption policy, see paras 8.34–8.42.

## VARIATION OR REVOCATION OF CONTACT ORDER UNDER ACA 2002, s 26

8.7 A contact order made under ACA 2002, s 26 may be varied or revoked by the court on the application by the child, the agency or a person named in the order. The adoption agency and any person in whose favour a contact order has been made may agree to change the terms of a s 26 order provided that the child, if of sufficient age and understanding, agrees, the prospective adopter(s) agree and the relevant persons have been informed of the change (AAR 2005, reg 47(2)).

## ADOPTION AGENCY'S POWER TO DISALLOW CONTACT

8.8 Pursuant to ACA 2002, s 27(2), the adoption agency is empowered to refuse to allow contact notwithstanding the existence of a s 26 contact order, but only if it is satisfied that it is necessary to do so in order to safeguard or promote the child's welfare and the refusal is decided as a matter of urgency and does not last for more than seven days. In the absence of a s 26 contact order there is no obligation on the adoption agency to allow contact between the child and any person. The agency may refuse to allow contact that would otherwise be required under a s 26 order, without seeking the court's approval. When a decision is taken by the adoption agency to refuse to allow contact, the agency is under a duty to inform the relevant person(s) as soon as any such decision is taken (AAR 2005, reg 47).

## PROCEDURE FOR MAKING AN APPLICATION FOR CONTACT UNDER ACA 2002, s 26

### Who may apply?

8.9 The persons who may apply for the court to consider the issue of contact within placement proceedings are those set out at paras 8.3–8.4.

### How should an application be made?

8.10 The procedure is governed by FPR 2010, Pt 14. The application must be made using Form A53 (FPR 2010, PD 5A), which is available at:

www.gov.uk/government/collections/family-law-forms

## Who should be made a respondent to the proceedings?

8.11 FPR 2010, r 14.3 requires the following persons to be made respondents to the application for an order under ACA 2002, s 26:

- the adoption agency authorised to place the child for adoption or which has placed the child for adoption;
- the person with whom the child lives or is to live;
- each parent with parental responsibility for the child;
- any guardian of the child; and
- the child, where:
  - the adoption agency or a parent with parental responsibility for the child opposes the making of the contact order;
  - the child opposes the making of the contact order;
  - the existing arrangement for contact is to be revoked;
  - relatives of the child do not agree to the arrangements for contact; or
  - the child is suffering or is at risk of suffering harm within the meaning of ChA 1989, s 31(9).

8.12 In addition, the court may at any time direct that a child who is not already a respondent to the proceedings be made a respondent to proceedings where:

(a) the child:

  (i) wishes to make an application; or
  (ii) has evidence to give to the court or a legal submission to make which has not been given or made by any other party; or

(b) there are other special circumstances (FPR 2010, r 14.3(2)).

8.13 The court may also at any time direct that any other person (which includes a father without parental responsibility) or body be made a respondent to the proceedings or that a party be removed (FPR 2010, r 14.3(3)). There is also an obligation for the court at the first hearing to consider whether the child or any other person should be a party to the proceedings, and if so, to give directions in accordance with FPR 2010, r 14.3(2) or (3) joining that child or person as a party.

8.14 The course of the proceedings will follow the procedure that applies in relation to the pending application for the placement order within which the application for the s 26 order is made.

## PROCEDURE FOR VARIATION OR REVOCATION OF CONTACT ORDER UNDER ACA 2002, S 26

### Who may apply?

8.15 An application for a variation or revocation of a contact order under ACA 2002, s 26 may be made by any person including the adoption agency or the local authority authorised to place or which has placed the child for adoption (ACA 2002, s 28(2) and FPR 2010, r 14.4(3)).

### How should an application be made?

8.16 The application should be made using Form A54 and providing the information and documents required. The form is available at:

www.gov.uk/government/collections/family-law-forms

### Who should be made a respondent?

8.17 The following persons should be made parties to the proceedings for a variation or revocation of a contact order under ACA 2002, s 26:

(a) the parties to proceedings leading to any placement order;
(b) the adoption agency authorised to place the child for adoption or which has placed the child for adoption;
(c) any prospective adopter(s) with whom the child is living;
(d) each parent with parental responsibility for the child; and
(e) any guardian of the child.

8.18 A father without parental responsibility is not automatically made a respondent unless provision in his favour has been made in any contact order. The court has a duty to consider whether he should be made a party to the proceedings at the first directions hearing, and may direct that he be made a respondent pursuant to FPR 2010, rr 14.3(3)(a) and 14.8(1)(b).

### Venue

8.19 The application should be made in the Family Court which made the placement order. The application will be allocated before the judge, if available, who made the placement order.

# POST-ADOPTION CONTACT

## General

8.20 When an application for an adoption order is before the court, it is required before making an adoption order to consider whether there should be arrangements for allowing any person contact with the child, and for that purpose the court must consider the existing or proposed arrangements and obtain the views of the parties to the proceedings (ACA 2002, s 46(6)).

8.21 Additionally, since 22 April 2014, where the child has been placed for adoption by an adoption agency or an agency is authorised to place the child for adoption and the court is making or has made an adoption order in respect of the child, the court may make a contact order pursuant to ACA 2002, s 51A. This section and s 51B were inserted in the ACA 2002 by the Children and Families Act 2014. Note, however, that an applicant, other than the child or the adopters or prospective adopters, will require permission from the court to make the application (ACA 2002, s 51A(4)(c)). In all other non-agency adoptions, contact arrangements may be made by agreement or by an order made under ChA 1989, s 8.

## Post-adoption contact where the child is placed by an adoption agency

### *What orders may the court make?*

8.22 Under ACA 2002, s 51A(2), the court may make an order:

(a) requiring the adoptive parent(s) or proposed adoptive parent(s) in whose favour the adoption order is or has been made to allow the child to visit or stay with the person named (see below) in the order or for the person named in the order and the child otherwise to have contact with each other; or
(b) prohibiting the person named in the order from having contact with the child.

### *Who are the person(s) who may be named in the order?*

8.23 Under ACA 2002, s 51A(3), the following persons may be named in an order made for contact or prohibiting contact with the child who is the subject of the adoption order:

(a) any person who (but for the child's adoption) would be related to the child by blood (including half-blood), marriage or civil partnership;
(b) any former guardian of the child;

(c) any person who had parental responsibility for the child immediately before the making of the adoption order;
(d) any person who was entitled to make an application for an order under ACA 2002, s 26 in respect of the child (contact with children placed or to be placed for adoption) by virtue of subs (3)(c), (d) or (e) of that section;
(e) any person with whom the child has lived for a period of at least one year. This period need not be continuous but must not have begun more than five years before the making of the application (ACA 2002, s 51A(6)).

## *Who may make an application for post-adoption order?*

8.24 An application for a contact order under ACA 2002, s 51A or prohibiting contact on the making of or where the court has made an adoption order may be made by the following person(s):

(a) a person who has applied for the adoption order or in whose favour the adoption order is or has been made;
(b) the child; or
(c) any person who has obtained and has been granted permission from the court to make the application (ACA 2002, s 51A(4)).

8.25 Note also that when making an adoption order the court is empowered on its own initiative to make an order not only in relation to post-adoption contact, but also prohibiting a person named in the order from having contact with the child (ACA 2002, s 51A(6)).

## *Factors that the court must consider on an application for permission to apply for an order under ACA 2002, s 51A*

8.26 Any person other than the adoptive or proposed adoptive parent(s) and the child will need the court's permission to make the application for contact with a child who has been placed for adoption by an adoption agency. In deciding whether to grant permission, the court is required to consider any risk there might be of the proposed application disrupting the child's life to such an extent that he would be harmed by it, as defined under the ChA 1989; the applicant's connection with the child; and any representations made to the court by the child or a person who has applied for the adoption order or in whose favour the adoption order is or has been made (ACA 2002, s 51A(5)).

## *The court's approach to an application for permission*

8.27 The court's approach to an application for post-adoption contact has been the subject of numerous cases decided before the ACA 2002 came into force, and therefore before the introduction of ACA 2002, s 51A. The settled approach before the ACA 2002 came into force was set out in *Re C (A Minor) (Adoption Order: Conditions)* [1989] AC 1, that on an adoption order being made, 'there should be a complete break but that each case has to be considered on its own particular facts' and that the court will not, except in the most exceptional case, impose conditions as to contact between the child and members of his family to which the adoptive parents do not agree, because to do so would result in friction which would not safeguard or promote the welfare of the child. When an agreement cannot be reached (at pages 17–18):

> the court will, with very rare exceptions, have to choose between making an adoption order without terms or conditions as to access, or to refuse to make such an order and seek to safeguard access to some other machinery, such as wardship. To do otherwise would be merely inviting future and almost immediate litigation.

8.28 In *Re R (Adoption: Contact)* [2005] EWCA Civ 1128, the Court of Appeal reviewed the issue of post-adoption contact in the light of the provisions in the ACA 2002, but concluded that although contact is more common, nonetheless the jurisprudence is clear that 'the imposition on prospective adopters of orders for contact with which they are not in agreement is extremely and remains extremely unusual' (at [49]).

8.29 In *Down Lisburn Health and Social Services Trust v H* [2006] UKHL 36 (a case decided before the ACA 2002 came into force), Baroness Hale, in a dissenting judgment, stated that the court was obliged not merely to decide whether 'adoption' was in the best interests of the child, but also to decide what sort of adoption would best serve those interests. If some form of open adoption were considered to be best, then that would have to be taken into account when deciding whether it would accord with the child's welfare. On further appeal to the ECtHR by the parents on the grounds of infringement of European Convention, Art 8 rights, the court, in dismissing the appeal, supported the decision taken by the House of Lords (now the Supreme Court).

8.30 In *Re P (Placement Order: Parental Consent)* [2008] EWCA Civ 535, Wall LJ took the view that the ACA 2002 'envisages the court exercising its powers to make contact orders post adoption where such orders are in the interests of the child concerned'.

8.31 Since then, in a series of cases, the issue of post-adoption contact and how the court should approach an application for such contact in the light of the changes brought about by the ACA 2002 and protection of European Convention rights has been considered by the Court of Appeal.

8.32 In *Re T (Adoption: Contact)* [2010] EWCA Civ 1527, the court applied the general approach to a contested claim for post-adoption contact by a member of the child's biological family, set out in *Re R* (see para 8.28) and referred to in *Oxfordshire County Council v X* [2010] EWCA Civ 581, where this approach was approved (at [8]). The court also held that there had been no breach of the appellant's right to a fair trial under European Convention, Art 6 because the appellant was legally represented and had the opportunity to cross-examine the guardian and submit full arguments to the judge on this issue. The court suggested that where the stance of adopters in relation to future contact remains ambivalent, this should be articulated in the Annex A report, and as a matter of good social work practice and elementary fairness, the same be communicated to the family members whose contact is in question, so that it can figure in the court's mandatory consideration of contact following adoption under ACA 2002, s 46(6) (see [16]). *Re R* (see para 8.28) suggests that permission is likely to be granted where the adopters have resiled from an earlier agreement on contact. For a case where the Court of Appeal allowed an appeal against the refusal of permission to a birth mother, see *Re B (Adoption Order: Contact Order)* [2011] EWCA Civ 509.

8.33 In *MF v LB of Brent and Others* [2013] EWHC 1838 (Fam), Ryder LJ granted a contact order in favour of family members when making an adoption order in respect of a seven-year-old boy. Having considered relevant case law relating to post-adoption contact, Ryder LJ held that the child's welfare throughout the child's life justified the continuation of his relationship with his biological family members and should contribute to the reassurance and stability of the child.

8.34 *Re B (A Child) (Post-Adoption Contact)* [2019] EWCA Civ 29 is the first case in which the court considered the issue of post-adoption contact under ACA 2002, s 51A. The parents of the child concerned had significant intellectual disability, with the mother being represented by the Official Solicitor. Despite attempts made to support the parents to care for their daughter, this proved unsuccessful. Consequently, the child was placed with foster carers, and care and placement proceedings were commenced. The foster carers were subsequently approved as adoptive parents for the child. During the course of the adoption proceedings, the parents applied for direct contact with their daughter for one hour twice a year. The adoptive parents suggested a meeting between them and the parents once a year with a view that these meetings may eventually lead to contact with the child as well. The first instance judge dismissed the parents' application. On appeal, the central issue raised was whether the introduction of ACA 2002, s 51A has altered the test from that stated in *Re R* and subsequently endorsed in *Oxfordshire County Council v X* [2010] EWCA Civ 581 and *Re T (Adoption: Contact)* [2010] EWCA Civ 1527. It was submitted on behalf of the parents that the introduction of ACA 2002, s 51A indicated an intention by the legislature that more parents would in future succeed in an application for direct contact post-adoption, and that if no change was intended the new provisions would be redundant. It was also argued that earlier case law in which some priority was afforded to the prospective adopters no longer represented the correct approach under ACA 2002, s 51A, and more particularly in the light of academic research, such as *The Role of the Social Worker in Adoption – Ethics and Human Rights: An Enquiry* (available at: www.basw.co.uk/system/files/resources/basw_55505-10_1.pdf) and *Contact after Adoption: A Follow Up in Late Adolescence* (available at: www.uea.ac.uk/contact-after-adoption/home). Reference was also made to observations made by King LJ in her keynote address at the Hersham/Levy lecture in June 2013 that 'the concept of public domain has changed forever as a result of the revolution in information technology' and social media such as Facebook, which enable adopted children and/or their birth parents to search for information. The address given by the President at the NAGALRO Annual Conference in March 2018 was also relied on. The Court of Appeal in *Re B* nevertheless dismissed the appeal and went on to make the following observation:

> 59. ACA 2002, s 51A has been brought into force at a time when there is research and debate amongst social work and adoption professionals which may be moving towards the concept of greater 'openness' in terms of post-adoption contact arrangements, both between an adopted child and natural parents and, more particularly, between siblings. For the reasons that I have given, the juxtaposition in timing between the new provisions and the wider debate does not indicate that the two are linked. The impact of new research and the debate is likely to be reflected in evidence adduced in court in particular cases. It may also surface in terms of advice and counselling to prospective adopters and birth families when considering what arrangements for contact may be the best in any particular case. But any development or change from previous practice and expectations as to post-adoption contact that may arise from these current initiatives will be a matter that may be reflected in welfare decisions that are made by adopters, or by a court, on a case by case basis. These are matters of 'welfare' and not of 'law'. The law remains, as I have stated it, namely that it will only be in an extremely unusual case that a court will make an order stipulating contact arrangement to which the adopters do not agree.
>
> …
>
> 61. Post-adoption contact is an important issue which should be given full consideration in every case [ACA 2002, s 46(6)]. Whilst there may not have been a change in the law insofar as the imposition of a contact regime against the wishes of prospective adopters is concerned, there is now a joined-up regime contained within the ACA 2002 for the consideration of contact both at the placement for adoption stage and later at the hearing of an adoption application. Further, and in contrast to the situation prior to 2014 where the issue of contact on adoption was determined under s 8 by applying the CA 1989, s 1 welfare provisions, issues under both s 26 and s 51A of the ACA 2002 will be determined by applying the bespoke adoption welfare provisions

in ACA 2002, s 1, where the focus is not just upon the welfare of the subject of the application during childhood but throughout their life.

62. A placement for adoption hearing has the potential for having an important influence upon the development of any subsequent long-term contact arrangements. As required by ACA 2002, s 27(4), the court must consider the issue of contact and any plans for contact before making a placement for adoption order. The court's order may well, therefore, set the tone for future contact, but the court must be plain that, as the law stands, whilst there may be justification in considering some form of direct contact, the ultimate decision as to what contact is to take place is for the adopters and that the court [sic] will be 'extremely unusual' for the court to impose a contrary arrangement against the wishes of adopters. Although Mr Recorder Norton was plainly most careful in his choice of words when speaking of contact at the time of the placement order in the present case, and I would not criticise him for anything that he said on that occasion, it is of note that his words were interpreted by the adopters as, in some way, flagging up that direct contact would be ordered at the final adoption hearing and that, as a result, the final adoption process has been delayed for a year and the adopters have felt less than fully settled in taking up the care of B as a result. At the placement order stage courts should therefore be careful to stress that, if there is any future issue as to contact, the law, as stated in *Re R*, will apply and, save for there being extremely unusual circumstances, no order will be made to compel adopters to contact arrangements with which they do not agree.

8.35 The court was asked (at [50]) to give guidance on the issue of post-adoption contact having regard to the research referred to during the hearing, and to endorse the good practice in relation to post-adoption contact as proposed by the local authority, i.e.:

a) adoption agencies to ensure that all prospective adopters and all adoption social workers fully understand the developing research when undergoing training and approval;
b) in every case where post-adoptive contact is a realistic option, the local authority should file, during the placement proceedings, the best information available as to the pool of 'open' adopters nationally and to ensure this is as specific to the subject children as possible;
c) the social work and children's guardian to consider the significance of the research studies in every case;
d) the court to provide full reasons on any s 26 contact application;
e) sibling contact to be considered as an entirely separate exercise to parental contact;
f) an open and frank dialogue between social workers, prospective adopters and birth parents and, if sufficiently mature, siblings about the child's needs, possibly with a face-to-face meeting as in this case.

8.36 The court declined to give any guidance but stated (at [60]) that 'it must be given that any social worker, children's guardian or expert who is required to advise the court on the issue of contact, will ensure that they are fully aware of any current research and its potential impact upon the welfare issues in each particular case'.

8.37 In *Re A (A Child) (Contested Adoption and Local Authority Conduct)* [2024] EWFC 182, a foster parent applied for adoption of a child, A, who had been cared by them for three years but whose father (Q), with whom A's sibling had been placed, was assessed as a good parent but with little insight into A's emotional needs. The father sought a revocation of the placement order. In dispensing with both parents' consent on the basis of the child A's requirements and making an adoption order, the court went on to make a post-adoption contact order in the following terms:

(a) supervised contact to ensure that the emotions following the hearing are under control and to allow mediation to take place;
(b) thereafter for visiting contact to enable Q to get used to taking A out with her sibling B and thereafter;
(c) monthly staying contact from Saturday morning to Sunday evening, i.e. 12 times a year;
(d) such other contact as the adoptive parents and Q may agree (see [293] of the judgment).

8.38 In *Re B (A Child: Post-Adoption Contact)* [2019] EWCA Civ 29, Sir Andrew McFarlane P approved the decisions in *Re R (Adoption: Contact)* (para 8.28); *Oxfordshire County Council v X, Y and J* (para 8.32); and *Re T (Adoption: Contact)* (para 8.32) (see above) and stated that, although:

> s 51A has introduced a bespoke statutory regime for the regulation of post-adoption contact following placement for adoption by an adoption agency, there is nothing to be found in the wording of s 51A or of s 51B which indicates any variation in the approach to be taken to the imposition of an order for contact upon adopters who are unwilling to accept it. (at [54])

He further stated that 'it will be in an extremely unusual case that a court will make an order stipulating contact arrangement to which the adopters do not agree' (at [59]; but see [52]–[54]). Contrast this decision with views expressed by the President on the issue of post-adoption contact in his address at the NAGALRO conference in 2018, which is available at:

> www.judiciary.uk/wp-content/uploads/2018/03/speech-by-lj-mcfarlane-nagalro.pdf

8.39 In *Re T and R (Refusal of Placement Order)* [2021] EWCA Civ 71, the Court of Appeal again confirmed the approach adopted in all the previous cases referred to above, making it clear that any suggestion that the insertion of the new s 51A into the ACA 2002 creating a specific statutory power to make orders for post-adoption contact heralded a different approach was put to rest by the decision in *Re B (A Child: Post-Adoption Contact* (see para 8.38). The court, however, acknowledged the value of the relationship between the siblings in this case.

8.40 The importance and value of maintaining sibling relationships was also acknowledged in *BT and GT (Children: Twins – Adoption)* [2018] EWFC 76 and in the research undertaken on post-adoption contact which is discussed below.

8.41 However, there is a large body of research that advocates that post-adoption contact may be in the best interests and welfare of the child. In 2021 the Nuffield Family Justice Observatory, in its report *Time to Re-think Post-adoption Contact*, confirmed that:

> there is a body or research that, when children are separated from their birth families and either adopted, placed in long-term local authority care, or live with a kinship carer, maintaining good quality contact with the people who are important to them is associated with a positive impact on their wellbeing.

It concluded that any contact system needs to accommodate the diverse needs of parents and children but that the status quo of letterbox contact is the least desirable option of all and that 'in making the system for the modern world we need to draw lessons from research about how to facilitate positive contact between birth parents, adoptive parents and children'. (Further information on the research referred to can be found at www.nuffieldfjo.org.uk/our-work.)

8.42 In September 2023 the Adoption Sub-Group of the Public Law Working Group published its interim report, *Recommendations for Best Practice in Respect of Adoption*, which was endorsed by the President. The interim report deals specifically with adoption and contact in Chapter 1, which opens with the main recommendation that:

> there should be a tailormade approach to the issue of contact for each adopted child which includes and promotes face-to-face contact with important individuals in that child's life if it can be safely achieved. The issue of contact needs to be actively considered throughout the child's minority, not only before the adoption order is made. The other recommendations are intended to support this overarching aim.

Paragraph 47 sets out some of the issues from the considerable research on post-adoption contact, as follows:

> i. There is considerable evidence that transparency and openness around the circumstances and experiences of the adoptee's birth family is beneficial to an adopted child.

ii. The purpose of contact post-adoption is for the adoptee about enabling a process to help them understand their experiences and develop a sense of identity. Existing relationships with birth parents must change to take into account their different role as a result of the legal process of adoption.
iii. Separating siblings can lead to an enduring sense of loss.
iv. There are strong indications that face-to-face contact helps adoptees develop a sense of identity, accept the reasons why they were adopted and move forward with their lives.

a) However, ensuring that contact is safe for the child is pivotal to positive outcomes.
b) Communication with and understanding from the parties involved in contact (birth parents or other relatives/adoptees/adopters) is an important component in its success.
c) Despite the research indicating the benefits of face-to-face contact, where it can be safely managed, the overwhelming majority of cases continue to recommend only letterbox contact. Where direct contact does occur it often happens without any formal agreement being in place.
d) Letterbox contact can prove problematic. A high number of arrangements stall as a result of one (or both) parties failing to maintain the arrangement. This leaves many adoptees without any effective contact from birth families.
e) The experience in Northern Ireland tends to suggest that a shift in mindset by professionals involved in the process of adoption and strong guidance from the judiciary can bring about a change in approach to post adoption contact without the need for changes in primary legislation

In its concluding paragraph, the group's recommendation is towards open adoption and the provision of 'opportunities to build and maintain relationships between the child, the adopters and birth parents and other related matters such as accessing birth records'. The consultation period for responses to the report ended on 30 November 2023. The report sets out comprehensively the extent of the research undertaken by the group and recommends how the current contact provisions in ACA 2002, s 26 and ss 51A and 51B can be utilised by all concerned in the adoption process, including the court, to achieve the desired goal. It is advised that the report should be read in full, which is available at:

www.judiciary.uk/wp-content/uploads/2023/09/11-Sep-23-Report-v3.pdf

8.43 When giving the Mayflower Lecture, *Adapting Adoption to the Modern World*, in November 2023 the President specifically dealt with the considerable research that has been undertaken and the numerous research projects that have looked into the issue of post-adoption contact and which indicate its importance. The President concluded the lecture as follows:

> I would conclude by stressing that adoption is a life changing and life enhancing process. Making an adoption order is one of the most significant decisions and actions the State can take. The plan for any adopted child is to ensure that they become settled on a pathway similar to any child whose life is centred around their birth parents and family, with provision for day to day care, a secure base, stimulation, connection and identity. In addition, an adopted child has needs beyond the 'typical child and family experience' that are stimulated by curiosity and the need to know about family history, relationships, and their past circumstances. The term 'open' is often used to give recognition to these issues in modern adoption – the modern approach is fundamentally different to the evidence and conclusions explored by the Joint Parliamentary Committee in pre-1970's adoption, where secrecy, denial and condemnation were prevalent. What we now know is that the concept of modern adoption needs to be developed further, so that services are improved, in particular with regard to provision for a continuing relationship with and knowledge of the birth family, with the child's needs being at the centre of all that we do. Every adopted child has a right to no less.

The lecture is available at:

> www.judiciary.uk/speech-by-sir-andrew-mcfarlane-adapting-adoption-to-the-modern-world/

8.44 In the second lecture addressed to the Parents of Traumatised Adopted Teens Organisation (POTATO group) on 17 May 2024, the President, while not seeking to offer any analysis to explain why some adoptions fail, focussed on what the Family Court can do which, in his view, could be 'used to a far greater extent to support adopters and their children in the post-adoption years than is currently the case'. The President referred in some detail to the research that has been undertaken on the issue of post-adoption contact and in particular to the extensive research undertaken by Beth Neill and her team at the University of East Anglia, and expressed his concern that the 'respect afforded to an adopter's autonomy on issues of contact has set the bar too high'. He questioned why, if the reality is that the court will not make a contact order, 'Parliament has given any power to the court to make post-adoption contact orders at all', and 'why the possibility that some, as yet unknown, prospective adopter may not accept contact with the child's birth family, be the trump card preventing social workers and the court from insisting that such contact will be of benefit to the child'. The President went on to add that where the child's needs:

> have been evaluated through the prism of the modern approach to post-adoption contact and the court concludes that it will be in the interests of that child to maintain a relationship with a member or members of their birth family, surely in accordance with its duty under ACA 2002, s 1, to afford paramount consideration to the child's welfare throughout his or her life, the court has a duty to say so in its order.

In particular, the President considered that courts should look at the child's relationship with family members wider than just the parents and, in particular, sibling relationships where the child has siblings who are not likely to move with the child. The President, having considered the result of research and all the reports on this issue. went on to suggest:

> Drawing this strand together, if there is to be a culture change with regard to future family contact, then as part of that culture change, it is likely that the almost absolute autonomy currently afforded by the courts to the adopters in matters of contact will have to be reviewed.

On the issue of how the court should use its power to make orders to influence the future development of contact, he suggested that:

> the likely template for contact arrangements post adoption should be set at the placement stage. This is not a change in the current approach. A court making a s 26 contact order, in keeping with the duty under s 1 and its lifelong focus, should have regard not only to the short-term contact arrangements required in the pre-adoption stage, but also in setting the course for the maintenance of family relations over the longer term if that is in the child's best interests. Also, there is nothing wrong, and I would suggest it should be good practice, for a s 26 contact order to contain a recital as to the court's view on contact arrangements post-adoption ... [and] that, where social work evidence is lacking on this important area of a case, the court will ask for an appraisal of the options set against the background of the modern approach and, if necessary, adjourn the case to obtain one.

The President also drew attention to the court's power under ACA 2002, s 51A(2) to make a contact order not only at the time of making the adoption order but also 'at any time thereafter', when he suggested that perhaps contact arrangements may be made the subject of review following an adoption order. In his concluding remarks, the President suggested:

> it seems clear that letterbox contact can no longer be seen as the appropriate regime for most cases, and should certainly not be the norm (as it has been for many years). Any contact arrangement will only be justified if it is for the benefit of the child, but that benefit is not to be confined to the short term. On the contrary the potential for some familial relationships to continue and be nurtured through contact may be of real benefit during the teen years and beyond into adulthood. Given the 'life-long' focus of s 1, adoption agencies and the court each has a duty to consider these matters more fully than may have been the case in the past. The question of contact should never be seen as an 'add on' issue, either at the placement order stage or at a final adoption. Rather, it should be centre stage and seen as an integral part of the child's support package as they move on towards adoption, adolescence and adulthood in the years to come.'

The lecture is available at:

> www.judiciary.uk/speech-by-the-president-of-the-family-division-adapting-adoption-to-the-modern-world-part-two/

For further information on this issue, see also articles by Andrew Bainham, Emeritus Reader in Family Law and Policy of Cambridge University, 'Is the wind of change about to blow through adoption?', published in [2024] Fam Law 176; and by Elsbeth Neil, Professor of Social Work, University of East Anglia, 'Maintaining children's birth family relationships in adoption? A theory of change', [2024] Fam Law 575.

8.45 It is evident from research as set out above that a child will require a tailor-made preparation if post-adoption contact is to succeed. In his Mayflower Lecture, the President offered some guidance on the degree of preparation that is likely to be required. The likely factors which are likely to be relevant in most cases in order to avoid delay in agreeing a plan for contact and the right solution for the child are:

1. Age of the child at removal from the parents.
2. Age of the child at placement with approved adopters.
3. The impact of genetic factors on the child's development.
4. The impact of risks to the child in the womb – Foetal Alcohol Syndrome, or drug use by the mother.
5. The lived experience of the child – domestic abuse, poor feeding and hygiene, comfort, sensitivity, playfulness and relationships
6. Tracking the child's health – weight, growth, sight, hearing.
7. A range of health factors which impact on the child such as a named developmental condition.
8. Parental neglect when evidenced by a significant failure to exercise parental responsibility as set out in law.
9. Significant risk and harm that fall within the experience of abuse – the direct actions of the parents that directly harm the child – physical violence and assaults, sexual abuse.

8.46 If permission to apply is granted, in deciding the issue of contact the court is required to apply the paramountcy test, i.e. the child's welfare throughout his life must be the paramount consideration, and must have regard to the factors set out in ACA 2002, s 1(4)). The court must also consider whether denial of contact will result in the infringement of rights under the European Convention and whether the acts and decisions of the adoption agency are proportionate. The court must therefore exercise care in assessing the effect which denial or restrictions on contact and/or the benefit of some contact is likely to have on the particular child in the particular circumstances of the case, bearing in mind the paramountcy of the welfare of the child. In *Re G (Adoption: Contact)* [2002] EWCA Civ 761, when considering the issue of contact with family members Ward LJ stated (at [14]) that, when one is looking at the benefits of contact:

> the benefit is the benefit that comes from the children simply knowing who the natural parental figures are. It is the sense of removing the ogre, as they reach adolescence and begin to search for their own identity ... That is why current research is in favour of some contact in adoption.

8.47 Where an adoption order is made, past case law indicates that it will require a fundamental change in the circumstances for the court to consider making a contact order and therefore also granting permission (*Re C (Minor) (Adopted Child: Contact)* [1993] 2 FLR 431). However, this approach is no longer tenable, as is evident from the extensive research on post-adoption contact and, in particular, the interim report of the Public Law Working Group and the President's two lectures *Adapting Adoption to the Modern World*, referred to above. In all proceedings relating to the removal of a child from the care of their birth parent(s) or family the issue of contact should no longer be sidelined. The issue should be given serious consideration at an early stage, and all professionals, local authorities, adoption agencies, Cafcass as children's guardian and the court, should approach the issue of post-placement contact and post-adoption contact on the basis of what is best for the child in the long term rather than, as at present, which is to take a short-term, least-resistance approach, by giving in to the views of the prospective adopters.

## *How to make the application for permission under ACA 2002, s 51A*

8.48 Where it is sought to make the application for permission to apply for an order for contact under ACA 2002, s 51A within current proceedings, the procedure under FPR 2010, Pt 18 should be followed. The application should be made on Form FP2. The applicant should set out the applicant's connection with the child; the reasons for making the application; and, importantly, provide all relevant information to establish to the court's satisfaction that there is no risk to the child if permission is granted, and that any opposition to contact by the adopters is contrary to the best interests of the child or is unreasonable in the circumstances of the case.

8.49 If a contact order is made, the court has the power to impose conditions and give directions on how it is to be carried into effect (ACA 2002, s 51B(1)(a) and (b)).

## POST-ADOPTION CONTACT WHERE THE CHILD IS NOT PLACED BY AN ADOPTION AGENCY

8.50 In all non-agency cases where an adoption order is sought by prospective adopter(s), for example a family member, all applications for contact should be made under a ChA 1989, s 8 child arrangement order. Consequently, the provisions set out in ChA 1989, s 1 will be relevant, i.e. the welfare of the child must be the paramount consideration, and the checklist set out in ChA 1989, s 1(3) must be taken into account:

- (a) the ascertainable wishes and feelings of the child concerned (considered in the light of his age and understanding);
- (b) his physical, emotional and educational needs;
- (c) the likely effect on him of any change in his circumstances;
- (d) his age, sex, background and any characteristics of his which the court considers relevant;
- (e) any harm which he has suffered or is at risk of suffering;
- (f) how capable each of his parents, and any other person in relation to whom the court considers the question to be relevant, is of meeting his needs;
- (g) the range of powers available to the court under this Act in the proceedings in question.

8.51 The court is required also to presume, unless the contrary is shown, that involvement (of some kind, either direct or indirect, but not any particular division of a child's time) of that parent in the life of the child concerned will further the welfare of the child (ChA 1989, s 1(2A) and (2B)).

## VARIATION AND REVOCATION OF CONTACT ORDER

8.52 An adoption order which is made subject to a contact order under ACA 2002, s 51A may be varied or revoked on the application made by the child, the adoptive parent(s), or a person named in the order and who has contact with the child.

### How should the application be made?

8.53 The application should be made using Form A54 and the procedure set out at paras 8.14–8.18. The form is available at:

www.gov.uk/government/collections/family-law-forms

# Chapter 9

# Adoption Order Application – Procedure

## INTRODUCTION

9.1 The procedure for an application for an adoption order is governed by FPR 2010, Pt 14. Additionally, the general rules which apply to all family proceedings and set out in Pts 1, 4 and 5 also apply. These relate to the court applying the overriding objective, the court's management powers and duties and the general provisions and prescribed forms set out in Pt 5, which are outlined at paras 4.69–4.83.

## STARTING PROCEEDINGS

### Who may apply?

9.2 Each of the applicant couple must have attained the age of 21, except the child's parent who must be over 18. At least one of the applicants must be domiciled in the British Isles or have been habitually resident in a part of the British Isles for at least one year preceding the application. In the case of a sole applicant, the person must be over 21 years of age, must not be married or a civil partner, or must satisfy the court that the spouse or civil partner cannot be found, or is permanently separated, or is mentally or physically unable to apply. Alternatively, the applicant is the partner of a parent of the child to be adopted or parent of the child and the other parent is dead or cannot be found and the domicile or residency conditions referred to above are satisfied (for more details, see Chapter 2).

### Who may be adopted?

9.3 The child to be adopted must be under the age of 18 when the application is issued (ACA 2002 s 49(4)) and must have lived with the applicants for the relevant probationary period unless the court has given permission to apply (ACA 2002, s 42(2)–(6)) (see further Chapter 3).

## Form of application

9.4 The application for an adoption order is made in Form A58. A serial number must be assigned to the person in whose favour the adoption order is to be made, to keep the applicant's identity confidential. The child's address should be omitted in the form and given instead on Form A65 (Confidential Information) (FPR 2010, PD 5A Forms), which should then be filed. The court officer will ensure that any notice sent out to any of the parties to the application does not contain information which discloses or is likely to disclose the identity of the applicant, and the proceedings on the application will be conducted with a view to securing that the person is not seen by or made known to any party who is not already aware of the applicant's identity except with the applicant's consent (FPR 2010, r 14.2).

## Documents to be filed with Form A58

9.5 The applicant must file three copies of the completed application form together with the documents listed in Form A58 and in particular:

- a certified copy of the full entry in the Register of Live Births that relates to the child or, where the child has been adopted, a certified copy of the entry in the Adopted Children Register;
- any written consent of the parent or guardian of the child being placed for adoption, and any notice of withdrawal of such consent;
- if the applicant is asking the court to dispense with the consent of any parent or guardian of the child being placed for adoption, a brief statement of the facts relied on in support of the request, and three copies of the statement (see paras 9.14–9.16);
- a copy of any placement order relating to the child;
- a copy of any final order relating to the child that has effect and a copy of any maintenance agreement or award relating to the child;
- if the applicant was party to the proceedings, a copy of any final order relating to full or half-siblings of the child that has effect;
- a copy of the relevant certificate of marriage, civil partnership or decree of divorce or dissolution of civil partnership, or death, as the case may be;
- a medical report in respect of each applicant and the child, except in the case of agency adoption (see FPR 2010, r 14.12 and PD 14D);
- if the applicant's name as entered on the application form differs from that on the applicant's marriage or civil marriage certificate, any documentary evidence which explains the reasons for the difference.

Where the child has not been placed by an adoption agency, for example where the application is made by a family member or foster carer and the applicant is not a parent of the child, the applicant must attach health reports to the application for an adoption order or a section 84 order. FPR 2010, PD 14C sets out the matters to be contained in the health reports in the Annex to the PD. The purpose is to build up a full picture of each child's health history and current state of health, including strengths and weaknesses. This will enable local authorities' medical advisers to base their advice to the court on the fullest possible information when commenting on the health implications of the proposed adoption (see FPR 2010, r 14.12(2) and PD 14D for the details of the information required in the health reports). The report must be prepared by a registered medical practitioner made not more than three months earlier on the health of the child and each applicant covering the matters set out in the Annex to PD 14D. Where the matter to be contained in the health report does not apply to the circumstances of a particular case, the reasons for not covering the matter should be given (FPR 2010, r 14.12 and PD 14D, para 1.3).

## Who should be made respondents?

9.6 FPR 2010, r 14.3 sets out the following persons who must be made respondents to the application:

- each parent who has parental responsibility for the child or guardian of the child unless that parent/guardian has given notice under ACA 2002, s 20(4)(a) that he/she does not wish to be informed of any application for an adoption order;
- any person in whose favour there is provision for contact;
- any adoption agency which has taken part at any stage in the arrangements for adoption of the child;
- any local authority or voluntary organisation which has parental responsibility for or is looking after or caring for the child;
- the child, where:
  - the parent has been granted permission to oppose the application (ACA 2002, s 4(3) or (5));
  - the child opposes the making of an adoption order;
  - the children and family reporter so recommends and the recommendation is accepted by the court;
  - the child is already an adopted child;
  - any party to the proceedings or the child is opposed to the arrangements for allowing any person contact with the child, or the person not being allowed contact with the child after the making of the adoption order;
  - the application is for a Convention adoption order or an order under ACA 2002, s 84 (prospective adopter(s) are asking for parental responsibility prior to the adoption abroad) (see Chapter 13);
  - the child has been brought into the United Kingdom pursuant to ACA 2002, s 83 (see Chapter 15);

- the application is for an adoption order other than a Convention order and the prospective adopter(s) intend to live in a country outside the British Isles after the making of the adoption order; or
- the prospective adopter(s) are the relatives of the child.

Where the adoption relates to a foreign child and it appears to the court that entry clearance was given for a purpose other than adoption, the court is likely to direct that the Home Secretary should be made a respondent to enable the Secretary of State to intervene if the application for adoption was made in breach of the purpose for which the entry visa was granted (*Re W (A Minor)* [1986] 1 FLR 179; [1985] 3 WLR 945. The usual practice in such cases is for the applicant to notify the Home Office of the intention to make the application to adopt. Where no response to the notification has been received or where an indication is given not to intervene in the proceedings, it is likely that the court will permit the proceedings to continue without the need for service of the application (see *Re B (Adoption: Immigration Status)* [2014] EWHC 1284 (Fam)).

## Steps to be taken by the court when the application is issued

9.7 FPR 2010, r 14.6 sets out the steps to be taken by the court as soon as practicable after the application has been issued:

> (i) if section 48(1) of the 2002 Act (restrictions on making adoption orders) applies, consider whether it is proper to hear the application;
> (ii) ... set a date for the first directions hearing [which must be within 4 weeks of issue unless otherwise directed by the court];
> (iii) appoint a children's guardian in accordance with rule 16.3(1) [unless it is not necessary];
> (iv) appoint a reporting officer in accordance with rule 16.30;
> (v) consider whether a report relating to the welfare of the child is required, and if so, request such a report in accordance with rule 16.33;
> (vi) set a date for the hearing of the application; and
> (vii) do anything else that may be set out in a practice direction; ...

9.8 Additionally, as soon as practicable, the court officer is required to take the following steps:

> (i) ... give notice of any directions hearing set by the court to the parties and to any children's guardian, reporting officer or children and family reporter;
> (ii) serve a copy of the application form (but, subject to sub-paragraphs (iii) and (iv), not the documents attached to it) on [any appointed children's guardian, children and family reporter and reporting officer; the local authority to whom notice of the intention to apply to adopt has been given; the adoption agency which placed the child for adoption with the applicants and any other person directed by the court to receive a copy] the persons referred to in Practice Direction 14A);

(iii) send a copy of the certified copy of the entry in the Register of Live Births or Adopted Children Register and any health report attached to an application for an adoption order to—

(aa) any children's guardian, reporting officer or children and family reporter; and

(bb) the local authority to whom notice under section 44 of the 2002 Act (notice of intention to adopt or apply for a section 84 order) has been given;

(iv) if notice under rule 14.9(2) has been given (request to dispense with consent of parent or guardian), ... inform the parent or guardian of the request and send a copy of the statement of facts to—

(aa) the parent or guardian;

(bb) any children's guardian, reporting officer or children and family reporter;

(cc) any local authority to whom notice under section 44 of the 2002 Act (notice of intention to adopt or apply for a section 84 order) has been given; and

(dd) any adoption agency which has placed the child for adoption; and

(v) do anything else that may be set out in a practice direction.

9.9 Where the child has been placed for adoption by an adoption agency, the court or the court officer will ask the adoption agency to file any relevant form of consent to the child being placed for adoption or to an adoption order; confirm whether any statement has been made by the parent of the wish not to be informed of any application for an adoption order, and if so, to file that statement and file any statement made by the parent withdrawing such a wish and prepare a report on the suitability of the prospective adopter(s) if one has not already been prepared (FPR 2010, r 14.6(2)(b)). In non-agency cases, the court or the court officer will ask for any relevant form of consent to an adoption order to be filed and ask the local authority to prepare a report on the suitability of the prospective adopter(s) if one has not already been prepared (FPR 2010, r 14.6(2)(a)).

## First directions hearing

9.10 Under FPR 2010, r 14.8, at the first directions hearing the court will:

(a) fix a timetable for the proceedings including a timetable for the filing of—

(i) any report relating to the suitability of the applicants to adopt a child [see paras 9.17–9.18];

(ii) any report from the local authority [see paras 9.17–9.18];

(iii) any report from a children's guardian, reporting officer or children and family reporter;

(iv) if a statement of facts has been filed, any amended statement of facts;
(v) any other evidence; and
(vi) give directions relating to the reports and other evidence;

(b) consider whether the child or any other person should be a party to the proceedings and, if so, give directions in accordance with rule 14.3(2) or (3) joining that child or person as a party;
(c) give directions relating to the appointment of a litigation friend for any protected party or child who is a party to, but not the subject of, proceedings unless a litigation friend has already been appointed [see para 9.16];
(d) consider ... whether the case needs to be transferred to another court and, if so, give directions to transfer the proceedings to another court;
(e) give directions about—

(i) tracing parents or any other person the court considers to be relevant to the proceedings;
(ii) service of documents;
(iii) ... disclosure as soon as possible of information and evidence to the parties;
(iv) participation and special measures directions where any party or witness is considered to be under any form of disability or is considered to be vulnerable; and
(v) the final hearing.

9.11 In the case of an adoption order with a foreign element (see Chapters 12–15), give any directions set out in FPR 2010, PD 14B.

9.12 The parties or their legal representatives must attend the first directions hearing unless the court directs otherwise (FPR 2010, r 14.8(4)).

9.13 Furthermore, the court may give directions at any stage in the proceedings either on its own initiative or on the application of a party or the children's guardian or where the direction concerns a report by a reporting officer or children and family reporter, the reporting officer or the children and family reporter (FPR 2010, r 14.8(5)). Notice of any date for a further directions or other hearing must be given by the court officer to the parties and to any children's guardian, reporting officer or children and family reporter.

## Requesting the court to dispense with parental consent

9.14 The applicant requesting the court to dispense with parental consent must give notice of the request in the application form or at any later stage by filing a written request setting out the reasons for the request and file a statement of facts setting out a summary of the history of the case and any other facts to satisfy the court that the parent or guardian cannot be found or is incapable of giving consent or that the welfare of the child requires the consent to be dispensed with (FPR 2010, r 14.9(2)). For dispensation of parental consent, see Chapter 6.

9.15 On receiving the notice for the request, the court officer will inform the parent or guardian of the request unless the parent or guardian cannot be found, and send a copy of the statement of facts filed to the parent or guardian of the child; any children's guardian, reporting officer or children and family reporter; any local authority to whom notice of intention to adopt has been given and any adoption agency which has placed the child for adoption (FPR 2010, r 14.9(4)(a)).

9.16 If the applicant considers that the parent or guardian is incapable of giving consent, the court will, unless a litigation friend has already been appointed for that parent or guardian, consider whether to appoint a litigation friend for the parent or guardian under FPR 2010, r 15.6(1) or give directions for an application to be made.

## Reports by adoption agency/local authority

9.17 Where a child has been placed for adoption by an adoption agency or the local authority, it must file a report on the suitability of the applicant to adopt a child; the matters set out in FPR 2010, PD 14C (Annex A report); and any other relevant matter relating to the welfare checklist (see Chapter 7) within the timetable fixed by the court (FPR 2010, r 14.11(1)–(3)). The court may also request a further report from the agency or the local authority to assist the court in any other matter.

9.18 In a non-agency application to adopt the local authority should be made aware of the application before it receives the notice of the first hearing. ACA 2002, s 44 requires the notice of the intention to adopt to be given not more than two years or less than three months before the date on which the application to adopt is made. The court may, however, permit an application to go forward if the circumstances of the case, the child's best interests, and rights under the European Convention justify that permission to proceed with the application should be granted (see, for example, *Re X (Time Barred Adoption)* [2024] EWHC 364, where the formal requirements for notice were given a purposive construction in an application for an adoption order).

9.19 On receipt of the report, the court officer will send a copy of the report to any children's guardian, reporting officer, or children and family reporter. All reports are confidential (FPR 2010, r 14.11(5) and (6)).

## Disclosure of confidential reports

9.20 The court will consider at the first directions hearing or at any stage of the proceedings whether a confidential report filed in the proceedings should be disclosed to any of the parties to the proceedings. When considering this issue, the court will have regard to the extent to which the document should be redacted so as not to disclose the identity or whereabouts of a person who has been assigned a serial number. The court may also direct that the report should not be disclosed to a party.

9.21 The court is likely to permit disclosure of all material which it is likely to take into account when reaching a decision which is adverse to a party, particularly since an adoption order has such far-reaching consequences. In so doing, the questions of whether disclosure of the material would involve a real possibility of significant harm to the child will be essential. If it would, the court should next consider whether the overall interests of the child would benefit from non-disclosure, weighing, on the one hand, the interests of the child in having the material properly tested and, on the other hand, both the magnitude of the risk that harm will occur and the gravity of the harm if it does occur.

9.22 If the court is satisfied that the interests of the child point towards non-disclosure, the next and final step is for the court to weigh that consideration, and its strength in the circumstances of the case, against the interest of the parent or other party in having an opportunity to see and respond to the material. In the latter regard, the court should take into account the importance of the material to the issues in the case. 'Non-disclosure should be the exception and not the rule. The court should be rigorous in its examination of the risk and gravity of the feared harm to the child and should order non-disclosure only when the case for doing so is compelling': *Re D (Minors) (Adoption Reports: Confidentiality)* [1995] 2 FLR 687, HL. In addition to the principles set out in *Re D*, the court must also have regard to the impact of the European Convention in relation to a party's right to have knowledge of, and the opportunity to comment on the observations and evidence adduced by the other party to the proceedings, and the parent's Art 6 rights to a fair trial: *Re B (Disclosure to Other Parties)* [2001] 2 FLR 1017, FD (at [34]–[43]). These principles were approved in *Re X (Adoption: Confidential Procedure)* [2002] EWCA Civ 828. In addition, the court held that any non-disclosure should be proportionate.

## The final hearing

9.23 Any person who has been given notice of the final hearing may attend the final hearing and be heard. The court may also direct any person to attend the hearing (FPR 2010, r 14.16(1) and (4)). A person whose application for permission to oppose the making of an adoption order has been refused is not entitled to be heard on the question of whether an adoption order should be made (FPR 2010, r 14.16(2)). The court cannot, however, make an adoption order unless the applicant and the child personally attend the hearing. Where a couple are the applicants, the court may make an order on the attendance of one only of the applicants if there are special circumstances. See also the President's Guidance: Listing Final Hearings in Adoption Cases, 11 April 2018, and Arrangements for Adoption Visits, 24 July 2018. (See *Family Law Practice 2024*, para 5.125.)

9.24 The Guidance emphasises the need to give to the respondents to an adoption application notice of each hearing and to be kept informed of the progress of the application. However, where a parent has applied for permission to oppose an application, the final hearing of the adoption case should not be listed on the same day. If the permission application has been refused, the final hearing should not be listed before 21 days so that any application for permission to appeal can be made. The visit to the court by the applicants and the child should be arranged at least 21 days after the adoption order has been made. The visit should, where possible, be at the same court where the adoption order was made, but should not be listed or referred to in any way. The court should ensure that the visit takes place outside court hours and that arrangements are made to avoid any possible risk of contact between those attending ordinary Family Court hearings and those attending the adoption visits.

### Permission to oppose an adoption application

9.25 The court cannot give permission to oppose an adoption application unless the court is satisfied that there has been a change of circumstances since parental consent was given or the placement order was made (ACA 2002, s 47((7)). For what constitutes 'change of circumstances', see paras 4.108–4.112.

## SERVICE OF COPIES OF ORDERS

9.26 Within seven days of the final order being made or such shorter period as the court may direct, a court officer must send:

(a) a copy of the order to the applicant;
(b) a sealed copy authenticated with the stamp of the court or certified as a true copy of the adoption order to the Registrar General;
(c) a copy of the final order to any other person with the permission of the court (FPR 2010, r 14.26(1)(a), (b) and (3)).

9.27 The court officer will also send notice of the making of an adoption order to any court in Great Britain which appears to the court officer to have made any order relating to parental responsibility for, and maintenance of, the child, and to the Principal Registry if it appears to the court officer that a parental responsibility agreement has been recorded at the Principal Registry (FPR 2010, r 14.26(2)).

## CUSTODY OF DOCUMENTS

9.28 There is a mandatory duty on the court for all documents relating to proceedings under the ACA 2002 while they are in the custody of the court to be kept in a place of special security (FPR 2010, r 14.23).

9.29 No document or order held by the court in proceedings under the ACA 2002 is open for inspection by any person, and no copy of such document or order or of an extract from any such document or order may be taken by or given to any person other than by directions given by the court or as provided for in the rules or any practice direction (FPR 2010, r 14.24) (see Chapter 20).

## DISCLOSING INFORMATION TO AN ADOPTED ADULT

9.30 An adopted person has the right on request to receive from the court which made the adoption order a copy of:

(a) the application form for an adoption order but not the documents that were attached to the form;
(b) the adoption order and any other orders relating to the adoption proceedings;
(c) orders containing any provisions for contact when the adoption order was made;
(d) a transcript or written reasons of the court's decision;
(e) a report made to the court by a children's guardian, reporting officer or a children and family reporter; a local authority; or an adoption agency.

9.31 The court will, however, remove any protected information from documents before they are sent to the adopted adult (FPR 2010, r 14.18 and PD 14F). 'Protected information' means information which would be protected information under ACA 2002, s 57(3) if the adoption agency gave the information and not the court (FPR 2010, r 14.18(4)).

## How to make the request for information

9.32 The request for information must be made in Form A64, which is available at:

www.justice.gov.uk/courts/procedure-rules/family/formspage

9.33 The form must have attached to it a full certified copy of the entry in the Adopted Children Register relating to the applicant.

9.34 The completed application form must be taken to the court which made the adoption order with evidence of the applicant's identity showing a photograph and signature, such as a passport or driving licence.

## COMMUNICATION OF INFORMATION RELATING TO PROCEEDINGS

9.35 Under FPR 2010, r 14.14, for the purposes of the law relating to contempt of court, information (whether or not it is recorded in any form) relating to proceedings held in private may be communicated:

(a) where the court gives permission;
(b) unless the court directs otherwise, in accordance with Practice Direction 14E; or
(c) where the communication is to—

 (i) a party;
 (ii) the legal representative of a party;
 (iii) a professional legal adviser [see para 9.36];
 (iv) an officer of the service or a Welsh family proceedings officer;
 (v) a welfare officer;
 (vi) the Director of Legal Aid Casework (within the meaning of section 4 of the Legal Aid, Sentencing and Punishment of Offenders Act 2012);
 (vii) an expert whose instruction by a party has been authorised by the court for the purposes of the proceedings; or
 (viii) a professional acting in furtherance of the protection of children [see para 9.37].

## Meaning of 'professional legal adviser'

9.36 FPR 2010, r 2.3 defines 'professional legal adviser' to mean a:

(a) barrister;
(b) solicitor;

(c) solicitor's employee;
(d) manager of a body recognised under section 9 of the Administration of Justice Act 1985;
(e) person who for the purposes of the Legal Services Act 2007 is an authorised person in relation to an activity which constitutes the conduct of litigation (within the meaning of that Act),

who is providing advice to a party but is not instructed to represent that party in the proceedings.

## Meaning of 'professional acting in furtherance of the protection of children'

9.37 FPR 2010, r 2.3 defines 'professional acting in furtherance of the protection of children' as including the following:

(a) an officer of a local authority exercising child protection functions;
(b) a police officer who is—

  (i) exercising powers under section 46 of the Act of 1989; or
  (ii) serving in a child protection unit or a paedophile unit of a police force;

(c) any professional person attending a child protection conference or review in relation to a child who is the subject of the proceedings to which the information regarding the proceedings held in private relates;
(d) an officer of the National Society for the Prevention of Cruelty to Children; or
(e) a member or employee of the Disclosure and Barring Service, being the body established under section 87(1) of the Protection of Freedoms Act 2012.

The persons referred to in the list are set out in FPR 2010, PD 14E, which is available at:

www.justice.gov.uk/courts/procedure-rules/family/rules_pd_menu

# Chapter 10

# Amendment, Revocation and Setting Aside of an Adoption Order

## AMENDMENTS

10.1 There are only two specific situations when the court which made the adoption order may amend the order on the application of the adopter(s) or the adopted person. First, it can do so to correct any error in the particulars contained in the order. Secondly, if satisfied that within the period of one year beginning with the date of the order any new name has been given to the adopted person, whether in baptism or otherwise, or has been taken by the adopted person, either in place of or in addition to a name specified in the particulars required to be entered in the Adopted Children Register (ACA 2002, Sch 1, para 4(1) and (2)).

10.2 The application for amendment of the order will inevitably occur when the proceedings have been concluded and therefore should be made using the procedure set out in FPR 2010, Pt 19. The application should set out the order that the applicant is seeking, the legal basis for it and why the order is being sought. It must be accompanied by written evidence on which the applicant intends to rely unless the information set out in the application notice provides sufficient information in support of the application and is verified by a statement of truth. The respondent(s) to the application will be those who were party to the original proceedings, but in view of the nature of the order sought the court may be asked to dispense with service on the respondent(s).

10.3 The court must send notice of the amendments made to the order to the Registrar General, specifying the amendments made with sufficient particulars to enable the Registrar General to identify the case (ACA 2002, Sch 1, para 4(3)). Any certified copy of the relevant entry in the Adopted Children Register must be a copy of the order as amended without the reproduction of any note or marking relating to the amendment. A copy or an extract of an entry in any register or record is deemed to be an accurate copy, provided that the marking and the cancellation have been omitted from it (ACA 2002, Sch 1, para 4(7) and (8)).

## REVOCATION AND SETTING ASIDE AN ADOPTION ORDER

10.4 The ACA 2002 refers to two instances when the court may revoke an adoption order or direction made following the making of an adoption order. These instances are first where a child of unmarried parents is adopted by one of the parents as a sole adoptive parent and the parents subsequently marry so that the adopted person becomes legitimated on the marriage of his natural parents, the court may, on the application of the parties concerned, revoke the order (ACA 2002, s 55, Sch 1, para 4(3) and (4)). This is the only instance referred to in the Act for a revocation of an order.

10.5 Secondly, the court may also revoke a direction in an adoption order for the making of an entry in the Register of Live Births, the Adopted Children Register or other records included in the order.

10.6 Save as above, an adoption order is considered to be irrevocable. On the making of an adoption order the parental responsibility of the parents and any other person with parental responsibility and orders made under the Children Act 1989 are extinguished and parental responsibility is transferred to the adopters. The child thereafter will be treated permanently as a child born to the adopters. The question therefore arises whether there is any situation in which an application may be made for an adoption order to be revoked or set aside. If so, what are the grounds which can be relied on for making the application, in which court and how can the challenge be made? The answer lies in case law where the court has been asked to either revoke the adoption order or for the adoption order made to be set aside. The Court of Appeal and High Court decisions set out below culminating in the very recent decision in *Re X and Y (Children: Adoption Order: Setting Aside)* [2025] EWCA Civ 2 confirm that it is only in exceptionally unusual circumstances, such as errors of law, mistake of facts, or serious procedural irregularities or misrepresentation of the facts, amounting to a denial of natural justice and a disregard of public policy, that the court may consider revoking or setting aside an adoption order. The bar for crossing the line is a high one. The Court of Appeal in *Re X and Y* (above) also ruled that the High Court per se does not have the power under the inherent jurisdiction to revoke or set aside an adoption order even in exceptional circumstances or on welfare grounds. The only way to challenge an adoption order is by way of appeal. If the high bar is crossed the appeal court may in its discretion exercise its inherent jurisdiction to revoke/set aside an adoption order. However, a simple procedural irregularity will not justify the revocation or setting aside of an adoption order validly made. The situation presented must also establish exceptionally unusual circumstances amounting to a denial of natural justice and the provisions of CPR 1998, Part 52 and PD 52B and PD 52C (see further below).

10.7 Case law suggests that an application for revocation of an adoption order is usually made when events occur later in the adopted person's life or experience of the adoptive parents results in the breakdown of the parent–child relationship. An application to set aside an adoption order is usually made when there has been serious irregularity. In *Re M (Minors) (Adoption)* [1991] 1 FLR 458 (CA) a step-parent adoption was made with the consent of the father who was not aware that the mother of his children was terminally ill at the time, and who died within 3 months of the order being made. The natural father was granted leave to appeal out of time to set aside the order on the ground that the father was under a mistaken belief and ignorance of the facts which was sufficient to vitiate his consent. Additionally, the court took account of the best interests of the children but clearly stated that the case should not be regarded as setting a precedent. In contrast in *Re B (Adoption: Jurisdiction to Set Aside)* [1995] Fam 239, [1995] 1 FLR 1 the application was made by an adopted child. He had been adopted by a Jewish couple. When working in the Middle East he faced difficulties. Subsequently he discovered that his father was an Arab Muslim. He applied for the adoption order to be set aside on the ground of irregularity and fundamental mistake. His application was refused on the ground that the court did not have the power to set aside an adoption order. On appeal it was argued that the High Court has the power under its inherent jurisdiction to set aside an adoption order on the grounds of fundamental mistake. His appeal was dismissed. The court accepted that there had been a fundamental mistake and that had an application to set aside the order been made shortly after the adoption order was made, the applicant might well have succeeded, but to grant the application on the basis of the current circumstances would result in a radical and impermissible distortion of the long-established adoption regime in this country ([339d]–[342g]). *Re K (Adoption: Foreign Child)* [1997] 2 FLR 221 (CA) concerned the adoption of a Bosnian child. Notice of the adoption was not given to the child's state-appointed guardian or any of the family members. A guardian ad litem for the child had not been appointed. The Home Office had not been served with the proceedings and there was no firm evidence of the death of the child's parents. The Court of Appeal granted leave to appeal, set aside the adoption order and remitted the case to be reheard in the High Court, where the order was revoked because of the numerous procedural errors in the adoption process, which were held to be sufficiently serious to amount to a denial of natural justice, and on public policy grounds in relation to the adoption of children from overseas. Contrast that case with *Webster v Norfolk County Council and Others* [2009] EWCA Civ 59, [2009] 1 FLR 1378 where the parents of three children, who had been adopted, following care and placement proceedings, on obtaining fresh medical evidence during proceedings in relation to their fourth child, sought leave to appeal out of time. The Court of Appeal while acknowledging the injustice that the parents might feel, refused the application for permission to appeal out of time. The reasons for the refusal were because there was no evidence of any irregularity, error or other grounds in the adoption process; the fact that the adoption order had been validly made and that it was only in highly exceptional and very particular circumstances that the court would consider setting aside the order. Additional reasons were the delay in appealing the order, the evidence now being relied on could have been introduced during the care proceedings and having regard to the interests of the children and the importance of not undermining the statutory principle of the irrevocability of an adoption order.

10.8 In *PK v Mr and Mrs K* [2015] EWHC 2316 (Fam), [2016] 2 FLR 576, the order was revoked on the application of an adopted 14-year-old teenager who had been adopted at the age of four. Subsequently, when she was six years of age, she was sent by her adoptive parents to Ghana to live with their extended family. While living with the extended family she was consistently abused. At the age of 14 she returned to England and was reunited with her biological mother and grandmother. The adoptive parents had clearly relinquished responsibility for her. Pauffley J having referred to the legal framework in relation to revocation of adoption orders as set out in previous cases (see [3]), granted the application for revocation of the adoption order for the reasons set out at [25]–[28]. Note, however, that the Court of Appeal has now ruled in *Re X and Y (Children: Adoption Order: Setting Aside)* [2025] EWCA Civ 2 that this case was wrongly decided for lack of jurisdiction (see below).

10.9 Similarly, in *AX v SX and Others* [2021] EWHC 1121 (Fam) the application was made by two adopted children. Within four years of the making of the adoption order one of the children located their natural mother and subsequently started having contact with her. Despite the fact that the adoptive parents agreed to contact between the children and the natural mother, the adoptive placement broke down and the children returned to live with their mother. In 2020 care arrangement orders were made in her favour. The children applied to have the adoption order revoked. The application was granted. Theis J acknowledged the transformative nature of the order in that it changes the child's status permanently and extinguishes the legal relationship between the natural parent and the child and that the child is treated in law as if born as the child of the adoptive parent(s). She also noted the strong public policy reason for not permitting the revocation of adoption order once made (see [80]). However, she took the view that she had jurisdiction to revoke an adoption order under the inherent jurisdiction of the High Court, albeit that any discretion is severely curtailed where an adoption order is validly made and can only be exercised in highly exceptional and very particular circumstances which amount to a fundamental breach of natural justice. She took the view that in exercising her discretion the welfare of the adopted person may, in appropriate cases, be taken into account, where the highly exceptional and particular circumstances of the case justify it. She acknowledged that the extent to which it can, or should, be will vary depending on the circumstances of the particular case. Note, however, that in *Re X and Y (Children: Adoption Order: Setting Aside)* (above, and see below) the Court of Appeal stated that this case was wrongly decided because it was based entirely on welfare grounds. (See also *Re PW (Adoption)* [2011] EWHC 3793 (Fam) where the application made for revocation was made when the applicant was 69 years of age. The application was refused; and *Re W (Inherent Jurisdiction: Permission Application; Revocation)* [2013] EWHC 1957 (Fam) where a local authority's application for permission to apply for revocation of the adoption order on the adopted child being taken into care was refused.)

10.10 In *Re F (R) (An Infant)* [1970] 1 QB 385, [1968] 3 All ER 1101 (CA) the Court of Appeal set aside an adoption order and remitted the case for a re-hearing because reasonable steps had not been taken to find the mother before the order was made and the mother had applied for leave to appeal within two months of the order being made. The court stated that the interests of the child have to be taken into account but stressed that, without laying down any general principles, a very exceptional case would have to be made out for the court in its discretion to extend the time for appeal. In *Re W (Adoption Order: Set Aside and Leave to Oppose)* [2010] EWCA Civ 1535, [2011] 1 FLR 2153 an adoption order was made by a circuit judge in the absence of the mother. The mother applied to set aside the adoption order on the ground that she did not have notice of the adoption proceedings and for leave to oppose the adoption on the ground of her change of circumstances. The application was heard by a High Court judge, not by way of appeal, but at first instance. The judge set aside the adoption order and granted permission to oppose the adoption application. The court held that when considering whether to grant leave to oppose the adoption application it is necessary for the applicant first to establish the change of circumstances and then for the court to be satisfied that in the exercise of the court's discretion it would be appropriate to apply the factors in ACA 2002, s 1. At this stage the applicant would need to establish the real possibility that the court would set aside the placement, namely that the appeal had a real prospect of success. It was only in exceptionally rare circumstances that an adoption order would be set aside where a care order and placement order had been made.

10.11 An order may be set aside on the grounds of misrepresentation of the facts and deceit by the adopters, as occurred in *Re J (Adoption: Appeal)* [2018] EWFC 8, where the mother and stepfather had lied about the existence of the natural father so that professionals had been unable to undertake the required statutory enquiries and the court had been misled about the child's history and paternity.

10.12 In *Re Human Fertilisation and Embryology Act 2008* [2016] EWHC 2273 (Fam), the order had been made as a result of errors at the fertility clinic in respect of the consent forms, and Ms Y being advised to adopt the child. Subsequently the parties applied for a declaration of parentage and for the revocation of the adoption order. The application in this instance was granted because of an error of law 'which went to the very root of the need for an adoption order' and therefore about the applicant's true legal status since under surrogacy law she was the legal parent of the child. In *Re J (A Minor; Revocation of Adoption Order)* [2017] EWHC 2704 (Fam), the adoption order had been made in error. The judge had subsequently sought to correct the error by revoking the order without jurisdiction to do so. However, see *Re B (Adoption: Jurisdiction to Set Aside)* [1995] Fam 239, where the court declined to revoke an order made in 1959; *Re W (Inherent Jurisdiction: Permission Application: Revocation and Adoption Orders)* [2013] EWHC 1957 (Fam), where the application was refused notwithstanding the recommendation of the consultant psychiatrist that all ties between the adopted child and the adopted parents should be severed. The court held that the court's inherent jurisdiction was the only vehicle for a revocation of the adoption order and that it would only be permissible in exceptional circumstances.

10.13 In *Re X and Y (Revocation of Adoption Orders)* [2024] EWHC 1059 (Fam), the application for revocation of the adoption order was made by the adoptive parent after the two children now aged 16 and 17 had returned to live with their birth parents (as had occurred in *AX v SX and Others* [2021] EWHC 1121 (Fam) (referred to above)). In this case, the application was refused on the ground that the court did *not* have power to revoke an adoption order on the grounds of welfare. Additionally, although the Court of Appeal had accepted a power to revoke an adoption order under the inherent jurisdiction where there had been a fundamental procedural irregularity, this case fell outside the scope of this decision because it was based entirely on welfare grounds. The adoptive parent appealed to the Court of Appeal.

## SETTING ASIDE AN ADOPTION ORDER

10.14 The court in *Re X and Y (Children: Adoption Order: Setting Aside)* [2025] EWCA Civ 2, having reviewed all the previous cases on the issue of revocation and setting aside of adoption orders, held that 'the key authority remains that in *Re B*, which stated that the courts should be strict in their refusal to allow adoption orders to be challenged otherwise than by way of appeal' ([61]). The court went on to add (at [62]–[63]):

> Evidently, the child's welfare is to be taken into account in deciding whether to grant permission to appeal out of time, but there is no support in *Re B* for the proposition that adoption orders can be set aside on welfare grounds. On the contrary, the development of the law in that direction has been at odds with the insistence in *Re B* on the inviolability of regularly made adoption orders as being the ultimate imperative. The requirement for an extension of time for appealing is an important

> filter in protecting adoption orders from challenge, and it should not be circumvented by the assumption of an original jurisdiction at first instance.
> There may nevertheless be very narrow and specific instances in which the High Court finds it necessary to entertain an application to revoke an adoption order, but they will only arise where for some reason an appeal, in or out of time, is not possible. That was the position in *G v G* (Hedley J), where the special statutory environment of surrogacy made it impracticable to bring an appeal.

The court also ruled (at [68]) that:

> … the statements about the extent and nature of the powers of the High Court, originating in *Re W*, continuing in *Re O*, and culminating in the summary in *AX v BX* at §80(5)–(7), are not correct and should not be followed. It further follows that the two cases in which adoption orders were set aside for welfare reasons (*Re PK* and *AX v BX*) were wrongly decided, albeit from the best of motives. As was made clear in *Re B*, the fact that an adoption has turned out badly and that revocation would serve the interests of the adopted person, whether a child or an adult, is not a reason for the court to supply a remedy that Parliament has chosen not to provide.

In its conclusion (at [70]) the court firmly held that 'there is no jurisdiction at first instance to set aside a validly made adoption order' and that adoption orders are transformative, have a peculiar finality and are intended to be irreversible, lasting throughout life, as if the child had been born to the adopter. That high degree of permanence, from which the benefits to the child of long-term security and stability should flow, is the unique feature that marks adoption out from all other orders made for children; it is, at its core, what adoption is all about' and that 'it would gravely damage the lifelong commitment of adopters to their adoptive children if there were a possibility of the finality of the adoption order being challenged on welfare grounds'.

## PRACTICE AND PROCEDURE

10.15 The procedure which should be adopted will depend on whether the application is one for revocation of the adoption order or for the order to be set aside. The distinction between whether the case merits an application for revocation or for the order to be set aside may be fine. Much will depend on the circumstances of the case and the grounds relied on to justify an interference with the final adoption order. Where the order is being challenged on procedural irregularity or error and within a reasonable time after the making of the adoption order, case law as set out above suggests that an appeal to set aside the order is the appropriate procedure. Inevitably, it will be necessary to apply for permission to appeal and where the time limit for an appeal has elapsed also to apply for permission to appeal out of time. In any event it is essential to act promptly on discovery of the mistake of fact or law, irregularity, error or other grounds relied on to justify the setting aside of the adoption order.

10.16 Where considerable time has elapsed, and the circumstances are exceptional, the appropriate procedure is to apply for permission to appeal out of time for a revocation or setting aside of the order under the inherent jurisdiction of the Appeal Court. The law sets a very high bar against any challenge to an adoption order and only in highly exceptional circumstances and very particular circumstances will the court consider it appropriate to revoke an adoption order as demonstrated by case law set out above. Appeals to the Court of Appeal are governed by the provisions of CPR 1998, Part 52 and PD 52B and PD 52C. (See *Family Court Practice 2024*, Part I, E.4 and *Emergency Remedies in the Family Court Division Appeals*, for a procedural guide.)

10.17 Where the failure to serve a party has been quickly identified, the court (whether the High Court or the Family Court) can correct the position by using its powers under FPR 2010, r 27.5 (see *Re X and Y (Children: Adoption Order: Setting Aside)* [2025] EWCA Civ 2, [63]–[64]). The High Court or Family Court may also be able to apply to correct any errors in judgments or orders under the slip rule under FPR 2010, r 29.16 ([66]).

## CANCELLATION

10.18 Where an adoption order is quashed or an appeal against an adoption order is allowed, the court must give directions to the Registrar General to secure that any entry in the Adopted Children Register and any marking of an entry in that register, the Register of Live Births or other records, as the case may be, in pursuance of the order is cancelled (ACA 2002, Sch 1, para 4(6)). In the case of a revocation of an order on legitimation, the court must communicate the revocation to the Registrar General (ACA 2002, Sch 1, para 4(4) and (6); FPR 2010, r 14.27(3)) with sufficient particulars to enable the Registrar General to identify the case. The Registrar General is under a duty to cancel or secure the cancellation of the entry in the register (ACA 2002, Sch 1, para 6).

# Chapter 11

# Consequences of Adoption

## INTRODUCTION

11.1 ACA 2002, Chapter 4 (ss 66–76), together with s 46, set out the effect of an adoption order after 30 December 2005 when the Act came into force. The provisions of the Adoption Act 1976 continue to apply to children adopted before 30 December 2005.

## MEANING OF ADOPTION UNDER ACA 2002, CH 4

11.2 ACA 2002, s 66(1) provides that 'adoption' means adoption by an adoption order made in England and Wales, Scotland or Northern Ireland or in the Isle of Man or any of the Channel Islands. It also includes a Convention adoption; an overseas adoption; and an adoption by the laws of England and Wales and effected under the law of another country.

## PARENTAL RIGHTS AND DUTIES

11.3 An adoption order is an order giving parental responsibility for a child to the adopter(s) (ACA 2002, s 46(1)). ChA 1989, s 3 defines 'parental responsibility' as 'all the rights and duties, powers, responsibilities and authority which by law a parent of a child has in relation to the child and his property'. It includes 'the rights, powers and duties which a guardian of the child's estate (appointed, before the commencement of section 5, to act generally) would have had in relation to the child and his property'. It includes, in particular, the rights of the guardian to receive or recover, in his own name, for the benefit of the child, property of whatever description and wherever situated which the child is entitled to receive and recover.

11.4 Until an adoption order is made, the natural parents, and any other person who has parental responsibility for the child, retain that parental responsibility, and their rights are unaffected, save as restricted by any determination made on a placement order (ACA 2002, s 46(3)(a) and (b)).

11.5 Under ACA 2002, s 46(2), an adoption order has the effect of extinguishing:

(a) the parental responsibility which any person other than the adopter(s) has for the adopted child immediately before the making of the adoption order;
(b) any order made under the ChA 1989 or the Children (Northern Ireland) Order 1995 (SI 1995/755, NI 2). This includes a residence order, contact order, specific issue order, prohibited steps order, parental responsibility order, guardianship order and a care or supervision order. The court may, however, make an order under the ChA 1989 when the adoption order is made;
(c) any order under the Children (Scotland) Act 1995 other than an excepted order;
(d) any duty arising by virtue of an agreement or an order of a court to make payments, so far as the payments are in respect of the adopted child's maintenance or upbringing for any period after the making of the adoption order.

Any order made in wardship proceedings will come to an end on the making of an adoption order: *Re O (Minors) (Adoption: Injunction)* [1993] 2 FLR 737.

11.6 The duty to make maintenance payments is unaffected where it arises under an agreement which constitutes a trust, or which expressly provides that the duty is not to be extinguished by the making of an adoption order (ACA 2002, s 46(4)). Hence, all previous orders are automatically extinguished. An adoption order is irrevocable unless the grounds for seeking a revocation are exceptional (see Chapter 10).

## STATUS CONFERRED BY ADOPTION

11.7 As from the date of the adoption, the child is treated in law as if born as the child of the adopter(s). The adopted child is the legitimate child of the adopter(s). If adopted by a couple or a partner of his parent, he is to be treated as the child of the relationship of the couple in question. The child is treated in law as if he were not the child of any person other than the adopter(s) or the child of the adopter and the biological parent of the child. Where a child is adopted by one of his natural parents as a sole adoptive parent, it does not affect any entitlement the child may have to property which depends on the relationship to that parent or in respect of anything else depending on that relationship (ACA 2002, s 67). The adopted child thus ceases to be the child of any previous marriage. These provisions do not apply to an adoption order made before the ACA 2002 came into force. In such cases the provisions under the Adoption Act 1976 will apply.

## ADOPTIVE RELATIVES

11.8 Relationships which are created by an adoption order may be referred to as 'adoptive relationships'; thus, an adopter may be referred to as an 'adoptive father', 'adoptive mother' or 'adoptive parent', as the case may be.

## PROHIBITED DEGREE OF RELATIONSHIP

11.9 An adopted child remains within the natural family for the purposes of the prohibited degrees of marriage and certain sexual offences within the family (ACA 2002, s 74). ACA 2002, s 74 as amended provides that s 67 does not apply for the purposes of a number of enactments, including the table of kindred and affinity in Marriage Act 1949, Sch 1; Civil Partnership Act 2004, Sch 1; and Sexual Offences Act 2003, s 27 (familial sex offences). Therefore, any sexual relationship between the adopted child and his natural parents, and marriage between the adopted child and the adoptive parents are prohibited, but relationships with any member of the adoptive family who is not within the prohibited degrees of consanguinity are not prohibited.

## NATIONALITY AND IMMIGRATION

11.10 A child who is not a British citizen acquires British citizenship from the date of the adoption order if he is adopted in the United Kingdom and one of his adoptive parents is a British citizen (British Nationality Act 1981, s 1(5)). An adopted child who is a British citizen retains his citizenship even if adopted by a person who is of foreign nationality (ACA 2002, s 74(2)).

## CHANGE OF NAME

11.11 If the prospective adopter(s) wish to give the child a new forename, an application for a change of name should be included in the application form. On the making of an adoption order, the child assumes the surname of his adopters, and if a change of forename has been applied for, an order to that effect will be made and registered (ACA 2002, s 77; Sch 1) (see also Chapter 10).

## STATE BENEFITS

11.12 The adoptive parent(s) are entitled to any state benefits in respect of the adopted child for which they are eligible. In calculating entitlement, the adopted child's resources, if any, will be taken into account, and set off against the amount receivable.

## INSURANCE

11.13 On the death of the child, any rights and liabilities under any insurance policy effected by the child's natural parent(s) for payment for funeral expenses are transferred to the adoptive parents as if the adoptive parents had taken out the policy (ACA 2002, s 76).

## PENSION

11.14 An adopted child's entitlement to a pension which is payable to him or for his benefit, where the child is in receipt of the pension when the adoption order is made, is not affected by an adoption order (ACA 2002, s 75).

## RULES OF INTERPRETATION

11.15 Rules of interpretation which are to apply to any instrument concerning the disposition of property subject to any contrary indication and to ACA 2002, Sch 4 are set out in s 69.

11.16 Where the disposition depends on the date of birth of a child or children of the adoptive parent(s), the disposition should be interpreted as if the adopted person had been born on the date of adoption. Where two or more persons are adopted on the same date they are to be treated as if they had been born on the same date in the order of their actual births (ACA 2002, s 69(2)); this does not affect any reference to a person's age. An adopted person retains any vested interest in possession, i.e. any qualifying interest, any interest expectant upon a qualifying interest and any contingent interest (other than a contingent interest in remainder) which the adopted person has immediately before the adoption, in the estate of a deceased person whether testate or intestate (ACA 2002, s 69(4)). Where it is necessary to determine for the purposes of a disposition of property effected by instrument, whether a woman can have a child, it is to be presumed that once she has attained the age of 55 she will not adopt a person after the execution of the instrument, and if she does, that child will not be treated as her child or, if she is adopting as part of a couple, as the child of the other one of the couple for the purposes of the instrument (ACA 2002, s 69(5)).

11.17 An indication contrary to any of the above need not appear on the face of the instrument; it is sufficient if it appears from any surrounding circumstances which are cogent and convincing (*Re Jones's Will Trusts, Jones v Squire* [1965] Ch 1124).

## PROPERTY DEVOLVING WITH PEERAGE

11.18 An adoption order does not affect the descent of any peerage or dignity or title of honour (ACA 2002, s 71(1)). Nor does it affect the devolution of any property limited (expressly or not) to devolve (as nearly as the law permits) along with any peerage or dignity or title or honour, provided a contrary intention is not expressed in the instrument and has effect subject to the terms of the instrument.

## TRUSTEES AND PERSONAL REPRESENTATIVES

11.19 Trustees and personal representatives who convey or distribute property without any notice of the adoption order or the revocation of such an order are protected (ACA 2002, s 72). This does not, however, prejudice any right of a person affected to follow the property or any property representing it, into the hands of a person other than a purchaser who has received it in good faith (ACA 2002, s 72(2) and (3)).

## TESTAMENTARY RIGHTS

11.20 An adopted person has the same rights as a biological child of his adoptive parents. A testamentary disposition made before the child was adopted by his adopters will be interpreted so as to give the adopted child inheritance rights under the disposition. Any disposition which discriminates against an adopted child would be contrary to European Convention, Art 14 (*Pla and Puncernau v Andorra (Application No 69498/01)* (2006) 42 EHRR 25, [2004] 2 FCR 630, ECtHR). The provisions of the ACA 2002 are not retrospective, so that, for example, an illegitimate child who is later adopted by his parent(s) cannot inherit under a will made prior to the provisions coming into effect. In such cases, the will may be challenged on the basis that it contravenes Art 14 (*Hand v George* [2017] EWHC 533 (Ch)). If the adopted child is disinherited by his adoptive parent(s), he may make a claim as a child of the deceased adopter for reasonable financial provision to be made for him out of the estate of the deceased under the Inheritance (Provision for Family and Dependants) Act 1975.

# Chapter 12

# Adoptions with a Foreign Element

## INTRODUCTION

12.1 Adoptions with a foreign element encompass any adoption of a child which took place outside England and Wales, and 'foreign adoption' therefore means any adoption made outside this jurisdiction. An 'overseas adoption' is defined in ACA 2002, s 87(1) to mean 'an adoption of a description specified by the Secretary of State, being a description of adoption effected under the law of any country or territory outside the British Islands, but ... does not include a Convention adoption'. Convention adoption is an adoption made under the 1993 Hague Convention on Protection of Children and Co-operation in Respect of Intercountry Adoption (1993 Hague Convention). Chapters 13–15 deal with these various types of adoptions with a foreign element. This chapter sets out the requirements of the 1993 Hague Convention.

12.2 The principles by reference to which the law on intercountry adoptions and the recognition of foreign adoptions has been formulated are enshrined in a number of international declarations and Conventions to which the United Kingdom is a party. These instruments provide the legal framework for the relevant domestic law. An appreciation of some of the background elucidates the reasons for, and the purpose of, the domestic process which has been laid down in respect of adoptions with a foreign element, and in particular those now known as 'Convention adoptions'. The relevant statutory provisions include, in particular, the Adoptions with a Foreign Element Regulations 2005 (SI 2005/392) (AFER 2005) and the 1993 Hague Convention.

12.3 The most important international instruments, which form the backbone of the legislative framework on the rights of the child, include:

- the United Nations Declaration on Social Legal Principles relating to the Protection and Welfare of Children with special reference to Foster Placements and Adoptions Nationally and Internationally, adopted by General Assembly Resolution 41/85 of 3 December 1986;

- the United Nations Convention on the Rights of the Child 1989 (UNCRC) (see paras 12.5–12.7);
- the 1993 Hague Convention (see paras 12.8–12.23);
- Recommendation 1443/2000, International adoption: respecting children's rights, adopted by the Parliamentary Assembly of the Council of Europe on 26 January 2000;
- the European Parliament's Resolution on Improving the Law and Co-operation between Member States on the Adoption of Minors, of 12 December 1996.

12.4 The central theme which runs through the international instruments is the principle that the best interests of the child must be the determining factor in any decision that is made relating to a child.

## THE UNCRC

12.5 The UNCRC recognises that the child, 'for the full and harmonious development of his or her personality, should grow up in a family environment, in an atmosphere of happiness, love and understanding'. UNCRC, Art 9 requires states to ensure that a child is not separated from his parents against their will, except where such separation is necessary for the best interests of the child, for example where there has been abuse or neglect of the child, but in any such case the parents should be given the opportunity to take part in any proceedings and to express their views. Where the separation of a child from his parents is inevitable, the state is obliged to respect the right of the child to maintain his relationship and for direct contact with his parents unless it is found to be contrary to the interests of the child.

12.6 Where, having taken account of the child's right to the preservation of family life, it is nevertheless considered that it is in the child's best interests that he should not live with his parents, the state is required to provide protection and assistance and to ensure alternative care for the child. UNCRC, Art 20(3) specifically states that such care could include, *inter alia*, foster placement, kafala of Islamic law, adoption or, if necessary, placement in suitable institutions for the care of children. When considering solutions, due regard must be paid to the desirability of continuity in a child's upbringing and to the child's ethnic, religious, cultural and linguistic background.

12.7 In states which recognise and permit adoption, the state is required to ensure that 'the best interests of the child shall be the paramount consideration'. In particular, under UNCRC, Art 21, states must:

> (a) Ensure that the adoption of a child is authorized only by competent authorities who determine, in accordance with applicable law and procedures and on the basis of all pertinent and reliable information, that the adoption is permissible

in view of the child's status concerning parents, relatives and legal guardians and that, if required, the persons concerned have given their informed consent to the adoption on the basis of such counselling as may be necessary;

(b) Recognize that inter-country adoption may be considered as an alternative means of [caring for the child], if the child cannot be placed in a foster care or an adoptive family or cannot in any suitable manner be cared for in the child's country of origin;

(c) Ensure that a child concerned in an inter-country adoption enjoys safeguards and standards equivalent to those existing in the case of national adoption;

(d) Take all appropriate measures to ensure that, in inter-country adoption, the placement does not result in improper financial gain for those involved in it;

(e) Promote, where appropriate, the objectives of the present article by concluding bilateral or multilateral arrangements or agreements, and endeavour, within this framework, to ensure that the placement of the child in another country is carried out by competent authorities or organs.

## THE 1993 HAGUE CONVENTION

12.8 The abuse of, and trafficking in, children led to the development of the Hague Convention of 29 May 1993. The Convention was ratified by the United Kingdom on 27 February 2003 and entered into force in the United Kingdom on 1 June 2003.

12.9 The preamble to the 1993 Hague Convention recognises that the child, for the full and harmonious development of his personality, should 'grow up in a family environment, in an atmosphere of happiness, love and understanding'. It requires each state to take appropriate measures to enable a child to remain in the care of his family of origin. It recognises that, if this is not possible, intercountry adoption may offer the advantage of a permanent family to a child for whom a suitable family cannot be found in his state of origin, but with the emphasis being on the need to take measures to ensure that intercountry adoptions are made in the best interests of the child and with respect to the child's fundamental rights. It confirms the desirability of establishing common provisions which take account of these principles, and those set out in the UNCRC, and the United Nations Declaration on Social and Legal Principles relating to the Protection and Welfare of Children with special reference to Foster Placements and Adoptions Nationally and Internationally.

### Objectives of the 1993 Hague Convention

12.10 The objectives of the 1993 Hague Convention are set out in Art 1:

a) to establish safeguards to ensure that intercountry adoptions take place in the best interests of the child and with respect for his or her fundamental rights as recognised in international law;

b) to establish a system of co-operation amongst Contracting States to ensure that those safeguards are respected and thereby prevent the abduction, the sale of, or traffic in children;

c) to secure the recognition in Contracting States of adoptions made in accordance with the Convention.

## Preconditions for adoption within the 1993 Hague Convention

12.11 The key requirements in respect of the natural parents or guardian of the child are set out in the 1993 Hague Convention, Art 4, which states that an adoption within the scope of the 1993 Hague Convention may take place only if the competent authorities of the state of origin:

a) have established that the child is adoptable;

b) have determined, after possibilities for placement of the child within the state of origin have been given due consideration, that an intercountry adoption is in the child's best interests;

c) have ensured that

  (1) the persons, institutions and authorities whose consent is necessary for adoption, have been counselled as may be necessary and duly informed of the effects of their consent, in particular whether or not an adoption will result in the termination of the legal relationship between the child and his or her family of origin,

  (2) such persons, institutions and authorities have given their consent freely, in the required legal form and expressed or evidenced in writing,

  (3) the consents have not been induced by payment or compensation of any kind and have not been withdrawn, and

  (4) the consent of the mother, where required, has been given only after the birth of the child; and

(d) have ensured, having regard to the age and degree of maturity of the child, that

  (1) he or she has been counselled and duly informed of the effects of the adoption and of his or her consent to the adoption, where such consent is required,

  (2) consideration has been given to the child's wishes and opinions,

  (3) the child's consent to the adoption, where such consent is required, has been given freely, in the required legal form, and expressed or evidenced in writing, and

  (4) such consent has not been induced by payment or compensation of any kind.

12.12 The 1993 Hague Convention, Art 5 imposes a duty on the competent authorities of the receiving state to determine that the prospective adopter(s) are eligible and suitable to adopt a child; to ensure that they have been counselled; and that the child is or will be authorised to enter and reside permanently in that state.

## Obligations of contracting states

12.13 The 1993 Hague Convention, Art 8 imposes the following obligations on contracting states:

(a) contracting states must designate a 'Central Authority' to discharge the duties imposed by the Convention (Art 6); and Central Authorities must co-operate with each other and promote co-operation to protect children and to achieve the other objects of the Convention (Art 7);
(b) states must accredit bodies to work as adoption agencies. These bodies must be non-profit making (Art 11; see para 12.15);
(c) states must take all appropriate measures to prevent financial or other gain in connection with adoption, and to deter all practices contrary to the object of the Convention.

12.14 The 1993 Hague Convention, Art 9 states that contracting states must also:

a) collect, preserve and exchange information about the situation of the child and the prospective adopters so far as is necessary to complete an adoption;
b) facilitate, follow and expedite proceedings with a view to obtaining the adoption;
c) promote the development of adoption counselling and post-adoption services in their States;
d) provide each other with general evaluation reports about experience with intercountry adoption;
e) reply, in so far as is permitted by the law of their State, to justified requests from other Central Authorities or public authorities for information about a particular adoption situation.

## Accredited bodies

12.15 The Central Authority (CA) in each state is obliged to take all appropriate measures to ensure that accreditation is granted only to, and maintained only by, bodies which have demonstrated the competence to carry out the tasks entrusted to them. Accredited bodies are required to be non-profit making and must be manned by qualified staff who have been appropriately trained and have experience to work in the field of intercountry adoption. The composition, operation and financial situation of accredited bodies must be subject to supervision by the competent authorities of the state. An accredited body should be permitted to act in another contracting state only if authorisation to do so has been given by the competent authorities in both states. The designation of the Central Authorities, and, where appropriate, the extent of their functions, with details of the accredited bodies, must be exchanged between the contracting states (see 1993 Hague Convention, Arts 10–13).

## Non-accredited bodies

12.16 Contracting states are permitted to allow non-accredited persons to make arrangements for intercountry adoption provided that such persons or bodies are subject to supervision of the competent authorities of that state. Where such arrangements are permitted, the contracting state must ensure that the persons or bodies meet the requirements of integrity, professional competence, experience and accountability of that state and that the persons are qualified by their ethical standards and by training or experience to work in the field of intercountry adoption (1993 Hague Convention, Art 22). In such cases the contracting state must provide to the Permanent Bureau of the Hague Conference on Private International Law the names and addresses of those persons and bodies. However, where such an arrangement is permitted, all reports on the prospective adopter(s) or the child must be prepared under the responsibility of the CA or other public body accredited to do so.

## Procedural requirements

### *The receiving state*

12.17 Prospective adopter(s) habitually resident in one contracting state, wishing to adopt a child who is habitually resident in another contracting state, must apply to the CA in the state of their habitual residence. If that CA is satisfied that the prospective adopter(s) are eligible and suitable to adopt a child, it must prepare a report, including information about their identity; eligibility and suitability to adopt; background; family and medical histories; social environment; reasons for seeking to adopt; ability to undertake an intercountry adoption; and the characteristics of the children whom they would be qualified to care for. The CA of the receiving state must then transmit the report to the state of origin (see 1993 Hague Convention, Arts 14 and 15).

### *The state of origin*

12.18 Under 1993 Hague Convention, Art 16, the state of origin must:

(a) satisfy itself that the child is adoptable; if it is so satisfied, it must prepare a report including information about the child's identity, adoptability, background, social environment, family history, medical and family histories and any special needs;
(b) give due consideration to the child's upbringing and to his ethnic, religious and cultural background;
(c) ensure that consents have been obtained in accordance with 1993 Hague Convention, Art 4; and

(d) determine, on the basis of the reports relating to the child and the prospective adopter(s), whether the envisaged placement is in the best interests of the child.

12.19 On completion of the report, the CA of the state of origin must transmit it to the CA of the receiving state, with proof of the necessary consents and the reasons for its determination on the placement, taking care not to reveal the identities of the mother and the father if, in the state of origin, these identities may not be disclosed. The CA must, before taking any decision to transfer the child into the care of the prospective adopter(s), ensure that the CA of the receiving state has the prospective adopter's/adopters' continued agreement for the child to be placed in their care with a view to adoption and has approved the placement; has determined that the prospective adopter(s) are eligible and suitable to adopt the child and that authorisation has been or will be given for the child to enter and reside permanently in the receiving state (1993 Hague Convention, Art 17). A mandatory duty is imposed on the CAs of the state of origin and the receiving state to ensure that permission for the child to leave the state of origin and to enter and live permanently in the receiving state has been obtained; for such transfer to take place in secure and appropriate circumstances and, if possible, in the company of the prospective adopter(s); and to keep each other informed about the progress of the adoption process (1993 Hague Convention, Arts 18 and 19).

## Duty to protect the child

12.20 The 1993 Hague Convention places a duty on a receiving state to protect the child once transfer has taken place. This includes a duty, where it appears to the CA that the continued placement of the child with the prospective adopter(s) is not in the child's best interests, to take all necessary measures to protect the child. In such a case the CA is required to remove the child from the prospective adopter(s) and to make alternative temporary arrangements for the care of the child pending consultation between the CAs of the two states. Where the placement breaks down, the receiving state is under a duty, in consultation with the CA of the state of origin, to arrange alternative long-term care. An alternative placement with a view to adoption by new prospective adopter(s) should be considered only if the CA of the state of origin has been duly informed of the arrangements and, it follows, their approval has been obtained. If all else fails, arrangements should be made for the child to be returned if his interests so require. Where the child is of sufficient age and maturity, he should be consulted and his consent should be obtained before any steps are taken (1993 Hague Convention, Art 21).

## Confidentiality, disclosure and preservation of documents

12.21 The competent authorities of a contracting state are under a duty to ensure confidentiality and safe custody of all information concerning the child and his biological parents and of all personal data, particularly reports on the child and prospective adopter(s), and that the child or his legal representatives have access to such information under appropriate guidance (1993 Hague Convention, Arts 30–31).

## Prohibition of payments

12.22 Improper financial or other gain from any activity related to an intercountry adoption is prohibited, but reasonable costs and expenses including professional fees involved in the adoption process are permitted (1993 Hague Convention, Art 32). This provision corresponds to that in ACA 2002, s 95. Directors and other administrative staff are prohibited from receiving remuneration which is unreasonably high in relation to the services rendered (1993 Hague Convention, Art 32(3)).

## Delay

12.23 Contracting states are required to deal with the adoption process expeditiously (1993 Hague Convention, Art 35). The ACA 2002 meets this requirement in providing in s 1(3) that delay in coming to a decision is likely to prejudice the child's welfare. The various regulations and guidelines also set out time limits within which the decision should be made.

# DOMESTIC LAW

12.24 It was not until 1 June 2003, when the Adoption (Intercountry Aspects) Act 1999 came into force, that action was taken to bring the law in England and Wales into line with the provisions of the 1993 Hague Convention. The UK Government has also issued advisory guidance on Convention adoptions, 'Intercountry adoption: information for adoption agencies', which is available at:

> www.gov.uk/guidance/intercountry-adoption-information-for-adoption-agencies

12.25 The Permanent Bureau has also issued a guide to good practice: *The Implementation and Operation of the 1993 Hague Intercountry Adoption Convention: Guide to Good Practice, Guide No. 1*, which is available at:

> www.hcch.net/upload/adoguide_e.pdf

12.26 The ACA 2002, together with such of the provisions of the Adoption (Intercountry Aspects) Act 1999 as remain in force, is now the primary legislative framework for adoptions with a foreign element which take place in England and Wales. The key secondary legislation includes the AFER 2005; the AAR 2005; the Adoption Agencies (Wales) Regulations 2005 (SI 2005/1313) (W 95); the Adopted Children and Adoption Contact Registers Regulations 2005 (SI 2005/924); the Paternity and Adoption Leave (Adoption from Overseas) Regulations 2003 (SI 2002/2788); the Suitability of Adopters Regulations 2005 (SI 2005/1712); and the Restriction on the Preparation of Adoption Reports Regulations 2005 (SI 2005/1711).

### Duties of local authorities and adoption agencies

12.27 Local authorities with social services responsibilities are required to establish and maintain an adoption service that extends to intercountry adoptions. Their duties, and the duties of adoption agencies, when arranging intercountry adoptions are the same as those relating to domestic adoptions. Those duties include:

(a) providing information about overseas adoption;
(b) offering counselling for both the prospective adopter(s) and the child;
(c) carrying out assessments of the eligibility and suitability of prospective adopter(s);
(d) carrying out assessments of the child; and
(e) matching children to prospective adopter(s).

12.28 Local authorities and accredited voluntary adoption agencies have to consider the requirements set out in the AFER 2005. These regulations deal with the process in relation to Convention and non-Convention adoptions, and adoptions of children from and to non-designated or restricted overseas territories (see Chapters 13, 14 and 15).

## TYPES OF ADOPTIONS WITH A FOREIGN ELEMENT

12.29 Adoptions with a foreign element may feature a number of scenarios, for example:

(a) adoptions of a child from a Convention country by a person who is habitually resident in the British Islands;
(b) adoption of a child, who is habitually resident in the British Islands, in a Convention designated country;
(c) adoption of a child from a foreign country by prospective adopter(s) who are habitually resident in the British Islands;

(d) adoption of a child, who is habitually resident in the British Islands, in a foreign country;
(e) adoptions of children from non-Convention and non-designated territories.

12.30 The first two of these are referred to as Convention adoptions. The provisions which apply to Convention adoption are dealt with in Chapter 13. Recognition of overseas adoptions to and from non-Convention but designated countries is considered in Chapter 14. An overview of the position of all other foreign adoptions is given in Chapter 15.

# Chapter 13

# Convention Adoptions

## INTRODUCTION

13.1 A 'Convention adoption' is an adoption effected under the law of a country outside the British Islands, in which the 1993 Convention on Protection of Children and Co-operation in Respect of Intercountry Adoption (1993 Hague Convention) is in force and certified in pursuance of Art 23(1) of that Convention (ACA 2002, s 66). The 1993 Convention places responsibility on the state where the mother/parents and child are living to assess their circumstances, to obtain the consent of the parent and to ensure that it is freely given, and to prepare a report and forward it to the Central Authority (CA). Similar responsibility is placed on the receiving state to assess the suitability of the prospective adoptive parents and prepare a report and forward it to the state of origin (Art 15).

13.2 Article 4 of the 1993 Hague Convention provides:

> An adoption within the scope of the Convention shall take place only if the competent authorities of the state of origin
>
> (a) have established that the child is adoptable;
> (b) have determined, after possibilities for placement of the child within the state of origin have been given due consideration, that an intercountry adoption is in the child's best interests;
> (c) have ensured that
>
> (1) the persons, institutions or authorities whose consent is necessary for adoption, have been counselled as may be necessary and duly informed of the effects of their consent, in particular whether the adoption will result in the termination of the legal relationship between the child and his or her family of origin,
> (2) such persons, institutions and authorities have given their consent freely, in the correct legal form, and expressed or evidenced in writing,

(3) the consents have not been induced by payment or compensation of any kind and have not been withdrawn, and
(4) the consent of the mother, where required, has been given only after the birth of the child; and

(d) have ensured, having regard to the age and degree of maturity of the child, that

(1) he or she has been counselled and duly informed of the effects of the adoption and of his or her consent to the adoption, where such consent is required,
(2) consideration has been given to the child's wishes and opinions,
(3) the child's consent to the adoption, where such consent is required, has been given freely, in the required legal form, and expressed or evidenced in writing, and
(4) such consent has not been induced by payment or compensation of any kind.

13.3 Article 5 of the 1993 Hague Convention provides:

An adoption within the scope of the Convention shall take place only if the competent authorities of the receiving State –

(a) have determined that the prospective adoptive parents are eligible and suited to adopt;
(b) have ensured that the prospective adoptive parents have been counselled as may be necessary; and
(c) have determined that the child is or will be authorised to enter and reside permanently in that State.

13.4 Article 17 of the 1993 Hague Convention provides for the CAs of the two contracting states to agree that the child may be placed with the prospective adopters and that the adoption may proceed.

13.5 The 1993 Hague Convention has been incorporated into domestic law by virtue of the Adoption (Intercountry Aspects) Act 1999. The aim of the Convention is to ensure that intercountry adoptions take place in the best interests of the child, and with respect for his fundamental rights as recognised in international law; and to establish a common basis and principles on which arrangements for intercountry adoptions should be made between contracting member states. Adoption orders made under the Convention are recognised in all member states (for details of Convention requirements, see also Chapter 12). Anyone who wishes to adopt a child from a 1993 Hague Convention country must comply with the provisions of the Convention and of the AFER 2005.

13.6 For advisory guidance on Convention adoptions issued by the Permanent Bureau at The Hague, see *The Implementation and Operation of the 1993 Hague*

*Intercountry Adoption Convention: Guide to Good Practice, Guide No. 1*, which is available at:

www.hcch.net/upload/adoguide_e.pdf

13.7 For the Government's guidance, see 'Intercountry adoption: information for adoption agencies', which is available at:

www.gov.uk/government/publications/intercountry-adoption-and-the-1993-hague-convention-a21

13.8 In undertaking the assessment, the adoption agency will apply the procedure which is set out in AAR 2005, Pt 4, as amended by the Adoption Agencies (Miscellaneous Amendments) Regulations 2013 (SI 2013/985) (AAR 2013). Part 4 now provides a two-stage approval process for prospective adopter(s). The procedure for stage 1 is set out in AAR 2005, regs 22–27 and applies when prospective adopter(s) notify the adoption agency that they want to adopt a child. Stage 2, set out in AAR 2005, regs 28–30G, applies where, within six months following the adoption agency's decision that the prospective adopter(s) may be suitable to adopt, the prospective adopter(s) notify the adoption agency that they wish to proceed to stage 2 of the approval process.

## CHILD ENTERING ENGLAND AND WALES WHERE THE UNITED KINGDOM IS A RECEIVING STATE

13.9 AFER 2005, Pt 3 applies where a person(s) habitually resident in the United Kingdom wishes to adopt a child who is habitually resident in a Convention country.

### Age and residency requirement

13.10 To qualify to adopt a child from a Convention country, if the application is to be made by an individual person, the prospective adopter must satisfy the authorities that he has attained the age of 21 and has been habitually resident in a part of the British Islands for a period of not less than one year immediately preceding the making of the application. Where the application is made by a couple, they must both have attained the age of 21 and satisfy the residency requirement (AFER 2005, reg 13(2)).

### Application

13.11 Prospective adopter(s) who wish to adopt a child who is habitually resident in a Convention country outside the British Isles must give notification in writing to an adoption agency that is accredited to undertake intercountry adoptions for a determination of eligibility and assessment as set out in Part 4 of the AAR 2005 or the corresponding Welsh provision of their suitability to adopt. Prospective adopter(s) must co-operate in providing the adoption agency with any information it requires for the purposes of the assessment (AFER 2005, reg 13(1)(a)(b)).

## Counselling and provision of information

13.12 Before carrying out the assessment, the adoption agency is required to provide to the prospective adopter(s) counselling services as required under AAR 2013, reg 24(1)(a). The adoption agency is also required to explain, and give written information, to the prospective adopter(s) the procedure in relation to, and the legal implications of, adopting a child from the state of origin (the state where the child is habitually resident) in question. The information given usually includes information about the process of assessment and matching; the role of the Department for Education (in Wales, the National Assembly); the immigration implications and processes; and the actions which the prospective adopter(s) will have to take once they have been approved as suitable persons to adopt a child. The prospective adopter(s) may need to attend meetings arranged by the adoption agency to assist in understanding the process and the issues which arise. In particular, prospective adopter(s) should be fully assisted in understanding the implications not only of UK adoption law, but also of the law of adoption in the child's state of origin. The requirement for the prospective adopter(s) to visit the child in the state of origin, to accompany him to the United Kingdom, and the costs and other consequences need to be addressed carefully. Written information on these matters must be provided. If the adoption agency to whom the application has been made is satisfied that the prospective adopter(s) have already received counselling and been provided with the relevant information from another authorised agency, this requirement can be dispensed with (AFER 2005, reg 14(2)).

## Assessment of eligibility and suitability

13.13 In carrying out the assessment on the suitability of the prospective adopter(s), the adoption agency must follow the procedure and apply the requirements relevant to domestic adoptions under AAR 2013, Pt 4, i.e. regs 22–30G (AFER 2005, reg 15(1)) (see Chapter 16). The adoption agency must place on the prospective adopter's/prospective adopters' case record any information obtained during the two-stage process in AAR 2013, Pt 4. In assessing eligibility and suitability, the adoption agency must check the age and residence of the prospective adopter(s), and their immigration status, under both British law and the law of the state of origin. It is important that this issue is addressed first. In the event of a favourable report, a 'prospective adopter's report' must be prepared for submission to the adoption panel. In a Convention adoption case, the prospective adopter's report must include the following information, as set out in AFER 2005, reg 15(4), in addition to that required in a domestic case:

(a) the State of origin from which the prospective adopter wishes to adopt a child;
(b) confirmation that the prospective adopter is eligible to adopt a child under the law of that State;
(c) any additional information obtained as a consequence of the requirements of that State; and
(d) the agency's assessment of the prospective adopter's suitability to adopt a child who is habitually resident in that State.

13.14 The decision about whether the prospective adopter(s) are suitable to adopt a child must be undertaken in accordance with AAR 2013, reg 30B.

## The agency's decision and notification

13.15 The adoption agency must notify to the prospective adopter(s) its decision on suitability. If the decision is that the prospective adopter(s) are not suitable to adopt a child, the agency must give its reasons, and a copy of the recommendation of the adoption panel. The prospective adopter(s) should be informed of their right to challenge the decision within 40 working days of the date on which the notification was sent, by submitting any representations the prospective adopter(s) wish to make to the agency or the Secretary of State for a review by an independent review panel. On receiving notice of the application for a review, the agency must within 10 days send to the Secretary of State all the documents and information which were passed to the adoption agency, and any relevant information in relation to the prospective adopter(s) which was obtained by the agency after the date on which the original decision was made. Thereafter, the agency must make the decision only after taking into account the recommendations of the independent review panel and the recommendation of the adoption panel made under AAR 2013, reg 30A. On the independent review panel's decision and its recommendations, the adoption agency must send to the Secretary of State a copy of the notification. Following approval, the adoption agency is required to review the approval in accordance with AAR 2013, reg 30D unless the adoption agency has received from the relevant CA written confirmation as required under the 1993 Hague Convention, Art 17.

## Procedure following decision on suitability

13.16 Once the adoption agency decides that the prospective adopter(s) are suitable to adopt a child from the state of origin in question, it must send the following documents and information to the CA (i.e. the Secretary of State in England or the National Assembly in Wales):

(a) written confirmation of the decision and any recommendation the agency may make in relation to the number of children the prospective adopter(s) may be suitable to adopt, their age(s), sex(es), likely needs and background(s);
(b) the enhanced criminal record obtained under AAR 2013, reg 25 or the corresponding Welsh provision;
(c) all the documents and information which were passed to the adoption panel in accordance with AAR 2013, reg 30(6) or (7);
(d) the record of the proceedings of the adoption panel, its recommendation and the reasons for its recommendation;
(e) confirmation that the child will be permitted to enter and live permanently in the United Kingdom if entry clearance or leave to enter or remain, as may be necessary, is granted and not revoked and a Convention adoption is made; and
(f) any other information relating to the case as the relevant CA or the CA of the state of origin may require (AFER 2005, reg 18).

13.17 If at any stage before an agreement is made under the 1993 Hague Convention, Art 17(c), the agency determines on a review under AAR 2013, reg 30D that the prospective adopter(s) are no longer suitable to adopt a child, the agency must inform the relevant CA (AFER 2005, reg 20(2)). If at any stage before any Convention adoption order is made and before the child's entry into the United Kingdom the prospective adopter(s) notify the adoption agency that they do not wish to proceed with the adoption of the child, the agency must inform the relevant CA and return the documents to that CA, which in turn must notify the CA of the state of origin of the decision and return the documents to that CA (AFER 2005, reg 20(3)).

## The role of the Central Authority

13.18 If the relevant CA is satisfied that the adoption agency has complied with the duties and procedures imposed by the regulations, it must send to the CA of the state of origin (the state in which the child is habitually resident) the following documents and information, as set out in AFER 2005, reg 18(2):

(a) the prospective adopter's report prepared under AAR 2013, reg 30 or the corresponding Welsh provision;
(b) a copy of the adoption agency's decision and the adoption panel's recommendation;
(c) any other information that the CA of the state of origin may require;
(d) if the prospective adopter(s) applied to the appropriate Minister for a review under ACA 2002, s 12, the record of the proceedings of the panel, its recommendations and the reason for the same; and

(e) a certificate in the form prescribed by AFER 2005, Sch 1 confirming that: the prospective adopter(s) are eligible to adopt; have been assessed and approved as eligible and suitable to be an adoptive parent(s); and that the child will be authorised to enter and reside permanently in the United Kingdom if entry clearance, and leave to enter or remain, as may be necessary, is granted and not revoked or curtailed and a Convention adoption order or Convention adoption is made.

13.19 If any documents need to be translated, notarised or legalised, the prospective adopter(s) are notified of this and given information on how to secure these services; the translated, notarised or legalised documents are then forwarded with the other documents. The relevant CA must notify the adoption agency and the prospective adopter(s) in writing that the certificate and all the documents and information have been forwarded to the CA of the state of origin (AFER 2005, reg 18(3)).

## The matching process

13.20 When a suitable child has been matched with the prospective adopter(s), the CA of the state of origin will send a report on the child as required under 1993 Hague Convention, Art 16 to the CA in the United Kingdom (UK CA). On receipt of the Art 16 information, the relevant CA must send that information to the adoption agency (AFER 2005, reg 19(1)).

## The adoption agency's role following the 1993 Hague Convention, Art 16 report

13.21 The adoption agency must consider the 1993 Hague Convention, Art 16 information, send a copy to the prospective adopter(s), and arrange a meeting with the prospective adopter(s) to discuss the information, the proposed placement and the availability of adoption support services. Where appropriate, it must counsel them and provide further information (AFER 2005, reg 19(2)). Thereafter, provided the prospective adopter(s) have visited the child in the state of origin and have confirmed in writing to the adoption agency that they wish to proceed to adopt the child, the adoption agency must notify the relevant domestic CA in writing that these procedures have been met and that it is content for the adoption to proceed (AFER 2005, reg 19(3)).

## Procedure to be followed by the Central Authority

13.22 On receiving this confirmation from the adoption agency, the relevant UK CA will notify the CA of the state of origin of the prospective adopter's/adopters' intention to go ahead and for the adoption process to proceed. It will also provide confirmation relating to entry clearance. For this purpose, it will liaise with the Home Office to obtain written confirmation on the immigration issue. If entry clearance and leave to enter and remain, as may be necessary, are granted and not revoked or curtailed and a Convention adoption order or a Convention adoption is made, the child will be authorised to enter and reside permanently in the United Kingdom. The CAs of both states will then reach an agreement that the adoption may proceed as required by 1993 Hague Convention, Art 17(c). Once the Art 17(c) agreement is reached, the relevant CA must notify the adoption agency and the prospective adopter(s) that the agreement is made. Should there be any difficulty over the immigration issue, the adoption agency is notified and must then provide the necessary support services to the prospective adopter(s). If the adoption cannot go ahead, all relevant documents sent to the adoption agency must be returned.

## Instances when proposed adoption may not proceed

13.23 Instances when a proposed placement may not proceed are where:

(a) before agreement is reached under 1993 Hague Convention, Art 17(c), the CA of the state of origin notifies the UK CA that it has decided that the placement should not proceed. The adoption agency will be notified of this decision and it must notify the prospective adopter(s) of the decision. The Art 16 information must be returned to the relevant CA which is under a duty to return the same to the CA of the state of origin (AFER 2005, reg 20(1));

(b) before the 1993 Hague Convention, Art 17(c) agreement is reached, the adoption agency, when undertaking its periodic review, determines that the prospective adopter(s) are no longer suitable to adopt a child. In this event it must notify the UK CA and return the Art 16 information. The CA of the state of origin must be notified and the relevant documents returned to it (AFER 2005, reg 20(2));.

(c) the prospective adopter(s) withdraw from the process and notify the adoption agency that they do not wish to proceed with the adoption. In this event the adoption agency must notify the relevant UK CA, which in turn must notify the CA of the state of origin and return all the relevant documents to it (AFER 2005, reg 20(3)).

## Procedure following the 1993 Hague Convention, Art 17(c) agreement

13.24 Following confirmation of 1993 Hague Convention, Art 17(c) agreement, if the prospective adopter is an individual person, he must notify the adoption agency of the date when he will enter the UK with the child; confirm to it when the child is placed with him; and must accompany the child on entering the United Kingdom. In the case of a couple, they must both accompany the child unless the adoption agency and the CA of the state of origin have agreed that only one of them needs to do so (AFER 2005, reg 21). Before the child enters the United Kingdom, the adoption agency must, as set out in AFER 2005, reg 22:

(a) send to the prospective adopter's/adopters' general practitioner written notification of the proposed placement, together with the report on the child's health history and current state of health as far as is known;
(b) send to the local authority, if that authority is not the adoption agency, and to the clinical commissioning group or in Wales the local health board in whose area the prospective adopter(s) live, and to the National Health Service Commissioning Board, notification of the proposed arrival date of the child; and where the child is of compulsory school age include in the notification to the local authority information about the child's educational history and whether the child has been or is likely to be assessed for special educational needs under the Education Act 1996 or the Children and Families Act 2014.

13.25 The prospective adopter(s) then have a choice – either to apply for an adoption order in the state of origin, or to continue the adoption process in the United Kingdom. If the child is placed with the prospective adopter(s) by the competent authority of the state of origin for a probationary period, and the prospective adopter(s), having applied for a Convention adoption in the child's state of origin, return to England or Wales with the child before the probationary period is completed, and the Convention adoption is then made in the state of origin, the relevant local authority must, if requested by the competent authority of the state of origin, provide a report about the placement and any other matter raised in the request. It must do so within such period as the competent authority reasonably requires (AFER 2005, reg 29).

13.26 For a recent example of the applications of the above provisions, see *A,C and B v District Council* [2022] EWHC 2962 (Fam), where a 17-year-old born in an Asian Convention country was adopted by her maternal aunt and uncle who were living in England.

## Convention adoption not made before entry

13.27 Where a Convention adoption has not been made before the child enters the United Kingdom and it is not intended to make such an application in the state of origin, the prospective adopter(s) must, within 14 days of entry into the United Kingdom with the child, notify the relevant local authority within whose area they have their home of the child's arrival in the United Kingdom and of their intention to adopt the child in accordance with ACA 2002, s 44(2). If the adopter(s) have changed their mind and do not wish to adopt, then they must give notice that they do not intend to give the child a home (AFER 2005, reg 24(1); and see para 13.29). If the prospective adopter(s) move to the area of another local authority, they must, within 14 days of the move, confirm to that local authority and give a similar notice in writing (AFER 2005, reg 24(2)).

13.28 Where the prospective adopter(s) have indicated an intention to proceed, the requirements and procedure in relation to a domestic adoption apply. The adoption agency must follow the procedure set out in AAR 2005, regs 24–27 (see Chapter 16). The information concerning the child received from the state of origin and the competent foreign authority is placed on the child's case records (AFER 2005, reg 25).

## Prospective adopter(s) unable to proceed

13.29 Where the prospective adopter(s) give notice to the relevant local authority that they do not wish to proceed with the adoption and no longer wish to give the child a home, they must return the child to that authority within seven days beginning with the day on which notice was given. The local authority is required to receive the child from the prospective adopter(s) and give notice to the UK CA of the decision of the prospective adopter(s) not to proceed with the adoption (AFER 2005, reg 26).

13.30 If, in the course of the reviews and inquiries which the local authority is obliged to make, it comes to the decision that the continued placement of the child is not in the best interests of the child, it must give notice to the prospective adopter(s) of its opinion and request that the child is returned to it. It must also inform the relevant CA of its decision. In this event, the prospective adopter(s) are under a duty to return the child within seven days of the date of the notice, unless Convention adoption proceedings in respect of the child were commenced before the notice was received. In the latter case, if the proceedings are still pending, the prospective adopter(s) are not obliged to return the child unless the court so directs (AFER 2005, reg 27).

## Breakdown of placement

13.31 Where a placement breaks down in any one or more of the circumstances set out below, the local authority is permitted to place the child for adoption with alternative prospective adopter(s) who are habitually resident in the United Kingdom, if it considers that such a placement would be in the best interests of the child. The circumstances are:

(a) the prospective adopter(s) do not wish to proceed with the adoption and give notice of their intention under AFER 2005, reg 26 (see para 13.29);
(b) the child is withdrawn from the placement under reg 27 (see para 13.30);
(c) an application for a Convention adoption is refused;
(d) a Convention adoption which is subject to a probationary period cannot be made; or
(e) a Convention adoption order or a Convention adoption is annulled under ACA 2002, s 89(1).

13.32 Where an alternative placement has been identified and the prospective adopter(s) have been appropriately assessed as eligible and suitable, the adoption agency must notify the UK CA in writing that alternative prospective adopter(s) have been identified and that the provisions in AFER 2005, regs 14–16, 18 and 19 have been complied with (see paras 13.9–13.22). If the child is of sufficient age and understanding, his views and feelings must be ascertained, and regard had to those wishes and feelings; his consent to the proposals should also be obtained (AFER 2005, reg 28(6)). The CA of the state of origin must be informed by the relevant UK CA of the proposed placement, and attempts should be made to reach an agreement with the state of origin for the placement to continue. If this cannot be achieved, and it is decided that it would not, after all, be in the best interests of the child to be placed with alternative prospective adopter(s) in England and Wales, the local authority must liaise with the relevant UK CA to arrange for the child to be returned to his state of origin (AFER 2005, reg 28).

## MODIFICATION OF STATUS OF ADOPTED CHILD FOR 1993 HAGUE CONVENTION ADOPTIONS

13.33 ACA 2002, s 88 makes provisions for the High Court to direct that ACA 2002, s 67(3), which provides that the child shall be treated in law as if he were not the child of any person other than the adopter(s), shall not apply or shall not apply to such extent as specified in the direction. This provision is relevant in those cases where the Convention state does not recognise the complete severance of all ties with the natural family. The conditions are that:

(a) under the law of the country in which the adoption was effected, the adoption is not a full adoption;
(b) the consents referred to in 1993 Hague Convention, Art 4(c) and (d) have not been given for a full adoption or that the United Kingdom is not the receiving state within the meaning of Art 2;
(c) it would be more favourable to the adopted child for such a direction to be given.

13.34 In relation to the ACA 2002, s 88 direction and an application for it, the Family Law Act 1986, ss 59 and 60 (declaration as to marital status) apply (ACA 2002, s 88(4)). The application should be made on Form A62.3. The application may be made by the adopter(s), the adopted person or the birth parent(s) of the child, or any other person. The respondent(s) will be the adopter(s) or the birth parent(s) (if not the applicant(s)), the adoption agency, the local authority to whom notice under ACA 2002, s 44 was given, the Attorney General and any other person that the court considers should be made a party to the proceedings, for example the child (FPR 2010, PD 5A and r 14.3).

## REGISTRATION OF CONVENTION ADOPTION

13.35 A Convention adoption is registered in accordance with the Adopted Children and Adoption Contact Registers Regulations 2005 (SI 2005/924) (ACACRR 2005) (see Chapter 19).

## APPLICATION FOR CONVENTION ADOPTION ORDER

13.36 Where prospective adopter(s) serve notice on the local authority of their intention to apply for a Convention adoption, the report under ACA 2002, s 44(5) (see Chapter 9) must include:

(a) confirmation that the certificate of eligibility and approval has been sent to the CA of the state of origin in accordance with AFER 2005, reg 18 (see paras 13.16–13.19);
(b) the date on which the Art 17(c) agreement was made and details of the reports of the visits and reviews made (AFER 2005, reg 30).

### How to apply for a Convention adoption order

13.37 The application should be made using Form A59. Three copies of the form together with any documents attached in support of the application and the court fee (unless exempt) should be sent to the Designated Family Centre for the area where the applicant lives. The procedure thereafter will follow that for domestic adoption orders (see Chapter 9), except that at the first directions hearing the court may also consider the matters set out in FPR 2010, PD 14B.

13.38 Before a Convention adoption order is made, as set out in AFER 2005, reg 31, the court must be satisfied that:

(a) the applicant, or both applicants in the case of a couple, has/have been habitually resident in any part of the British Islands for a period of not less than one year immediately preceding the date of the application;
(b) the child to be adopted was, on the date of the Art 17(c) agreement, habitually resident in a Convention country outside the British Islands; and
(c) where one member of a couple (in the case of an application by a couple) or the applicant (in the case of an application by one person) is not a British citizen, the Home Office has confirmed that the child is authorised to enter and reside permanently in the United Kingdom.

Note that a Convention adoption order may not be made in relation to a child who has attained the age of 19 years (ACA 2005, s 47(9)).

13.39 Pursuant to ACA 2002, s 66(1)(c), an adoption effected under the law of a Convention country outside the British Islands and certified in pursuance of Art 23(1) of the 1993 Hague Convention is an adoption under English Law.

### Procedure on making of a Convention adoption order

13.40 Where a court in England and Wales makes a Convention adoption order, a copy of the order must be sent to the relevant UK CA, which must then issue a certificate in the form in AFER 2005, Sch 2, confirming that the adoption has been made in accordance with the Convention. A copy of the certificate is then sent to the state of origin, the adoptive parent and the adoption agency or the relevant authority. Similarly, where a Convention adoption is made in the state of origin and a certificate under 1993 Hague Convention, Art 23 is received by the relevant UK CA, it must send a copy of the certificate to the adoptive parent and the adoption agency or relevant local authority (AFER 2005, reg 32).

## REFUSAL, WITHDRAWAL OR ANNULMENT OF CONVENTION ADOPTION

13.41 If an application for a Convention adoption order is refused or withdrawn, the prospective adopter(s) must return the child to the relevant local authority within the period specified by the court (AFER 2005, reg 33).

13.42 Pursuant to ACA 2002, s 89, the High Court may, on an application made to it, by order annul a Convention adoption or Convention adoption order on the ground that it is contrary to public policy. The application for annulment must be made on Form A63. The procedure is governed by FPR 2010, Pt 14. The application may be made by the adopter(s); the adopted person; a birth parent; the relevant CA; the adoption agency or the local authority to whom notice was given under ACA 2002, s 44; the Home Secretary; or any other person. The respondent(s) to the application (if not the applicant(s)) will be the adopter(s), the birth parent(s); the adoption agency and the local authority to whom notice under ACA 2002, s 44 has been given (FPR 2010, r 14.3).

13.43 Where a Convention order is annulled under ACA 2002, s 89(1), a copy of the order must be served on the relevant UK CA, which in turn must forward a copy to the CA in the state of origin (AFER 2005, regs 33 and 34).

## REQUIREMENTS WHERE THE UNITED KINGDOM IS THE STATE OF ORIGIN

13.44 Where prospective adopter(s) who are habitually resident in a Convention country outside the British Islands wish to adopt a child habitually resident in the British Islands, the requirements and procedure set out in AFER 2005, regs 35–51 must be followed.

### Counselling and information for the child

13.45 Where an adoption agency is considering whether a child is suitable for an adoption in accordance with the 1993 Hague Convention, it must provide a counselling service for, and information to, that child in accordance with AAR 2013, reg 13 and, as set out in AFER 2005, reg 36(1), it must:

(a) explain to the child in an appropriate manner the procedure in relation to, and the legal implications of, adoption under the Convention for that child by a prospective adopter habitually resident in the receiving State; and
(b) provide him with written information about the matters referred to in sub-paragraph (a).

13.46 If the child has already received counselling and information from another agency, it is not necessary to repeat the process.

### Counselling and information for the parent, guardian and others

13.47 The domestic provisions set out in AAR 2013, reg 14 relating to counselling and providing information to the parent(s) or guardian of the child and to other significant persons applies to Convention adoptions. This duty is also owed to the child's father who does not have parental responsibility where his identity is known (AFER 2005, reg 37).

## Permanence report and panel's recommendation

13.48 A permanence report must be prepared in accordance with AAR 2013, reg 17 (see Chapter 16). In addition to the usual requirements, it must include a summary of the possibilities for placing the child within the United Kingdom, and an assessment of whether an adoption by a person(s) in the particular receiving country is in the child's best interests (AFER 2005, reg 38(1)).

13.49 The adoption agency should have received the 1993 Hague Convention, Art 15 report (see para 13.1), prepared by the receiving state, on the eligibility and suitability of the prospective adopter(s), including information about the person's/persons' identity, background, family and medical history, social environment, reasons for seeking to adopt and ability to undertake an intercountry adoption. This report, together with the adoption agency's observations on it and the other reports and information required under AAR 2013, reg 17(2D), must be placed before the adoption panel. In addition to the matters set out in AAR 2013, reg 17, the adoption panel must, when making its recommendation, consider and take into account the 1993 Hague Convention, Art 15 report and the adoption agency's observations on it (AFER 2005, reg 39).

13.50 If the decision of the adoption agency is in the affirmative, it must notify the relevant UK CA of its decision; provide details of the child; the reason it considers the child may be suitable for such an adoption; whether prospective adopter(s) have been identified, and if so, any relevant information; and any other information that may be required. The child's name will be placed on the Convention list of children maintained by the UK CA (the 'Convention list'), which is available for consultation by other authorities within the British Islands. If the adoption agency decides that a Convention adoption is no longer in the child's best interests, it must inform the relevant UK CA, so that the child's name may be removed from the Convention list (AFER 2005, reg 41).

## Role of the relevant UK CA

13.51 Where the relevant CA receives the 1993 Hague Convention, Art 15 report from the CA of the receiving state and it relates to prospective adopter(s) who are habitually resident in that receiving state and wish to adopt a child who is habitually resident in the British Islands, the relevant CA must satisfy itself that the prospective adopter, if an individual person, meets the age requirement specified in ACA 2002, ss 50 and 51 (see Chapters 2 and 5), and that in the case of a couple, they are both, or in the case of an adoption by an individual person, that person is, habitually resident in a Convention country outside the British Islands. It must then consult the Convention list and may, if it considers appropriate, consult any Convention list maintained by another CA within the

British Islands to find an appropriate match (AFER 2005, reg 42(1) and (2)). Where a match between the prospective adopter(s) and the child has been identified, the criteria set out above are satisfied, and the 1993 Hague Convention, Art 15 report has been received, the CA need not consult the Convention list, and must send the Art 15 report to the local authority which referred the child's details to the CA. Where a match is still to be identified, a copy of the 1993 Hague Convention, Art 15 report may be circulated among other CAs within the British Islands with a view to finding a possible match from its Convention list. If a match is found, that CA must send the Art 15 report to the relevant local authority which referred the child's details to that CA (AFER 2005, reg 42(3)–(5)).

## Proposed placement and referral to the adoption panel

13.52 The adoption agency is required to have regard to the 1993 Hague Convention, Art 15 report when considering placing a child with particular prospective adopter(s), and to place the report together with all other relevant matters specified in the relevant regulations (see Chapter 16) before the adoption panel. The adoption panel must consider the 1993 Hague Convention, Art 15 report when it makes its recommendation (AFER 2005, regs 43–44). If the decision is against placement, the Art 15 report must be returned together with any other documents and information provided to the UK CA, which must then forward these to the receiving state (AFER 2005, reg 45). Where the decision is in the affirmative, the adoption agency must prepare a 1993 Hague Convention, Art 16 report (see para 13.16), which must include the information set out in AAR 2013, Sch 1 and the reason for the adoption agency's decision. This report, together with any court orders, for example placement orders made in respect of the child and confirmation that the parent or guardian of the child consents to the adoption, must be sent to the relevant UK CA for forward transmission to the CA of the receiving state (AFER 2005, reg 46).

## Precondition for placement

13.53 Before agreement is reached under 1993 Hague Convention, Art 17(c), the relevant UK CA must have confirmation from the CA of the receiving state that:

(a) the prospective adopter(s) have agreed to adopt the child and have received necessary counselling;
(b) the prospective adopter, if an individual person, has confirmed that he will accompany the child to the receiving state. In the case of a joint application by a couple, it may be agreed that only one of them should do so;
(c) it is content that the adoption should proceed;

(d) where a Convention adoption is to be effected, it has explained to the prospective adopter(s) the need to make an application in England or Wales for a parental responsibility order under ACA 2002, s 84(1); and
(e) the child is or will be authorised to enter and reside permanently in the Convention country if a Convention adoption is effected or a Convention adoption order is made.

13.54 In addition, the adoption agency is required to confirm that the prospective adopter(s) have visited the child; the agency has met the prospective adopter(s) and explained to them the need to make an application for a parental responsibility order under ACA 2002, s 84(1) (see paras 13.52–13.54) before the child is removed from the United Kingdom and the prospective adopter(s) have confirmed that they are content for the adoption to proceed (AFER 2005, reg 47).

### Local authority's report

13.55 In the case of an application for a Convention adoption order, the local authority's report under ACA 2002, ss 43(a) and 45(5) must include a copy of the 1993 Hague Convention, Art 15 and Art 16(1) reports and written confirmation of the agreement under Art 17(c).

## PARENTAL RESPONSIBILITY ORDER UNDER ACA 2002, S 84

### Conditions that must be met

13.56 Pursuant to ACA 2002, s 84(1), the High Court may on an application made by person(s) who intend to adopt a child outside the British Isles make an order giving parental responsibility for the child to the applicant(s). For the court to make the order, it has to be satisfied that the domicile/residency conditions and the requirements set out in AFER 2005, reg 48 are met. The reg 48 requirements are that:

(a) the competent authorities of the receiving state have:

    (i) prepared a 1993 Hague Convention, Art 15 report;
    (ii) determined and confirmed in writing that the prospective adoptive parent(s) are eligible and suitable to adopt;
    (iii) ensured and confirmed in writing that the prospective adoptive parent(s) have been counselled as may be necessary; and
    (iv) determined and confirmed in writing that the child is or will be authorised to enter and reside permanently in that state;

(b) the adoption agency has:

  (i) prepared the Art 16(1) report; and
  (ii) confirmed in writing that it has complied with the requirements imposed upon it under AAR 2013, Pt 3; and
  (iii) obtained and made available to the court the reports and information referred to in AAR 2013, reg 17(2D); the recommendation made by the adoption panel in accordance with reg 18, where applicable, and reg 33; and the adoption placement report prepared in accordance with reg 31(2);

(c) the adoption agency includes in its report submitted to the court, in accordance with ACA 2002, s 43(a) or s 44(5) as modified respectively by AAR 2013, reg 11, details of any reviews and visits carried out as consequence of AAR 2013, Pt 6; and
(d) the prospective adopter, if an individual person, has confirmed in writing that he will accompany the child on taking the child out of the United Kingdom to travel to the receiving state, or in the case of a couple, the agency and competent foreign authority have confirmed that it is necessary for only one of them to do so.

13.57 In addition, AFER 2005, reg 10 sets out further requirements which must be satisfied prior to the making of the order (see paras 14.18–14.22).

13.58 The procedure for seeking an order ACA 2002, s 84 is governed by FPR 2010, Pt 14 and PD 5A.

## How to make the application

13.59 The application should be made on Form 61. The applicant(s) will be the prospective adopter(s) who are seeking parental responsibility before applying for an adoption order in a Convention state. The respondents will be the persons who are respondents to an application for a domestic adoption order and the procedure that will be followed will be the same (see Chapter 9). However, at the first directions hearing, in addition to the matters referred to in FPR 2010, r 14.8(1), the court will also consider, as set out in FPR 2010, PD 14B, para 2:

(a) whether the requirements of the ACA 2002 and the AFER 2005 appear to have been complied with, and if not, consider whether it is appropriate for the case to be transferred to the High Court;
(b) whether all relevant documents are translated into English, and if not, fix a timetable for translating any outstanding documents;

(c) whether the applicant needs to file an affidavit setting out the full details of the circumstances in which the child was brought to the United Kingdom, of the attitude of the birth parent(s) and of compliance with any of the requirements of the AFER 2005;
(d) giving directions about the production of the child's passport and visa; the need for a Cafcass or Welsh family proceedings officer and representative of the Home Office to attend future hearings and personal service on the birth parent(s) (via the CA in the case of a Convention adoption order), including information about the role of Cafcass or Welsh family proceeding officer and the availability of legal aid for them to be represented in the proceedings; and
(e) fixing a further directions appointment within six weeks and timetabling a date by which Cafcass or the Welsh family proceedings officer should file an interim report in advance of the next appointment.

## Consequence of removal of a child from the United Kingdom without a parental responsibility order

13.60 It is an offence:

(a) to remove a child from the UK without a parental responsibility order or authority given under the relevant Scottish or Northern Irish legislation;
(b) to make arrangements to remove a child without a parental responsibility order or authority given under the relevant Scottish or Northern Irish legislation. This includes:

    (i) any arrangement made for the purposes of facilitating the removal of the child;
    (ii) any steps taken to initiate or take part in any negotiations for the purpose of making arrangements for the removal of the child or to cause another person to take any such steps.

See further the *Statutory Guidance on Adoption*, which is available at:

www.gov.uk/government/publications/adoption-statutory-guidance-2013

# Chapter 14

# Overseas Adoptions

## INTRODUCTION

14.1 An 'overseas adoption' is defined in ACA 2002, s 87(1) as an adoption of a description specified in an order made by the Secretary of State, being an adoption 'effected under the law of any country or territory outside the British Islands but does not include a Convention adoption'. ACA 2002, s 87(2) provides that regulations may prescribe the requirements to be met in respect of an adoption of any description effected after the commencement of the regulations for it to be an overseas adoption for the purposes of the Act. ACA 2002, s 87(3) provides that the Secretary of State must exercise his powers under the section to secure that subsequently effected adoptions of any description are not overseas adoptions for the purposes of the Act if he considers that they are not likely, within a reasonable time, to meet the prescribed requirements. The specification of overseas adoption from 3 January 2014 is now governed by the Adoption (Recognition of Overseas Adoptions) Order 2013 (SI 2013/1801), which defines an overseas adoption to mean an adoption other than a Convention adoption effected under the law of a country or territory listed in the Schedule to the Order. The Schedule sets out the 87 designated overseas countries (see the Appendix to this chapter). The Order excludes customary or common law adoptions (Art 2). For overseas adoption prior to 3 January 2014, the specification of overseas adoption was governed by the Adoption (Designation of Overseas Adoptions) Order 1973 (SI 1973/19) and the Adoption (Designation of Overseas Adoptions) (Variation) Order 1993 (SI 1993/690) and applies to the list of countries set out in the Order. Any adoption that was recognised as an overseas adoption prior to 3 January 2014 continues to be recognised as such.

14.2 In cases where the foreign country where the adoption order was made is not a designated country, application for recognition may be made under the common law (see paras 14.26–14.33).

14.3 Where a child has been adopted in one of the designated countries, the adoption is recognised in the United Kingdom as a valid adoption and it is not necessary to seek an adoption order in the domestic courts.

## REGISTRATION IN THE UNITED KINGDOM OF OVERSEAS ADOPTION

14.4 The adopter (s) or any person with parental responsibility or the adoptee on reaching the age of 18 years may apply to register an overseas adoption that is recognised in the United Kingdom in the Adopted Children Register pursuant to the ACACRR 2005. The application should be made in writing to the Registrar General, exhibiting evidence of the adoption (ACACRR 2005, reg 5).

## ENTRY TO THE UNITED KINGDOM

14.5 When bringing into the United Kingdom a child who is the subject of an overseas adoption, entry clearance is required, but since an overseas adoption is recognised as a full adoption in England and Wales, entry clearance with unlimited leave to remain will be granted to the adopted child to enter, provided the adoptive parent(s) can establish their British nationality or right to remain in the United Kingdom and can establish the validity of the adoption order (see *Re G (Children)* [2014] EWHC 2605 (Fam); and *Re V (A Child) (Recognition of Foreign Adoption)* [2017] EWHC 1733 (Fam), where the court under its inherent jurisdiction recognised the Nigerian adoption order at common law for immigration purposes because the parents were temporarily resident in the United Kingdom and the child lived in Nigeria), or have applied for and registered the child as a British citizen before the child is brought into the United Kingdom. Where a final overseas adoption has not yet been made, the child may nevertheless be permitted to enter the United Kingdom for a limited period to enable the overseas adoption to be finalised. When the final order is made, it should be registered in the Adopted Children Register under the ACACRR 2005 (ACA 2002, Sch 1, para 3) (see Chapter 19). The adopter(s) must have been habitually resident in England and Wales at the time the adoption was effected. Application for registration may be made to the Registrar General in writing with supporting documents of the adoption, by the adopter(s), anyone with parental responsibility for the child or the adopted child when he attains the age of 18 years (ACACCR 2005, regs 3 and 4). An application should also be made for British citizenship for the child.

# ANNULMENT OF AN OVERSEAS ADOPTION

## Grounds for the application

14.6 The High Court may on an application made under ACA 2002, s 89(2) order that an overseas adoption, or a determination by the overseas authority which includes determinations to revoke or annul an adoption order, shall cease to be valid in England and Wales on the ground that the order or determination is contrary to public policy or that the authority which purported to authorise the adoption or make the determination was not competent to entertain the case. The court may also decide the extent, if any, to which a determination under ACA 2002, s 91 has been affected by a subsequent determination under that section.

14.7 ACA 2002, s 91 applies where an authority of (*inter alia*) any British overseas territory has power under the law of that country or territory to authorise or review the authorisation of an adoption order made in that country or territory, or to give or review a decision revoking or annulling such an order. If such an authority makes such a determination in the exercise of that power, then that determination has effect for the purpose of effecting, confirming or terminating the adoption in question, or as the case may be. Save as aforesaid, the validity of an overseas adoption or a determination under ACA 2002, s 91 cannot be called into question in proceedings in any court in England and Wales (ACA 2002, s 89(4)).

14.8 The provisions of ACA 2002, s 89 echo those in 1993 Hague Convention, Art 24 (see Chapters 12 and 13), which provides that the recognition of an adoption may be refused in a contracting state only if the adoption is manifestly contrary to its public policy, taking into account the best interests of the child. Applying the principles of the 1993 Hague Convention and the UNCRC, it would appear that the court would have to be satisfied that there were exceptional circumstances to justify annulling an order on public policy grounds. Such grounds may exist where there have been serious breaches of the provisions of ACA 2002, s 83 or of the principles set out in the Conventions, or, for example, there is evidence of child trafficking or fraud.

## Procedure for application for annulment

14.9 The procedure to seek an annulment is governed by FPR 2010, Pt 14 and r 14.22. The application must be made using Form A63.

### Parties to the application

14.10 The applicant(s) will be the adopters; the adopted person; any parent; the relevant CA; the adoption agency; the local authority to whom notice under ACA 2002, s 44 (notice of intention to adopt or apply for an order under ACA 2002, s 84) has been given; the Secretary of State for the Home Department; or any other person. The respondent(s) to the application will be the adopter(s), parent(s) (if not the applicant(s)), the adoption agency and the local authority to whom notice under ACA 2002, s 44 has been given.

### Timing of the application

14.11 The application for an order under ACA 2002, s 89 must be made within two years beginning with the date on which the overseas adoption or determination under ACA 2002, s 91 to which it relates was made.

### Which court?

14.12 ACA 2002, s 89 specifically notes that the High Court may make an order to annul the overseas adoption order, so it follows that the application should be issued in the High Court.

### First directions hearing

14.13 At the first directions hearing the court will, in addition to any matters referred to FPR 2010, r 14.8(1), also consider the matters set out in FPR 2010, PD 14B.

## TAKING CHILDREN OUT OF THE UNITED KINGDOM FOR ADOPTION

### Restrictions

14.14 ACA 2002, s 85 provides that a child who is a Commonwealth citizen or is habitually resident in the United Kingdom 'must not be removed from the United Kingdom to a place outside the British Islands for the purposes of adoption' unless, as set out in ACA 2002, s 85(1) and (2):

(a) the prospective adopter(s) have parental responsibility for the child by virtue of an order made under ACA 2002, s 84; or
(b) the child is removed under the authority of an order under Adoption (Scotland) Act 1978, s 49 or Adoption (Northern Ireland) Order 1987 (SI 1987/2203 (NI 22)), art 57.

14.15 Removing a child from the United Kingdom includes arranging to do so, and the circumstances in which person(s) (which includes a local authority) arrange to remove a child from the United Kingdom include those where they:

(a) enter into an arrangement for the purposes of facilitating such a removal of the child;
(b) initiate or take part in any negotiations of which the purpose is the conclusion of an arrangement within (a) above; or
(c) cause another person to take any step mentioned in (a) or (b) above.

14.16 An 'arrangement' includes an agreement (whether or not enforceable) (ACA 2002, s 85(3)).

14.17 It is a criminal offence for any person(s) to remove a child from the United Kingdom in contravention of the above provisions (ACA 2002, s 85(4)). A person(s) charged with the offence cannot, though, be convicted unless it is proved that they knew or had reason to suspect that the step taken would contravene ACA 2002, s 89(1) (ACA 2002, s 89(5)).

## Preconditions for removing a child from the United Kingdom

14.18 The High Court is empowered if satisfied that the applicant(s) 'intend to adopt a child under the law of country or territory outside the British Islands' to make a parental responsibility order for the child to the applicant(s) (ACA 2002, s 84(1)). If an order is made, it has the effect of extinguishing the parental responsibility of the natural parents or any other person and any existing parental responsibility order in favour of any person (ACA 2002, s 84(5); AFER 2005, reg 11).

14.19 The decision to remove a child for adoption outside the United Kingdom is generally made by a local authority, which may decide that the interests of a child in its care would best be served by the child's being adopted by identified person(s) in another country. The prospective adopter(s) in such cases is usually a relative(s) of the child or someone who is known to the family. Before a child is removed from the United Kingdom, it is necessary for the person(s) seeking to adopt the child under the law of a country or territory outside the British Islands to apply, under ACA 2002, s 84, for an order from the High Court giving parental responsibility for the child to the prospective adopter(s).

14.20 An order for parental responsibility for a child under ACA 2002, s 84 may not be made unless the following conditions are met:

(a) the requirements prescribed by regulations are satisfied (ACA 2002, s 84(3));

(b) at all times during the preceding 10 weeks the child's home was with the applicant, if an individual person, or, in the case of an application by two people, both of them (ACA 2002, s 83(4)). Whether a child has had his home with the applicant(s) is a question of fact and does not require that each of the applicants should be physically present throughout the 10 weeks. There is also no requirement that the home for the 10-week period should be in England and Wales (*Re A (Adoption: Removal)* [2009] EWCA Civ 41).

14.21 AFER 2005, reg 10 sets out the requirements which must be satisfied before an order under ACA 2002, s 84 may be made. Where the child is placed for adoption by an adoption agency, the court must be satisfied that:

(a) in the case of a child placed by an adoption agency, that agency has:

   (i) confirmed to the court that it has complied with the requirements set out in AAR 2005, Pt 3. These include requiring the adoption agency to open the child's case record; provide counselling and information; where the child is of sufficient age and understanding, ascertain his wishes and feelings regarding the placement and contact with his natural family; and consider the child's religious and cultural upbringing. Counselling must also be provided to the natural parents and others with whom the child has had a relationship, and their wishes and feelings must be ascertained and considered. The legal implications of the placement and the adoption must be explained to them. The adoption agency is also required to obtain information about the child's extended family and prepare a permanence report which must be placed before the adoption panel. The adoption panel must have recommended the adoption, and the agency must have decided that the placement is in the best interest of the child. In coming to the decision, the adoption agency must apply the welfare test and consider all the factors set out in ACA 2002, s 1(4)–(6);
   (ii) has submitted to the court:

      (1) the reports and information referred to in AAR 2005, reg 17(2) and (3) as appropriate, i.e. the child's permanence report; the child's health report and the reports of any other examination recommended by the medical adviser; information relating to the health of the child's natural parents; and any other information presented to the adoption panel at its request;
      (2) the recommendation made by the adoption panel in accordance with AAR 2005, regs 18 and 33;
      (3) the adoption placement report prepared in accordance with AAR 2005, reg 31(2)(d);

(4) the reports and information obtained in respect of the visits and reviews referred to in AAR 2005, reg 36;
(5) the report referred to in ACA 2002, s 43, i.e. on the suitability of the prospective adopter(s), and on any other relevant matter referred to in ACA 2002, s 1;

(b) in the case of a child placed by an adoption agency, the relevant foreign authority (see below) has:

(i) confirmed in writing that the prospective adopter(s) have been counselled and have had explained to them the legal implications of adoption;
(ii) prepared a report on the suitability of the prospective adopter(s) to be adopted parent(s);
(iii) determined and confirmed in writing to that agency that they are eligible and suitable to adopt in the country or territory in which the adoption is to be effected; and
(iv) confirmed in writing that the child is or will be authorised to enter and reside permanently in that foreign country or territory; and

(c) in the case of a child placed by an adoption agency, confirmation in writing has been received from the prospective adopter, if an individual person, that he will accompany the child when taking him out of the United Kingdom and entering the country or territory where the adoption is to be effected. In the case of a couple, confirmation is required from the agency and the foreign relevant authority that only one of them should accompany the child.

14.22 The reference to the 'relevant foreign authority' which is required to provide the details set out under (b) above including the confirmation relating to the child being authorised to enter and reside permanently in that foreign country or territory (see para 14.21(b)(iv)), is a reference to the foreign equivalent of an adoption agency in England and not a government department (*Re G (Adoption: Placement Outside the Jurisdiction); Re G (Adoption: Placement Outside the Jurisdiction) (No 2)* [2008] EWCA Civ 105).

14.23 The adoption agency is not required to notify the Department for Education of the decision to place the child with prospective adopter(s) overseas.

## PROCEDURE

14.24 The application for a parental responsibility order will follow the same procedure as that for a domestic adoption order, and in particular it will be necessary to establish that the adoption agency has been authorised to place the child for adoption, or each parent or guardian with parental responsibility has consented, and if not, that his consent should be dispensed with. The court will also apply the adoption welfare test when considering the application (see Chapters 4–7). For a full list of the provisions of ACA 2002 which apply, see AFER 2005, reg 11. See also paras 13.56–13.58.

14.25 For the relations between ACA 2002, s 85 and ChA 1989, Sch 2, para 19, which provide for the local authority to arrange for a child in its care to be placed with carer(s) outside England and Wales with the approval of the court, see *ECC v M and Others* [2008] EWHC 332 (Fam).

## Recognition under common law

14.26 An adoption order which is made in a country which is not a Convention country or made in an overseas designated country may, in some instances, be given recognition under the common law in exceptional cases. In such cases proceedings will need to be issued for recognition by the court under its inherent jurisdiction and a declaration pursuant to Family Law Act 1986, s 57.

14.27 The principles which apply in determining whether to recognise the foreign adoption under common law were first set out in *Re Valentine's Settlement* [1965] Ch 831. These were:

(a) the adoptive parents must have been domiciled in the foreign country at the time of the foreign adoption;
(b) the child must have been legally adopted in accordance with the requirements of the law of the foreign country;
(c) the foreign adoption had the same essential characteristic as those of an English adoption; and
(d) there must be no reason of public policy for refusing recognition of the adoption.

14.28 Since then, there has been some shift towards relaxing these principles. Recognition may be granted where the adoption was granted by a foreign court where both parents were then habitually resident, or where adoption recognition is in the child's best interests. In *S v S (No 3) (Foreign Adoption Order: Recognition)* [2016] EWHC 2470 (Fam), it was held that when determining an application for the recognition of a foreign adoption at common law and an application for a declaration pursuant to Family Law Act 1986, s 57 the court must ensure that it acts in a manner that is compatible with the Art 8 rights of the parents and the child. In *Re N (A Child)* [2016] EWHC 3085 (Fam), Sir James Munby P held that: (i) the principles in *Re Valentine's Settlement* remained good law until the Court of Appeal directed otherwise; (ii) recognition at common law of a foreign adoption depends upon and only upon the four criteria identified in *Re Valentine's Settlement*; and (iii) the fourth principle of public policy operates in a limited and narrow manner. He rejected the proposal that there was the need to add additional criteria to these principles of the child's best interests to be considered when deciding whether to recognise a foreign adoption order at common law. The *Re Valentine's Settlement* criteria were also applied in *FX and MJX v Cafcass Legal* [2020] EWHC 1227 (Fam) to grant a declaration under the inherent jurisdiction recognising the foreign adoption. See also *Z v Z (Recognition of Brazilian Adoption Order)* [2013] EWHC 747 (Fam) and *Re G (Children)* [2014] EWHC 2605 (Fam).

14.29 However, in S v S (No 3) (Foreign Adoption Order: Recognition) [2016] EWHC 2470 (Fam), a s 57 declaration was made to recognise a child's foreign adoption notwithstanding the fact that neither the domicile nor the residency criteria under the rule in *Re Valentine's Settlement* were met, on the ground that a refusal of recognition would be a breach of the rights of both the child and the parents under European Convention, Art 8. The evidence before the court established that there were family ties between the parents and the child. Strict application of the common law rule in *Re Valentine's Settlement* would constitute an interference in the Art 8 right to respect for family life. It would be contrary to public policy to apply those rules in a way that would result in a breach of the fundamental rights of the parties and would constitute an interference in the Art 8 rights to respect for family life of the parents and the child that could not be said to be either necessary or proportionate (see the discussion at [101]–107]). See also *Re V (A Child) (Recognition of Foreign Adoption)* [2017] EWHC 1733 (Fam).

14.30 More recently, in *KA v FA and Others* [2024] EWHC 2855 (Fam), the application was for recognition of a Nigerian adoption under common law. The mother was domiciled in Nigeria at the time of the adoption but the father was not. He was domiciled in England. Therefore, the first factor of the *Re Valentine's Settlement* which requires both parents to have been domiciled in Nigeria was not met. They required court-determined recognition of the Nigerian adoption order to enable the mother and the children to enter the United Kingdom. The court held that to apply the test strictly would result in a breach of the Art 8 rights of the parents and the children to respect for family life. It would impact on the parental responsibility of the parents and deny the children all the rights which result from an adoption order, such as inheritance rights. It would also impact on their emotional stability, security and welfare. In the circumstances, the court granted the application.

14.31 *Re G (Recognition of Nigerian Adoption)* [2024] EWHC 2769 (Fam) is another example of an application for an order for recognition of a Nigerian adoption under common law because, although prior to 3 January 2014 Nigerian adoption orders were recognised as designated overseas adoptions, as from that date such orders can now only be recognised if they are recognised under common law under ACA 2002, s 66(1)(e) (see further in Chapter 15). The Secretary of State has by Order made pursuant to CAA 2006, s 9 imposed a restriction on bringing a child from Nigeria to the United Kingdom. The reasons for the restriction are set out in the *Adoptions: Restricted List* document published in April 2023. The concerns regarding Nigerian adoptions are stated to be as follows:

> The specific areas of concern included:
>
> - difficulties confirming the background and adoptability of children;
> - unreliable documentation;
> - concerns about corruption in the Nigerian adoption system;
> - evidence of organised child trafficking within Nigeria; and
> - concerns about weaknesses in checks completed by Nigerian authorities in relation to adoption applications from prospective adopters who are habitually resident in the United Kingdom and therefore are likely to in fact be intended to be intercountry adoptions. This includes weaknesses in pre and post adoption monitoring procedures. There is an absence of checks as to whether the adoption is intended to be an intercountry adoption in light of the habitual residence of applicants and accordingly whether prospective adopters have been assessed and approved by a UK adoption agency and issued with relevant UK authority documentation (e.g. certificate of eligibility to adopt) to proceed with an intercountry adoption from Nigeria.

Further information is available at:

> https://assets.publishing.service.gov.uk/media/640b4369d3bf7f02fa988cec/Adoptions_-_restricted_list_-_April_2023.pdf

14.32 In *Re G* the application related to G, a girl who was born in Nigeria and had been abandoned at birth. She was found by an anonymous person and taken to the local maternity and orphanage home. G was adopted by the applicant, a Nigerian citizen, in one of the states of Nigeria in 2016. The applicant was then married to an Italian but estranged from him; he had consented to the adoption. Following the adoption G remained in Nigeria in the care of the applicant's extended family while the applicant took up employment first in Italy and then in England. Prior to making the application for recognition of the adoption under common law the applicant had twice applied for permission for G to join her. On both occasions the application was refused. The applicant therefore applied to the court for recognition of the Nigerian adoption. At the date of the application the applicant had indefinite leave to remain in England. The application was opposed by the Secretary of State for the Home Department. The court confirmed that the criteria for recognition at common law remained those set out in *Re Valentine's*

*Settlement* (see para 14.28). There was no dispute that the last two of the criteria were satisfied. The issue was whether the applicant had been domiciled in Nigeria when the adoption order was made and whether the applicant had met the Nigerian legal requirements that the prospective adopters must give 12 months' notice before the application is made. On the issue of the applicant's domicile, on the evidence the court held that when the applicant became estranged from her Italian husband and returned to Nigeria, her Nigerian domicile of origin was revived. On the second issue, the court, having scrutinised the legal process which the Nigerian's authorities undertook before the final adoption order was made, was satisfied that process was substantially the same as would have applied in England and that the Nigerian court had disapplied the 12 months' requirement in the best interests of the child. The court also went on to rule that even if the *Re Valentine's Settlement* criteria were not met the court was satisfied 'that there exists de facto family life between Mrs B and G for the purposes of Article 8 of the ECHR'; and:

> that the strict application of the common law rules in *Re Valentine's Settlement* and the concomitant refusal to recognise G's Nigerian adoption would constitute an interference in G's and Mrs B's Article 8 rights which could not be said to be necessary or proportionate in a democratic society. Where family life exists between Mrs B and G, I am clear that the court cannot refuse to recognise or engage with the actual situation on the ground. Here, G is ultimately dependent on Mrs B; has been adopted by her in Nigeria; and recognises her as 'mommy' despite their geographical separation. In that context, a decision to refuse to recognise G's adoption would not take into account the actual reality, namely that G cannot be integrated into her adoptive family by means of the creation of a permanent legal relationship in this jurisdiction. G would be Mrs B's daughter in Nigeria but not recognised as such in the UK where her mother lives; has indefinite leave to remain and intends to stay. [48]

The court therefore made a declaration recognising G's Nigerian adoption by the applicant at common law. (See also *Re C (A Child) (Recognition of Nigerian Adoption)* [2025] EWHC 204 (Fam).)

14.33 Family Law Act 1986, s 57 empowers the High Court or the Family Court to make a declaration in respect of 'any person whose status as an adopted child depends on whether he has been adopted by that person by either a Convention adoption, or overseas adoption, within the meaning of the ACA 2002 or an adoption recognised by the law of England and Wales and effected under the law of any country outside the British Islands'. The application should be made to the Family Court and allocated to be heard by a High Court Judge or a judge nominated to sit as a Deputy High Court Judge. The declaration sought is for confirmation that the child/person is or is not the adopted child of that person (Family Law Act 1986, s 57(1) and (2)). The court, however, has jurisdiction to make such a declaration only if the applicant is domiciled in England and Wales on the date of the application or has been habitually resident in England and Wales throughout the period of one year before the application is made.

## *Procedure*

14.34 FPR 2010, Part 5A requires the application to be made on Form C65. The procedure set out in FPR 2010, Part 19 applies to this application. The document filed with the Form C65 must set out the details required under FPR 2010, r 19.3. These are:

(i) the declaration that the applicant wants the court to make, i.e. a declaration that the child who is the subject of the proceedings is for the purposes of ACA 2002, s 67 the adopted child of the applicant (FPR 2010, r 19.3(b)(i));
(ii) that the application is made under Family Law Act 1986 (FPR 2010, r 19.3(c));
(iii) details of any representative capacity in which the application is made or in which a respondent might appear, for example, a child by their litigation friend (FPR 2010, r 19.3(d) and (e));
(iv) the applicant's interest in the application as required under Family Law Act 1986, s 55;
(v) the grounds on which the application is made and the legal basis of the application (FPR 2010, r 19.3(b)(ii));
(vi) particulars of every person whose interest might be affected and his relationship to the applicant or the child (for example, the parent(s) of the child) to enable the court to decide whether they or any other person should be joined as a party (FPR 2010, r 8.20((2) and (4)).

14.35 The applicant must send a copy of the application and all supporting documents to the Attorney General at least one month before the application is made to enable the Attorney General to decide whether to intervene in the proceedings. If the decision is made to intervene, the court must send to the Attorney General any subsequent documents filed at court. The court may also when giving directions consider whether to request the Attorney General to argue any questions relating to the proceedings. If the Attorney General accedes to the request, they must serve a summary of the arguments on all the parties to the proceedings (FPR 2010, r 8.21).

## APPENDIX – LIST OF THE 87 DESIGNATED OVERSEAS COUNTRIES

Albania
Andorra
Armenia
Australia
Austria
Azerbaijan
Belarus
Belgium
Belize
Bolivia
Brazil
Bulgaria
Burkina Faso
Burundi
Canada
Cape Verde
Chile
China, The People's Republic of
Colombia
Costa Rica
Cuba
Cyprus, The Republic of
Czech Republic
Denmark (including the Faroe Islands and Greenland)
Dominican Republic
Ecuador
El Salvador
Estonia
Fiji
Finland
France
Georgia
Germany
Greece
Guinea
Hungary
Iceland
India
Ireland, The Republic of
Israel
Italy
Kazakhstan
Kenya
Latvia
Lesotho
Liechtenstein
Lithuania
Luxembourg
Macedonia, The Former Yugoslav Republic of
Madagascar
Mali
Malta
Mauritius
Mexico
Moldova, The Republic of
Monaco
Mongolia
Montenegro
Netherlands, The (including the Caribbean part of the Netherlands (the islands of Bonaire, Sint Eustatius and Saba))
New Zealand
Norway
Panama
Paraguay
Peru
Philippines
Poland
Portugal
Romania
Rwanda
San Marino
Senegal
Seychelles
Slovakia
Slovenia
South Africa
Spain
Sri Lanka
Swaziland
Sweden
Switzerland
Thailand
Togo
Turkey
United States of America, The
Uruguay
Venezuela
Vietnam

## Chapter 15

# Intercountry Adoptions – Other than Convention Adoptions/'Overseas Adoptions'

## INTRODUCTION

15.1 Adoptions from countries that are not Convention member states (see Chapters 12 and 13) or from designated overseas countries or territories (see Chapter 14) are generally not recognised in the United Kingdom, and restrictions are imposed by ACA 2002, s 83 on bringing children into the United Kingdom by person(s) who are habitually resident in the British Islands. Section 83 also provides for regulations to be made which (a) require a person intending to bring or cause another to bring a child into the United Kingdom to apply to an adoption agency for an assessment of their suitability to adopt the child and to give the agency any information the adoption agency requires for the purpose of the assessment; and (b) in relation to the child where notice of intention is given to impose functions on the local authority to which notice is give and provide for modifications or exemption from any provisions which apply to domestic adoptions.

15.2 The Secretary of State is empowered to impose further restrictions or extra conditions in certain cases or suspension of intercountry adoption from a country or territory outside the British Islands, which may include a country which is listed as a Convention country or a designated country. The relevant provisions which apply are set out in the ACA 2002, the Children and Adoption Act 2006 (CAA 2006), the Adoptions with a Foreign Element (Special Restrictions on Adoptions from Abroad) Regulations 2008 (SI 2008/1807) and the AFER 2005, which contain specific regulations relating to intercountry adoptions from these countries. The restrictions, conditions or suspension that apply with regard to the movement of children are considered in outline in this chapter.

## RESTRICTIONS ON BRINGING CHILDREN INTO THE UNITED KINGDOM

15.3 ACA 2002, s 83 sets out the restrictions which apply where a person habitually resident in the British Islands:

> (a) brings, or causes another to bring, a child who is habitually resident outside the British Islands into the United Kingdom for the purpose of adoption by the British resident, or
> (b) at any time brings, or causes another to bring, into the United Kingdom a child adopted by the British resident under an external adoption [a non-Convention adoption] effected within the period of twelve months ending with that time.

15.4 It is a criminal offence for a person to bring, or to cause another to bring, a child into the United Kingdom at any time in circumstances where ACA 2002, s 83 applies unless the requirements of the AFER 2005 have been satisfied. A person guilty of this offence is liable on summary conviction to imprisonment for a term not exceeding six months or a fine or both, or on conviction on indictment to imprisonment for a period not exceeding twelve months or a fine or both (ACA 2002, s 83(1), (7) and (8)).

15.5 There is no statutory definition or guidance on what is meant by the phrase 'for the purposes of adoption'. In *Re A and B (Adoption: section 83 ACA 2002)* [2024] EWHC 2837 (Fam), there were a number of issues for determination. The primary issue for determination was whether the applicant, who was a British citizen habitually resident in England, had brought her two nieces from Pakistan to England 'for the purposes of adoption' in breach of ACA 2002, s 83(1)(a). The court's first task was to determine the meaning of the phrase 'for the purposes of adoption' and then to decide whether on the facts of the case the applicant had breached this provision. The court held that 'for the purposes of adoption' means 'with the intention of adopting' the children by an adoption order through the English courts. The word 'purpose' should be given its ordinary meaning, i.e. the reasons or intent behind an action or decision; the phrase designated an action with a specific objective. It is neither appropriate nor necessary to import the word 'sole' or dominant' before 'purpose'. In arriving at this decision the court referred to: (a) the explanatory notes to the ACA 2002, which use the words 'with the intention of adopting, in relation to section 84'; (b) the Home Office Guidance 2024, *Adopted Children and Children Coming to the UK for Adoption Caseworker Guidance*, which in reference to s 83 uses the words 'for the purpose of being adopted' (AFER 2005, regs 3–9); and (c) the provisions of ACA 2002, s 84, which deal with the reverse situation of removal of children from the British Isles for adoption and use the words persons who 'intend to adopt' a child under the law of a country or territory outside the British Isles. On this basis, on the facts the court ruled that the applicant, who had applied for and had been granted a guardianship order and permission to remove her nieces from Pakistan through a legal process and had been granted entry visas from the Home Office for the children, had brought them to England to provide them with a permanent home and to give them 'love, home and sense of belonging' after the children's father, who had been the children's only carer, died. There was thus no breach of ACA 2002, s 83(1)(a) and the AFER 2005 were not engaged. Had the court concluded that there had been such breaches, the court would nevertheless have had the power to disapply the statutory provisions and regulations where 'to refuse the application would be materially to deny the Article 8 ECHR rights of the children and the Applicant' (see [40]–[43]).

15.6 Applying the decision in *Re TY (Preliminaries to Intercountry Adoption)* [2019] EWHC 2979 (Fam), the court also held that the court has the power to disapply non-compliance with statutory provisions where to do otherwise would be incompatible with ECHR rights of the parties and/or the children. The court also identified the following factors, extracted from previous decisions of the court, which should be considered in interpreting non-compliance (at [44]–[46]):

> 'i) The focus of the court's analysis should be upon the consequence of the non-compliance as opposed to the imperative wording of the provision (*Re X* at [37]); "the emphasis ought to be on the consequences of non-compliance" (per Lord Steyn in *Regina v Soneji and another* [2005] UKHL 49, [2006] 1 AC 340, at [23]);
>
> ii) If there is a breach of a statutory procedural requirement, the modern approach is to look at the underlying purpose of the requirement, whether departure from it contravenes the letter of the statute and if so, whether it renders it a nullity; (*Re X* at [39]/[41]); a "purposive" interpretation should be adopted (*Re X* at [39]);
>
> iii) The consequences of making or not making the order (or in this case of allowing the application to proceed) should be considered; this would be particularly pertinent if the consequences could be lifelong and irreversible (*Re X* at [54]);
>
> iv) The Human Rights Act 1998 requires an interpretation which gives effect to the rights enshrined therein (*Re X* at [44]);
>
> v) Relevant to the exercise of discretion (in considering whether to adhere strictly to the letter of the statute or not) would be whether the parties had acted in good faith (*Re A & B* at [45], [52], [65]);
>
> vi) Consideration should be given to whether any party suffer prejudice if the application is allowed to proceed (*Re X* [65], cited in *KB & RJ* at [38]).'
>
> vii) It is essential to recognise and give effect to the rights of the child and the parties for a family life under Art 8 of the ECHR and Art 6 of the UN Convention on the Rights of the Child. Any interference with those rights must be proportionate and justified. It is not unconstitutional for a public authority court or tribunal to disapply a provision of subordinate legislation which would otherwise result in acting incompatibly with Convention Rights.

15.7 In contrast in *A v B and Another* [2024] EWHC 3198 (Fam), on the facts the applicant was found to be in breach of ACA 2002, s 83. The applicant, a British citizen and habitually resident in England who had previously adopted a child from Morocco, applied to adopt a child X who was born in Morocco and was a Moroccan citizen. The child X had been abandoned and was placed in an orphanage, and was declared to be 'an abandoned child' by the Moroccan court. Morocco is not a member of the 1993 Hague Convention but is a member of the 1996 Hague Convention on Jurisdiction, Applicable Law, Recognition, Enforcement and Co-operation in Respect of Parental Responsibility and Measures for the Protection of Children (1996 Hague Convention). Morocco being an Islamic country, adoption, the legal relationship and obligations of the person in whose care an abandoned child is placed are regulated by the process known as kafala and incorporated in the kafala law 2002. Under that law kafala may come into existence either by agreement by virtue of a court order or by notarial kafala. Adoption where all legal rights and obligations of the biological parents are extinguished on the making of an adoption order is forbidden. Pursuant to the 1996 Hague Convention, Art 23, judicial kafala is recognised in the United Kingdom. In this instance the applicant, having been assessed and approved by the Inter-country Adoption Centre as a suitable prospective adopter, applied to the Moroccan court for kafala of the child X. She went through the local matching and assessment process and was granted a kafala order in respect of X. The kafala order, however, merely grants her guardianship of the child who is the subject of the order. The child therefore does not have the same legal rights as that of a child who is the biological child of the applicant. It was therefore the applicant's intention to apply for an adoption order in England as she had done with her previous adopted child. She brought X to England on 6 May 2023 and he continued to live with her and her first adopted child. She applied for an adoption order on 28 September 2023.

15.8 On the evidence the court distinguished the earlier case of *Re A and B (Adoption: section 83 ACA 2002)* [2024] EWHC 2837 (Fam) and held that the applicant had brought the child to England for the purposes of adoption and was in breach of ACA 2002, s 83. However, the court ruled that non-compliance of the statutory provisions is not an absolute bar to the court making an adoption order. Any breach of the terms of ACA 2002, s 83 does not fetter the court's power to make an adoption order. In exceptional circumstances the court will weigh into the balance the circumstances leading to the non-compliance, including the gravity and nature of the acts. Pursuant to Human Rights Act 1998, s 3, the court will then adopt a purposive interpretation of the legislation if it finds that the regulatory requirements have been complied with in substance, and that to approach the situation strictly would result ina breach of the Art 8 rights of the applicant and the child for respect of family life and would not be in the best interests and welfare of the child. In such an instance the court is empowered to read down the provisions of ACA 2002, s 83 and disapply the requirements of s 83 and those of the AFER 2005.

15.9 The issue of whether a case falls within the restrictions under s 83 and, if so, whether non-compliance will be considered to be a bar to the court making an adoption order is a factual determination based on the evidence in each case. It is only where the circumstances are considered to be exceptional that the court may make an adoption order.

15.10 Additionally, in some instances pursuant to CAA 2006, s 9, the Secretary of State may by order declare that special restrictions set out in CAA 2006, Pt 2 are to apply to bringing a child into the United Kingdom from certain named states where there is reason to believe that, because of the practices taking place in the other country in connection with the adoption of children, it would be contrary to public policy to further the bringing of children into the United Kingdom.

15.11 The Secretary of State is required, pursuant to CAA 2006, s 9(7), to publish reasons for imposing the 'restriction order' and to keep each such restricted country under review to determine whether the restriction should remain (CAA 2006, s 10). (See under para 14.31 for the reasons for the restrictions in respect of Nigeria.) The reasons given for the other countries (for the list, see para 15.14) on which a restriction order has been made can be found at:

> https://assets.publishing.service.gov.uk/media/640b4369d3bf7f02fa988cec/Adoptions_-_restricted_list_-_April_2023.pdf

The Secretary of State must also publish a list of the restricted countries ('the restricted list') (CAA 2006 s 9(8)).

15.12 The provision in CAA 2006, s 9 applies irrespective of whether the other country is a Convention country or not.

15.13 CAA 2006, s 11(2), however, permits the processing of cases from countries that are the subject of the restriction order where the relevant authority is satisfied that the case should proceed despite the restrictions.

15.14 Currently, there are six restricted countries under CAA 2006, Pt 2, namely: Cambodia (SI 2008/1808), Guatemala (SI 2008/1809), Nepal (SI 2010/951), Haiti (SI 2013/2265), Ethiopia (SI 2018/517) and Nigeria (SI 2021/64). Details of the full list is available at:

> https://assets.publishing.service.gov.uk/media/640b4369d3bf7f02fa988cec/Adoptions_-_restricted_list_-_April_2023.pdf

15.15 CAA 2006, s 12(1) permits the Secretary of State to make regulations providing for the imposition of extra conditions in certain cases.

## Exceptions to suspension

15.16 The Adoptions with a Foreign Element (Special Restrictions on Adoptions from Abroad) Regulations 2008 (SI 2008/1807) set out the procedure to be followed by the relevant authority (Secretary of State in England and National Assembly for Wales) when a request from a prospective adopter(s) to be treated as an exception to the general suspension is being considered, and the matters to be taken into account in determining whether a case merits an exception to the suspension. The procedure requires the relevant authority to seek information from the prospective adopter(s) to enable the authority to determine whether a case is exceptional. The relevant authority is also entitled to make further inquiries from other departments and from the British Consulate in the foreign country. The relevant authority may also take into account matters that are not listed in the Regulations.

15.17 Where a child has been identified for adoption, the inquiries undertaken will be more extensive. Furthermore, when dealing with an application for exceptional treatment, the relevant authority is likely to impose further conditions.

## What the prospective adopter(s) must do to apply for exceptional treatment

15.18 The prospective adopter(s) who wish to adopt a child from any of the aforesaid six countries must contact the Intercountry Adoption Team. An application must be made in writing, setting out the reasons why the case should be treated as an exception having regard to the grounds on which the restrictions were imposed.

15.19 The application should be sent to one of the following addresses:

- *For England:*
  Intercountry Adoption Casework Team
  Department for Education
  Level 0, Riverside
  Bishopsgate House
  Feethams
  Darlington DL1 5QE
  Tel: +44 370 0002288
  Email: ica.darlington@education.gov.uk
  www.gov.uk/guidance/intercountry-adoption-information-for-adoption-agencies

- *For Wales:*
  Improving Outcomes for Children Advisory Group
  Welsh Government
  Cathays Park
  Cardiff CF10 3NQ
  Tel: +44 (29) 203000 257305 or +44 (29) 203000257382
  Fax: +44 (29) 2082 3142
  Email: lookedafterchildren@gov.wales

- *For Scotland:*
  The Scottish Executive
  Young People and Looked After Children Unit
  Education Department
  Area 2B (S)
  Victoria Quay
  Edinburgh EH6 6QQ
  Tel: +44 (131) 244 7137
  Fax:+44 (131) 244 3547
  Email: intercountry.adoption@scotland.gsi.gov.uk
  Contact person: Dominic Brack

- *For Northern Ireland:*
  Family and Children's Policy Directorate
  Department of Health
  Room A3.3, Castle Buildings
  Stormont
  Belfast BT4 3SQ
  Tel: +44 (28) 905 205 49
  Emails: Jennifer.mooney@health-ni.gov.uk;
  intercountry.adoption@health-ni.gov.uk
  Contact person: Jennifer Mooney

- *For the Isle of Man:*
  Children and Families
  Manx Care
  2nd Floor Murray House
  Mount Havelock
  Douglas IM1 2SF
  Tel: +44 (1624) 686179
  Email: Julie.Gibney@gov.im
  (Agency Decision Maker/Assistant Director, Children and Families

15.20 The prospective adopter(s) must also inform their local authority or the local adoption agency of their intention to adopt a child from overseas. The Department for Education charges a fee of £2,500 for processing the application. The fee is exempt from VAT. Once an application is received and accepted, the department will inform the applicant about how to pay the fee. The fee includes case management but no other costs.

## REQUIREMENTS FOR BRINGING CHILDREN INTO THE UNITED KINGDOM

### Application

15.21 A person(s) intending to bring or to cause another to bring a child into the United Kingdom in circumstances where ACA 2002, s 83(1) applies must also apply in writing to an adoption agency for an assessment of his suitability to adopt a child and give the adoption agency any information it may require for the purposes of the assessment (ACA 2002, s 83(4), and AFER 2005, reg 3). The local authority/adoption agency will need to undertake an assessment on eligibility and suitability before the matter can proceed any further. The assessment covers all the issues required to be covered for a domestic adoption. The Guidance issued by the Home Office on adoption provides further guidance. The Guidance is available at:

> https://assets.publishing.service.gov.uk/media/665f1df3d470e3279dd3358f/Adoption+guidance.pdf

15.22 Reference should also be made to the Annex C report, which is available at:

> https://assets.publishing.service.gov.uk/government/uploads/system/uploads/attachment_data/file/270102/annex_c_adoptions_with_a_foreign_element.pdf

### The agency's decision and notification

15.23 The same rules apply as set out at paras 13.15–13.17. The adoption agency must inform the prospective adopter(s) that they should not bring or cause the child to be brought into the United Kingdom until they have received notification from the Department for Education, and it must also warn them that if they go ahead without the appropriate certificate having been issued and served on them they will be at risk of being prosecuted for an offence under ACA 2002, s 83 and will not be able to adopt the child.

## Referral of case to the department

15.24 Once a decision is made in a case under ACA 2002, s 83 on the suitability of the prospective adopter to adopt a child, as set out in AAR 2005, reg 30, the agency must send to the Secretary of State:

(a) written confirmation of the decision and any recommendation the agency may make in relation to the number of children the prospective adopter may be suitable to adopt, their age range, sex, likely needs and background;
(b) all the documents and information which were passed to the adoption panel in accordance with regulation 25;
(c) the record of the proceedings of the adoption panel, its recommendation and the reasons for its recommendation;
(d) if the prospective adopter applied to the Secretary of State for a review by an independent review panel of a qualifying determination, the record of the proceedings of that panel, its recommendation and the reasons for its recommendation; and
(e) any other information relating to the case which the Secretary of State or the relevant foreign authority may require.

## Role of the appropriate department

15.25 On receipt of the information from the agency, the application will be checked to ensure that the relevant statutory requirements and procedures have been followed and that all the relevant information has been provided. Further information may be sought from the agency if any information is missing or the correct procedure has not been followed, or the prospective adopter(s) will be notified if any further information is required from them.

15.26 When all the statutory and procedural information has been complied with, a certificate will be issued to the relevant foreign authority where the child is habitually resident confirming that the prospective adopter(s) have been assessed and approved as eligible and suitable to adopt a child, and subject to any entry clearance and immigration requirements, the child will be permitted to enter and live in the United Kingdom. The certificate and all relevant documents will be forwarded to the foreign authority. The adoption agency and the prospective adopter(s) will be notified when this has been done. For details of the requirements in relation to the adopter(s) and the child, which the Home Office has issued under the Immigration Rules, see:

www.ind.homeoffice.gov.uk

15.27 Before entry clearance is granted, the Home Office will require the prospective adopter's/adopters' representative in the foreign country where the child is to apply to the British Government representative for an entry clearance and provide all the necessary documents requested. The representative will need to ascertain the wishes and feelings of the child on the adoption, having regard to the age and understanding of the child; and the representative will need to be satisfied that the evidence of parental consent to the adoption has been given freely and with full understanding of its implications; that the parents agree to the child leaving the country to come to the UK for adoption; and that there is no objection from the local authorities to the proposed adoption outside that country.

15.28 On completion of all the administrative procedures, the entry clearance application and all documents will be sent to the Home Office. On receipt of the documents by the Home Office, the applicant(s) will be required to give an undertaking that on the child entering the United Kingdom they will notify the local authority social services department of their intention to adopt the child and to apply for an adoption order; and that they will be financially responsible for the child and for the cost of repatriation of the child to the country of his origin if necessary. The adopter(s) will also be required to comply with AFER 2005, reg 3. Further enquiries will be made by the Home Office with the Department for Education or the National Assembly in the case of Wales in relation to the adoption by the prospective adopter(s). Further detailed information is set out in the *Statutory Guidance on Adoption: For local authorities, voluntary adoption agencies and adoption support agencies* (Department for Education, July 2013) (*Adoption Statutory Guidance 2013*), which is available at:

www.gov.uk/government/publications/adoption-statutory-guidance-2013

15.29 However, the fact that the assessment of the prospective adopter(s) has been positive does not necessarily mean that their application will be accepted by the relevant foreign authority or that a child who is a suitable match is available. Note also that the prospective adopter(s) will be charged the relevant consular fees for the service to be provided by the Home Office.

## Fees for services provided by local authority/adoption agency

15.30 ACA 2002, s 95 prohibits any payment (other than excepted payments) to be made for or in consideration of, *inter alia*, the adoption of a child, or preparing, causing to be prepared or submitting a report about the suitability of a child for adoption, or of a person to adopt a child, or about the adoption or placement for adoption of a child. Local Authorities (Prescribed Fees) (Adoptions with a Foreign Element) (Wales) Regulations 2005 (SI 2005/3114) (W 234), reg 3 provides that where facilities are provided by a local authority in Wales in connection with:

(a) the adoption of a child brought into the United Kingdom for the purposes of adoption; or
(b) a Convention adoption, an overseas adoption or any other adoption effected under the law of a country or territory outside the British Islands,

it may charge a fee to a prospective adopter. The facilities in question are those provided in the discharge of any function imposed by or in accordance with the AFER 2005 or by the ACA 2002 or the Welsh equivalent provisions, and the submission of a report to a relevant foreign authority where the child is habitually resident, except with regard to:

(a) facilities provided under AFER 2005, reg 5;
(b) the provision of counselling which is not followed by receipt of a written application for assessment of suitability;
(c) the provision of information prior to the receipt of a written application for an assessment of suitability to adopt a child under AFER 2005, reg 14(1);
(d) the provision of information to prospective adopter(s), meeting with prospective adopter(s) or providing counselling to prospective adopter(s) in accordance with AFER 2005, reg 19(2); and
(e) the submission of a report in accordance with AFER 2005, reg 30.

15.31 The fees charged must be reasonable and limited to the local authority's costs and expenses properly incurred in providing the facilities. The fees charged must not include any element in respect of the costs and expenses incurred by the local authority in connection with any complaint made about any aspect of the local authority's service or representation submitted to the local authority in respect of the assessment process or in respect of a review of a qualifying determination under ACA 2002, s 12.

## Further requirements before the child is brought into the United Kingdom

15.32 Before bringing the child into the United Kingdom, each prospective adopter must:

(a) receive in writing a confirmation from the Secretary of State that a certificate has been issued confirming to the relevant foreign authority the matters set out above;
(b) notify the adoption agency, before visiting the child in the foreign state, of the details of the child to be adopted; provide the agency with any further information and reports received from the foreign authority; and discuss with the agency the proposed adoption and information received;
(c) visit the child in the state of origin; and

(d) confirm in writing to the adoption agency, after the visit, that he has done so and wishes to proceed with the adoption; provide the agency with any additional reports and information received on or after that visit; and notify the adoption agency of the expected date of entry into the United Kingdom with the child.

15.33 The prospective adopter, if an individual person, must accompany the child on entering the United Kingdom. In the case of a couple, they must both do so unless the adoption agency and the relevant foreign authority have agreed that only one of them should do so.

## PROCEDURE FOLLOWING ARRIVAL IN THE UNITED KINGDOM

### What the prospective adopter(s) must do

15.34 On return to the United Kingdom, the adopter(s) must confirm in writing that the visit has taken place; provide the adoption agency with any additional reports and information received on or after the visit; and inform the adoption agency of the expected date of the child's arrival in the United Kingdom. The prospective adopter(s) must also, within 14 days of the date on which the child is brought into the United Kingdom, give notice to the relevant local authority of the child's arrival in the United Kingdom and of their intention to apply for an adoption order in accordance with ACA 2002, s 44(2) and (3), or not to give the child a home. In a case where the prospective adopter(s) have given notice as set out above and subsequently move their home into another local authority, the prospective adopter(s) must confirm this information in writing to the new local authority within 14 days of that move (AFER 2005, reg 4). The requirement of giving the local authority 14 days' notice is to enable the social work checks and weekly visits to be undertaken and for advice to be offered.

15.35 The requirement of compliance with ACA 2002, s 44(3), which requires at least three months' notice of intention to adopt to be given, is to enable the local authority to undertake its investigations and assessments. The court may, however, allow an application to proceed where there are exceptional circumstances, such as those which occurred in *Re TY (Preliminaries to Inter-country Adoption)* [2019] EWHC 2979 (Fam). The applicant in that case had adopted her nephew (T) in Jamaica in 2014 but he was not able to enter the United Kingdom until 2018 due to delay by the Home Office in issuing a visa. The applicant did not give notice to the local authority within the 14 days of T's arrival in the United Kingdom, and the requirement of giving three months' notice of the intention to apply for an adoption in compliance with ACA 2002, s 44(3) was not complied with. The local authority, however, had confirmed that its investigation and assessments could be completed before that period because much of that work had already been undertaken during the application for adoption in Jamaica. The court, applying the decision in *Re X (A Child) (Surrogacy: Time Limit)* [2014] EWHC 3135 (Fam), held that, given the exceptional circumstances of the case, it would not be appropriate to prevent the application proceeding simply on the basis of non-compliance with time limits. Additionally, the court ruled that, given the long-standing relationship between the applicant and T, it would be an unjustified and disproportionate interference with their rights under European Convention, Art 8 ([27]–[32]). As to the requirement for T to have his home with the applicant, see para 3.12, and [33]–[36] of the judgment. More recently, in *Re X (Time Barred Adoption)* [2024] EWHC 364 (Fam), a step-parent adoption, Mr X gave notice of his intention to adopt the son of his wife, who was Ukrainian. The notice given fell short of the required 'not less than three months notice' in ACA 2002, s 44(3) when he made the application to adopt. The issue was whether the court was precluded from making an adoption order. The court held that the breach did not preclude an adoption order being made because the provision was a technical matter. Following the cases referred to above, the court granted permission to proceed with the application on the grounds that, on the facts of the case, the subsection should be given a purposive construction and that non-compliance of the time limit did not cause any disadvantage or prejudice to any of the parties or the court. Additionally, that pursuant to Human Rights Act 1998, s 3, the statutory provisions should be read down so they did not breach the Art 8 rights of the parties and the child and that it was in the best interests of the child to grant the application. Breach of the provisions of s 44(3) will not be a bar to making an application nor to the application succeeding.

## What the local authority must do

15.36 When notice of intention to adopt has been given to the local authority, it must:

(a) if it has not already done so, set up a case record in respect of the child and place on it any information it has received from the relevant foreign authority, any other adoption agency involved, the prospective adopter(s), the entry clearance officer and the Secretary of State, or as the case may be;
(b) send to the prospective adopter's/adopters' general practitioner written notification of the arrival in England or Wales of the child, together with a written report of the child's health history and current state of health, so far as is known;
(c) send to the clinical commissioning group or (in Wales) local health board in whose area the prospective adopter(s) have their home, and to the National Health Service Commissioning Board, if the prospective adopter's/adopters'

home is in England, written notification of the arrival in England or Wales of the child;

(d) ensure that the child and the prospective adopter(s) are visited within one week of receipt of the intention to adopt, and thereafter at intervals of not less than once a week until a review required by regulations (see point (f) below) is carried out, and thereafter at such frequency as the authority may decide;

(f) carry out a review of the child's case not more than four weeks after receipt of the notice of intention to adopt, and:

    (i) visit and, if necessary, review not more than three months after that initial review, and
    (ii) thereafter not more than six months after the date of the previous visit,

    unless the child no longer has his home with the prospective adopter or an adoption order is made;

(g) when carrying out the review, consider the following matters:

    (i) the child's needs, welfare and development, and whether any changes need to be made to meet his needs or assist his development,
    (ii) the arrangements for the provision of adoption support services and whether there should be any reassessment of the need for those services, and
    (iii) the need for further visits and review;

(h) ensure that:

    (i) advice is given as to the child's needs, welfare and development,
    (ii) written reports are made of all visits and reviews of the case and placed on the child's case records, and
    (iii) on such visits, where appropriate, advice is given as to the availability of adoption support services.

## Application for adoption

15.37 The prospective adopter(s) should apply for and obtain an adoption order in the United Kingdom. The procedure to be followed is the same as for a domestic application, save that the application must be made within two years of giving notice of intention to adopt, and the minimum period of time the child must have lived with the applicants before an adoption order is made is six months if the statutory conditions referred to above have been complied with. If they have not been complied with, the child must have lived with the applicants for at least 12 months before an adoption order is made.

The recent case of *SR and MF v AE (By her Guardian Allison Baker)* [2023] EWFC 127, where the subject of the proceedings was 18 years old, illustrates the application of the above provisions.

## Application for adoption not made

15.38 If the prospective adopter(s) fail to make an application for an adoption order within two years of the receipt by the local authority of the notice of intention to adopt, the local authority must review the case. The matters it should consider when carrying out the review are:

(a) the child's needs, welfare and development, and whether any changes need to be made to meet his needs or assist his development;
(b) the arrangements, if any, in relation to the exercise of parental responsibility for the child;
(c) the terms upon which leave to enter the United Kingdom was granted and the immigration status of the child;
(d) the arrangements for the provision of adoption support services for the adoptive family and whether there should be any reassessment of the need for those services;
(e) in conjunction with the appropriate agencies, the arrangements for meeting the child's health care and educational needs (AFER 2005, reg 5(4)).

# CONSEQUENCES OF PLACEMENT

## Change of name

15.39 In a case where the child is brought into the United Kingdom in circumstances where ACA 2002, s 83(1) applies (see paras 15.1–15.4) then, whether or not the child is in England and Wales, a person may not cause the child to be known by a new surname, unless the court gives permission to do so or each parent or guardian of the child gives written consent (AFER 2005, regs 6 and 7).

## Return of the child

15.40 ACA 2002, s 35 is modified (by AFER 2005, reg 8) to provide that:

(a) where a child enters the United Kingdom in circumstances where s 83(1) applies and the prospective adopter gives notice to the local authority of their wish to return the child, the local authority must:

(i) receive the child from the prospective adopter within seven days of receipt of the notice, and
(ii) give notice to the Secretary of State or, as the case may be, the National Assembly for Wales, of the prospective adopter's wish to return the child;

(b) where a child enters the United Kingdom in circumstances where s 83(1) applies and the local authority:

(i) is of the opinion that the child should not remain with the prospective adopters, and
(ii) gives notice to them of its opinion,

the prospective adopters must, within seven days of the giving of notice, return the child to the local authority;

(c) if the agency gives notice under (2)(b) (above), it must also give notice to the Secretary of State or, as the case may be, the National Assembly for Wales.

## Consequences of failure to return the child

15.41 A prospective adopter who fails to comply with a requirement to return the child within seven days of notice being given under ACA 2002, s 35(2) commits a criminal offence, and is liable, on summary conviction, to imprisonment for a term of not more than three months or a fine, or both (ACA 2002, s 35(4)).

## Effect of notice to return the child if proceedings are pending

15.42 Where a local authority gives notice to the prospective adopter(s) that it is of the opinion that the child should not remain with them, but before the notice was given an application for an adoption order, special guardianship order or care arrangement order, or for leave to apply for a special guardianship order or care arrangement order, was made in respect of the child, and the application has not been disposed of, the prospective adopter(s) are not required to return the child to the local authority unless the court so orders (ACA 2002, s 35, as modified by AFER 2005, reg 8).

## Requirement for child to live with prospective adopters

15.43 Where the prospective adopter(s) have complied with the statutory and procedural requirements for applying to adopt a child who is habitually resident outside the United Kingdom, as outlined above, and make an application for an adoption order, ACA 2002, s 42(3) does not apply to them. ACA 2002, s 42(3) requires that, if the applicant, or one of the applicants, is the partner or a parent of the child, the child must have had his home with the applicant(s) for six months before the application. Furthermore, the provision which requires that the child should have had his home with the applicants for a minimum period where one of the applicants is not a partner of the child's parent or a local authority foster carer (ACA 2002, s 42(4) and (5)) is reduced to six months in the case of an intercountry adoption application. Where the child has been brought into the United Kingdom without having complied with the statutory requirement imposed in ACA 2002, s 83(4) and the AFER 2005, the period for which the child must have had his home with the prospective adopter(s) is 12 months (AFER 2005, reg 9).

# Chapter 16

# Adoption Agencies

## INTRODUCTION

16.1 Each local authority has a statutory duty to maintain within its area a service referred to as 'the adoption service' designed to meet the needs in relation to adoption of: (a) children who may be adopted, their parents and guardians; (b) persons wishing to adopt a child; and (c) adopted persons, their parents, natural parents and former guardians (ACA 2002, s 3(1)). A local authority is required to maintain and operate its adoption service in accordance with the provisions set out in ACA 2002, Chapter 2, ss 2–15 and detailed statutory regulations made under the Act. The main statutory regulation for the provision of adoption services is the AAR 2005. This is supplemented by the *Statutory Guidance on Adoption: For local authorities, voluntary adoption agencies and adoption support agencies* (Department for Education, July 2013) (*Adoption Statutory Guidance 2013*), which is available at:

> www.gov.uk/government/publications/adoption-statutory-guidance-2013

16.2 There are separate national minimum standards for inspection of adoption agencies, which are available at:

> www.gov.uk/guidance/social-care-common-inspection-framework-sccif-independent-fostering-agencies/23-fostering-for-adoption

and for adoption, *Adoption: national minimum standards* (Department for Education, July 2014) (NMS 2014), which is available at:

> www.gov.uk/government/publications/adoption-national-minimum-standards

16.3 Steps taken by the agencies and how and when decisions are made by the agencies will necessarily be relevant and impact on the outcome of proceedings. This chapter attempts to give an overview of the statutory requirements.

## THE ADOPTION PANEL

16.4 Each adoption agency is required to maintain a list of persons (the central list) who are considered to be suitable to be members of an adoption panel. The panel must include one or more social workers who have at least three years' relevant post-qualifying experience and a medical adviser to the adoption agency (or at least one, if more than one medical adviser is appointed) (AAR 2005, reg 3). The adoption agency may constitute one or more adoption panels, but any two or more local authorities may jointly establish 'a joint adoption panel' (AAR 2005, reg 4(1) and (3); and see *Adoption Statutory Guidance 2013*, para 1.34). The role of the panel is to consider every case referred to it and make recommendations to the agency on whether the child should be placed for adoption; the suitability of the prospective adopter(s) to adopt a child; and whether the child should be placed for adoption with a particular prospective adopter(s) (AAR 2005, regs 18, 26 and 32).

### Constituting an adoption panel

16.5 The adoption agency must appoint panel members from the persons on the central list. Where two or more local authorities jointly constitute a joint adoption panel, the appointment of members must be by agreement between the authorities. Panel members appointed must include a chair who is an independent person (see para 16.6) and who has the skills and experience necessary for chairing an adoption panel, and one or two persons who may act as chair ('the vice chairs') if the chair is absent or that office is vacant. The adoption agency must ensure that individual members have between them the experience and expertise necessary to discharge effectively the functions of the panel. The local authority may pay to any member of an adoption panel constituted by it, a reasonable fee (AAR 2005, reg 4(1)–(3)).

16.6 As set out in AAR 2005, reg 4(7), a person (P) is not an independent person if:

(a) in the case of a registered adoption society, P is a trustee or employee of that society; or
(b) in the case of a local authority, P is:

    (i) an elected member of that authority; or

(ii) employed by that authority for the purposes of the adoption services or of any of that local authority's functions relating to the protection or placement of children; or

(c) P is the adoptive parent of a child who was placed for adoption with P by the adoption agency (A) or placed for adoption with P by another adoption agency where P had been approved as suitable to be an adoptive parent by agency A, unless at least 12 months has elapsed since the adoption order was made in respect of that child.

## Meetings/Composition of adoption panel

16.7 In order to conduct its business, the panel must have at least the following members apart from the chair, or one of the vice chairs, as set out in AAR 2005, reg 6:

(a) one or more social workers who have at least three years' relevant post-qualifying experience;
(b) one other independent person (see para 16.6 or definition);
(c) an agency adviser (see para 16.8);
(d) an agency medical adviser.

16.8 The adoption agency is required to appoint a senior member of staff or, where local authorities agree to constitute joint adoption panels as necessary, appoint a senior member of staff of one of them, as an 'agency adviser', who must be a social worker of at least five years' relevant post-qualifying experience and relevant management experience. The role of the agency adviser is:

- to assist the agency with the maintenance of the central list and the constitution of the adoption panel;
- to be responsible for the induction and training of persons on the central list;
- to be responsible for liaison between the agency and the adoption panel;
- to monitor the performance of persons in the central list and members of the panel and the administration of the panels;
- to give such advice to an adoption panel as it may request in relation to any case or generally (AAR 2005, reg 8(1) and (2)).

16.9 The agency adviser therefore is not a panel member but attends the panel meetings to advise on any matters that arise during the meetings (see also *Adoption Statutory Guidance 2013*, paragraphs 1.27–1.47).

16.10 The adoption agency is required to appoint at least one registered medical practitioner to be the agency's medical adviser who must be consulted in relation to the arrangements for access to and disclosure of health information which is required or permitted by the AAR 2005 (reg 8(3) and (4); see also the medical adviser's role under reg 15, discussed at paras 16.34–16.35).

16.11 On adoption panels generally, see also NMS 2014, paras 17.1–17.11 (see also paras 16.39–16.42).

16.12 The objective is that this group of people will pool their experiences and expertise, offer an informed perspective and bring knowledge and scrutiny to the adoption agency's work.

## Term of office

16.13 A member of an adoption panel may remain in office until they resign or until their office is terminated by the adoption agency which appointed them (AAR 2005, reg 1(2)).

16.14 A medical adviser member may hold office only for so long as he is the medical officer of the adoption agency.

## Resignation and termination of office

16.15 Any adoption panel member may resign from office at any time by giving one month's notice in writing to the adoption agency (AAR 2005, reg 4(5)). Where an adoption agency is of the opinion that a person included in the central list is unsuitable or unable to remain in the list, the agency may remove that person's name from the list by giving them one month's written notice with the agency's reasons for its action. An adoption agency may terminate a member's office at any time if it is of the opinion that any member of the adoption panel appointed by it is unsuitable or unable to continue as a panel member by giving the member notice terminating the appointment. The notice of termination must be given in writing and must set out the reasons for the termination (AAR 2005, regs 3(3) and 4(6)).

## Functions of the adoption panel

16.16 The adoption panel has its own identity, separate from that of the agency. An adoption agency may not delegate decision-making to the panel, but it is required to refer to the panel the question as to whether adoption is in the best interests of the child. The adoption panel is required to consider the case of every child referred to it by the adoption agency and make a recommendation to the agency as to whether the child should be placed for adoption.

16.17 In considering what recommendation to make, the adoption panel is under a mandatory duty to have regard to the adoption agency's obligations to exercise its powers in relation to the adoption of a child set out in ACA 2002, s 1(2),(4), (5) and (6), namely that the paramount consideration of any decision relating to the child is the welfare of the child throughout the child's life. In determining this issue, regard must be taken of the factors set out in s 1(4), and, in particular in this regard in relation to Wales, consideration of the child's religious persuasion, racial origin and cultural and linguistic background (s 1(5)), and the other available options, before determining that adoption is the best outcome for the child. It must be satisfied that the agency's proposal for adoption was arrived at after having explored and discounted all the available options.

16.18 The panel also:

(a) must consider and take into account the reports and any other information passed to it by the adoption agency;
(b) may request the agency to obtain any other relevant information which the panel considers necessary; and
(c) must obtain legal advice in relation to the case before it makes its recommendations (AAR 2005, reg 18(6)).

16.19 Where the adoption panel recommends that the child should be placed for adoption, it must consider and may at the same time give advice to the agency about:

(a) the arrangements the agency proposes to make for allowing any person contact with the child; and
(b) where the agency is a local authority, whether it should apply for a placement order (AAR 2005, reg 18(3)).

16.20 An adoption panel should make a written record of its proceedings, recommendations, and the reasons for its recommendations. (See further the *Adoption Statutory Guidance 2013*, paragraphs 2.70–2.71 and the NMS 2014.)

## DECIDING WHETHER A CHILD SHOULD BE PLACED FOR ADOPTION

### Outline

16.21 A child is 'looked after' if he is being voluntarily accommodated by the local authority or is the subject of a care order under the ChA 1989, or if care proceedings in respect of him have been issued. The local authority has a duty to such children to identify a permanence plan by the four-month review. The range of options available must be considered at the review. The options include rehabilitation of the child with his parent(s) or birth family, with appropriate support; placement with foster carer(s) or in a residential institution; and placement for adoption. The views of the child, his parent(s) and others with parental responsibility must be ascertained, and the options explained to them.

16.22 As set out in AAR 2005, regs 11–17, an adoption agency's duties towards a child whom the agency is considering for adoption include the following:

(a) to open the child's case records;
(b) to provide counselling and information for the child and ascertain the child's wishes and feelings;
(c) to provide counselling and information for, and ascertain the wishes of, the child's parent(s) or guardian, and others;
(d) to obtain information about the child;
(e) to obtain information about the child's family;
(f) to prepare the child's permanence report for the adoption panel (see also *Adoption Statutory Guidance 2013*, Chapter 2 and NMS 2014, para 12).

## The child's case record

16.23 The adoption agency is under a duty to set up a child's case record and place on it:

(a) all the information gathered by it in relation to the duties referred to above;
(b) the child's permanence report;
(c) a written record of the proceedings of the adoption panel, its recommendations and reasons for them, and any advice given by the panel to the agency;
(d) a record of the agency's decision and any written notification of that decision given to the parent or guardian and, where appropriate, the father of the child (see para 16.47);
(e) any parental consent obtained for the placement of the child for adoption;
(f) any advance consent obtained for the adoption of the child;
(g) any form or notice of withdrawal of consent under ACA 2002, s 19 or s 20, or notice under s 20(4)(a) or (b);
(h) a copy of any placement order in respect of the child;
(i) any other documents or information obtained by the agency which it considers should be included in the case record (AAR 2005, reg 12(1)).

## Counselling, etc for the child

16.24 Where an adoption agency is considering adoption for a child, it must, unless it is satisfied that these duties have been carried out by another agency, as far as is reasonably practicable (ACA 2002, s 1(4) and (5), and AAR 2005, reg 13):

(a) provide a counselling service for the child;
(b) explain to the child, in an appropriate manner, the procedure in relation to, and the legal implications of, adoption for the child, and provide him with appropriate written information about these matters; and
(c) ascertain the wishes and feelings of the child regarding the possibility of placement for adoption with a new family and his adoption; his religious and cultural upbringing; and contact with his parent(s), guardian, other relatives or any other person the agency considers relevant (see also *Adoption Statutory Guidance 2013*, paragraphs 2.22–2.26).

16.25 The needs of children from minority cultural backgrounds must be addressed. There may be language or cultural issues to be considered, so that effective communication is achieved when information is given to the child. When giving information to the child, it is important to ensure that the child understands the reasons for the agency's decision to place the child for adoption, and the effect of the order on the child and his parent(s). The effect it will have on contact should also be clearly explained. When seeking to ascertain the child's wishes and feelings, it is essential that the child understands that his views are only one of the factors which will be taken into account.

## Counselling, etc for the parent(s) or guardian and others

16.26 When considering adoption for a child, an adoption agency is required, unless it is satisfied that these duties have been carried out by another agency, so far as is reasonably practicable:

(a) to provide a counselling service for the parent(s) or guardian of the child;
(b) to explain to them the procedure in relation to both placement and adoption; the legal implications of giving consent to placement for adoption and advance consent to the placement for adoption; and the legal implications of adoption, and to provide them with written information about these matters;
(c) to ascertain the wishes and feelings of the parent(s) or guardian of the child and any other relevant person regarding the child; the placement of the child for adoption and his adoption, including any wishes and feelings about the child's religious and cultural upbringing and contact with the child if the child is authorised to be placed for adoption or the child is adopted.

16.27 Where the parent's/parents' or other relevant person's first language is not English, the adoption agency must establish whether the person(s) need an interpreter to explain the above matters. It is important to ensure that the information given is understood and that the person(s) are able to make an informed decision. Cultural and religious differences and any disabilities, including learning difficulties or intellectual impairment, must be taken into account to impart meaningful information. Similar factors should be considered when offering counselling (see below). The effect of adoption on contact between the parent(s) or other person and child must be made clear. The right to apply for contact under ACA 2002, ss 26 and 46 and the court's duty to consider arrangements for contact should be explained. Any information gathered during this process should be recorded and placed on the child's case record. Any consent or advance consent of any parent(s) or guardian in relation to placement orders must be in Form 100 and Form 103, respectively, and in relation to adoption in Form A103, and in Form 104 for advance consent (FPR 2010, PD 5A). Where counselling is offered but not accepted, there is a continuing duty to support the parent(s) or guardian throughout the adoption process, and to continue to offer counselling. It is also important that the parent's/parents' wishes and feelings are clearly recorded on the child's case records.

16.28 Both the ACA 2002 and the regulations specifically require consideration to be given to the effect of the loss of relationship between the child and his original family, including his relatives and others who may play a significant role in his life, and the wishes of the relatives too must be considered. At every stage of the process in coming to a decision relating to the adoption of the child, those concerned in making the decision are required to consider the adoption welfare test and all the matters set out in ACA 2002, s 1(4)–(7). It would seem that only in very exceptional circumstances could the information-gathering process not include the extended family (see further paras 16.29–16.39).

## Notification to fathers and relatives

16.29 In the case of the father of a child who does not have parental responsibility, but whose identity is known to the adoption agency, the service available to the parent with parental responsibility must also be made available to the father, unless the agency is satisfied that these duties have been carried out by another agency. In addition, the agency should ascertain, so far as is possible, whether the father wishes to acquire parental responsibility for the child, under ChA 1989, s 4 (acquisition of parental responsibility by father) or s 4ZA (acquisition of parental responsibility by female partner), or intends to apply for a care arrangement (residence) order, contact order or any other order under the ChA 1989, for example, the discharge of a care order, or apply for contact under ChA 1989, s 34 if the child is in care (AAR 2005, reg 14(3) and (4)); see also *Adoption: Statutory Guidance 2013*, paragraphs 2.39–2.47). There is, however, no duty to seek out the father or other relatives unless it is in the interests of the child to do so and to assist in finding prospective adopter(s) or long-term carer(s) for the child (*Re C (Child v XYZ County Council)* [2007] EWCA Civ 1206; see also *Re M and N (Twins: Relinquished Babies: Parentage)* [2017] EWFC 31). The view of the birth family, although relevant, is not determinative (*Re JL and AO (Babies Relinquished for Adoption)* [2016] EWHC 440 (Fam)).

16.30 As in the case of relatives, so in the case of the father without parental responsibility, there may be exceptional circumstances which permit the local authority not to contact him. An example arose in *Re M (Adoption: Rights of Natural Father)* [2001] 1 FLR 745, where the evidence disclosed that the father was violent and dangerous, and had subjected the mother to serious domestic violence in the presence of an older child. The father also had a series of criminal convictions for violent offences. The court excused the local authority from trying to locate and seek to interview the father. However, it was stressed that only in exceptional circumstances would it be appropriate to depart from the general rule that a father should be informed. Where it was felt that it would not be in the interests of the child to do so, authority from the court should be sought. It was also held that, on the particular facts of the case, the interference with the father's rights was justified. See also *A Local Authority v A Mother* [2017] EWHC 1515 (Fam).

16.31 The principles which apply in such cases were summarised by Cobb J in *Re A (Relinquished Baby: Risk of Domestic Abuse)* [2018] EWHC 1981 (Fam) at [19], as follows:

- i) Each case is fact-sensitive (*Re RA* [*(Baby Relinquished for Adoption)* [2016] EWFC 25, [2017] 1 FLR 1610] at [31]);
- ii) The outcome contended for here is 'exceptional' (*A Local Authority v the mother* [[2017] EWHC 1515 (Fam)] at [1]/[7]);
- iii) The paramount consideration is the welfare of A; section 1(2) Adoption and Children Act 2002 ('ACA 2002');
- iv) The court must have regard to the welfare checklist in section 1(4) ACA 2002;
- v) It is a further requirement of statute (section 1(4)(f)(iii) ACA 2002) that the court has regard to the wishes and feelings of the child's relatives;
- vi) Respect can and indeed must be afforded to the mother's wish for a confidential and discreet arrangement for the adoption of her child, although the mother's wishes must be critically examined and not just accepted at face value; overall the mother's wishes carry 'significant weight' albeit that they are not decisive (*Re JL and AO* [[2016] EWHC 440 (Fam)] at [47], [48] and [50], and see also *Re RA* at [43(vi)]);
- vii) Article 8 rights are engaged in this decision; however, in a case where a natural parent wishes to relinquish a baby, the degree of interference with the Article 8 rights is likely to be less than where the parent/child relationship is to be severed against the will of the parent (*Re TJ* [[2017] EWFC 6] at [26]);
- viii) Adoption of any kind still represents a significant interference with family life, and can only be ordered by the court if it is necessary and proportionate (*Re RA* at [32]);

ix) A high level of justification is still required before the court can sanction adoption as the outcome, and a thorough 'analysis' of the options is necessary (*Re JL & AO* at [32]); 'analysis' is different from 'assessment' – a sufficient 'analysis' may be performed even though the natural family are unaware of the process (*Re RA* at [34]). As I said in *Re RA* at [38]:

> 'in order to weigh up all of the relevant considerations in determining a relinquished baby case it may be possible (it may in some cases be necessary) and/or proportionate to perform the analysis without full assessment of third parties, or even their knowledge of the existence of the baby. The court will consider the available information in relation to the individual child and make a judgment about whether, and if so what, further information is needed'.

16.32 In *Re C (A Child: Care Proceedings: Adoption)* [2018] EWHC 3332 (Fam), the issue was whether the local authority should notify the father about the birth of the child where the young mother clearly wished the child to be adopted. Cohen J applied the principles referred to above and went on to add (at [32]):

> First, I fully subscribe to the principle that the remedy sought by the mother is exceptional and the circumstances needed to justify that outcome have to be exceptional, but that does not mean that there has to be one magnetic factor. The combination of circumstances, none in themselves exceptional, may, when aggregated, satisfy the test. Secondly, in considering whether the test is met one needs to conduct a holistic exercise considering all the circumstances. This includes an assessment, imperfect though it will necessarily be, of what the paternal family is likely to be able to offer. Thirdly, the fact that the mother could, if she had known, have declined to name the father and thus avoid this problem with which she and the court are now faced is not a relevant factor, although its impact on the mother may be relevant.

16.33 In *Re A, B and C (Adoption: Notification of Fathers and Relatives)* [2020] EWCA Civ 41, the court considered three consolidated appeals where the mothers had concealed their pregnancies and did not wish the fathers and other relatives to know of the births. The Court of Appeal reviewed all the relevant past case law, including those cases referred to at paras 16.29–16.32 and paras 16.37–16.39, on the issue of whether a father (putative or otherwise) and extended family members should be notified when a mother relinquishes her child for adoption. The court noted that there was uncertainty on the core principles that applied in such cases. The court emphasised the need for consistency of approach and expressed the view that there is no hierarchy as between a putative father and other relatives and the outcome will depend on the facts of the case and balancing the various factors including the competing rights of the child, the parents and other family members. The court (at [89]) summarised the principles governing decisions (by local authorities or by the court) as to whether a putative father or a relative should be informed of the existence of a child who might be adopted (see para 5.7 for the summary of the principles).

16.34 See also *Re A Local Authority R, Q, R, S (through their Children's Guardian Kayleigh Jennings)* [2023] EWHC 1971 (Fam), where the court accepted that the birth of a child outside marriage would be contrary to the religious and cultural heritage of the mother's family and disclosure to them would have serious negative effect on the lives of the mother and the wider family. The court made a declaration for non-disclosure.

## Steps to be taken when a child is placed for adoption on the basis that the child's father or extended family are not notified

16.35 In order to assist practitioners, the court in *Re A, B and C (Adoption: Notification of Father and Relatives)* [2020] EWCA Civ 41 (see above) approved the agreed collective statement of the local authorities and the parties on the steps (although not binding) to be taken when faced with these situations. These are as follows:

1. A local authority should take these steps as soon as it is notified that a mother, or mother and father, are expressing a wish that an infant is placed for adoption without notification to either the child's father or extended family:

    (i) The local authority files should be checked for background information about the mother and extended family and for contacts with other relevant agencies, such as health and police.

    (ii) The allocated social worker, ideally accompanied by an adoption worker, should undertake at least one visit but preferably a series of visits to the mother, or mother and father, if she/they are willing, to discuss:

    - The decision to place the child for adoption.
    - The reasons for not notifying the child's father, or extended family, where possible gathering details about the father's background and that of the family.
    - The mother's background and information about her family.
    - Any cultural issues and how they have affected the decision made by the mother, or mother and father.
    - The implications of adoption for the child.
    - The legal process required to achieve adoption.
    - Other possible options for the care of the child.
    - The adoption counselling service and how to access it.
    - Whether the mother, or mother and father, require any other form of support and how that might be achieved.

    No assurance should be offered to a parent during the social work visit/s that notice of the birth of the child will be withheld from the father and/or extended family members.

    (iii) The mother, or mother and father, must be provided with written information, where available, about the process and adoption counselling services.

(iv) Where the father is identified, the local authority should check its records for any background information known about him.

(v) The placement team must be informed immediately and it should begin the process of finding a suitable placement, preferably with 'foster for adoption'/early permanence carers.

(vi) CAFCASS must be informed as soon as the local authority is notified so that it can allocate a worker to the case for the purpose of meeting with the mother, or mother and father, to discuss and where appropriate take consent for adoption.

2. The local authority should critically examine all information that it receives and, in circumstances where the mother states the identity of the father is unknown to her, the local authority should carefully consider her statement and her explanation to consider whether there is any basis for considering that the statement might be false. If the local authority does form that view, it should consider if there is any reasonable way by which the identity of the birth father could be established.
3. The social worker should, as a matter of urgency, seek legal advice to ascertain whether the matter should be placed before the court in all cases where:

   (i) the mother opposes notification to the father, if identified;
   (ii) the mother knows the identity of the father but is unwilling to disclose this information;
   (iii) the local authority has reason to doubt the reliability of the mother's claim that the identity of the father is unknown, or
   (iv) the mother is opposed to any notification to her family or the father's family.

4. The legal advisors will need to consider and advise as a matter of urgency whether a Part 19 application or other proceedings should be issued.
5. If a decision is made that a Part 19 application is not required, the local authority should immediately notify CAFCASS, and provide detailed reasons for that decision, to allow CAFCASS to consider this information prior to meeting with the mother, or mother and father, when discussing consent under section 19 or for any later adoption application.
6. As non-means/non-merits tested public funding is unavailable to parents for a Part 19 application (and emergency funding may be difficult to access on an emergency basis even if merits and means tests are met), a local authority should provide the mother, or mother and father, with advice concerning access to independent legal advice and how that might be obtained and funded (including by the local authority considering the funding of such advice). A list of specialist solicitors available in the area should be provided.
7. Where an application is to be made, the social worker should prepare a detailed statement setting out the information gathered and providing the local authority's position regarding the wish of the mother, or mother and father, to relinquish the child without notifying the father and/or extended family members.

16.36 Other cases where this issue has been considered include those discussed at paras 16.37–16.39. The procedure for making the application to the court for directions and the court's approach are set out in paras 16.130–16.131.

16.37 In *Re L* [2007] EWHC 1771 (Fam), the court excused the local authority from trying to locate the father where the mother was not aware of his whereabouts. *A and B v P Council* [2014] EWHC 1128 (Fam) concerned the question of whether the natural father of a nine-year-old boy should be notified of an application by the boy's stepfather to adopt him. The court concluded that this was an exceptional case, which, on the facts, justified the court exercising its discretion to direct that the father not be given notice.

16.38 *Re H (A Child) (Adoption: Disclosure); Re G (A Child) (Adoption: Disclosure)* [2001] 1 FLR 646 concerned two unmarried mothers, each of whom had placed her child for adoption with the local authority on the basis she would not be asked to disclose the identity of the child's father. In *Re H*, the mother and father had lived together and had had an older child with whom the father had contact. The mother had concealed the second pregnancy from the father and the extended family. In *Re G*, the mother and father had never lived together, but the relationship had ended and they were not in contact with each other. In each case, the local authority sought the guidance of the court on whether the father should be consulted about the adoption and whether he should be joined as a party. In directing, in *Re H*, that the father should be informed, and in *Re G* that he should not, the facts of the cases were distinguished on the basis of the relationships between the parents. However, generally on the issue of confidentiality and the involvement of a father without parental responsibility in adoption proceedings, Dame Elizabeth Butler-Sloss P said (at pages 661–662):

> A considerable confidentiality is clearly important, but it ought not, in the majority of cases, deprive the father of his right to be informed and consulted about his child. In my view, social workers counselling mothers ought to warn them that at some stage, the court will have to make a decision in adoption proceedings as to whether to add the father as a respondent to the proceedings. The father should therefore be told as soon as possible in order to reduce delay, and certainly before the child is placed with prospective adopters. If the mother refuses to disclose the identity of the father, her reasons must be carefully considered and, unless those reasons are cogent it would be wise for the local authority to seek legal advice at an early stage. If necessary the local authority should follow the prudent course adopted by [one of the authorities in the case] of an application to the court for directions on whether to notify the father.

16.39 In *Re J (Adoption: Contacting Father)* [2003] EWHC 199 (Fam), [2003] 1 FLR 933, the mother had a baby at the age of 16 years, at which time her relationship with the father had ended and they had no contact with each other.

They had not lived together. She gave the local authority details of the father on the basis that the father would not be informed. The child was diagnosed as suffering from severe cystic fibrosis. The local authority sought a declaration from the court that it was in the child's best interests for the father to be informed. The mother objected. The court declared that it was lawful for the local authority to place the child for adoption without informing the father and seeking his views. There had been no family life within the context of European Convention, Art 8 between the father and the mother; the fact that it was unlikely that the father or his family would wish to care for the child outweighed any potential advantage to the child.

## Information about the child

16.40 An adoption agency is required to obtain so far as is reasonably practicable, two specific types of information:

(a) the information specified in AAR 2005, Sch 1, Pt 1 – this information includes the child's personal details and information about his cultural background, legal status, care history, a physical description and a description of his personality and interests, likes and dislikes, his educational history, his relationships with his family and others, arrangements for contact, and any other relevant information which might assist the adoption panel and the adoption agency; and
(b) to make arrangements for the child to be examined by a registered medical practitioner and for such other medical and psychiatric examination or tests as may be recommended by the agency's medical adviser, and in each case to obtain a written report on the child's health. This is known as the child's health report. It must record any treatment which the child is receiving, any need for health care, and the matters set out in AAR 2005, Sch 1, Pt 2. The adoption agency must also make arrangements for such medical and psychiatric examination of, and other tests on, the child, to be carried out as recommended by the agency's medical adviser and for written reports of such examination and tests to be obtained. No medical examination may be carried out, however, if the child is of sufficient understanding to make an informed decision and refuses to submit to the examination or other tests.

16.41 The medical examination need not be carried out if the medical adviser advises that it is not necessary (AAR 2005, reg 15(2); see also *Adoption Statutory Guidance 2013*, paragraphs 2.53–2.61, and the impact of the Data Protection Act 1998).

## Information about the child's family

16.42 The adoption agency must obtain, so far as is practicable, the information about the child's family specified in AAR 2005, Sch 1, Pt 3, and the information about each of the child's natural parents and brothers and sisters of the full blood or half-blood, as specified in AAR 2005, Sch 1, Pt 4.

## The permanence report

16.43 The adoption agency is under a duty to prepare a written report, referred to as the child's 'permanence report', prepared by a qualified person as required by the Restriction on the Preparation of Adoption Reports Regulations 2005 (SI 2005/1711). As set out in AAR 2005, reg 17, the report must include:

(a) the information specified in AAR 2005, Sch 1, Pts 1 and 3;
(b) a summary, written by the agency's medical adviser, of the child's state of health, his health history and any need for health care which might arise in the future;
(c) the wishes and feelings of the child on placement for adoption and adoption, his religious and cultural upbringing. and contact with his parent(s), guardian or other relative or with any other relevant person;
(d) the wishes and feelings of the child's parent(s) or guardian, or his natural father not having parental responsibility, and any other person the agency considers relevant on placement, adoption, religious and cultural upbringing and contact with the child;
(e) the views and proposals, if any, of the agency about the child's need for contact with and his parent(s), guardian, relatives or other relevant persons;
(f) an assessment of the child's emotional and behavioural development and related needs;
(g) an assessment of the parenting capacity of the child's parent and father without parental responsibility;
(h) a chronology of the decisions and actions taken by the agency with respect to the child;
(i) an analysis of the options for the future of the child which have been considered, and the reason adoption is considered the preferred option;
(j) any other information that the agency considers relevant. The welfare principle, the factors set out in the welfare checklist, issues relating to the child's religious persuasion, racial origin and cultural and linguistic background, and the no order principle, will be relevant considerations. The *Adoption Statutory Guidance 2013*, paragraphs 2.62–2.68 provides additional details on matters which should be included in the child's permanence

report. This includes, in particular, the need to ensure that the views of the child's guardian and any expert reports and agreed documents in care proceedings are disclosed to the agency decision maker.

16.44 Copies of the report, edited where appropriate, should be provided to the parent(s). A copy may also be provided to the child, if he is of sufficient age and understanding.

## THE ADOPTION PANEL'S DECISION

### Documents to be sent to the panel

16.45 The adoption agency must send the permanence report to the adoption panel, together with the child's health report, any other reports obtained under AAR 2005, reg 15, and information about the health of both the child's parents, but medical information should only be sent to the panel if the medical adviser so advises. It must also obtain and send to the panel any other relevant information requested by the panel (AAR 2005, reg 17(2); see *Adoption Statutory Guidance 2013* and the table at paragraph 2.69). The panel must also be supplied with any other relevant information, such as expert reports or a summary (see *Re B (Placement Order)* [2008] EWCA Civ 835 at [81]).

### The role of the adoption panel

16.46 The adoption panel has its own identity, separate from that of the agency. An adoption agency may not delegate decision-making to the panel, but it is required to refer to the panel the question as to whether adoption is in the best interests of the child. This requirement, however, is not absolute.

16.47 If the panel recommends that adoption is in the best interests of the child, it may at the same time give advice to the agency about the arrangements which the agency proposes to make for allowing any person contact with the child. Where the agency is a local authority, the panel may also recommend that the authority apply for a placement order in respect of the child. The adoption panel is required to consider the case of every child referred to it by the adoption agency and to make a recommendation to the agency as to whether the child should be placed for adoption.

16.48 In considering what recommendation to make, the adoption panel must have regard to the welfare principle; the factors set out in the welfare checklist; issues relating to the child's religious persuasion, racial origin and cultural and linguistic background; the duty to consider the whole range of powers available;

and the no order principle. The panel must also consider and take into account the reports and other information submitted to it by the adoption agency and described above. It may request the agency to obtain any other additional, relevant information, which the panel considers necessary, and must obtain legal advice in relation to the case. It must thus be satisfied that the agency's proposal for adoption was arrived at having explored and discounted all the options available (AAR 2005, reg 18; see *Adoption Statutory Guidance 2013*, paragraphs 2.70–2.71, and the NMS 2014).

## ADOPTION AGENCY'S DECISION

16.49 The adoption agency is under a mandatory duty to take into account the recommendation of the adoption panel in coming to a decision about whether the child should be placed for adoption, but no member of the adoption panel must take part in any decision made by the adoption agency. The adoption panel, therefore, is a separate entity from the agency, providing an important independent element, and providing impartiality and objectivity. The decision of the panel has to be considered independently by the adoption agency under the AAR 2005, which have to be complied with. These principles were endorsed in *Re P-B (A Child) (Adoption: Application for Placement Order)* [2006] EWCA Civ 1016, [2007] 1 FLR 1106. Additionally, in *Hofstetter and Hofstetter v Barnet London Borough Council* [2009] EWHC 3282 (Admin) the court (at [129]–[133]) set out the need for the agency to clarify the respective role of the panel and the agency decision makers; for the agency decision makers to be reminded of their role and the care with which they should carry out their functions; and for steps to be taken to ensure that as and when each decision is taken the reasons for it are made clear. In relation to the approach to be taken by the agency decision maker, Charles J suggested that, 'with a view to ensuring that the agency decision-maker approaches the making of the decision in the case, and thus a reconsideration of the case, with an open mind, and as the decision-maker it would be a good discipline and appropriate for him or her to take' the following steps:

- (i) list the material taken into account;
- (ii) identify the key arguments on both sides;
- (iii) ask whether he or she agrees with the process and approach of each of the relevant panels and is satisfied as to its fairness, and that both panels have properly addressed the arguments;
- (iv) consider whether any information he or she has that was not before the relevant panel has an impact on its reasons or recommendation;
- (v) identify the reasons given for the relevant recommendations that he or she does, or does not, wish to adopt; and

(vi) state: (a) the adopted reasons by cross-reference, repetition or otherwise; and (b) any further reasons for his or decision, when informing the prospective adopters of that decision.

16.50 The adoption agency's decision, with reasons for it, must be recorded in the child's case record. The agency must also notify the child's parent(s) or guardian of its decision, in writing. The father of the child who does not have parental responsibility should also be notified if his identity and whereabouts are known and if the agency considers it appropriate to do so (AAR 2005, reg 19, and see further under paras 16.43–16.44).

## SUMMARY OF PROCESS FOR DECIDING WHETHER A CHILD IS TO BE PLACED FOR ADOPTION

16.51 When considering whether a child should be placed for adoption:

(a) The agency sets up the child's case record.
(b) The agency provides counselling and information to the child and the parent(s) or guardian of the child, and ascertains their wishes and feelings.
(c) The agency obtains information about the child.
(d) The agency obtains information about the family.
(e) The agency prepares the child's permanence report.
(f) The agency sends the matter to the adoption panel for its recommendation and advice.
(g) On receiving the panel's recommendation, the agency decides whether or not the child should be placed for adoption, and sends written notification of the decision to the child's parent(s) or guardian.
(h) Where the child's parent(s) are prepared to consent to placement under ACA 2002, s 19 or s 20, the agency should ask Cafcass to appoint an officer of the service.

## ASSESSING AND APPROVING PROSPECTIVE ADOPTER(S)

### Counselling and information

16.52 Once it has been decided that a child is to be placed for adoption, the next step in the process is to assess and approve the prospective adopter(s) in accordance with the provisions set out in Part 4 of AAR 2005, which provides for a two-stage process. The first stage, set out in AAR 2005, regs 21–27, deals with the pre-assessment decision. This requires that before an application for assessment is accepted and before placing a child with prospective adopter(s), as set out in AAR 2005, reg 21, the adoption agency is under a duty to:

(a) provide a counselling service for the prospective adopter(s);
(b) in the case of a child from outside the United Kingdom (an ACA 2002, s 83 case – see Chapter 15), explain to the prospective adopter(s) the procedure for adopting a child from the country in question and the legal implications of so doing;
(c) in any other case, explain the legal implications of, and procedure in relation to, placement for adoption and adoption; and
(d) provide written information about the above matters.

16.53 See also *Adoption Statutory Guidance 2013*, Chapter 3 on preparing, assessing and approving prospective adopters.

16.54 The prospective adopter(s) should also be informed of the legal requirements which they will have to meet before they can be considered as prospective adopters(s). In this respect, it is always advisable for prospective adopter(s) to seek legal advice. The procedure for making the application to the agency to be considered as prospective adopter(s) should be explained. This includes giving information about enquiries, police checks and health checks that will be made. It also includes ensuring that the prospective adopter(s) know and understand the various stages of the assessment, approval, matching and placement process before the adoption application can be made; and explaining the review and complaints procedure. The prospective adopter(s) should also be informed that if the criminal record checks reveal that they or any adult member of their household has been convicted of a specified offence as defined in the *Adoption Statutory Guidance 2013* at paragraph 3.2, which includes conviction for sexual offences of a child or a person with a mental disorder, or offences concerning the possession of indecent images of children and offences involving bodily injury to a child, this will disqualify them. See also the *Draft Statutory Guidance* of July 2014, which is available at:

> https://assets.publishing.service.gov.uk/media/5a7c1dfbed915d210ade1af8/Draft_adoption_statutory_guidance.pdf

16.55 If, following the above information procedure, the adoption agency receives an application by a prospective adopter(s) for an assessment of their suitability to adopt a child, the adoption agency is required to set up a case record in respect of the applicant(s) and consider their suitability to adopt a child.

## Preparation for adoption

16.56 Where the agency is considering a person's/persons' suitability to adopt, the agency is required to make arrangements for the prospective adopter(s) to receive such preparation for adoption as the agency considers appropriate, as set out in AAR 2005, reg 24, including the provision of information about:

(a) the age range, sex, likely needs and background of children who may be placed for adoption by the adoption agency;
(b) the significance of adoption for a child and the child's family;
(c) contact between a child and the child's parent(s) or guardian or other relatives where a child is authorised to be placed for adoption or is adopted;
(d) the skills which are necessary for an adoptive parent(s);
(e) the adoption agency's procedures in relation to the assessment of a prospective adopter(s) and the placement of a child for adoption; and
(f) the procedure in relation to placement for adoption and to adoption.

## The prospective adopter's/adopters' case record

16.57 When an adoption agency receives a written application, in the form provided by the agency, from a prospective adopter(s), the agency must set up a case record in respect of the prospective adopter(s) and consider their suitability to adopt a child. The agency may ask the prospective adopter(s) for any further information it may reasonably require (AAR 2005, reg 21). The case record must include the information set out in AAR 2005, regs 22(3) and 23.

## Police checks

16.58 In assessing suitability to adopt, the agency must first take steps to obtain, in respect of the prospective adopter(s) and any member of their household who is over the age of 18, an enhanced criminal record certificate within the meaning of Police Act 1997, s 115, including the matters specified in s 115(6A).

16.59 If a prospective adopter or a member of his household aged 18 or over has been convicted of a specified offence committed at the age of 18 or over, or has been cautioned by a constable in respect of any such offence which he admitted when the caution was administered, he is not to be considered suitable to adopt a child. The specified offences are:

(a) an offence against a child;
(b) an offence specified in AAR 2005, Sch 3, Pt 1 (rape and sex offences);
(c) a breach of any of the prohibitions and restrictions relating to pornography in relation to prohibited goods, which include indecent photographs of

children under the age of 16 years (see Customs and Excise Management Act 1979, s 170, and Customs Consolidation Act 1876, s 42);

(d) any other offence involving bodily injury to a child, other than an offence of common assault or battery.

16.60 In addition, an adoption agency may not consider a person suitable to adopt a child if he, or any member of his household aged 18 or over, has been convicted of, or cautioned for any of the following offences (and, when cautioned, admitted the offence), even though these offences have been repealed:

(a) an offence specified in AAR 2005, Sch 3, Pt 2, para 1 committed at the age of 18 or over (rape and sex offences); or
(b) offences which fall within AAR 2005, Sch 3, para 2 or para 3 (other sex offences and offences of indecency).

16.61 Where an adoption agency becomes aware that a prospective adopter or a member of his household has been convicted of or cautioned for any of these offences, the agency must notify the prospective adopter as soon as possible that he cannot be considered suitable to adopt a child (AAR 2005, reg 23).

16.62 Where the police check discloses an offence which does not fall within AAR 2005, reg 23(3) or (4), the adoption agency has a discretion whether or not to proceed with the application. Its decision and reasons for it must be placed on the prospective adopter's case record. The information received by the agency is confidential and, if the application is a joint one, must not be disclosed to the person's partner or spouse (Police Act 1997, s 124; see also *Adoption Statutory Guidance 2013*, paragraphs 3.24–3.32).

## Further information

16.63 If the adoption agency forms a view, after carrying out the police checks and the preparation work described above, that the prospective adopter(s) may be suitable to adopt a child, the agency must obtain the information required under AAR 2005, Sch 4, Pt 1 and the following:

(a) a written medical report from a registered practitioner about the health of the prospective adopter(s) following a full examination, covering the matters set out in AAR 2005, Sch 4, Pt 2, unless the agency has received advice from its medical adviser that such a report is unnecessary;
(b) references, and it must prepare a report of each of the interviews with the persons nominated by the prospective adopter(s) to provide references for them;

(c) it must ascertain from the local authority in whose area the prospective adopter(s) have their home whether it has any information on the adopter(s) which may be of relevance to the assessment, and if so, obtain a written report from that authority (see *Adoption Statutory Guidance 2013*, paragraphs 3.33–3.41).

## Prospective adopter(s)' – first stage report

16.64 A written report (prospective adopter's report) must then be prepared by the agency, which must include the information set out in AAR 2005, Sch 4, Pt 1 and the following, as set out in AAR 2005, reg 25(5):

(a) the information about the prospective adopter(s) as specified in AAR 2005, Sch 4, Pt 1;
(b) a summary, written by the agency's medical adviser, of the state of health of the prospective adopter(s);
(c) any relevant information from the local authority in whose area the prospective adopter(s) live;
(d) the observations of the agency on the police checks, the preparation for adoption and the provision of information about adoption;
(e) the agency's assessment of the prospective adopter's/adopters' suitability to adopt a child; and
(f) any other information which the agency considers relevant.

16.65 In relation to an intercountry adoption case under ACA 2002 s 83 (see Chapter 15), the prospective adopter's/adopters' report must also include the following further information:

(a) the name of the country from which the prospective adopter(s) wish to adopt ('country of origin');
(b) confirmation that the prospective adopter(s) meets the obligations requirements to adopt from the country of origin;
(c) additional information obtained as a consequence of the requirements of the country of origin; and
(d) the adoption agency's assessment of the prospective adopter(s) suitability to adopt a child who is habitually resident outside the British Islands.

## Matters to be taken into account

16.66 In making any report in respect of the suitability of any person to adopt, as set out in Suitability of Adopters Regulations 2005 (SI 2005/1712) (SAR 2005), reg 3, the adoption agency must take into account:

(a) any information obtained as a consequence of providing counselling services to the prospective adopter(s);
(b) any information obtained in consequence of the preparation for adoption (see paras 16.56–16.57);
(c) any information received as a consequence of obtaining an enhanced criminal record certificate (see paras 16.58–16.62);
(d) the information about the prospective adopter(s) obtained under AAR 2005 Sch 4, Pt 1;
(e) in the case of a Convention adoption, any additional information obtained about the prospective adopter(s) which is required in preparation of the prospective adopter's/adopters' report as a consequence of AFER 2005, reg 15(4) (see also para 16.64);
(e) the written reports of the medical practitioner, the referees and the local authority (see para 16.63).

16.67 Where the agency is assessing the suitability of a couple to adopt, it should also have regard to the need for stability and permanence in their relationship (SAR 2005, reg 4(2)). Where a person is putting himself forward as a single prospective adopter, and that person is in a relationship, the stability and permanence of the relationship may nevertheless be a relevant factor to be considered and assessed.

16.68 Where the adoption agency is of the opinion that the prospective adopter(s) are unlikely to be considered suitable to adopt a child, it may proceed to make the prospective adopter's/adopters' report even though it has not obtained all the information required by the regulations (AAR 2005, reg 25(7)). In coming to its decision, the matters taken into account by the adoption agency may be limited to any information received which is specified in AAR 2005, Sch 4, Pt 1; the medical report; the referee's report; and the report from the local authority in whose area the prospective adopter(s) live (SAR 2005, reg 5).

16.69 On obtaining and assessing all the information required under regs 25–26, the adoption agency is required to decide whether the prospective adopters are suitable to adopt a child or not, and make a record of its decision in the prospective adopter's/adopters' report. Regulation 27(2) requires the adoption agency, where reasonably practicable, to make its decision within two months from the date on which it notified the prospective adopter(s) that it had decided to proceed with the pre-assessment process. A longer period may be necessary where there has been delay in obtaining the information set out above; or where the prospective adopter(s) so request, or for other good reason.

16.70 If the adoption agency decides that the prospective adopter(s) are not suitable to adopt a child the agency must, as soon as practicable after making the decision, notify the prospective adopter(s) in writing of its decision and the reasons for its decision (AAR 2005, reg 27(5)).

16.71 If the adoption agency decides that the prospective adopter(s) are suitable to adopt a child, it should notify the prospective adopter(s) of its decision and that their application will be presented to the adoption panel, give them a copy of the prospective adopter's report, and invite them to send any observations in writing to the agency within 10 working days beginning with the date on which the notice is sent. At the end of the 10 days, or earlier if a response is received from the prospective adopter(s), the adoption agency must send to the adoption panel the prospective adopter's report, the prospective adopter's/adopters' observations; the report of the registered medical practitioner; the reports on the interviews with the referees; the local authority's report; and any other relevant information obtained by the agency (AAR 2005, reg 25(8)). The agency should also obtain any other relevant information requested by the panel, and send it to the panel (AAR 2005, regs 8–10).

16.72 The adoption agency must also explain to the prospective adopter(s) that they must notify the adoption agency within six months of the date on which notification is given if they wish to continue with the assessment process (AAR 2005, reg 27(4)).

16.73 Once the adoption agency receives confirmation from the prospective adopter(s) that they wish to continue with their application to adopt a child, the adoption process enters the second stage. AAR 2005, reg 29 requires the adoption agency to prepare a written plan in conjunction with the prospective adopter(s) ('the prospective adopter(s)' assessment plan'), which includes the procedure for assessing the prospective adopter's/adopters' suitability to adopt; the applicable time scale; details of the arrangements for the prospective adopters to receive any additional counselling or preparation for adoption; details of any training and information about the prospective adopters'/adopters' role in the assessment process. Information should also be given on the process for submitting representations to the independent review panel (IRP) or applying to the Secretary of State for a review by an IRP under reg 30B(5)(c) and information on any other matter that the agency considers relevant. The agency should provide any necessary training and assessment in order to provide a report of the asscssment plan.

16.74 The time scale for completing the second stage is four months, but this period can be extended if necessary, either at the request of the adoption agency or if the prospective adopter(s) need more time to complete the second stage process.

## Prospective adopter(s)' – second stage report

16.75 The adoption agency is required to prepare a written report which includes all the information set out in AAR 2005, reg 30. This is not dissimilar to the report prepared under reg 25 in the first stage of the process, but in particular includes specific information about the prospective adopter's/adopters' family; a summary written by the agency's medical adviser of the state of health of the prospective adopter(s); the agency's assessment of the prospective adopter's/adopters' suitability to adopt, and any other information which the agency considers relevant.

## Procedure where a prospective adopter is considered unsuitable to adopt

16.76 Where the adoption agency, having received all the relevant information in relation to the assessment of the prospective adopter(s), concludes that the prospective adopter(s) are unlikely to be considered suitable to adopt a child, it may prepare the prospective adopter's/adopters' report notwithstanding that the agency may not have received all the required information. In this event the adoption agency must notify the prospective adopter(s) of their decision; give them a copy of their report; invite them to send any observations in writing to the agency within 40 working days beginning with the date on which the notification is sent, and explain to them that the adoption agency may in exceptional circumstances extend this time scale. As soon as possible after any observations are received, the adoption agency must decide whether or not to refer the case to an adoption panel or to proceed to make a decision under AAR 2005, reg 30B without such referral.

16.77 If the agency decides to refer the case to the adoption panel, it must send to the adoption panel the prospective adopter's/adopters' report and the prospective adopter's/adopters' observations; the written reports and references, if so advised by the agency's medical adviser, and other relevant information obtained by the agency.

# FUNCTION OF THE ADOPTION PANEL

16.78 On receiving the documents and information, the panel is required to consider the case and make a recommendation to the agency as to whether the prospective adopter(s) are suitable to adopt a child. In considering what recommendation to make, the adoption panel must consider and take into account all the information and reports submitted to it; it may request the agency to obtain other relevant information; and it may obtain legal advice (AAR 2005, reg 30A(2)). Where the agency's decision is that the prospective adopter(s) are unsuitable to adopt, the panel may request that a further prospective adopter's/ adopters' report be prepared covering all the matters set out in reg 30(2) or recommend that the prospective adopter(s) are not suitable to adopt a child (AAR 2005, reg 30A (3)).

16.79 Where the adoption panel makes a positive recommendation to the adoption agency, the panel may advise the agency about the number of children the prospective adopter(s) may be suitable to adopt, their age(s), sex(es), likely needs and background(s) (AAR 2005, reg 30A(4)).

16.80 Before making its recommendations, the panel may invite the prospective adopter(s) to attend a meeting of the panel (AAR 2005, reg 30A(5)).

## Determining suitability to adopt

16.81 It is for the adoption agency to decide whether a prospective adopter(s) are suitable to adopt; no member of the panel may take any part in the agency's decision. In determining the suitability of a prospective adopter(s), as set out in SAR 2005, reg 4, the adoption agency must take into account:

(a) the prospective adopter's report;
(b) the medical report and the report of the referees;
(c) the recommendation of the adoption panel;
(d) any other relevant information obtained by the agency at the request of the panel;
(e) where AFER 2005, reg 12 applies, any additional information obtained as a consequence of AFER 2005, Pt 3, Ch 1;
(f) the need for stability and permanence.

16.82 Where the agency is considering the suitability of a couple to adopt, it should have regard to the need for stability and permanence in their relationship (SAR 2005, reg 4(2)).

## Notification to prospective adopter(s)

16.83 Where the adoption agency decides that the prospective adopter(s) are suitable to adopt a child, it must notify them in writing of the decision (AAR 2005, reg 30B (4)).

16.84 If the decision is negative, the adoption agency must notify the prospective adopter(s) in writing that it proposes not to approve them as suitable to adopt a child (a 'qualifying determination') with its reasons. The notification must include the recommendation of the adoption panel if that recommendation is different from the decision reached. It must also advise them that they may, within 40 working days, beginning with the date on which the notification is sent, either submit any representations they wish to make to the agency, or apply to the Secretary of State (in Wales, the National Assembly) for a review of the qualifying determination by an independent review panel (AAR 2005, reg 30B(5)).

16.85 If the prospective adopter(s) do not make any representations or apply for a review, the adoption agency should proceed to make its decision and notify the prospective adopter(s) of it in writing, together with its reasons. If, on the other hand, representations are made, these, together with all the relevant information, must be resubmitted to the adoption panel for further consideration. The panel must reconsider the case and make a fresh recommendation (AAR 2005, reg 30B(7)). The adoption panel is required to reconsider the case and make a fresh recommendation of the prospective adopter's/adopters' suitability to adopt a child.

16.86 The agency must then make a decision on the case on the basis of matters set out at para 16.81 (a)–(f). Where the referral to the adoption panel was made on receipt of representations, the agency must also take into account both the original recommendation of the panel and the fresh recommendation. Where the prospective adopter(s) have applied for an independent review, the adoption agency must make a decision only after taking into account any recommendation of the independent review panel (see para 16.87) and the original recommendation of the adoption panel (AAR 2005, reg 30B(8)–(9)). It must then send a written notification of its decision to the prospective adopter(s). If the decision is negative, it must also state its reason for the decision and send a copy of the adoption panel's recommendation if this is different from the agency's decision. (AAR 2005, reg 30B(10). It is also required to send to the Secretary of State a copy of the notification sent to the prospective adopter(s) (AAR 2005, reg 30B(11)).

## INDEPENDENT REVIEW OF QUALIFYING DETERMINATION

### Independent review panel

16.87 If prospective adopter(s) seek an independent review of a qualifying determination as described at para 16.84, the review is undertaken by a panel constituted for the purpose by the Secretary of State or the National Assembly for Wales. The review panel is independent of adoption agencies. The review is not an appeal process; nor does it deal with complaints against an adoption agency. A separate procedure for making complaints is available. The independent review panel cannot overturn the decision of the adoption agency. It may only review the information before it and request further information. It can then make a recommendation to the adoption agency as to the suitability or otherwise of the prospective adopter/adopters to adopt a child of the specified age range, sex, needs and background, but not a specific child. The adoption agency is required to take into account any recommendation of the independent review panel when making its final decision on the prospective adopter's/adopters' suitability to adopt a child (Independent Review of Determinations (Adoption and Fostering) Regulations 2009 (SI 2009/395) (IRD(AF)R 2009), reg 11).

## Processing an application for review

16.88 The prospective adopter(s) must, within 40 days (in Wales, 20 days) from the date of the qualifying determination, apply for a review. The application must be made in writing and set out the reasons/grounds for the request for review (AAR 2005, reg 30B(5)(c), (5A)). The application should be acknowledged by the Secretary of State.

16.89 A panel is then constituted by the Secretary of State or the National Assembly for Wales.

16.90 The prospective adopter(s) and the adoption agency must be notified of the date, time and venue of the panel meeting.

## Procedure to be followed by the adoption agency

16.91 Where an adoption agency receives notification of a prospective adopter's/adopters' request for a review, the agency is obliged, within 10 working days of receipt of that notification, as set out in AAR 2005, reg 30C, to send to the Secretary of State the following information:

(a) all the documents and information which was placed before the adoption panel in accordance with AAR 2005, reg 30;
(b) any relevant information in relation to the prospective adopter(s) which was obtained by the agency after the documents and information were passed to the adoption panel;
(c) the qualifying determination and the reasons for it (see reg 30B(5)(a) and (b)).

## Appointment of the panel and conduct of review

16.92 Upon receipt of the application for review, the Secretary of State must take the following steps:

(a) notify the agency which made the qualifying determination that an application has been made by sending to the agency a copy of the application;
(b) send a written acknowledgement to the applicant and notify the applicant that the agency has been notified of the application for a review;
(c) fix a date, time and venue for the panel to meet for the purpose of reviewing the application;
(d) inform the agency concerned and the applicant of the steps set out above under (c); and
(e) inform the applicant in writing that the applicant may, if the applicant so wishes, provide to the panel further details of the grounds of the application within a period of three weeks before the review meeting and orally at the meeting (IRD(AF)R 2009, reg 18).

## Who may attend before the independent review panel?

16.93 The prospective adopter(s) may attend the meeting of the panel with a McKenzie friend. Prospective adopter(s) who have any disability may bring a helper. Where English is not the prospective adopter's/adopters' first language, an interpreter may also be brought. The expenses of the helper or interpreter will not, though, be paid by the panel. It will be for the prospective adopter(s) to make the necessary arrangements and meet the expenses. The independent review panel may ask the prospective adopter(s) questions. The adoption agency may be represented. It is advisable for the person who carried out the original assessment to attend so that any questions the panel may have may be addressed.

## Procedure of the independent review panel

16.94 It is the duty of the independent review panel to review the qualifying determination and make a recommendation to the adoption agency which made it as to whether a prospective adopter(s) is suitable to be an adoptive parent(s). The panel will consider and take into account the agency's determination and reasons and the adoption panel's recommendations. It will also have regard to all the information which was presented to the adoption panel, and any other information that has come to light since its decision, together with the grounds for review and information provided by the prospective adopter(s). The panel may request the adoption agency to obtain any other relevant information which the panel considers necessary or to provide such other assistance the panel may request. It may also obtain such legal advice as it considers necessary in relation to the case. Where the panel makes a recommendation that the applicant is suitable to adopt a child, the panel may consider and give advice to the adoption agency about the number of children the applicant may be suitable to adopt (IRD(AF)R 2009, reg 11).

### Recommendation of the independent review panel

16.95 The independent review panel's recommendation will be that of the majority. The panel may either give its decision on the date fixed for the review or reserve its decision. The recommendation of the panel, with its reasons for it, and whether the recommendation was a unanimous one or by a majority, has to be recorded immediately in a document, which must be signed and dated by the chairman. It is the duty of the Secretary of State or the National Assembly for Wales (as the case may be), without delay, to send a copy of the recommendation to the adoption agency which made the qualifying determination and to the prospective adopter(s) (IRD(AF)R 2009, reg 20).

## REVIEW OF APPROVAL

16.96 Where an adoption agency has approved a person as suitable to adopt a child, the agency is under a duty to review the approval whenever it considers it necessary to do so, and in any event must do so not more than one year (in Wales, two years) after approval, and thereafter at intervals of not more than one year (in Wales, two years) (AAR 2005, reg 30D). This is to ensure that there has not been any change in the circumstances of the prospective adopter(s), such as the separation of a couple, the birth of a child or a criminal conviction. The review should encompass all the relevant factors under SAR 2005, reg 4.

16.97 In carrying out the review, the adoption agency must make such inquiries and obtain such further information as it considers necessary in order to review whether the prospective adopter(s) continue to be suitable to adopt a child, and must seek and take into account the views of the prospective adopter(s) (AAR 2005, reg 30D(3).

## TERMINATION OF APPROVAL

16.98 If the adoption agency considers that the prospective adopter(s) are no longer suitable to adopt a child, it must:

(a) prepare a prospective adopter's/adopters' review report, which must include the agency's reasons and any other information which the agency considers relevant;
(b) notify the prospective adopter(s) that their case has been referred to the adoption panel; and
(c) give them a copy of the report, inviting them to send any observations to the agency within 10 working days beginning with the date on which the report is sent (AAR 2005, reg 30D(4).

16.99 If the prospective adopter(s) make representations, these, together with the prospective adopter's/adopters' review report, are resubmitted to the adoption panel. If the adoption panel requires further information, the adoption agency must provide it (AAR 2005, reg 30D(5).

16.100 The panel is required to consider the review report, together with the prospective adopter's/adopters' observations and any other information passed to it, following which the panel must make a recommendation to the agency as to whether the prospective adopter(s) continue to be suitable. Thereafter, the adoption agency must decide whether the prospective adopter(s) continue to be suitable to adopt a child. If the decision is negative, the procedure outlined above in respect of qualifying determinations must be followed (AAR 2005, reg 30D(4)–(8)). See also NMS 2014, Standard 13.

## MATCHING AND APPROVAL OF PLACEMENTS

16.101 An adoption agency is under a duty to take certain steps relating to the proposed placement of a child for adoption. These include an information-gathering and information-giving process; an assessment of the adoptive family's needs; the preparation of an adoption placement report; and the submission of the information to the adoption panel for its recommendation and decision. At this stage, the agency needs to consider and compare alternative prospective adopter(s) for a particular child and assess their respective abilities to meet that child's needs.

### The proposed placement

16.102 When the adoption agency has identified prospective adopter(s) for a child, and is considering placing the child with them, as set out in AAR 2005, reg 31, the adoption agency is under a duty:

(a) to provide the prospective adopter(s) with the child's permanence report and any other relevant information;
(b) to meet the prospective adopter(s) to discuss the placement;
(c) to ascertain the views of the prospective adopter(s) about the placement and the agency's proposals for contact with the child;
(d) to provide a counselling service for, and any further information to, the prospective adopter(s).

### Assessment of needs and preparation of the adoption placement report

16.103 Where the adoption agency considers that the proposed placement should proceed, if the agency is a local authority, it must, before placing a child for adoption, carry out an assessment of the needs of the child and the prospective adopter(s) and any children of the prospective adopter(s), to ascertain whether the prospective adoptive family needs adoption support services. Where the agency is a registered adoption society, it must notify the prospective adopter(s) that they may request that such an assessment be carried out by the local authority in whose area they live. If they do so request, the agency must pass to the relevant authority, at its request, a copy of the child's permanence report and the prospective adopter's/adopters' report (AAR 2005, reg 31(2)).

16.104 The agency must also consider the arrangements for allowing any person contact with the child, and whether the parental responsibility of any parent(s) or guardian or of the prospective adopter(s) is to be restricted to any extent. As set out in AAR 2005, reg 31(2)(d), it must prepare a written report, referred to as 'the adoption placement report', which should include:

(a) the reason for proposing the placement;
(b) the information gathered by the agency when it informed the prospective adopter(s) of the placement (see paras 16.43 and 16.51);
(c) where the agency is a local authority, its proposal for the provision of adoption support services for the adoptive family;
(d) the proposal for contact between the child and any person;
(e) any other relevant information.

## Referral to the adoption panel

16.105 Once an adoption agency decides to place the case before the adoption panel for its consideration, the agency must notify the prospective adopter(s) of its intention to do so and give them a copy of the adoption placement report. The notification must include an invitation to the prospective adopter(s) to make any observations in writing to the agency within 10 days beginning with the date on which the notification is sent.

16.106 At the end of the 10-day period, or earlier if the observations have been received, the agency must send to the adoption panel the adoption placement report; the child's permanence report; the prospective adopter's report; and its observations. If the adoption panel requests further information in connection with the placement, the agency must provide that information to the panel (AAR 2005, reg 31(3)–(5)).

16.107 Where an adoption agency (A) intends to refer a proposed placement to the adoption panel and another agency (B) made the decision that the child should be placed for adoption or that the prospective adopter(s) are suitable to be adoptive parent(s), agency A may only refer the proposed adoption placement to the panel if it has consulted agency B about the proposed placement. When the decision is taken by agency A, it must open a child's record if it concludes that the child should be placed for adoption or open a prospective adopter's/adopters' record if the decision relates to the suitability of the prospective adopter(s) (AAR 2005, reg 31(6)–(8)).

### Functions of the adoption panel in relation to a proposed placement

16.108 The adoption panel must consider all the information placed before it and any other information provided to it. Where the decision was taken by a local authority, the panel must consider the local authority's proposals for the provision of adoption support services for the adoptive family; the arrangements the adoption agency proposes for allowing contact with the child; and whether the parental responsibility of any parent or guardian or of the prospective adopter(s) should be restricted, and if so, the extent of the proposed restrictions.

16.109 When making a recommendation for the placement of a child for adoption with a particular prospective adopter(s), the panel is permitted to give advice to the agency about any of the matters referred to above. The panel may make the recommendation for the placement with a particular prospective adopter(s) only if:

(a) all three decisions – to recommend that the child be placed for adoption, that the prospective adopter(s) are suitable to adopt a child, and that the child be placed with the prospective adopter(s) – are made at the same meeting; or
(b) the adoption agency, or another adoption agency, has already made a decision that the child should be placed for adoption and that the prospective adopter(s) are suitable to adopt a child.

16.110 In other words, the recommendation on the placement may not be made before the recommendations that the child be placed for adoption, and that the prospective adopter(s) are suitable to adopt (AAR 2005, reg 32(1)–(5)).

## THE ADOPTION AGENCY'S DECISION

16.111 On receiving the adoption panel's recommendation, the adoption agency must decide whether or not the child should be placed for adoption with the prospective adopter(s). In making that decision, it must take into account the recommendation of the adoption panel and apply the welfare principle and the adoption welfare test. No member of the adoption panel may take part in this decision. As set out in AAR 2005, reg 33, the agency must then:

(a) notify the prospective adopter(s) of the decision in writing;
(b) notify in writing the parent or guardian, if his whereabouts are known, and the father of the child, if his identity is known, that the child is to be placed for adoption;
(c) if the decision is to place the child with the prospective adopter(s), explain to the child, in an appropriate manner having regard to the age and understanding of the child, its decision; and
(d) place on the child's case records:

    (i) the prospective adopter's/adopters' report,
    (ii) the adoption placement report and the prospective adopter's/adopters' observations,
    (iii) the written record of the proceedings of the adoption panel and its recommendation and reasons for the recommendation, and
    (iv) any advice given by the panel to the agency and the record of the notification of the agency's decision.

## PLACEMENT AND REVIEWS

### Procedure to be followed before placement

16.112 Once the decision is taken to place a child with the identified prospective adopter(s), the adoption agency must, as soon as possible, send the prospective adopter(s) an adoption placement plan in respect of the child. The adoption placement plan must include the information set out in AAR 2005, Sch 5 (the adoption placement plan) (AAR 2005, reg 35(1) and (2)).

16.113 Where the child already has his home with the prospective adopter(s), the adoption agency must notify the prospective adopter(s) in writing of the date on which the child is placed for adoption with them by that agency (AAR 2005, reg 35(5)).

16.114 A child who is less than six weeks old should not be placed for adoption unless the parent(s) or guardian of the child have agreed in writing that the child may be placed for adoption, save in cases where there is a placement order in place in respect of that child (AAR 2005, reg 35(4)).

16.115 The agency is authorised to place the child for adoption with the prospective adopter(s) only after:

(a) it has been notified by the prospective adopter(s) that they wish to proceed with the placement;

(b) it has sent to the prospective adopter's/adopters' general practitioner written notification of the proposed placement, together with a written report of the child's health history and current state of health;

(c) it has sent to the local authority (if that authority is not the adoption agency) and integrated care board or local health board (Wales) in whose area the prospective adopter(s) have their home, and to the National Health Service Commissioning Board if the prospective adopter(s)' home is in England, written notification of the proposed placement; and

(d) where the child is of compulsory school age, it has included in the notification to the local education authority in whose area the prospective adopter(s) have their home, written notification of the proposed placement; and information about the child's educational history, and whether the child has been or is likely to be assessed for special educational needs under the Children and Families Act 2014.

16.116 The adoption agency must notify the prospective adopter(s) in writing of any change to the adoption placement plan and must place on the child's case records a copy of the adoption placement plan and any amendments made to that plan. Where the child is less than six weeks old and a placement order has not been made, but the parent(s) have agreed to the placement, a copy of the agreement must be placed on the child's record (AAR 2005, reg 35).

## Reviews

16.117 Where an adoption agency is authorised to place a child for adoption but has not done so, the agency must carry out a review of the child's case not more than three months after the date on which the agency was first authorised to place the child, and thereafter not more than six months after the date of the first review, until the child is placed for adoption (AAR 2005, reg 36(1)).

16.118 Where a child has been placed for adoption, the agency must carry out a review not more than four weeks after the date on which the child was placed for adoption (the first review); and again not more than three months after the first review; and thereafter not more than six months after the date of the previous review, unless the child is returned to the agency by the prospective adopter(s) or an adoption order is made. The adoption agency must also ensure that the child and the prospective adopter(s) are visited within one week of the placement, and thereafter at least once a week for four weeks until the first review and thereafter at such frequency as the agency decides at each review. Written reports of each such visit must be made. Advice and assistance to the prospective adopter(s) must also be provided as the agency considers necessary (see AAR 2005, reg 36(1)–(4)).

## Matters to be considered on review

16.119 When carrying out a review, an adoption agency is under an obligation to ascertain, so far as is reasonably practicable, the views of the child having regard to his age and understanding and to take account of the views of the prospective adopter(s) with whom the child is placed for adoption, and the views of any other person the agency considers relevant. In addition, as set out in AAR 2005, reg 36(5) and (6), the agency must have regard to the following matters:

(a) whether the adoption agency remains satisfied that the child should be placed for adoption;
(b) the child's needs, welfare and development, and whether any changes need to be made to meet his needs or assist his development;
(c) the existing arrangements for contact and whether they should continue or be altered;
(d) the arrangements in relation to the exercise of parental responsibility for the child, and whether they should continue or should be altered;
(e) the arrangements for the provision of adoption support services for the adoptive family and whether there should be any reassessment of the need for those services;
(f) in consultation with the appropriate agencies, the arrangements for assessing and meeting the child's health care and educational needs;
(g) the frequency of the reviews.

16.120 Where the child is subject to a placement order but has not been placed at the time of the six-month review, the local authority must establish why the child has not been placed and consider what further steps should be taken in that respect and whether it remains satisfied that the child should be placed for adoption (AAR 2005, reg 36(7)).

## Notification of review

16.121 Any decision taken by the agency in consequence of the review must, as far as is reasonably practicable, be notified to:

(a) the child if he is of sufficient age and understanding;
(b) the prospective adopter(s); and
(c) any other relevant person.

16.122 The adoption agency must record in writing, in the child's case record, all the information it obtains during review visits, including the views expressed by the child; details of any proceedings of any meeting arranged by the agency to consider any aspect of the review of the case; and details of any decision made in the course of the review (AAR 2005, reg 36(8)–(10)).

## INDEPENDENT REVIEWING OFFICER

### Appointment of an independent reviewing officer

16.123 ChA 1989, s 25A, as amended, requires the local authority that is looking after a child, to appoint an independent reviewing officer (IRO) for that child's case. The IRO's function is to participate in the review process, monitor the local authority's functions and refer a case to Cafcass where appropriate (ChA 1989, s 25B). The local authority is under a general duty to review the child's case in accordance with Care Planning, Placement and Case Review (England) Regulations 2010 (SI 2010/959), Pt 6. Additionally, AAR 2005, reg 37(1) imposes a duty on a local authority, or a registered adoption society which is a voluntary organisation providing accommodation for a child, to appoint an IRO in respect of each child authorised to be placed for adoption, to carry out the functions set out in the ChA 1989. (Although the AAR 2005 refers to the functions of an IRO appointed under the Regulations to be those set out in s 26(2A), the Act does not contain such a provision. The functions of the IRO must therefore be the same as those of an IRO appointed under CA 1989, s 25B.)

### Qualification of the independent reviewing officer

16.124 The IRO must be a social worker registered in the register maintained under the Children and Social Work Act 2017 or in the register maintained by Social Care Wales under Regulation and Inspection of Social Care (Wales) Act 2016, s 80, or in a corresponding register maintained under the laws of Scotland and Northern Ireland. The IRO must have sufficient relevant social work experience to undertake the duties required of the independent reviewing officer under ChA 1989, s 26(2A) (AAR 2005, reg 37(2) and (3)).

16.125 As set out in AAR 2005, reg 37(4) and Care Planning Placement and Case Review (England) Regulations 2010, reg 46, a person who is an employee of the adoption agency may not be appointed as IRO if he is involved in the management of the case, or under the direct management of:

(a) person involved in the management of the case; or
(b) a person with management responsibilities in relation to a person involved in the management of the case; or
(c) a person with control over the resources allocated to the case.

### Functions of the independent reviewing officers

16.126 As set out in AAR 2005, reg 37(5)–(7), the IRO must, so far as is reasonably practicable:

(a) attend any meetings in connection with the review of the child's case and chair any such meeting that he attends;

(b) take steps to ensure that the review is conducted in accordance with AAR 2005, reg 36 and, in particular, to ensure that:

   (i) the child's views are understood and taken into account;
   (ii) the persons responsible for implementing the decision taken in consequence of the review are identified;
   (iii) any failure to review the case as provided for in the regulations (see para 16.83), or to take steps to make arrangements agreed at the review, is brought to the attention of persons at an appropriate level of seniority within the adoption agency (Care Planning Placement and Case Review (England) Regulations 2010, reg 36 and Pt 8);

(c) assist the child to obtain legal advice, if the child wishes to take proceedings on his own account, without the need for an adult to act for him, for example to apply for the revocation of a placement order, in which case, the IRO should ensure that the child has access to a suitable solicitor; or in all other cases to establish whether an appropriate adult is able and willing to provide such assistance to bring proceedings on the child's behalf. In the event that the child is not able to bring proceedings on his own account and no appropriate adult is available or willing to act on the child's behalf, and there is a risk of the child's human rights being breached. the IRO should consider whether it is appropriate to refer the case to Cafcass Legal. (Note also that pursuant to the Advocacy Services and Representations Procedure (Children) (Amendment) Regulations 2004, as amended, the local authorities have duties to make arrangements for the provision of advocacy services for children making or intending to make complaints under ChA 1989, ss 24D and 26(3).)

16.127 The adoption agency is required to inform the IRO of any significant failure to make arrangements agreed at a review and any significant change in the child's circumstances after a review that affects those arrangements. Significant changes include changes to the child's permanence plan such as placement breakdown. The IRO's role is to ensure that the local authority has made the appropriate arrangements and taken steps to implement any changes in the child's care plan. Where possible, if there is a problem, the IRO will seek to resolve any issues with the child's care plan through negotiations with the team responsible for the child's case.

## CONTACT

16.128 Where it has been decided to place a child for adoption, the adoption agency is required to consider what arrangements it should make for allowing any person contact with the child (the 'contact arrangements'). In doing so, the adoption agency is required to take account of the wishes and feelings of the parent(s) or guardian of the child. Where the father of the child does not have parental responsibility, but it is appropriate to take into account his wishes and feelings, the adoption agency must do so. It must take into account any advice given by the adoption panel and be guided by the welfare principle and the factors set out in the adoption welfare checklist (AAR 2005, reg 46(3)).

16.129 As set out in AAR 2005, reg 46(4), any arrangements the agency makes relating to contact must be notified to:

(a) the child if he is of sufficient age and understanding;
(b) the parent or guardian of the child if their whereabouts are known;
(c) the father of the child, if appropriate;
(d) any other person in whose favour there was a contact order; and
(e) any other relevant person.

16.130 Where an adoption agency decides that a child should be placed for adoption with a particular prospective adopter(s), the adoption agency is required to review the arrangements for contact in the light of the views of the prospective adopter(s) and any advice given by the adoption panel. If it is then proposed to make any changes to the arrangements which affects any person mentioned in para 16.129, it must seek the views of that person and take those views into account when deciding the arrangements for contact while the child remains in the placement. The adoption agency must set out the contact arrangements it should make for allowing any person contact with the child while placed for adoption with the prospective adopter(s). Any arrangements made must be placed in the placement plan and kept under review (see AAR 2005, reg 46(5)–(7)).

16.131 Pursuant to ACA 2002, s 7, an adoption agency may refuse contact that would otherwise be required by virtue of an order, if it is satisfied that it is necessary to do so to safeguard or promote the child's welfare. The refusal must be decided upon as a matter of urgency and should not have effect for more than seven days. ACA 2002, s 27(3) provides that regulations may make provisions as to the steps to be taken by the agency when it seeks to refuse contact; and the circumstances in which, and conditions upon which, the terms of an order made under ACA 2002, s 26 may be varied by agreement. AAR 2005, reg 47(1) requires the agency, as soon as the decision is made to refuse contact, to inform the child, if he is of sufficient age and understanding, and the person in whose favour the order under ACA 2002, s 26 was made and the prospective adopter(s) of the decision, the date of the decision, reasons for the decision and duration of the period (AAR 2005, reg 47(1) and (3)). As set out in AAR 2005, reg 47(2) and (3), the terms of the order under ACA 2002, s 6 may be varied by agreement between the agency and any person for whose contact with the child the order provides, subject to:

(a) the agreement of the child, if he is of sufficient age and understanding;
(b) where the child has been placed with prospective adopter(s), consultation with them before the agreement is reached; and
(c) written confirmation by the agency to the persons referred to at para 16.129 of the terms of that agreement (see also Chapter 7 and *Adoption Statutory Guidance 2013*, paragraphs 7.1–7.47, and NMS 2014, paragraph 8).

## THE ADOPTION AND CHILDREN ACT REGISTER

16.132 The Register is maintained by the Secretary of State. It contains information about children who are suitable for adoption; those who the adoption agency is satisfied ought to be placed for adoption; and prospective adopter(s) who are suitable to adopt a child. Where an adoption agency has determined that a child should be placed for adoption but is not placed due to the unavailability of prospective adopter(s), it must refer to the Register for inclusion in the Register within three months of the decision to place the child for adoption. Similar provisions apply in relation to prospective adopter(s) and, subject to the agreement of the prospective adopter(s), their details must be submitted for inclusion in the Register within three months. The Register is open for search to adoption agencies and prospective adopter(s), but see ACA 2002, s 129 in relation to disclosure of information contained in the Register. See, further, the Adoption and Children Act Register (Search and Inspection) Regulations 2017 (SI 2017/978).

## PROCEDURE FOR APPLYING FOR DIRECTIONS ON NOTIFICATION TO FATHERS AND RELATIVES

16.133 Where a local authority has to decide whether or not to notify a child's father or family members of their plan to place the child for adoption, especially when it concerns a baby that has been relinquished and the mother requests confidentiality, the issue needs to be determined at an early stage and with urgency and speed. If there is uncertainty on how to proceed and proceedings have not as yet been issued, an application should be made to the court for directions following the procedure set out in FPR 2010, Pt 19. Although it is not mandatory for a respondent to be named in the application for directions, it would be appropriate to consider the mother to be named as a respondent. The father with or without parental responsibility or family members should be served with or notified of the application or provided with any of the evidence filed in support of the application.

## Venue

16.134 The application must be heard in the High Court. Upon issue of the proceedings in the Family Court, the application should be referred to the designated family judge for consultation with the Family Division Liaison Judge as to whether the application should be allocated to a High Court Judge or a s 9 Deputy High Court Judge sitting in the Family Court or whether the proceedings should be transferred to the Family Division of the High Court.

## First initial directions hearing

16.135 Once that decision is made, the application should be listed for urgent initial directions on whether the child should be joined as a party and for a Cafcass officer to be appointed to act as the children's guardian in the application, and for the listing of a case management hearing.

## Case management

16.136 The Cafcass officer appointed as guardian for the child should attend the case management hearing. At the hearing the court will consider whether any further evidence should be filed to support the application, including the issue relating to the rights under the Convention for the Protection of Human Rights and Fundamental Freedoms of all the parties concerned, including those of the father and family members and give directions:

(a) for the guardian to file a report providing an analysis and recommendations;
(b) consider whether the mother should provide her account in a written statement and/or whether she should be required to give oral evidence;
(c) for filing of written submissions; and
(d) for listing of the final hearing of the application with specific directions for the application to be given priority.

The parties will be required to give a time estimate, allowing sufficient time for evidence and submissions, and for a reasoned judgment to be given.

16.137 Where the local authority has commenced proceedings under the ChA 1989, s 31 for a care order and/or under ACA 2002 for a placement order, any application for the father and/or members of the extended family to be notified of the proceedings, served with the application or joined as parties, should be made within the care proceedings following the procedure set out in FPR 2010, Pt 18. The directions in the Pt 18 proceedings will, where appropriate, follow those set out in para 16.136.

Chapter 17

# Intermediary Services for Persons Adopted before 30 December 2005

## INTRODUCTION

17.1 ACA 2002, s 98(1) provides for regulations to be made to assist persons adopted before 30 December 2005, who have attained the age of 18 years, to obtain information about their adoption, and to facilitate contact between them and their relatives. ACA 2002 s 98(1A), which was inserted into the Act by the Children and Families Act 2014 and came into force from 25 July 2014, provides for regulations to be made for the purposes of facilitating contact between persons with a prescribed relationship to a person adopted before 30 December 2005. For these purposes, 'relative' means any person who (but for his adoption) would have been related to the adopted person by blood (including half-blood), marriage or civil partnership (ACA 2002, s 98(7)). 'Prescribed relationship' means a relationship whereby a person (who is not a relative of the adopted person) is related to the adopted person: (a) by blood (including half-blood), marriage or civil partnership; or (b) by virtue of the adopted person's adoption (Adoption Information and Intermediary Services (Pre-Commencement Adoptions) Regulations 2005 (SI 2005/890) (AIIS(PCA)R 2005), reg 2A). It also makes provision for regulations to require registered adoption support agencies, the Registrar General and adoption agencies to disclose information or restrict the disclosure of information. The section thus provides the framework for a very specific service to be provided to persons who were adopted before 30 December 2005, and the birth families of such persons, to obtain information about each other and to facilitate contact between them. The aim is to address the difficulties faced by this class of adopted persons who, but for these provisions, would have had little or no information enabling them to trace persons from whom they have been separated by adoption.

17.2 Pursuant to ACA 2002, s 98, the AIIS(PCA)R 2005, as amended by the Adoption Information and Intermediary Services (Pre-Commencement Adoptions) (Amendment) Regulations 2014 (SI 2014/2696), which came into force 31 October 2014 and the Adoption Information and Intermediary Services (Pre-Commencement Adoptions) (Amendment) Regulations (SI 2015/1685), which defines 'the corresponding Welsh regulations', identify the agencies which are to provide the services (known as 'intermediary services'), and to whom such services may be provided. The AIIS(PCA)R 2005 set out the procedure to be adopted by both the applicant who seeks such services and the agency which provides them. This regulatory structure enables an intermediary agency to seek information to assist an adopted adult person and his adult birth relatives to obtain information about each other, subject to obtaining the necessary consents; to facilitate contact; and to offer support and advice to the persons concerned. The right to request this service is additional to the right which the adopted person has, on reaching the age of 18, to apply to the Registrar General for the information needed to obtain a certified copy of his birth record. It is also additional to the adopted person's right to apply to the appropriate adoption agency for access to his adoption records (see Chapters 19 and 20).

## WHO CAN PROVIDE INTERMEDIARY SERVICES?

17.3 Only a registered adoption support agency or an authorised adoption agency can provide intermediary services. The adoption support agency must be registered under Care Standards Act 2000, Pt 2 to provide intermediary services. These services are available only to adopted persons who have attained the age of 18 and must be provided in accordance with the requirements set out in the regulations. An adoption agency which is the appropriate agency in relation to an adopted person, and which provides information solely about that person's adoption, does not provide an intermediary service (AIIS(PCA)R2005, reg 4(2)). If these conditions are met, the agency constitutes an adoption support service for the purposes of ACA 2002, s 2(1) (see AIIS(PCA)R 2005, regs 3 and 5(3)).

## SERVICES TO BE PROVIDED

17.4 The intermediary agency is required to provide services:

(a) to assist a person adopted before 30 December 2005 who has attained the age of 18 to obtain information in relation to his adoption;
(b) to facilitate contact between that person and their relatives; and
(c) to facilitate contact between a person with a prescribed relationship to the relatives of the adopted person or a relative of an adopted person to contact the adopted person or a person with a prescribed relationship to the adopted person (AIIS(PCA)R 2005, regs 4 and 5). The services also include securing counselling, advice and other information to such persons and assisting a

relative of the adopted person to contact an adopted person (AIIS(PCA)R 2005, regs 5 and 10).

Regulation 5(2), which required for priority to be given to applications in respect of adoptions before 12 November 1975, was revoked as from 31 December 2014 (SI 2014/2696).

17.5 The intermediary agency should have the expertise to investigate; to gather information and assess it; and to contact, advise, prepare, support and counsel the individuals concerned. AIIS(PCA)R 2005, reg 4(2) distinguishes between the provision of an intermediary service by the intermediary agency and the function of the adoption agency to disclose information to the adopted person in relation to his adoption. The adoption agency is the first point of contact for an adopted person seeking information about his adoption and his family. The intermediary agency therefore needs to establish clearly what information is being sought by the applicant and whether the usual steps have already been taken to trace the person he wishes to contact or about whom he seeks more information.

## PROCEDURE ON RECEIPT OF THE APPLICATION

17.6 The intermediary agency may receive an application for intermediary services from:

(a) an adopted person for assistance in contacting a relative (see para 17.1 for meaning);
(b) a relative of an adopted person for assistance in contacting:

   (i) the adopted person, or
   (ii) a person with prescribed relationship (see para 17.1 for meaning) to the adopted person, or

(c) a person with a prescribed relationship to an adopted person for assistance in contacting a relative of an adopted person (AIIS(PCA)R 2005, reg 5).

On receipt of the application, before proceeding further, the intermediary agency must take reasonable steps to confirm:

(a) the identity of the applicant or any person acting on his behalf;
(b) the age of the applicant, to ensure that he is 18 or over;
(c) that any person acting on the applicant's behalf is authorised to do so;
(d) in the case of an application by a relative of the adopted person, that the applicant is related to the adopted person;

(e) in the case of an application by a person with a prescribed relationship to the adopted person, that the applicant does have a prescribed relationship with that person (AIIS(PCA)R 2005, reg 11).

The applicant and the subject of the application must both be aged 18 or over. If, during the course of the inquiry, it is discovered that the subject of the application is or may be under the age of 18, the application should not be proceeded with (AIIS(PCA)R 2005, reg 5).

## RESTRICTION ON PROCEEDING WITH AN APPLICATION FROM A RELATIVE FOR ASSISTANCE

17.7 In any case where the intermediary agency receives an application from a person who is a relative or from a person with a prescribed relationship to the adopted person for assistance in contacting the adopted person it must not proceed until it has confirmation from the adoption agency of the absence of any veto from the adopted person, or without the consent of the adopted person (AIIS(PCA)R 2005, reg 5A(1) and (2)). The requirement for obtaining the adopted person's consent does not apply where the adopted person has died, or the intermediary agency determines that the adopted person is incapable of giving informed consent.

17.8 In all instances where consent of the adopted person is required, the intermediary agency must take all reasonable steps to ensure that the adopted person has sufficient information to make an informed decision (AIIS(PCA)R 2005, reg 5A (6) and (7)).

17.9 The appropriate adoption agency must, if the adopted person has notified it in writing that they do not wish to be contacted or that they only wish to be contacted in certain circumstances, keep a written record of the veto on the adopted person's case record and ensure that it is made known to any intermediary agency that contacts it in relation to an application for assistance in making contact with the adopted person ((AIIS(PCA)R 2005, reg 8).

17.10 In the case of an application by a person with a prescribed relationship to the adopted person for assistance in contacting a relative of the adopted person, the intermediary is prohibited from proceeding with the application if the adopted person does not consent to the disclosure. However, the regulations provide for an exception to this mandatory provision in two circumstances. These are: (a) where the intermediary has taken all reasonable steps to locate the adopted person without success; or (b) where the applicant is either the spouse, civil partner, child, grandchild or great grandchild of the adopted person and the applicant is seeking to contact a relative of the adopted person to obtain information about the medical history of the adopted person's relatives, unless that information, taken on its own or together with other information possessed by the person to whom it is disclosed, would enable the adopted person, any relative of the adopted person or any person with a prescribed relationship to the adopted person to be identified or traced (AIIS(PCA)R 2005, reg 5A(3) and (4)).

## DISCRETION WHETHER OR NOT TO PROCEED

17.11 The intermediary agency is not obliged to proceed with or continue with the application where it considers that it would not be appropriate to do so. In deciding whether it is appropriate to proceed or continue to proceed with the application, the agency must have regard to:

(a) the welfare of the applicant, the person in relation to whom the information is sought, and any other person who may be identified or otherwise affected by the application. Where the subject of the application is under 18 years of age, the agency must not proceed further with the application in relation to that subject;
(b) any views of the appropriate agency that was involved in the adoption, having regard to the information disclosed by them;
(c) any information obtained from the Adoption Contact Register; and
(d) all the other circumstances of the case (AIIS(PCA)R 2005, reg 6).

## CONSENT TO DISCLOSURE

17.12 Save where the subject has died or is incapable of giving consent, the intermediary agency must not disclose to the applicant any identifying information without the subject's consent. Where the subject has died or is determined to be incapable of giving consent, the agency is permitted to disclose only such identifying information (which, whether taken on its own or together with other information possessed by the applicant, would enable the subject to be identified), as it considers appropriate having regard to the factors set out above under para 17.11. The intermediary agency must take all reasonable steps to ensure that any person whose consent is required is given sufficient information to enable them to make an informed decision as to whether to give their consent.

## VETO BY THE ADOPTED PERSON

17.13 When the appropriate adoption agency has been identified, it is important to establish whether a veto exists, or whether the subject of the application has at any time expressed his views to the agency about future contact with any relative of his, or about his being approached in relation to contact. A veto applies where the subject is the adopted person and that person has notified the appropriate agency in writing that he does not wish to be contacted by an intermediary agency in relation to an application under the regulations; or that he wishes to be contacted only in specified circumstances or by specified persons (AIIS(PCA)R 2005, reg 8). It is the duty of the adoption agency, before the veto is registered, to take appropriate steps to advise and counsel the person of the implications, particularly where the veto is in absolute terms. The adopted person should also be informed of his right to amend or withdraw the veto at any time, and as to how this can be done, if he wishes to do so. Where the veto is a qualified one, the agency should ensure that the specified circumstances are clearly identified, and the person is advised about the need for him to be informed of special circumstances that could affect him, for example, a serious medical condition. ACA 2002, s 80 makes specific provision for recording information in Part 2 of the Adoption Contact Register about the wishes of the relatives of an adopted person regarding contact with the adopted person. An adopted person also has a right to specify the relatives with whom he does or does not wish to have contact. Both these provisions reflect respect for the person's right to privacy.

17.14 The agency must keep a written record of such a veto on the adopted person's case record and ensure that it is made known to any intermediary agency which requests information (AIIS(PCA)R 2005, reg 8(2)). If no veto is in place, the intermediary agency must ascertain from the adoption agency whether the subject has at any time expressed a view to the agency about future contact with any relative, or about being approached with regard to such contact; ascertain the agency's views as to whether the application is appropriate having regard to the relevant criteria (see para 17.11); and seek any other information required to trace the subject, enable him to make an informed decision on whether or not to consent to the disclosure sought, and offer him and the applicant counselling (AIIS(PCA)R 2005, reg 12).

## COUNSELLING

17.15 Once the identification is confirmed, the agency is required to provide written information about the availability of counselling, which must include details of the persons who offer such counselling services, and the fees that may be charged by such persons for the service (AIIS(PCA)R 2005, reg 10), to any person who:

(a) makes the application;
(b) is the subject of such an application and is considering whether to consent to the disclosure about himself to the applicant; or
(c) is an adopted person considering whether to consent to the application proceeding.

17.16 If the person concerned asks for counselling services to be provided, the intermediary agency must secure the provision of such services for him, by providing the service itself or arranging for counselling services to be provided, if the person is in England or Wales by another adoption agency or registered support agency; or if the person is in Scotland by a Scottish adoption agency; or if the person is in Northern Ireland by an appropriate voluntary organisation within the meaning of the Adoption (Northern Ireland) Order 1987 (SI 1987/2203) (NI 22), Art 2(2), or a Regional Board or any Health and Social Trust. If the person is outside the United Kingdom, the request should be made to any person or body outside the United Kingdom who appears to the agency to correspond in its functions to those provided in the United Kingdom (AIIS(PCA)R 2005, reg 10(3)–(5)).

17.17 The intermediary agency must take all reasonable steps to seek any other information required to trace the subject of the inquiry, to enable that person to make an informed decision whether to consent to the disclosure sought. The AIIS(PCA)R 2005 also require the intermediary agency to seek information for counselling the subject and the applicant before the decision is taken by him (AIIS(PCA)R 2005, reg 12).

17.18 These provisions clearly recognise the importance of counselling as a support service to assist the individuals concerned with the difficult feelings they will undoubtedly experience, and to help them to deal with the outcome of the inquiry and any decisions which they make. The further and perhaps more specialised services provided by the adoption support agency should also be considered in difficult cases. Before doing so, the intermediary agency must verify that the adoption support agency is registered to provide the particular service and has the expertise to do so.

## SOURCES OF INFORMATION

17.19 The intermediary agency has four main sources from which it may seek information: appropriate adoption agencies; a local authority; the Registrar General; and the courts.

## Contacting the appropriate adoption agency

17.20 The intermediary agency must take reasonable steps to contact the appropriate agency which was involved in the adoption, since that agency should have information on the adopted person's case records. The steps taken may include:

(a) requesting in writing from the Registrar General any information that may be relevant (see further paras 17.23–17.24);
(b) requesting in writing from the court that made the adoption order information about the identity of the appropriate adoption agency; and
(c) making enquiries of the local authority for the area where the adoption took place.

17.21 Where the appropriate agency has been identified, the intermediary agency must take all reasonable steps to contact that agency in order to ascertain whether a veto exists (see para 17.13) which prevents the disclosure of any information. Where there is no veto, the intermediary agency must take all reasonable steps to ascertain whether the adopted person has at any time expressed their views to the agency about:

(a) any future contact with any relatives of his, or
(b) any future contact between people with a prescribed relationship to him and his relatives, or
(c) his being approached with regard to such contact.

The intermediary agency must also ascertain the views of the appropriate agency as to whether the application for disclosure is appropriate (see under para 17.11).

17.22 The intermediary agency must also take all reasonable steps to seek any other information required for:

(a) tracing the adopted person and, where the adopted person is not the subject, any other subject;
(b) enabling the adopted person to make an informed decision as to whether to consent to: the disclosure of the identifying information about him; an application proceeding to facilitate contact between a relative of his and a person with a prescribed relationship to him; or contact with the applicant;
(c) enabling any other subject to make an informed decision as to whether he consents to the disclosure of identifying information about him or contact with the applicant;
(d) counselling the subject and, where they are not the subject, the adopted person, in relation to that decision; and
(e) counselling the applicant (AIIS(PCA)R 2005, reg 12).

The appropriate adoption agency is required to take all reasonable steps to provide the information requested from it and may disclose such information, including identifying information as is necessary, where a veto against disclosure does not exist (AIIS(PCA) 2005, reg 12(4)). The adoption agency may charge an intermediary agency such fee as it determines to be reasonable for providing the information requested or for giving its views (AIIS(PCA) 2005, reg 18(4)).

## The Registrar General

17.23 The intermediary agency should, where appropriate, request from the Registrar General such information as may assist it to proceed with the application. The request for information should be in writing to the Registrar General to identify the appropriate adoption agency; details of the court that made the adoption order; information that the Registrar General may hold that would enable an application to be made for a certified copy of any entry in the Adopted Children Register; and information from the Adoption Contact Centre (AIIS(PCA)R 2005, reg 13(1)). If the application for information is from a person with a prescribed relationship to an adopted person for assistance in contacting a relative of an adopted person, it may also request from the Registrar General such information as the Registrar General may hold from the Register of Live Births that would enable the adopted person with whom the applicant has a prescribed relationship to obtain a certified copy of the adopted person's record of birth (AIIS(PCA)R 2005, reg 13(2)). Information on the Adoption Contact Register may assist the intermediary agency to make an informed decision on whether to proceed with the application.

17.24 The Registrar General is under a duty to take all reasonable steps to comply with the written request for information from the intermediary agency (AIIS(PCA)R 2005, reg 14(1)). The Registrar General is entitled to charge an intermediary agency a fee of £36 for processing an initial request for information and £14 for providing information in response to any subsequent request made in relation to the same applicant (AIIS(PCA)R 2005, reg 18(3)) (see also Chapter 19).

## The court

17.25 Where the Registrar General certifies that he does not have the information, a request in writing should be made to the court that made the adoption order. The appropriate court fees not exceeding £20 may be payable for providing the information (AIIS(PCA)R 2005, reg 18(5)). The court which made the adoption order generally has the information filed in the proceedings. A request to the court may become appropriate, for instance where the local authority or the adoption agency has lost the records, or the records have been destroyed. On receiving the request, the court must disclose any information requested by the intermediary agency that is contained in the court records. If the court does not have the information, it must inform the intermediary agency in writing of the fact. The information given must include details of the searches that have been made of the records; if the court considers that the information may be found in the records of another court, it must provide that information to the intermediary agency with details of the court (AIIS(PCA)R 2005, reg 15).

## DISCLOSURE

17.26 The intermediary agency must obtain the consent of the person concerned before disclosure of any identifying information is made. 'Identifying information' means information which, whether taken on its own or together with other information in the possession of the applicant, would enable the applicant to identify or trace the subject. Before obtaining such consent, the agency should ensure that the subject has had enough information to make an informed decision whether to give consent. If the subject has died or is incapable of giving his consent, the agency may disclose such information as it considers appropriate having applied the criteria set out in AIIS(PCA)R 2005, reg 6 (see para 17.11) (AIIS(PCA)R 2005, reg 7). Information which is not identifying information may be disclosed where it would be appropriate to do so (AIIS(PCA)R 2005, reg 9).

17.27 An agency must not proceed with an application and should not disclose information where the subject is the adopted person and he has notified the appropriate agency (i.e. the agency involved in the adoption) that he does not wish to be contacted by an intermediary agency in relation to such an application, or that he wishes to be contacted only in specified circumstances (AIIS(PCA)R 2005, reg 8(1)).

17.28 Any information received by the intermediary agency must be treated as confidential. Disclosure may be made to the Registrar General, the court or the appropriate adoption agency for the purpose of obtaining information under AIIS(PCA)R 2005, reg 12 or reg 13 (see paras 17.19–17.25). Information may also be disclosed to the appropriate adoption agency to ascertain its views. Such information as is necessary to enable the subject to make an informed decision may be disclosed to the subject. Where counselling services are provided in connection with the application, such disclosure as is necessary may be made to the person who is to provide the counselling services (AIIS(PCA)R 2005, reg 16).

## FEES

17.29 The intermediary agency may charge such fees as it deems reasonable for processing the application, for providing counselling services or for making arrangements for such services to be provided outside the United Kingdom (AIIS(PCA)R 2005, reg 18(1) and (2)). (See also paras 17.19–17.25.)

## OFFENCE

17.30 It is an offence, punishable on summary conviction by a fine not exceeding level 5 on the standard scale, which is currently unlimited for offences committed after 13 March 2015, for an intermediary agency to disclose information in contravention of AIIS(PCA)R 2005, reg 7 without reasonable excuse (AIIS(PCA)R 2005, reg 17).

## Chapter 18

# Adoption Support Services and Agencies

## INTRODUCTION

18.1 In the past, local authorities and voluntary adoption agencies and societies worked together to meet the needs of children placed for adoption, the natural families of adopted children and the prospective adopter(s). The framework for the assessment and provision of adoption support services is now set out in ACA 2002, ss 3 and 4; and the Adoption Support Services Regulations 2005 (SI 2005/691), as amended by the Adoption Support Services (Amendment) Regulations 2014 (SI 2014/1563) (ASSR 2005). Guidance on the Regulation is currently set out in *Statutory Guidance on Adoption: For local authorities, voluntary adoption agencies and adoption support agencies* (Department for Education, July 2013) (*Adoption Statutory Guidance 2013*), which is available at:

> www.gov.uk/government/publications/adoption-statutory-guidance-2013

18.2 Whilst the guidance does not have the same force as the statutory provision, it is issued under the provisions contained in statute and should therefore be complied with unless exceptional circumstances justify a variation (*B v Lewisham London Borough Council* [2008] EWHC 738 (Admin) at [20]).

18.3 In relation to Wales, the statutory framework in addition to the ACA 2002 is provided under the Regulation and Inspection of Social Care (Wales) Act 2016; the Adoption Support Services (Wales) Regulations 2018 (SI 2018/286) (W 66); the Regulated Adoption Services (Service Providers and Responsible Individuals) (Wales) Regulations 2019 (SI 2019/762) (W 145), in force on 29 April 2019; and the Statutory Guidance, which is available at:

> www.gov.wales/sites/default/files/publications/2019-04/guidance-for-providers-and-responsible-individuals-of-regulated-adoption-services.pdf

## STATUTORY OBLIGATIONS ON MAINTENANCE OF SUPPORT SERVICES

18.4 ACA 2002, s 3 requires each local authority to provide and maintain services collectively referred to in ACA 2002, s 2(1) as 'adoption support services', which must include making and participating in arrangements for the provision of adoption services designed to meet the needs, in relation to adoption, of children who may be adopted, their parents and guardians, prospective adopters and adopted persons, their parents, natural parents and former guardians (ACA 2002, s 3(1) and (2)).

18.5 Additionally, if a request is made by any of these persons or any other person prescribed by regulation for their need for adoption services to be assessed, the local authority is required to undertake such an assessment, and if a need for the provision of support services to be provided is established and a decision is taken to provide those needs, further obligations are imposed on the local authority on how those needs should be met as set out in ACA 2002, s 4(5)–(11) and the regulations made under the ACA 2002.

18.6 When ACA 2002, s 4A comes into force, where the person who applies for the assessment is an adopted person or the parent of an adopted person, the local authority must prepare a personal budget for that person as set out in ACA 2002, s 4A and any regulation made as provided under ACA 2002, s 4A(4)–(7) (inserted by the Children and Families Act 2014, s 5, but not yet in force).

18.7 The local authority may secure the provisions of these services by registered adoption agencies or by other persons prescribed by regulations as long as these are provided in conjunction with the local authority's other social services and with registered adoption societies in its area so that help may be given in a coordinated manner without duplication, omission or avoidable delay (ACA 2002, s 3(4) and (5)). The additional bodies prescribed under ASSR 2005, reg 5 (as amended) who may be enlisted to provide adoption support services include:

(a) another local authority;
(b) a registered adoption support agency, defined, in relation to England, as an adoption support agency in respect of which a person is registered, under Care Standards Act 2000, Pt 2; or, in relation to Wales, an agency registered as a provider in Wales of such services under Regulation and Inspection of Social Care (Wales) Act 2016, Pt 1;
(c) an individual falling within Adoption Support Agencies (England) and Adoption Agencies (Miscellaneous Amendments) Regulations 2005 (SI 2005/2720) (ASAR 2005), reg 4(4);

(d) a local health board, a clinical commissioning group and the National Health Service Commissioning Board (see also the *Adoption Statutory Guidance 2013*, referred to at para 18.1).

18.8 ACA 2002, s 3A (inserted by the Children and Families Act 2014) provides for the Secretary of State to give directions requiring one or more named local authorities in England, or one or more descriptions of local authority in England, to make arrangements for all or any one of their functions which relate to:

(a) the recruitment of persons as prospective adopters;
(b) the assessment of prospective adopter's/adopters' suitability to adopt a child; or
(c) the approval of prospective adopters as suitable to adopt a child

to be carried out on their behalf by one or more other adoption agencies. The Secretary of State may also by order require all local authorities in England to make arrangements for all or any of their functions as set out above to be carried out on their behalf by one or more other adoption agencies. The direction may, in particular, specify who is to carry out the function or require the local authority or authorities to determine who is to carry out the functions.

18.9 Similarly, ACA 2002, s 3A empowers the Welsh Ministers to direct two or more authorities to enter into arrangements with each other in relation to the provision of the services maintained under ACA 2002, s 3(1), in relation to those matters set out in ACA 2002, s 3A(3).

## MEANING OF ADOPTION SUPPORT SERVICES

18.10 ACA 2002, s 2(6) defines 'adoption support services' to mean '(a) counselling, advice, and information and (b) any other services prescribed by regulations' in relation to adoption (see also the *Adoption Statutory Guidance 2013*).

18.11 ASSR 2005, reg 3 prescribes the following other services:

(a) financial support;
(b) services to enable groups of adoptive children, adoptive parents and natural parents or former guardians of an adoptive child to discuss matters relating to adoption;
(c) assistance, including mediation services, in relation to arrangements for contact between an adoptive child and a natural parent, natural sibling,

former guardian or a related person of the adoptive child. 'Related person' includes grandparent, brother, sister, uncle or aunt whether of the full blood or half-blood or by marriage, or any person with whom the adoptive child has a relationship which appears to the local authority to be beneficial having regard to the welfare checklist set out in ACA 2002, s 1 (ACA 2002, s 144(1) and ASSR 2005, reg 2);

(d) services in relation to the therapeutic needs of an adoptive child;

(e) assistance for the purpose of ensuring the continuance of the relationship between an adoptive child and his adoptive parent(s), including training for the adoptive parent(s) to meet any special needs of the child and, subject to ASSR 2005, reg 3(4), respite care. If respite care takes the form of providing accommodation, it must be provided by or on behalf of a local authority under ChA 1989, s 23 or by a voluntary organisation under ChA 1989, s 59;

(f) assistance where disruption of an adoptive placement or of an adoption arrangement following the making of an adoption order has occurred or is in danger of occurring. This includes making arrangements for the provision of mediation services and organising and running meetings to discuss disruptions in such placements and arrangements.

The services referred to in (b) to (f) above may include giving assistance in cash (ASSR 2005, reg 3(3)).

## PERSONS TO WHOM ADOPTION SUPPORT SERVICES ARE PROVIDED

18.12 ASSR 2005, reg 4 and the corresponding Welsh regulation prescribe the following services that must be provided, and to whom.

### Counselling, advice and information

18.13 ASSR 2005, reg 4(1) provides that counselling advice and information must be available to:

(a) children who may be adopted, their parents and guardians;

(b) persons wishing to adopt a child;

(c) adopted persons, their adoptive parents, natural parents and former guardians;

(d) children who are natural siblings (whether full or half-blood) of an adoptive child;

(e) children of adoptive parents (whether or not adopted);

(f) related persons in relation to adoptive children.

See also para 18.11(c).

## Financial support

18.14 Financial support under ASSR 2005, Pt 3 must be payable to an adoptive parent of an agency adoptive child (ASSR 2005, reg 4(3)).

18.15 Note, however, that financial support is only payable in the circumstances specified in ASSR 2005, reg 8 (see also ASSR 2005, reg 9 in relation to payment to a former foster parent).

18.16 See also the decision in *Re M (Care Proceedings: Adoption Support)* [2016] EWCA Civ 61 at [42], where King LJ stated that:

> One can only hope that, even in the straightened [sic] times in which we live, local authorities appreciate that failure to find the funds necessary to support those who adopt disadvantaged children is all too often a false economy, and ultimately it is the children who pay the price when an adoptive placement breaks down.

## Services to enable discussion

18.17 ASSR 2005, reg 4(4) sets out that services to enable groups of adoptive children, adoptive parents, natural parents and former guardians of adoptive children to discuss matters relating to adoption must extend to:

(a) an adoptive parent of an agency adoptive child;
(b) an agency adoptive child;
(c) a natural parent, or a former guardian of an agency adoptive child.

## Contact

18.18 ASSR 2005, reg 4(5) requires that services relating to contact (see para 18.12(c)) must extend to:

(a) an adoptive parent of an agency adoptive child;
(b) an agency adoptive child;
(c) a child who is a natural sibling, whether of the full or half-blood, of an adoptive child;
(d) a natural parent, former guardian or related person in relation to an agency adoptive child.

## Therapeutic services

18.19 As set out in ASSR 2005, reg 4(6), services to meet the therapeutic needs of an adoptive child must extend to:

(a) an agency adoptive child;
(b) an adoptive child, in circumstances where the restrictions in ACA 2002, s 83 (restrictions on bringing children in from overseas) apply; and
(c) an adoptive child in the case of a Convention adoption.

18.20 Since May 2015, application for financial assistance for therapeutic support may be made to the Adoption Special Guardianship Support Fund by local authorities and regional adoption agencies. The ASGSF lists the following as eligible for assistance:

> children and young people up to and including the age of 21, or 25 with an education, health and care plan, who:
>
> - are living (placed) with a family in England while waiting for adoption
> - were adopted from local authority care in England, Wales, Scotland or Northern Ireland and live in England
> - were adopted from abroad and live in England with a recognised adoption status
> - were in care before an SGO was made
> - left care under a special guardianship order that was subsequently changed to an adoption order, or vice versa
> - are under a residency order or child arrangement order (CAO) and were previously looked after
> - were previously looked after but where the adoption, special guardianship, residency or CAO placement has broken down, irrespective of any reconciliation plans

The application must be made within three months of assessing a family's support needs. The local authority that places the child for adoption is responsible for assessing the needs for support for three years post-adoption, thereafter it becomes the responsibility of the local authority where the child lives. For further details, see:

> www.gov.uk/guidance/adoption-support-fund-asf

## Services to ensure continuance of relationship and to assist in case of disruption of relationships

18.21 Pursuant to ASSR 2005, reg 4(7), assistance for the purpose of ensuring the continuance of the relationship between an adoptive child and his adoptive parent(s), and assistance where disruption of the placement has occurred or is in danger of occurring, must extend to:

(a) a child mentioned at para 18.19;
(b) an adoptive parent(s) of such a child; and

(c) a child of such an adoptive parent(s), irrespective of whether the child is that person's/persons' natural child or an adopted child.

## DUTY TO PROVIDE INFORMATION

### To whom should information set out in ACA 2002, s 4B be provided?

18.22 Children and Families Act 2014, s 6 amended the ACA 2002, as from 25 July 2014, to insert s 4B, which imposes a further duty upon the local authority to provide specified information (see para 18.23) to:

(a) any person who has contacted the authority to request information about adopting a child;
(b) any person who has informed the authority that he wishes to adopt a child;
(c) any person within the authority's area who the authority is aware is a parent of an adopted child; and
(d) any person within the authority's area who is a parent of an adopted child and has contacted the authority to request any of the specified information (see para 18.23).

### What is the specified information which should be provided?

18.23 The specified information referred to above is:

(a) information about the adoption support services available to people in the authority's area;
(b) information about the right to request an assessment under ACA 2002, s 4 (assessments, etc. for adoption support services), and the authority's duties under that section and regulations made under it;
(c) information about the authority's duties under ACA 2002, s 4A (adoption support services: personal budgets) and regulations made under it;
(d) any other information prescribed by regulations.

### Prescribed information required to be provided under regulation

18.24 Pursuant to ASSR 2005, reg 2A(1) (inserted by the Adoption Support Services (Amendment) Regulations 2014 (SI 2014/1563) of 9 June 2014), the local authority is also required to provide to the persons listed at para 18.22 the following information:

(a) the address and phone number of the local authority's adoption support services adviser appointed under regulation 6;
(b) the address and phone number of the web based information service supported and funded by the Department for Education to provide information to the public about adoption and the adoption process in England;
(c) information about the availability of assessments for adoption support services for person who are outside the area of the local authority;
(d) where appropriate, information about priority in school admissions for looked after children (including those placed for adoption) and adopted children as set out in the School Admissions Code issued under section 84 of the School Standards and Framework Act 1998;
(e) information about the right to make a representation (including a complaint) under the Children Act 1989 Representations Procedure (England) Regulations 2006;
(f) information about the procedure under section 26B of the Local Government Act 1974, for making a complaint to the Local Government Ombudsman; and
(g) information about any other relevant services provided by the local authority.

18.25 Additionally, as set out in ASSR 2005, reg 2A(2), the local authority must provide to any person who has requested information about adopting a child, and any person who has informed the authority that he wishes to adopt a child:

(a) details of where to find information about statutory adoption pay and statutory adoption leave; and
(b) information about a prospective adopter's right to receive the child's permanence report (prepared in accordance with regulation 17 of the Adoption Agencies Regulations 2005), including a summary of the medical adviser's report on the health of the child, in accordance with regulation 31 of those Regulations.

## Circumstances in which information need not be provided

18.26 ASSR 2005, reg 2B(1) and (2) provides that a local authority is not required to provide the above information to a person who:

(a) has already received that information from the local authority within the preceding twelve months and the information has not changed substantively in that time, or
(b) has informed the local authority that they do not want to receive that information,

unless the local authority is satisfied that there are valid reasons for providing that information.

18.27 The local authority must give reasons for refusing to provide information where the information is being sought by a person who has contacted the local authority about adopting a child, or by a person within the local authority's area who is a parent of an adopted child and is seeking information about services specified at para 18.23.

## ADOPTION SUPPORT SERVICE ADVISER

18.28 The local authority must appoint an adoption support services adviser, whose function is to:

(a) give advice and information to those who may be affected by the adoption or proposed adoption of a child, including information about services that may be appropriate and how to obtain those services;
(b) give advice, information and assistance to the local authority, including advice, information and assistance concerning the assessment of needs for adoption support services, the availability of such services and the preparation of plans required under ACA 2002, s 4(5);
(c) consult with and give advice, information and assistance to another local authority where appropriate.

18.29 The person appointed as adoption support services adviser must have sufficient knowledge and experience of the process of adoption and its effect on persons likely to be affected by adoption, for the purposes of the work he is to perform (ASSR 2005, reg 6; see also the guidance set out in *Adoption Statutory Guidance 2013*, paragraphs 9.9–9.17).

## SERVICES FOR PERSONS OUTSIDE THE AREA

18.30 Pursuant to ACA 2002, s 4, a local authority is obliged to provide adoption support services to the following persons who are outside its area:

(a) an agency adoptive child whom the authority has placed for adoption, or who has been adopted after being placed for adoption by the authority;
(b) an adoptive parent of such a child;
(c) a child of such an adoptive parent, whether adopted or not.

18.31 This duty ceases three years after the adoption order is made, except in relation to any financial support provided by the local authority where the decision to provide support was made before the adoption. The local authority is not prevented from providing adoption support services to persons outside its area where it considers it appropriate to do so, and, therefore, it is within its discretion to do so even if the case falls outside the regulations (ASSR 2005, reg 7). For provisions in relation to Wales, see the Regulation and Inspection of Social Care (Wales) Act 2016; the Adoption Support Services (Wales) Regulations 2018 (SI 2018/286) (W 66); the Regulated Adoption Services (Service Providers and Responsible Individuals) (Wales) Regulations 2019 (SI 2019/762) (W 145); and the Statutory Guidance in force on 29 April 2019 (see para 18.3).

## FINANCIAL SUPPORT

### Circumstances in which financial support is payable

18.32 As set out in ASSR 2005, reg 8, financial support is payable to an adoptive parent(s) for the purpose of supporting the placement of the adoptive child, or the continuation of the adoption arrangements after an adoption order is made only where:

(a) it is necessary to ensure that the adoptive parent(s) can look after the child. It is implicit, having regard to the meaning given to the phrase 'adoptive parent' in the regulations, that this includes offering the service at every stage of the adoption process;
(b) the child needs special care which requires greater expenditure or resources by reason of illness, disability, emotional or behavioural difficulties or the continuing consequences of past abuse or neglect. This would cover situations such as those which arose in *A v Essex County Council* [2003] EWCA Civ 1848, [2004] 1 WLR 1881;
(c) it is necessary for the local authority to make special arrangements to facilitate the placement or adoption by reason of:

    (i) the age or ethnic origin of the child; or
    (ii) the desirability of the child being placed with the same adoptive parent(s) as his sibling (whether of the full blood or half-blood) or with a child with whom he has previously shared a home;
    (iii) such support is to meet recurring costs in respect of travel for the purpose of visits between the child and a related person.

(d) the local authority considers it appropriate to make a contribution to meet the legal costs, including fees payable in court, in relation to an adoption; expenditure for the purpose of introducing an adoptive child to his adoptive parent(s), and expenditure necessary for accommodating and maintaining the child, including the provision of furniture and domestic equipment, alterations to and adaptations of the home, provision of means of transport and provision of clothing, toys and other items necessary for the purpose of looking after the child.

18.33 See also the *Adoption Statutory Guidance 2013*, paragraphs 9.26–9.27.

## Remuneration for former foster parent

18.34 Where adoptive parent(s) have been local authority foster parent(s) and an element of remuneration was included in the payments made by the local authority to the adoptive parent(s) in relation to their fostering the child, financial support may include an element of remuneration. But this may be done only where the decision to pay was taken before the adoption order was made, and the local authority considers it to be necessary to facilitate the adoption. However, the element of remuneration ceases to be payable at the end of two years from the date of the adoption order, unless the local authority considers its continuation to be necessary having regard to the exceptional needs of the child or any other exceptional circumstances (ASSR 2005, reg 9; and see *Adoption Statutory Guidance 2013*, paragraphs 9.28–9.29). Remuneration to an adoptive parent(s) for the care of the child is not permitted. The payment to the foster carer(s) is an exception by reason of the particular circumstances in which the placement arises.

## Payment of financial support

18.35 Where a local authority decides that financial support should be given, it may be paid in a single payment, except where the local authority and the adoptive parent(s) agree that it should be paid by instalments, or periodically, if it is provided to meet a need which is likely to give rise to recurring expenditure (ASSR 2005, reg 10).

## Cessation of financial support

18.36 As set out in ASSR 2005, reg 11, financial support ceases to be payable to an adoptive parent if the child:

(a) ceases to have a home with the adoptive parent;
(b) ceases full-time education or training and commences employment;
(c) qualifies for income support or jobseeker's allowance in his own right;
(d) attains the age of 18 years, unless he continues in full-time education or training, when it may continue until the end of the course or training he is then undertaking.

## Conditions attached to financial support

18.37 Where financial support is payable periodically, it is not payable until the adoptive parent, or, in the case of an adoption by a couple, each adoptive parent, has agreed to the following conditions:

(a) that he will inform the local authority immediately if he changes his address, or the child dies; or any change occurs which would lead to the payments ceasing; or there is a change in his financial circumstances or the financial needs or resources of the child, which may affect the amount of financial support payable to him, and where the information is given orally, that he will confirm it in writing within seven days;
(b) that he will complete and supply the local authority with an annual statement of his financial circumstances, the financial needs and resources of the child and his address, and whether the child still has a home with him.

18.38 The local authority may impose such other conditions as it considers appropriate, including the timescale within which, and purposes for which, any payment of financial support should be utilised (ASSR 2005, reg 12(1) and (2)).

## Termination and suspension of payment

18.39 Non-compliance with any condition imposed on the provision of financial support entitles the local authority to suspend or terminate payment. It also entitles the local authority to recover all or any part of the financial support it has paid. Where the non-compliance consists of failure to provide an annual statement, a written reminder must be sent to the person to provide the statement, and the person given 28 days from the date on which the notice was sent within which to comply before any steps are taken to suspend or terminate the financial support (ASSR 2005, reg 12(3); and see *Adoption Statutory Guidance 2013*, paragraphs 9.30–9.31).

## Assessment for financial support

18.40 In determining the amount of financial support to pay, the local authority is required to take account of any other grant, benefit, allowance or resource available to the person in respect of his needs as a result of the adoption of the child. As set out in ASSR 2005, reg 15(3), the local authority must also take account of:

(a) the person's financial resources, including any tax credit or benefit which would be available to him if the child lived with him;
(b) the amount required by the person in respect of his reasonable outgoings and commitments (excluding outgoings in respect of the child); and
(c) the financial needs and resources of the child.

18.41 These considerations *may*, however, be disregarded where financial support is being considered in respect of the initial costs of accommodating an agency adoptive child; recurring costs in respect of travel for the purposes of visits between the child and a related person; any special arrangements or special care required by reason of illness, disability, emotional or behavioural difficulties or the continuing consequences of past abuse or neglect of the adoptive child; or where it is necessary to make special arrangements to facilitate the placement by reason of the child's age, sex, ethnicity or the desirability of placing a sibling in the same household. The considerations at para 18.40(a)–(c) may also be disregarded where the local authority is considering including an element of remuneration paid to adoptive parent(s) who have been the foster parent(s) of the child (ASSR 2005, reg 15(5)).

18.42 Additionally, the local authority *must* disregard the matters set out at para 18.40(a)–(c) where it is considering providing financial support in respect of legal costs, including fees payable to a court, where an adoption order is applied for in respect of an agency adoptive child; or expenditure for the purposes of introducing an agency adoptive child to his adoptive parent(s) (ASSR 2005, reg 15(4); see *Adoption Statutory Guidance 2013*, paragraphs 9.32–9.38).

## REQUEST FOR ASSESSMENT

18.43 Pursuant to ACA 2002, s 4 and ASSR 2005, reg 13, local authorities are required to undertake an assessment of adoption support services needs at the request of:

(a) a child who may be adopted, his parent(s) and guardian;
(b) a person wishing to be adopted;
(c) an adopted person, his adoptive parent(s), natural parent(s) and former guardian(s);
(d) a child of an adoptive parent(s) (whether or not adopted);
(e) a natural sibling (whether of full blood or half-blood) of an adoptive child;
(f) a relative of the adopted child or other related person with whom the child has a beneficial relationship.

18.44 Where a request for an assessment is made by a person falling within any one or more of the above categories, and the request relates to a particular support service, or it appears to the local authority that the person's needs for adoption support services may be adequately assessed by reference to a particular adoption support service, the local authority may carry out the assessment by reference only to that service (ASSR 2005, reg 13(2); and see also paras 18.4–18.9).

18.45 Regulation 13(3) specifically excludes assessment for a service if the person in question does not come within the description of persons who are eligible for that particular service.

## Matters to be taken into consideration on assessment

18.46 ASSR 2005, reg 14(1) provides that, in carrying out an assessment of a person's needs for adoption support services, the following matters are considered relevant:

(a) the needs of the person being assessed and how these might be met;
(b) the needs of the adoptive family and how these might be met;
(c) the needs, including developmental needs, of the adoptive child and how these might be met;
(d) the parenting capacity of the adoptive parent(s);
(e) wider family and environmental factors;
(f) where the child is or was placed for adoption or matched for adoption, the circumstances that led to the child's being so placed or matched;
(g) any previous assessments of needs for adoption support services undertaken in relation to that person.

## Interview and report

18.47 The local authority must, where it considers it appropriate to do so, interview the person requesting assessment. Where the person is an adoptive child, it must also interview the adoptive parent(s). In any event, the local authority must prepare a report of the assessment (ASSR 2005, reg 14(3)).

## Referrals to other agencies

18.48 Where it appears to the authority that the person who is being assessed may have a need for services by a primary care trust, or a local health board, or a local education authority, it must consult the appropriate body as part of the assessment (ASSR 2005, reg 14(4); see *Adoption Statutory Guidance 2013*, paragraphs 9.39–9.51).

# THE PLAN

## Preparation of the plan

18.49 If, following an assessment, the authority decides to provide any adoption support services to a person on more than one occasion and those services are not limited to the provision of advice or information, it must prepare a plan for the provision of those services and keep the plan under review (ACA 2002, s 4(5)).

18.50 Where the local authority considers that there may be a need for the provision to that person of services by a clinical commissioning group or, in the case of Wales, by a health authority, or a local health board or an education authority, it must notify and consult with that clinical commissioning group health authority, local health board or local education authority before preparing the plan, and nominate a person to monitor the provision of the services (ACA 2002, s 4, and ASSR 2005, reg 16(3) and (4); see *Adoption Statutory Guidance 2013*, paragraphs 9.52–9.54).

## Notice of assessment

18.51 On completing the assessment but before deciding whether to provide adoption support services, the local authority is required to give notice of the proposed decision to the person requesting the services and allow that person an opportunity to make representations. The notice must contain:

(a) a statement of the person's needs for adoption support services;
(b) where the needs relate to financial support, the basis upon which financial support is determined;
(c) whether it is proposed to provide adoption support services to him;
(d) the services, if any, which it is proposed to provide;
(e) if financial support is to be paid, the proposed amount that would be payable and any conditions attached to it;
(f) where the local authority is required to prepare a plan (see paras 18.49–18.50), the notice must be accompanied by a copy of the draft plan;
(g) details of the right to make representations and the time within which they must be made.

18.52 The local authority must not make a decision until the person has made representations or notified the local authority that he is satisfied with the proposed decision, and, where applicable, with the draft plan; or the time limit has expired (ASSR 2005, reg 17). The regulation does not specify the time limit within which the representation should be made, but see *Adoption Statutory Guidance 2013*, paragraph 9.56, which suggests a period of 28 days as good practice; and see paragraphs 9.47–9.67 generally on the issue of the preparation of the plan procedure to be followed.

## Notice of decision

18.53 Written notice of the decision, together with reasons for it, and where appropriate a copy of the plan, must be given to the person requesting the assessment, together with details of the person who has been nominated to monitor the plan.

18.54 Where the local authority has decided to provide financial support, as set out in ASSR 2005, reg 18, the notice must also include details of:

(a) the method of determination of the amount;
(b) where the payment is to be made in instalments or periodically:

    (i) the amount of financial support,
    (ii) the frequency with which payment will be made,
    (iii) the period for which financial support will be paid,
    (iv) when the first payment is to be made;

(c) where the amount is to be paid in a single payment, the date on which it is to be paid;
(d) if conditions are to be imposed pursuant to ASSR 2005, reg 12, details of the conditions, the date by which the conditions are to be met and the consequences of failing to meet those conditions;
(e) the arrangements and procedure for review, variation and termination of financial support;
(f) the responsibilities of the local authority when carrying out the review (see paras 18.56–18.59) and that of the adoptive parent as set out in ASSR 2005, reg 12 (see para 18.37).

18.55 If the person to whom the notice is to be given is a child and it appears to the local authority that the child is not of sufficient age and understanding for him to be given such notice, or in all the circumstances it would be inappropriate to give him such notice, the notice should be given to the adoptive parent, or to the adult whom the local authority considers most appropriate (ASSR 2005, reg 22).

## REVIEWS

### Services other than financial support

18.56 Where the local authority is providing, or in the preceding 12 months has provided, adoption support services for a person, it must review the provision of such services. The duty to review arises where the local authority becomes aware of any change in the person's circumstances; at any stage in the implementation of the plan as the authority considers appropriate; and in any event, annually. The procedure for assessment, set out in ASSR 2005, regs 14 and 15 (see paras 18.40–18.48), applies to a review as it does to an initial assessment.

18.57 If the local authority proposes to vary or terminate the provision of adoption support services, then before making the decision it must give the person affected an opportunity to make representations. Notice of the proposal must therefore be given to him and he must be allowed sufficient time to make the representations (ASSR 2005, reg 19(1)).

18.58 The notice must contain the information set out at paras 18.49–18.50 and, if the local authority proposes to revise the plan, a draft of the plan should be enclosed with the notice (ASSR 2005, reg 19(5)).

18.59 The local authority should not make a decision until it has received the representations of the person affected, or the time for making representations has expired. When coming to its decision, the local authority is required to have regard to the representations made. It may vary or terminate the provision of adoption support services and, where appropriate, revise the plan. Notice of the decision must be given, together with reasons for the decision, and, where appropriate, a copy of the revised plan (ASSR 2005, reg 19(6); see *Adoption Statutory Guidance 2013*, paragraphs 9.62–9.67).

## Financial support paid periodically

18.60 The local authority is required to review the provision of financial support:

(a) annually, on receipt of the adoptive parents' financial statement under ASSR 2005, reg 12;
(b) if any relevant change of circumstances or any breach of a condition comes to its notice; and
(c) at any stage in the implementation of the plan as it considers appropriate.

18.61 In carrying out the review, the local authority must apply the same considerations as when carrying out an assessment.

18.62 The local authority has a right to review, suspend or cease payment of financial support and seek to recover all or part of the financial support it has paid if any conditions on the provision of such support have not been complied with. Where the breach consists of failure to provide the annual statement, a reminder should be sent, with a notice that compliance should take place within 28 days.

18.63 If the local authority proposes to reduce or terminate the financial support or revise the plan, it is under a duty first to notify the person of the proposal, give the person an opportunity to make representations, and allow the person time to do so. The notice must contain a statement of the person's needs and the basis upon which the financial support is assessed, whether the local authority proposes to provide financial support and, if so, the amount and any conditions attached.

18.64 When carrying out the review, the local authority should consider the representations made and give notice of its decision, with reasons, and a revised plan, if appropriate, to the person assessed (ASSR 2005, reg 20; see *Adoption Statutory Guidance 2013*, paragraphs 9.39–9.42).

## RECOVERY OF EXPENSES BETWEEN LOCAL AUTHORITIES

18.65 Where it appears to a local authority that another local authority could, by taking any specified action, help in the exercise of any of its functions, it (the 'paying authority') may request the help of that other local authority, specifying the action in question (ACA 2002, s 4(10)). Where a local authority (the 'recovering authority') provides adoption support services to any person in consequence of such a request from another local authority, the recovering authority may recover the expenses of providing those services from the paying authority. This provision does not, however, apply where the recovering authority has provided counselling, advice and information under ACA 2002, s 2(6)(a), or the recovering authority is providing services to the following persons, set out in ASSR 2005, regs 23 and 7(1), who are outside the authority's area:

(a) an agency adoptive child whom the authority has placed for adoption or who has been adopted after having been placed for adoption by the authority;
(b) an adoptive parent(s) of such a child;
(c) a child of such an adoptive parent(s) (whether or not adopted).

## FEES

18.66 Pursuant to ACA 2002, s 11, adoption agencies are permitted to charge fees prescribed by regulations, to persons to whom facilities are provided as part of the adoption service. They are also permitted to pay fees to persons providing or assisting in providing such facilities. Local authorities may also charge for the facilities of the adoption service in connection with the adoption of a child brought into the United Kingdom for the purpose of adoption, a Convention adoption, an overseas adoption or an adoption effected under the law of a country or territory outside the British Islands.

## ADOPTION SUPPORT AGENCIES

### Statutory framework

18.67 ACA 2002, s 3(4) permits a local authority to provide any of the requisite facilities by securing the provision of these services by registered adoption agencies, or by other persons who are within a description prescribed by regulations. This is in conjunction with the local authority's other social services and with registered adoption societies in its area.

18.68 ACA 2002, s 9(1) makes provision for regulations to be made relating to the exercise by local authorities, voluntary adoption agencies and adoption support agencies of their functions in relation to adoption. ACA 2002, s 10(1) identifies some of the areas, which such regulations should cover. These include:

(a) the persons who are fit to be employed for the purposes of functions relating to adoption and in this case to also make provision for prohibiting persons from working in prescribed positions unless they are registered;
(b) the fitness of premises;
(c) the management and control of operations;
(d) the number of persons, or persons of any particular type, working for the purposes of those functions;
(e) the management and training of persons working for the purposes of those functions; and
(f) keeping information.

18.69 Children and Social Work Act 2017, s 39 makes the following provisions in relation to registration:

(1) Social Work England is required to keep a register of social workers in England;
(2) the Secretary of State may, through regulations, also require Social Work England to keep a register of those who are undertaking education or training in England to become social workers;
(3) the Secretary of State is required, through regulations, to authorise Social Work England to appoint a member of staff as a registrar and make provision about the functions of the registrar. It also allows regulations to make other provision in connection with the keeping of a register;
(4) a list of examples of provisions that may be included in regulations made under point (3) (above), such as provision about who can be registered and stay registered; different categories of registration; suspension and removal from the register, etc.

18.70 The provision relating to registration in Children and Social Work Act 2017, s 39(2)–(4) is in force as at 1 April 2018, pursuant to Children and Social Work Act 2017 (Commencement No 3) Regulations 2018 (SI 2018/346), reg 4(j). Consequently, ACA 2002, s 10(2) has been amended to provide that regulations made in relation to persons who are fit to work for local authorities, voluntary adoption agencies and adoption support agencies may in particular make provision for prohibiting persons from working in prescribed positions unless they are registered in, or in a particular part of:

(a) the register of social workers in England maintained under Children and Social Work Act 2017, s 39;
(b) any register of social care workers in England maintained under an Order in Council under Health Act 1999, s 60 or any other register maintained under such an Order in Council so far as it relates to social care workers in England; or
(c) the register maintained under Regulation and Inspection of Social Care (Wales) Act 2016, s 80.

18.71 In relation to voluntary adoption agencies and adoption support agencies, ACA 2002, s 10(3) provides that the regulations may cover, among others, matters relating to the fitness and qualifications and registration of personnel in managerial positions; impose requirements as to the financial position of an agency; make provision requiring the appointment of a manager; in the case of a voluntary adoption agency, make provision for the welfare of the children placed by the agency, including the promotion and protection of their health; and in the case of an adoption agency, make provision as to persons who are fit to carry on the agency.

18.72 ACA 2002, s 10(4) particularises some of the matters, which may be covered by subsidiary legislation on the conduct of such agencies, to include:

(a) the facilities and services to be provided;
(b) the keeping of accounts;
(c) notifying the registration authority of events which occur in the premises used for the purposes of an agency;
(d) notifying the registration authority when the manager of an agency proposes to be absent, making arrangements for running the agency in the manager's absence, and notifying any intention to change the identity of the manager;
(e) notifying the registration authority of changes in ownership of an agency or of the identity of any of its officers, and requiring the payment of the appropriate fee to the registration authority; and
(f) requiring arrangements to be made for dealing with complaints made by or on behalf of those seeking or receiving any of the services provided by the agency and requiring the agency or manager to take steps for publicising the arrangements.

18.73 Consequently, the following regulations have been made which apply to England:

- the Adoption Support Agencies (England) and Adoption Agencies (Miscellaneous Amendments) Regulations 2005 (SI 2005/2720) (ASAR 2005);
- the Adoption Information and Intermediary Services (Pre-Commencement Adoptions) Regulations 2005 (SI 2005/890) (AIIS(PCA)R 2005), which deal

with services offering assistance to an adopted person who was adopted before 30 December 2005 to obtain information and facilitate contact with his birth family and vice versa (this is discussed in Chapter 17);
- the Disclosure of Adoption Information (Post-Commencement Adoptions) Regulations 2005 (SI 2005/888) (DAI(PCA)R 2005), which deal with similar services for persons adopted after 30 December 2005.

## The prescribed adoption support services

18.74 ASAR 2005, reg 3 lists the prescribed adoption support services as follows:

(a) any services prescribed in ASSR 2005, reg 3(1)(b)–(f) that are provided in the case of an adoption of a child by his natural parent or the partner of his natural parent;
(b) assistance to adoption agencies in preparing and training adoptive parents;
(c) assistance to adopted persons who have attained the age of 18, or relatives of such persons,

to facilitate contact between such adopted persons and their relatives. 'Relative' here means any person who, but for his adoption, would be related to him by blood, including half-blood, marriage or civil partnership.

18.75 Where a child is adopted by his natural parent or the partner of his natural parent, respite care that consists of the provision of accommodation must be accommodation provided by or on behalf of a local authority under ChA 1989, s 23 (accommodation of looked after children) or by a voluntary organisation under ChA 1989, s 59.

## Providers of services who are excepted as adoption support agencies

18.76 The regulations specifically except from being regarded as an adoption support agency a barrister or solicitor who is providing adoption support services in the course of their practice. Also excepted is any undertaking, as set out in ASAR 2005, reg 4, which merely provides:

(a) services to enable groups of adoptive children, adoptive parents and natural parents or former guardians of an adoptive child to discuss matters relating to adoption; or
(b) respite care in relation to adoption, and which is a care home, children's home or domiciliary care agency in respect of which a person is registered under Care Standards Act 2000, Pt 2; or

(c) respite care in relation to adoption consisting of child minding or day care within the meaning of ChA 1989, Pt 10A and which is registered for providing child minding or day care under that Part; or
(d) if the undertaking is carried on by an individual who only provides adoption support services under a contract for services with either an agency in respect of which a person is registered under Care Standards Act 2000, Pt 2 as the person carrying on the agency or an adoption agency.

An undertaking is also not an adoption agency merely because it provides counselling in relation to an adopted person who has attained the age of 18.

## Fitness of the registered provider

18.77 A person must not carry on an agency unless he is fit to do so. As set out in ASAR 2005, reg 7(1)–(3), a person is not regarded as fit unless the person:

(a) is an individual who carries on the agency otherwise than in partnership with others and satisfies certain specified requirements (which are set out in para 18.78); or in partnership with others, where he and each of the partners satisfy the requirements as to fitness and registration set out under ASSR 2005, reg 7(3) and (4) (see paras 18.79–18.80); or
(b) is a partnership and each of the partners satisfies the requirements set out at paras 18.79–18.80; or
(c) is an organisation which has given the registration authority details of the person (referred to as the 'responsible individual') who is responsible for supervising the management of the agency, and that individual satisfies the requirements set out in ASAR 2005, reg 7(3) (see paras 18.79–18.80).

18.78 As set out in ASAR 2005, reg 7(4), a person must not carry on an agency if:

(a) he has been made bankrupt, or sequestration of his estate has been awarded, or he is a person in relation to whom a moratorium period under a debt relief order applies, and he has not been discharged from the bankruptcy or sequestration and the bankruptcy order has not been annulled or rescinded; or
(b) he is a person in respect of whom a bankruptcy restrictions order or an interim bankruptcy restrictions order under Insolvency Act 1986, Sch 4A, or a debt relief restrictions order or an interim debt relief restrictions order under Insolvency Act 1986, Sch 4ZB has effect; or
(c) he has made a composition or arrangement with his creditors and has not been discharged in respect of it (see also NMS 2014, Standard 19).

## The responsible individual

18.79 As set out in ASAR 2005, reg 7(2) and (3), an organisation is prohibited from carrying on an agency unless it fulfils two conditions concerning a person known as the 'responsible individual', namely:

(a) it has given notice to the registration authority of the name, address and position in the organisation of a person (the 'responsible individual') who is a director, manager, secretary or other officer of the organisation and is responsible for the supervision and management of the agency; and
(b) the responsible individual is a person of suitable integrity and good character to carry on the agency, is physically and mentally fit to do so, and has made available full and satisfactory information or documentation of each of the matters specified in ASAR 2005, Sch 2.

18.80 The information required under ASAR 2005, Sch 2 includes:

(a) where appropriate, an enhanced criminal record certificate issued under Police Act 1997, s 115. The certificate must cover such matters as, for example, whether the person's name appears on the list kept under Protection of Children Act 1999, s 1, of individuals considered unsuitable to work with children;
(b) proof of identity with a recent photograph;
(c) two written references, one of which must be from the person's most recent employer, if any;
(d) if the person has previously worked with children or vulnerable adults, then, so far as is reasonably practicable, verification of the reason the employment came to an end;
(e) documentary evidence of qualifications; and
(f) a full employment history, together with a satisfactory written explanation of any gaps.

## The registered manager

18.81 The person who is registered under Care Standards Act 2000, Pt 2 as the person carrying on the agency ('the registered provider') is under a duty to appoint a manager ('the registered manager') to manage the agency, if the registered provider is an organisation or a partnership, or is not fit to manage an agency, or is not, or does not intend to be in full-time day-to-day charge of the agency. In this case the registered provider must immediately notify the registration authority of the name of the person appointed as the manager and the date the appointment takes effect.

18.82 The person appointed must be of suitable integrity and good character; have the qualifications, skills and experience necessary to manage the agency; and be physically and mentally fit to do so. A person will not be regarded as fit to manage an agency unless full and satisfactory information is available in relation to them as regards their integrity, character, qualification skills and experience and their physical and mental health (ASAR 2005, reg 8; and see paras 18.79–18.80).

### Training and standards of work

18.83 The registered provider must ensure that the registered manager undertakes from time to time such training as is appropriate to ensure that he has the experience and skills necessary for managing the agency (ASAR 2005, reg 10(3)). If the registered provider is an individual, they must undertake, or if it is an organisation, it shall ensure that the responsible individual undertakes, and in the case of a partnership that one of the partners undertakes, such training as is appropriate to ensure that they have the experience and skills necessary for managing the agency.

## STATEMENT OF PURPOSE AND CHILDREN'S GUIDE

18.84 The regulations contain provisions requiring the compilation of certain documents relating to the objectives and methods of working of adoption support agencies.

### Statement of purpose

18.85 ASAR 2005, reg 5(1) and Sch 1 require that the person who is the registered provider or registered manager (the 'registered person') must compile, in relation to the agency, a written statement of purpose, which must consist of the following matters:

(a) the aims and objectives of the agency;
(b) the name and address of the registered provider and, where applicable, the registered manager and the responsible individual;
(c) any conditions in force in relation to the registration under Care Standards Act 2000, Pt 2 of the registered provider and, if applicable, the registered manager;
(d) the relevant qualifications and experience of the registered provider and, if applicable, the registered manager;
(e) the number, relevant qualifications and experience of the staff working for the purposes of the agency;

(f) a description of the organisational structure of the agency;
(g) a description of the services offered by the agency;
(h) the procedures for assessing the needs of those requesting adoption support services from the agency;
(i) the system in place to monitor and evaluate the provision of services to ensure that the services provided by the agency are effective and of an appropriate quality standard;
(j) a summary of the complaints procedure;
(k) the name, address and telephone number of the registration authority.

18.86 A copy of the statement of purpose must be provided by the registered person to the registration authority (in England, the Commission for Social Care; in Wales, the National Assembly). As set out in ASAR 2005, reg 5(2) and (3), a copy must also be made available, upon request, for inspection by:

(a) any person working for the purposes of the agency;
(b) any person receiving adoption support services from the agency or acting on behalf of a child receiving such services from the agency;
(c) any person making enquiries about receiving adoption services from the agency on his behalf or on a child's behalf; and
(d) any local authority.

## The children's guide

18.87 The registered person, in relation to an agency which provides adoption support services, is also under an obligation to provide a written guide to the agency, the 'children's guide'. It should include a summary of the agency's statement of purpose; a summary of the complaints procedure; and the address and telephone number of the registration authority.

18.88 The guide should be in a form which is age-appropriate and appropriate to the understanding and communication needs of the children to whom the agency provides adoption support services. The registered person must provide a copy of the children's guide to the registration authority; to any adult acting on behalf of a child to whom the agency provides adoption support services; and, subject to the child's age and understanding, to the child (see ASAR 2005, reg 5(4)–(6)).

## Review

18.89 Both the statement of purpose and the children's guide must be kept under review and, where appropriate, revised by the registered person. Within 28 days of any revision, the registered person must notify the registration authority of the revision. A copy of any revision to the children's guide should also be made available to any adult who is acting on behalf of a child to whom the agency supplies adoption support services, and, subject to his age and understanding, to each such child (see ASAR 2005, reg 6).

## ARRANGEMENTS FOR THE PROTECTION OF CHILDREN

18.90 The registered person is required to make arrangements for the protection and safety of children receiving adoption support services from the agency. The registered person in relation to an adoption agency (and, in Wales, the local authority) which provides adoption support services is required to prepare and implement a written policy, which is intended to safeguard from abuse or neglect children receiving adoption services from the agency or the local authority and sets out the procedure to be followed if an allegation of abuse or neglect is made. The regulation requires that this procedure should provide, in particular, for:

(a) liaison and co-operation with any local authority which is, or may be, making child protection enquiries in respect of the child. This includes any enquiries carried out by a local authority in connection with its duty under the ChA 1989 relating to the protection of children;
(b) written records to be kept of any allegations of abuse or neglect, and the actions taken in response; and
(c) arrangements to be made for persons working for the purposes of the agency and adults and children to whom the agency has provided adoption support services to have access to information that would enable them to contact:

    (i) the local authority in whose area the agency is situated and any other local authority on behalf of whom the agency is providing adoption support services to a child, and
    (ii) the registration authority,

regarding any concern about a child's welfare and safety.

18.91 'Child protection enquiries' means any enquiries carried out by a local authority in the exercise of any of its functions conferred by or under the ChA 1989 relating to the protection of children (ASAR 2005, reg 12).

## RECORDS

18.92 As set out in ASAR 2005, reg 14, the registered person is under a duty to maintain records, indicating in respect of each person to whom the agency is providing adoption support services:

(a) full names and date of birth;
(b) whether the person is an adoptive child or an adopted person who has attained the age of 18 or, if not, his relationship to an adoptive child or adopted person;
(c) description of the services requested;
(d) description of needs as assessed by the agency or a local authority;
(e) description of the services provided; and
(f) whether the services were provided on behalf of a local authority or another person or organisation.

18.93 The records must be retained for such period as the registered provider considers appropriate. In Wales, the records must be kept for 75 years from the date of the last entry.

## COMPLAINTS

18.94 The registered person is required to establish a written procedure for considering complaints made by or on behalf of any person who has requested, or to whom the agency has provided, adoption support services or to whom such services have been refused.

18.95 The procedure formulated must include provision:

(a) for an opportunity for informal resolution of a complaint at an early stage;
(b) to ensure that no person who is the subject of a complaint takes part in its consideration other than, if the registered person considers it appropriate, at the informal resolution stage only;
(c) for dealing with complaints about the registered person or the responsible individual; and
(d) in the case of an agency providing adoption support services to children, for complaints to be made by a person acting on behalf of a child.

18.96 The registered person is required to provide a copy of the complaints procedure to every person working for the purposes of the agency. A copy must also be provided upon a request made on behalf of any person to whom the agency has provided adoption support services, or any person acting on behalf of a child. In this event, the copy of the complaints procedure must also contain the name, address and telephone number of the registration authority and details of the procedure (if any) which has been notified to the registered person by the registration authority for making complaints to the registration authority that relate to the agency (ASAR 2005, reg 16).

18.97 The registered person must take the following steps if a complaint is made:

(a) ensure that the complaint is fully investigated;
(b) ensure, so far as is reasonably practicable, that, within 28 working days of the complaint being received by the agency, the complainant is informed of the outcome of the investigation and of the action (if any) which it is proposed to take in response to the complaint; and
(c) ensure that a written record is made of any complaint, details of the investigation made, the outcome and any action taken in consequence. The record must be retained for at least three years from the date it is made.

18.98 As set out in ASAR 2005, regs 16 and 17, the registered person is also required to:

(a) take all reasonable steps to ensure that a child is enabled to make a complaint and that a person is not subjected to any reprisals by the agency for making the complaint;
(b) at the request of the registration authority, supply a statement containing a summary of any complaints made during the preceding 12 months and the action taken in response.

## STAFF

### Fitness

18.99 The registered person must ensure that the agency has a sufficient number of suitably qualified, competent and experienced persons working for the purposes of the agency, having regard to the size of the agency, its statement of purpose and the need to safeguard and promote the health and welfare of children to whom the agency provides adoption support services.

18.100 ASAR 2005, reg 19 and Sch 2 require that the personnel employed by the agency should be fit to work for the purposes of the agency in that they must:

(a) be of integrity and good character;
(b) have the qualifications, skills and experience necessary for the work to be performed, with documentary evidence of any relevant qualification;
(c) be physically and mentally fit for the work they are required to undertake; and
(d) have provided full and satisfactory information relating to a criminal record certificate under Police Act 1997, ss 113 and 115; references; verification of the reason any previous employment ended, particularly if the position held was one which included work with children or vulnerable adults; and their full employment histories.

## Employing staff

18.101 The registered person is required to ensure that all permanent staff employed by the agency to carry out its functions: (a) satisfactorily complete a period of probation; (b) receive appropriate training, supervision and appraisal, and are enabled from time to time to gain further qualifications appropriate to the work they perform; and (c) that every member of staff is provided with a job description outlining his responsibilities (ASAR 2005, reg 20).

## Disciplinary procedure

18.102 As set out in ASAR 2005, reg 21, the registered person/local authority is required to operate a disciplinary procedure, which, in particular, provides for the suspension of an employee where necessary in the interests of the safety or welfare of the persons to whom the agency provides adoption support services and that any failure on the part of an employee to report an incident of abuse or suspected abuse of a child to the following persons is a ground on which disciplinary proceedings may be instituted:

(a) the registered person;
(b) an officer of the registration authority;
(c) a police officer;
(d) an officer of the NSPCC; or
(e) an officer of a local authority in whose area the agency is situated, or (in England only) in whose area the child is living or in whose area the child is placed for adoption, if this is a different authority.

## Records of staff

18.103 The registered person is required to maintain and keep up-to-date records of each person working for the purposes of the agency, for a period of at least 15 years from the date of the last entry. The record must contain personal details of the person; his address; qualifications relevant to, and experience of, working with persons receiving adoption support services; and (in relation to an agency which provides adoption support services to children) qualifications relevant to, and experience of, work involving children (ASAR 2005, reg 22 and Sch 3).

# FINANCES AND ACCOUNTS

18.104 The registered provider is required to ensure that the agency is financially viable; to ensure adequate accounts are maintained and, if requested, to provide the registered authority with such information and documents as it may require to assess the financial viability of the agency, including the annual accounts of the agency certified by an accountant and certificate of insurance in respect of liability of death, injury, public liability, damage and loss (ACA 2002, s 10(4)(b); ASAR 2005, reg 25).

## NOTICES TO THE REGISTRATION AUTHORITY

### Notice of absence

18.105 Written notice of any proposed absences of the registered person or manager for a continuous period of 28 days or more must be given to the registration authority at least one month in advance unless a shorter period is accepted by the registration authority. The notice must set out the prescribed information (ASAR 2005, reg 26(2)–(5)).

### Notice of changes

18.106 Written notice to the registration authority must be given by the registered person of the following events:

(a) a person other than the registered person carries on or manages the agency;
(b) a person ceases to carry on or manage the agency;
(c) where the registered person is an individual, they change their name;
(d) where the registered provider is a partnership, any change in the membership of the partnership;
(e) where the registered provider is an organisation, any change in its name or address, or of a director, manager, secretary or similar officer, or in the identity of the responsible individual;
(f) where the registered provider is an individual, a trustee in bankruptcy is appointed or the registered provider makes any composition or arrangement with his creditors; or
(g) where the registered provider is a company, a receiver, manager, liquidator or provisional liquidator is appointed in respect of the registered provider.

18.107 If more than one person is registered in respect of an agency and one of the registered persons dies, written notice to the registration authority must be given by the surviving person without delay and in the case of a single registered person by their personal representatives (ASAR 2005, reg 27).

## NOTIFICATION OF CONVICTION

18.108 Written notice setting out details of any criminal conviction of the registered person/responsible individual or manager must be given to the registration authority by the individual concerned (ASAR 2005, reg 9).

## NOTICES TO THE RELEVANT AUTHORITY

18.109 Notice of the following events must be given by the registered person without delay as indicated and, if given orally, confirmed in writing within 14 days:

(a) a referral to the Secretary of State pursuant to Protection of Children Act 1999, s 2(1)(a), of an individual working for an agency to the registration authority;
(b) the death or serious injury of a child in the course of receiving adoption support services, (i) to the registration authority; (ii) relevant authority (see para 18.111); (iii) clinical commissioning group; (iv) local health board in whose area the child was living at the time of death; or (v) when serious injury was sustained and in the event of a death, to the Secretary of State.

18.110 The 'relevant authority' means the local authority in whose area the agency is situated. In relation to a child who has died or sustained serious injury in the course of receiving adoption support services, it means any local authority on behalf of which the agency was providing the services to the child under ACA 2002, s 3(4)(b).

## FEES

18.111 Fees may be charged by adoption agencies for providing facilities as part of the adoption service, and the fees which may be paid by adoption agencies to persons providing or assisting in providing such facilities. Fees may also be charged for providing counselling in connection with the disclosure of information in relation to a person's adoption and for services or facilities provided for adoption with a foreign element.

# Chapter 19

# The Registers

## INTRODUCTION

19.1 Under ACA 2002, ss 77 and 78, the Registrar General is required to maintain, at the General Register Office (which is part of the Office for National Statistics at PO Box 2, Southport PR8 2JD, tel 0300 123 1837, www.gov.uk/general-register-office) an Adopted Children Register, and an index to that register. No entries may be made in this register other than entries directed by the court in its adoption order or required to be made under ACA 2002, Sch 1 (ACA 2002, s 77(3)). The Adopted Children Register is not open to public inspection or search (ACA 2002, s 77(2)), but any person may search the *index* and obtain certified copies of any entry in the register. The Registrar General is not permitted to furnish any person with any information contained in, or with any copy or extract from, any such register, except in accordance with ACA 2002, s 78(3) or under an order of court. ACA 2002, s 78 provides the machinery whereby an adopted person might apply to the Registrar General for particulars to enable him to obtain a copy of his birth certificate, provided he is 18 years of age.

19.2 The question whether the adopted person's right to information contained in the register was absolute or subject to public policy considerations has been addressed in a number of cases. The general principle is that the application for disclosure must be made on notice to the Registrar General, and the applicant has to establish the reasonableness of the order sought. The court nevertheless has a discretion whether to grant the application and may refuse disclosure on public policy grounds where, for example, the evidence shows that there was a real risk of a serious crime being committed or serious danger to a member of the public (*Re H (Adoption: Disclosure of Information)* [1995] 1 FLR 236; *R v Registrar General ex parte Smith* [1991] 1 FLR 255). In *D v Registrar General* [1997] 1 FLR 715, the court ruled that its discretion should be exercised only in exceptional circumstances and where an exceptional need for disclosure is established. This principle was applied by the court in *FL v Registrar General* [2010] EWHC 3520 (Fam), when refusing the application to order disclosure. The above cases relate to adoption pre-ACA 2002, but the principles are equally applicable post-ACA 2002, and were considered in *In the matter of X (Adopted Child: Access to Court File)* [2014] EWFC 33. The High Court may also under its inherent jurisdiction make an order directing the Registrar General not to disclose details of an adoption which are recorded in the register without the court's permission (*Re X (A Minor) (Adoption Details: Disclosure)* [1994] 2 FLR 450, CA; *Re W (Adoption Details: Disclosure)* [1998] 2 FLR 625). Where an order restricting disclosure is sought, an application should be made for the application to be transferred to a High Court judge (President's Direction: Adopted Children Register: Restriction on Disclosure of 17 December 1998 [1999] 1 FLR 35).

19.3 The Adopted Children and Adoption Contact Registers Regulations 2005 (SI 2005/924) (ACACRR 2005) are the main regulations which apply to registration. The Adoption and Children Act Register (Search and Inspection) Regulations 2017 (SI 2017/978) provides for the search and inspection of the Adoption and Children Act Register by prospective adopters who an adoption agency is satisfied are suitable to adopt a child in accordance with the AAR 2005.

## THE ADOPTED CHILDREN REGISTER

### Role of the Registrar General

19.4 The Registrar General is required to maintain in the General Register Office the Adopted Children Register, which contains details of the date of birth of the adopted person or country of birth (or registration district or sub-district) of the adopted child. It also sets out the name, surname and sex of the child, and details of the adoptive parent(s) and the date the adoption order was made, or the adoption effected. Although this register is not open to public inspection or search (ACA 2002, s 77(2)), any person may search the *index* and obtain a certified copy of any entry in the Adopted Children Register subject to the terms, conditions and regulations as to payment of fees and otherwise, applicable under the Births and Deaths Registration Act 1953 and the Registration Service Act 1953, in respect of searches in the index, certified copies of entries in the Register of Live Births and the supply of certified copies of entries. However, a person is not entitled to have a certified copy of an entry in the Adopted Children Register relating to an adopted person who has not attained the age of 18 years unless the applicant provides the Registrar General with the full names and date of birth of the adopted person and the full names of the adoptive parent(s) (ACA 2002, s 78(2)–(4), and ACACRR 2005, reg 10). The terms, conditions and regulation as to payment of fees and otherwise, applicable under the Births and Deaths Registration Act 1953 and the Registration Service Act 1953 in respect of searches in the index kept in the General Register Office of certified copies of entries, and the supply of certified copies of entries in those certified copies, also apply in respect of searches and supplies of certified copies of any entry in the Adopted Children Register (ACA 2002 s 78(4)). The Registrar General is also required to make traceable the connection between any entry in the Register of Live Births or other records which has been marked 'Adopted', and any corresponding entry in the Adopted Children Register (ACA 2002, s 79(1)).

19.5 The ACA 2002 provides three separate procedures for the disclosure of information by the Registrar General:

(a) Under ACA 2002, s 79(4), where a person was adopted before ACA 2002, ss 56–65 (the provisions on disclosure of information relating to a person's adoption) came into force, the court may, in exceptional circumstances, order the Registrar General to give to the adopted person information kept by the Registrar pursuant to ACA 2002, s 79(1) (see para 19.1) and any other information which would enable an adopted person to obtain a certified copy of the record of his birth (ACA 2002, s 79(3); see also ACA 2002, Sch 2, discussed at para 19.7).
(b) On an application made in writing by the appropriate adoption agency for the like information as set out under (a) above (ACA 2002, s 79(5), and ACACRR 2005, reg 11), the appropriate agency is:

    (i) if the person was placed for adoption by an adoption agency, that agency, or (if different) the agency which keeps the information in relation to the person's adoption;
    (ii) in any other case, the local authority to which notice of intention to adopt was given (ACA 2002, s 65).

(c) An adopted person who is under 18 years of age and intends to marry or form a civil partnership, and whose record of birth is kept by the Registrar General, may apply for information. The application must be made in writing and signed by the adopted person (ACACRR 2005, reg 13). The Registrar General is under a duty to inform the applicant whether or not it appears from the information contained in the Register of Live Births or other records that the applicant and the intended spouse or civil partner may be within the prohibited degrees of relationship for the purposes of the Marriage Act 1949 or the Civil Partnership Act 2004. A fee may be payable before the information is disclosed (ACA 2002, s 79(8)).

19.6 In addition, pursuant to DAI(PCA)R 2005, reg 20, the Registrar General is required to:

(a) disclose to any person (including an adopted person), at his request, any information which the person requires to assist him to make contact with the appropriate adoption agency; and

(b) disclose to the appropriate agency any information which the agency requires about an entry relating to the adopted person on the Adoption Contact Register on payment of any fee required by the Registrar General.

## Disclosure to a person adopted before the ACA 2002

19.7 A person adopted before the commencement of ACA 2002, ss 56–65 may apply for a certified copy of the record of his birth, provided he has attained the age of 18 years. The application must be made to the Registrar General, in writing, by the adopted person and signed by him. The Registrar General is under a duty to give the applicant any information necessary to enable the applicant to obtain a certified copy of the record of his birth, subject to the following:

(a) Before giving any information to the applicant, the Registrar General must inform the applicant that counselling services are available, and identify where such services may be obtained (see ACA 2002, Sch 2, para 2(1)(a)–(d), (2) and (3)).
(b) If the applicant chooses to receive counselling from a person or body whose details are provided to the applicant by the Registrar General, the Registrar General must send to the person or body chosen by the applicant the information to which the applicant is entitled (ACA 2002, Sch 2, para 2(4)).
(c) Where the adopted person seeking the information was adopted before 12 November 1975, the Registrar General must not give information to the applicant unless the applicant has attended an interview with a counsellor arranged by a person or body from whom counselling services are available as provided under ACA 2002, Sch 2, para 4(1)(a)–(b).
(d) Where the Registrar General is prevented by reason of (c) above from giving information to a person who is not living in the United Kingdom, the Registrar General may give the information to any body which the Registrar General is satisfied is suitable to provide counselling to the adopted person, and which has notified the Registrar General that it is prepared to provide such counselling (ACA 2002, Sch 2, para 4(2)).

19.8 Where the Registrar General declines to provide the information to a person adopted before the ACA 2002 came into force, the court may, in exceptional circumstances, order the Registrar General to give the information which would enable an adopted person to obtain a certified copy of the record of his birth (ACA 2002, s 79(3) and (4)). If the application is granted, the Registrar General is obliged to pass on the information to the adopted person directly.

19.9 In all other cases, to obtain information relating to the connection between any entry in the Register of Live Births and with any other record which has been marked 'Adopted' and any corresponding entry in the Adopted Children Register, an application may be made with the leave of the court. Permission will only be granted in exceptional circumstances.

19.10 ACA 2002, s 98 provides for regulations to be made in connection with those who were adopted before 30 December 2005 to obtain information about their adoption and to facilitate contact between them and their birth families. For further information, see the AIIS(PCA)R 2005 and Chapter 17.

## Disclosure to a person adopted after the ACA 2002

19.11 A person adopted after ACA 2002 came into force, who wishes to trace the connection between any entry in the Register of Live Births or other records which has been marked 'Adopted' and any corresponding entry in the Adopted Children Register, must apply through the appropriate adoption agency and not seek the information directly from the Registrar General (see ACA 2002, s 60(2)).

19.12 DAI(PCA)R 2005, reg 19 imposes a duty on the adoption agency, if it does not have the information, to seek it from the Registrar General. The application must be made in writing and provide the following information:

(a) the name, date of birth and country of birth of the adopted person;
(b) the name of the adoptive father and mother; and
(c) the date of the adoption order.

19.13 However, in exceptional circumstances the agency may apply to the High Court for an order restricting such disclosure (ACA 2002, s 60(2)(a) and (3); see also paras 19.1–19.3 and para 20.21).

# THE REGISTRATION OF ADOPTION ORDERS

19.14 Every adoption order must contain a direction to the Registrar General to make an entry in the Adopted Children Register in the form prescribed by regulation made by the Registrar General with the approval of the Secretary of State. If the order is made in England, this is ACA 2002, Sch 1 and ACACRR 2005, reg 2(1); if the order is made by a court in Wales, this is Sch 2. The adoption order must also contain a direction that the entry in the Register of Live Births or record in question is marked with the word 'Adopted'. Where the adoption order relates to a child who has been previously adopted, the order must contain a direction to the Registrar to mark the previous entry in the Adopted Children Register with the word 'Re-adopted' (ACA 2002, Sch 1, para 1(2) and (3)). For registration of adoption in Scotland, Northern Ireland, the Isle of Man and the Channel Islands, see ACA 2002, Sch 1, para 2.

19.15 For the duty imposed on the court officer to send to the Registrar General and other relevant bodies and organisations a copy of any final order made in relation to adoption proceedings, see FPR 2010, rr 14.26 and 14.27; and in relation to any amendments, rectification and cancellation of registers and other records, see ACA 2002, Sch 1, paras 4–6. In proceedings in Wales, a party may request that an order be drawn up in Welsh as well as English (FPR 2010, r 14.25(2)).

19.16 'Records' includes certified copies kept by the Registrar General of entries in any Register of Births, and 'Register of Live Births' means the Register of Live Births made under the Births and Deaths Registration Act 1953 (ACA 2002, s 82(1)).

19.17 A certified copy of an entry in the Adopted Children Register which is sealed or stamped with the seal of the General Register Office is evidence of the adoption to which it relates (ACA 2002, s 77(4)). Where an entry in the Adopted Children Register contains a record of the date of birth of the adopted person, or of the country or district of his birth, a certified copy of the entry in the Adopted Children Register is, without further proof, as sufficient evidence of that adoption, as if it were a birth certificate. Adoption records in Scotland, Northern Ireland and the Isle of Man or Channel Islands are admissible as evidence of adoption in England and Wales (ACA 2002, s 107).

## THE REGISTRATION OF CONVENTION AND OVERSEAS ADOPTIONS

19.18 In the case of registration of Convention and overseas adoption orders, these may be registered if, at the time the order is made, the adoptive parent or, in the case of a couple, both adoptive parents, are habitually resident in England or Wales (see ACA 2002, Sch 1, para 3, and ACACRR 2005, reg 3) (see also Chapters 13–15).

### The applicant(s)

19.19 The persons who are qualified to make the application for registration are:

(a) the adoptive parent or, in the case of a couple, one of the adoptive parents of the adopted child;
(b) any other person who has parental responsibility, within the meaning of ChA 1989, s 3, for the adopted child;
(c) the adopted person if he has attained the age of 18 years (ACACRR 2005, reg 4).

## Form of application

19.20 The application must be in writing and signed by the person making it. It must be in the form prescribed by ACACRR 2005, reg 2(2). As set out in ACACRR 2005, reg 5, it must be accompanied by the following documents and information:

(a) in the case of a Convention adoption, a copy of the certificate sent to the adoptive parents by the relevant CA in accordance with AFER 2005, reg 32, and the date on which the adoption was effected;
(b) in the case of an overseas adoption, the evidence in accordance with Adoption (Recognition of Overseas Adoptions) Order 2013 (SI 2013/1801), art 3, or an order made under ACA 2002, s 87(1) that the adoption has been effected, and the date on which the adoption was effected;
(c) particulars of the child, namely:

    (i) the child's full name on adoption and any previous names,
    (ii) the child's sex,
    (iii) the child's date of birth,
    (iv) the place and country of the child's birth,
    (v) the full names and any previous names of the child's natural mother and father,
    (vi) the full name, any previous names, address and occupation of the adoptive parent(s), and
    (vii) the capacity in which the person is making the application;

(d) where the documents or information are not in English or Welsh, a translation into English of the application, signed and endorsed by the translator with:

    (i) the name and address and occupation of the translator; and
    (ii) a statement to the effect that the translation is true and accurate.

19.21 If the Registrar General is satisfied that he has sufficient particulars relating to a child adopted under a Convention or overseas adoption to enable an entry to be made in the Adopted Children Register, he is under a duty to make an entry. Further, if he is satisfied that an entry in the Register of Live Births or other records relates to the child, he must secure that the entry is marked 'Adopted', followed by the name, in brackets, of the country in which the adoption order was made; or, in the case of an overseas adoption, secure that the overseas register of births is so marked (ACA 2002, Sch 1, paras 3(1) and (2)).

## THE ADOPTION CONTACT REGISTER

19.22 ACA 2002, s 80(1) requires the Registrar General to continue to maintain the Adoption Contact Register, in two parts, to assist the adopted persons and their natural families who wish to express their views about contact with each other.

### The two parts of the Adoption Contact Register

19.23 In order to make an entry in Part 1 of the Adoption Contact Register, the adopted person must give notice expressing his wish to make contact with his relatives. 'Relatives' includes any person who would have been related to the adopted person, but for the adoption, by blood (including half-blood), marriage or civil partnership (ACA 2002, s 81(2)). The notice must be in the form set out in ACACRR 2005, Sch 3. The adopted person has a right to withdraw the notice at any time.

19.24 As set out in ACA 2002, s 80(3), the Registrar General may make an entry in Part 1 of the Adoption Contact Register only if:

(a) a record of the adopted person's birth is kept by the Registrar General;
(b) the adopted person has attained the age of 18 years;
(c) the Registrar General is satisfied that the adopted person has such information as is necessary to enable him to obtain a certified copy of the record of his birth.

19.25 An entry in Part 1 of the Adoption Contact Register must contain the full name, address and date of birth of the adopted person together with the following information:

(a) any relative with whom the adopted person wishes to have contact together with the name of that relative, if known;
(b) any relative with whom the adopted person does not wish to have contact, together with the name or that relative, if known.

19.26 A fee of £15 is payable to make the entry (ACACRR 2005, regs 6(1) and 9(1)).

19.27 An entry in Part 2 of the Adoption Contact Register contains information about person(s) who have given notice expressing their wishes, as relatives of an adopted person, to make contact with the adopted person. Such a person must have attained the age of 18, and the Registrar General must be satisfied that the person is a relative of the adopted person and has such information as is necessary to enable him to obtain a certified copy of the record of the adopted person's birth

(ACA 2002, s 80(4) and (5)). The fee payable for entry in Part 2 of the Adoption Contact Register is £30 (ACACRR 2005, reg 9(2)).

19.28 The notice expressing the wish to make contact must be in the form set out in ACACRR 2005, Sch 4 (reg 7(2)). The information required to be given is the full name, address, and date of birth of the relative of an adopted person, together with the following additional information:

(a) the name of the adopted person with whom it is sought to have contact; or
(b) the fact that the person does not wish to have contact with the named adopted person.

19.29 ACA 2002, s 80(6) makes provision for regulations to be made for the disclosure of information to persons included in both sections of the Adoption Contact Register. ACACRR 2005, reg 8 requires the Registrar General to give an adopted person whose name is in Part 1 of the Adoption Contact Register, in writing, the name of any relative of the adopted person whose name appears in Part 2 of the Adoption Contact Register, and who has asked for contact with the adopted person. The Registrar General must also provide an address, at or through which the adopted person can contact the relative.

19.30 The Adoption Contact Register is not open to the public for inspection or search (ACA 2002, s 81(1)).

Chapter 20

# The Disclosure of Information

## INTRODUCTION

20.1 ACA 2002, ss 56–65 regulate the information that adoption agencies must keep in relation to an adopted person and information they are required to disclose to an adult adopted person; that which they may release to an adult adopted person, birth families and others; and information that the court is required to disclose to an adult adopted person. Pursuant to those sections, the following regulations provide for, or authorise the circumstances in which, how and to whom disclosure should be made:

- the Adoption Information and Intermediary Services (Pre-Commencement Adoptions) Regulations 2005 (SI 2005/890), as amended by SI 2014/2696 and 2015/1685 (AIIS(PCA)R 2005);
- the Adopted Children and Adoption Contact Registers Regulations 2005 (SI 2005/924) (ACACRR 2005); and
- the Disclosure of Adoption Information (Post Commencement Adoptions) Regulations 2005 (SI 2005/888) (DAI(PCA)R 2005).

20.2 The first of these regulations relates to adoptions before 30 December 2005 and is dealt with in Chapter 17; the requirements of the second can be found in Chapter 19. The DAI(PCA)R 2005, discussed in this chapter, deal with adoption after 30 December 2005.

20.3 All applications for disclosure relating to adoptions after 30 December 2005 must now be made through the appropriate adoption agency and not to the Registrar General. This is the only gateway.

## INFORMATION TO BE KEPT BY ADOPTION AGENCIES

20.4 DAI(PCA)R 2005, Pt 1 regulates the information (referred to as 's 56 information') which an adoption agency which placed the child for adoption must keep and store in secure conditions, or to which the case records have been transferred in relation to an adopted person, and the form and manner in which such information should be kept. The records must include:

(a) any information that has been supplied to the agency by a natural parent or relative or other significant person in the adopted person's life with the intention that the adopted person may, should they wish, be given that information;
(b) any information supplied by the adoptive parent(s) or other persons which is relevant to matters arising post-adoption;
(c) any information that the adopted person has requested should be kept;
(d) any information given to the adoption agency in respect of an adopted person by the Registrar General pursuant to a request made by the agency or given to the agency relating to an entry on the Adoption Contact Register that would enable an adopted person to obtain a certified copy of the record of his birth;
(e) any information disclosed to the adoption agency about an entry relating to the adopted person on the Adoption Contact Register;
(f) any information relating to disclosure made for the purposes of research; disclosure required for the purposes of inquiries, etc.; of views obtained under ACA 2002, ss 61(3) or 62(3) or (4), and information obtained for the purposes of providing counselling required to be recorded in accordance with DAI(PCA)R, 2005, regs 10, 14 and 18; and
(g) the record of any agreement under DAI(PCA)R, 2005, reg 11 (DAI(PCA)R 2005, reg 4(3)).

20.5 The adoption agency is not required to keep any information under (a)–(c) above if the adoption agency considers that it would be prejudicial to the adopted person's welfare or that it would not be reasonably practicable to keep it (DAI(PCA)R, reg 5).

However, note that any s 56 information kept by the adoption agency which, whether taken on its own or with other information, would enable a person to be identified, and information received or kept by the agency from the Registrar General or an entry in the Adoption Contact Register, is classified under ACA 2002, s 57 as 'protected information'. This information must, at all times, be kept in secure conditions, and, in particular, all appropriate measures must be taken to prevent theft, unauthorised disclosure damage, loss or destruction: (DAI(PCA)R 2005, reg 4(4)).

20.6 The records must be kept for at least 100 years (DAI(PCA)R 2005, reg 6). See also NMS 2014, Standard 27.

## General Data Protection Regulation

20.7 The General Data Protection Regulation (GDPR) extends the data rights of individuals (data subjects) and places a range of new obligations on organisations that process EU residents' personal data. The Data Protection Act 2018 modifies the GDPR and applies a broadly equivalent regime known as the 'applied GDPR' (see www.itgovernance.co.uk/dpa-2018).

## Transfer of information

20.8 An adoption agency is permitted to transfer a copy of the child's case records or the case records of the prospective adopter(s) or part of that record to another adoption agency when it considers this to be in the interests of the child or the prospective adopter(s). Such a situation would arise, for example, if the adoptive family moves home from one area to another. The agency must keep a written record of any such transfer (AAR 2005, reg 43).

20.9 Where a registered adoption agency intends to cease to act, or to exist as such, it must transfer any s 56 information it holds in relation to a person's adoption:

(a) to another adoption agency, having first obtained the approval of the registration authority for such transfer;
(b) to the local authority in whose area the society's principal office is situated;
(c) in the case of a society which amalgamates with another registered adoption society to form a new registered adoption society, to the new body (DAI(PCA)R 2005, reg 7(1)).

Where the activities of a registered adoption society that transfers its records to another adoption society were based principally in the area of a single local authority, it must give notice of the transfer to that authority (DAI(PCA)R 2005, reg 7(2)).

20.10 An adoption agency to which the information is transferred must give written notification of the transfer to the registration authority (DAI(PCA)R 2005, reg 7(3)).

## PERMITTED GENERAL DISCLOSURE

20.11 The disclosure of s 56 information by an adoption agency is either discretionary or mandatory (ACA 2002, s 58).

### Discretionary disclosure

20.12 The adoption agency has a discretion to disclose s 56 information:

(a) that is not 'protected information' as it thinks fit for the purposes of carrying out its functions as an adoption agency (ACA 2002, s 58(2); DAIPCA)R 2005, reg 8(1)). This discretion enables the agency to share information provided by the birth family and others who may have played a significant role in the child's life with the adoptive parent(s) and vice versa, subject of course to the consent of the interested parties. The information given to the birth family will include information about how the child is getting on at school and with the adoptive family, and any achievements of the child. Information passed on to the adoptive parent(s) may include medical information relating to the birth family, and other information which may assist the adoptive parent(s) with the care of the child;
(b) within which there is protected material, to:

    (i) a registered adoption support agency or another adoption agency which provides services to the adoption agency in connection with any of its functions under ACA 2002, s 61 or s 62 (see Chapter 18); or
    (ii) a person who is authorised in writing by the Secretary of State to obtain information for the purposes of research; or
    (iii) another adoption agency as it thinks fit for purposes related to its functions or the receiving agency's function as an adoption agency (DAI(PCA)R 2005, reg 8(2), as amended by SI 2018/152, reg 2(a)).

20.13 Before such information is disclosed, the agency should seek the views, on the disclosure sought, of the person to whom the information relates. It must also ensure that the agency requesting the information has the skills to conduct the work for which the information is required. It would be prudent, when providing the information, to obtain an undertaking from the agency that the information will be used for the specified purpose only.

20.14 Where the information is required for research, a similar undertaking should be obtained, with an added provision that any published report or finding should not disclose any material which could identify any person involved in an adoption.

## Disclosure in pursuance of agreement

20.15 ACA 2002, s 57(5) permits disclosure of protected information in pursuance of a prescribed agreement to which the adoption agency is a party. As set out in DAI(PCA)R 2005, reg 11(1), the prescribed agreements are:

(a) an agreement made between the adoption agency, and a person aged 18 or over at the time the agreement was made, as to the disclosure of protected information about him; or
(b) an agreement made between the adoption agency and each of the following persons as to the disclosure of protected information about them or about the adopted person:

    (i) the adoptive parent(s) of the adopted person;
    (ii) each person who, before the adoption was made, was a parent with parental responsibility for the adopted person.

20.16 As set out in DAI(PCA)R 2005, reg 11(2), where an agreement is reached, the adoption agency is under a duty to keep a written record of the agreement, which must include:

(a) the full names and signatures of the persons who are parties to the agreement;
(b) the date on which it is made;
(c) the reasons for making it;
(d) the details of the information which it was agreed should be disclosed; and
(e) details of any agreed restrictions on the circumstances in which the information may be disclosed.

20.17 Before entering into such an agreement, the agency should ensure that the person concerned is aware of and understands the legal implications. Where necessary, counselling should be offered to the person before the agreement is signed. Any agreement reached must be for the benefit of the child's welfare. It would be prudent to renew the terms of the agreement periodically to ensure that it remains valid.

## Mandatory disclosure for purposes of inquiries, etc

20.18 DAI(PCA)R 2005, reg 9 requires an adoption agency to disclose s 56 information, including protected information, for the purposes of inquiries and investigations and inspection to:

(a) those holding an inquiry under ss 3 and 4 of the Children Act 2004 or under the Inquiries Act 2005;

(b) the Secretary of State;
(c) the registration authority, for example in connection with inspection of the agency's services;
(d) subject to the provisions of Local Government Act 1974, ss 29(7) and 32(3) (investigations and disclosure), the Commission for Local Administration in England, for the purposes of any investigation conducted in accordance with Local Government Act 1974, Pt 3. This relates to cases where a complaint is being investigated by a local government ombudsman, but disclosure should be limited and restricted;
(e) any person appointed by the adoption agency for the purposes of the consideration by the agency of any representations (including complaints);
(f) a panel constituted under ACA 2002, s 12 to consider a qualifying determination in relation to the disclosure of s 56 information;
(g) a court having power to make an order under the ACA 2002 or under the ChA 1989;
(h) the Public Services Ombudsman for Wales for the purposes of an inquiry held by him under Public Services Ombudsman (Wales) Act 2005, s 2.

20.19 In any case where discretionary or mandatory disclosure is made, the adoption agency is required to make a written record, which must include:

(a) a description of the information disclosed;
(b) the date on which the information was disclosed;
(c) the person to whom the disclosure was made;
(d) the reason for the disclosure (DAI(PCA)R 2005, reg 10).

## DISCLOSURE TO AN ADOPTED ADULT

20.20 An adult adopted person has a right to ask for disclosure from the adoption agency and the court. Where the application is made to an adoption agency the adopted person has a right, save in exceptional circumstances, to receive, from the appropriate adoption agency (see paras 20.1 and 20.12 and Chapter 19), any information which would enable him to obtain a certified copy of any record of his birth, unless the High Court or Family Court orders otherwise, and certain information disclosed to the adopter(s) by the agency (ACA 2002, s 60(2)). Any person adopted on or after 30 December 2005 must apply to the appropriate adoption agency for this information rather than to the Registrar General. Where the agency does not have the requested information, it must apply to the Registrar General for it on behalf of the adopted person (see further Chapter 19).

## Withholding of information on the ground of exceptional circumstances

20.21 The High Court has the power, on an application made to it by an appropriate adoption agency, to prevent disclosure of such information if it is satisfied that the circumstances are exceptional. The application by an adoption agency to withhold information must be made in accordance with the procedure set out in FPR 2010, Pt 19.

## Information from the court

20.22 An adult adopted person also has a right, at his request, to receive from the court which made the adoption order a copy of the following:

(a) the application form for the adoption order, but not the documents attached to that form;
(b) the adoption order and any other orders relating to the adoption proceedings;
(c) orders containing any provision for contact with the child after the adoption order was made; and
(d) any other document or order referred to under (a)–(c) above (ACA 2005, s 60(4); FPR 2010, rr 14 and 18 and PD 14F, para 1.1).

20.23 In addition, the adopted adult is also entitled to receive:

(a) any transcript or written reasons of the court's decision; and
(b) a report made to the court by a children's guardian, reporting officer or children and family reporter; a local authority or an adoption agency (FPR 2010, r 14.18 and PD 14F, para 2).

The court will remove protected information from documents before they are sent to the adopted adult (FPR 2010, r 14.18(2) and PD 14F, para 3).

20.24 The request for information must be made by the adult adopted person in Form 64 and must have attached to it a full certified copy of the entry in the Adopted Children Register relating to the applicant (FPR 2010, PD 14F, para 1.2). The form must be taken to the court which made the adoption order, along with evidence of the applicant's identity showing a photograph and signature, such as a passport or driving licence (FPR 2010, PD 14F, para 1.3). Note, however, that the entitlement to information and documents does not apply to a document or order in so far as it contains information which is protected information (ACA 2002, s 60(5)).

## DISCLOSURE OF PROTECTED INFORMATION ABOUT ADULTS

### Who may apply for protected information about adults?

20.25 Any adult person may apply to the appropriate agency for protected information, provided that none of the information sought relates to a child at the time of the application, but disclosure will not be made unless the adoption agency considers it appropriate to do so.

### Manner in which the application should be made

20.26 The application for disclosure should be made in writing, setting out the reasons for seeking the disclosure and providing proof of identity (DAI(PCA)R 2005, reg 12).

### Steps the agency should take and factors it must apply when making its decision

20.27 On receiving the application for disclosure of protected information, the adoption agency must take reasonable steps to confirm the identity of the applicant or any person acting on his behalf, and if the latter, that the person is authorised to do so (DAI(PCA)R 2005, reg 13).

20.28 In deciding whether to disclose the information, the adoption agency must take all reasonable steps to obtain the views of any person to whom the information relates as to the disclosure of the information about him. Any views obtained must be recorded in written form (ACA 2002, s 61(3) or s 62(3) or (4); DAI(PCA)R 2005, reg 14). As set out in ACA 2002, s 61(5), it must also consider:

(a) the welfare of the adopted person;
(b) any views obtained from interested parties;
(c) any prescribed matters; and
(d) all the other circumstances of the case.

The adoption agency may decide not to proceed with an application from any person for disclosure of protected information; or it may decide to disclose information against the express views of the person the information is about, or not to disclose information about a person where that person has expressly expressed a view that the information should not be disclosed.

## Reasons for decision taken

20.29 The adoption agency is required to give written notification of its decision, stating the reason for it and advising the person concerned or the person to whom the protected information relates (the relevant person), as the case may be, of his right to apply to the Secretary of State within 40 days of the date on which the notice was sent for a review by an independent review panel under ACA 2002, s 12, where the decision relates to one or more of the qualifying determinations referred to in para 20.30 (DAI(PCA)R 2005, reg 15(2)).

## Independent review

20.30 As set out in DAI(PCA)R 2005, reg 15(1), the qualifying determinations in relation to which a review may be applied for are:

(a) not to proceed with an application from any person for disclosure of protected information;
(b) to disclose information against the express views of the person the information is about;
(c) not to disclose information about a person to the applicant where that person has expressed the view that the information should be disclosed.

20.31 Upon receiving an application for review, the Secretary of State will notify the adoption agency which must, within 10 days of receipt of the notification, send to the Secretary of State the following documents and information:

(a) a copy of the application for disclosure of information;
(b) a copy of the notification given to the relevant person of the determination and his right to a review;
(c) the record of any views obtained by the agency under ACA 2002, s 61(3); and
(d) any additional information requested by the panel (DAI(PCA)R 2005, reg 15(3)).

20.32 The adoption agency must not take any action in accordance with its original determination before the independent review panel has made its recommendation; or if the person has not applied for a review within that 40-day period, before the end of that period (DAI(PCA)R 2005, reg 15(4)). Where a review takes place, the panel's decision takes the form of a recommendation which the agency is required to consider in taking any decision whether to proceed with its original determination (DAI(PCA)R 2005, reg 15(5)).

## DISCLOSURE OF PROTECTED INFORMATION ABOUT CHILDREN

20.33 The procedure for making the application is the same as that set out at para 20.26.

20.34 Where a person applies for disclosure of protected information that relates to a child, the agency is not required to give that information unless it considers it appropriate to do so (ACA 2002, s 62(2)).

### Steps the agency must take on receipt of the application

20.35 As required under ACA 2002, s 62(3) and (4), before it decides whether or not to disclose the information, the adoption agency must take all reasonable steps to obtain:

(a) the views of any parent or guardian of the child; and
(b) the views of the child, if the agency considers it appropriate to do so having regard to his age and understanding and to all the other circumstances of the case; and
(c) so far as the information is about a person who has at the time attained the age of 18 years, his views as to the disclosure.

20.36 Any views obtained must be recorded in writing (DAI(PCA)R 2005, reg 14).

### Factors the agency must consider

20.37 In deciding whether it is appropriate to proceed with the application or disclose information relating to a child:

(a) where the child is an adopted child, the child's welfare must be the paramount consideration;
(b) in the case of any other child, the agency must have particular regard to the child's welfare (ACA 2002, s 62(6)).

20.38 In deciding whether it is appropriate to proceed with the application, or disclose the information, the agency must consider:

(i) the welfare of the adopted person (where s 62(6)(a) (above) does not apply);
(ii) any views obtained under ACA 2002, s 62(3) and/or (4) (see paras 20.34–20.35) (i.e. if the subject of the application for disclosure is about a person

who is at the time a child, from the parent(s) or guardian of a child, the child if appropriate having regard to his age understanding);

(iii) any prescribed matters; and

(iv) all the other circumstances of the case (ACA 2002, s 62(7)).

20.39 Any views obtained must be recorded in writing.

20.40 Thus, the agency has a discretion whether to disclose the information. Even where it considers it might be appropriate to disclose information, it should do so only if it is satisfied that it would be in the interests of the child. The applicant does not have a right to request a review of the decision since it concerns a child (see *Adoption Statutory Guidance 2013*, Chapter 11).

## COUNSELLING

### Provision of counselling

20.41 An adoption agency is under a duty to provide written information about the availability of counselling services to any person:

(a) seeking information under ACA 2002, ss 61 and 62 as outlined at paras 20.25–20.32 and paras 20.33–20.40; or

(b) considering objecting or consenting to the disclosure of information by the agency (whose views have been sought under ACA 2002, s 61(3) or s 62(3) or (4)); or

(c) who has entered into or is considering entering into an agreement with the agency to share protected information (see paras 20.15–20.17).

20.42 The information provided must include information about the fees that may be charged by the person providing counselling (DAI(PCA)R 2005, reg 16).

20.43 When counselling is requested, the agency must itself provide counselling, or make arrangements for it to be provided by:

(a) another adoption agency or a registered adoption support agency;

(b) if the person is in Scotland, a Scottish adoption agency;

(c) if the person is in Northern Ireland, an adoption agency registered under Adoption (Northern Ireland) Order 1987 (SI 1987/2203) (NI 22), art 4 and any Board; or

(d) if the person is outside the United Kingdom, any person or body outside the United Kingdom who appears to the agency to correspond in its function to an adoption agency or an adoption support agency (DAI(PCA)R 2005, reg 17).

20.44 The agency must ensure that an adoption support agency which provides counselling is registered to provide such services. It must also satisfy itself that the adoption support agency has appropriately qualified and experienced staff to provide the necessary services to meet the needs of the particular person.

### Disclosure of information for counselling

20.45 An adoption agency is permitted to disclose any information, including protected information, which is required for the purposes of providing counselling to any person with whom it has made arrangements to provide counselling. It must make a written record of any such disclosure made in the person's case records (ACA 2002, s 63(3); DAI(PCA)R 2005, reg 18).

## CONFIDENTIAL INFORMATION

20.46 Great efforts are made to protect the anonymity of adopters in confidential adoption proceedings. In *Re R (Children) (Secure Editing of Documents)* [2007] EWHC 876 (Fam), the President of the Family Division approved the following guidance:

> 19. Wherever sensitive confidential information is to be protected, the following procedure should apply:
>
> (1) The court should identify that a case falls into this category and make a clear statement that special restrictions will apply.
> (2) A direction should be given that information of a clearly specified kind shall not be contained in any document filed, gathered or circulated in the proceedings. It is insufficient to allow the information to be withheld.
> (3) In considering whether to order documentary disclosure, the court should bear in mind the risk that confidential information may inadvertently be compromised, and avoid making unnecessarily wide orders. It is notoriously burdensome to edit large amounts of documentation accurately and mistakes are easily made.
> (4) The chain of possession should be spelled out. The documents should in the first instance be gathered by one appropriately selected party and only released once they have been carefully checked.
> (5) Responsibility for the process should be given to one or more named individuals. The Guardian's solicitor, where there is one, may be the obvious candidate. The solicitor for the party who wishes to withhold the information might well be given the opportunity to check the edited documents before they go to the party from whom the information is to be withheld. A timetable can be imposed to avoid delay.
> (6) There should always be a second editor where there is a significant volume of material to be edited, or where the potential consequences of inadvertent disclosure are serious.

(7) The editing/checking process should be carried out by someone who knows the details of the case and the importance of the task. It is not an administrative task that can be delegated. Where appropriate the person(s) carrying out the task should be identified by name ('AB') rather than by title ('the Mother's solicitor').

(8) The editor(s) should know exactly what they are trying to protect. It is obviously not sufficient to say 'the mother's name and address' if the editor does not know what they are.

(9) The procedure should be tailored to the circumstances of the case.

## Serial number

20.47 Applications for an adoption order are given a serial number where it is intended to keep the identity of the prospective adopter(s) confidential. Similarly, when any other application is made in the proceedings for contact; prohibiting contact; or the revocation or variation of an order (FPR 2010, r 14.2).

## Reports filed in the proceedings

20.48 Any report filed by a children's guardian, reporting officer or a children and family reporter is confidential and may only be disclosed to the party in the proceedings with the court's permission and in the form directed by the court. The court also has the power to direct non-disclosure of the report to a party (FPR 2010, r 14.3) but such a direction will only be made where there are exceptional circumstances and there is a compelling case for non-disclosure, for example where there is a real risk of harm to the child or to protect the European Convention, Art 8 rights of the child and the prospective adoptive parent(s), but consideration of this right must be balanced against the right to a fair trial under Art 6 (*Re X (Adoption: Confidential Procedure)* [2002] EWCA Civ 828; *Re B (Disclosure to Other Parties)* [2001] 2 FLR 1017).

## Proceedings heard in private

20.49 Adoption proceedings are held in private. Any information related to the proceedings may only be communicated where the court gives permission to do so, and as set out in FPR 2010, r 14.14. The duty of confidentiality also applies to documents in the control of an adoption agency or a local authority.

## Documents held by the court

20.50 All documents relating to adoption proceedings in the custody of the court are required to be kept in a place of special security (FPR 2010, r 14.23). The documents or order are not open to inspection by any person, and access to such document or extract thereof or of the order cannot be taken or given to any person (FPR 2010, r 14.24).

## Access to information held by the court

20.51 Pursuant to ACA 2002, s 60(4), an adopted person has the right to request and to receive from the court which made the adoption order certain documents and orders relating to the adoption, but this right is not absolute. In *In the matter of X (Adopted Child: Access to Court File)* [2014] EWFC 33, the court considered whether the right to access to information is absolute or subject to public policy consideration. The court summarised the principles as follows (at [29]):

> i) The court has a discretion whether to disclose information contained in its own file to the applicant.
>
> ii) In considering whether or not to exercise that discretion the court should have regard to all the circumstances of the case and should exercise its discretion justly.
>
> iii) The public policy of maintaining public confidence in the confidentiality of adoption files is an important consideration.
>
> iv) The duration of time that has elapsed since the order was made, and the question of whether any or all of the affected parties are deceased, are important considerations.
>
> v) The nature of the connection between the applicant with the information sought from the court file is an important consideration.
>
> vi) The potential impact of disclosure on any relevant third parties, and any safeguards that could be put in place to mitigate this, is an important consideration.

# Index

*References are to page numbers*